DE-COLONIZATION, HERITAGE, AND ADVOCACY

DE-COLONIZATION, HERITAGE, AND ADVOCACY

AN OXFORD HANDBOOK OF APPLIED ETHNOMUSICOLOGY

VOLUME 2

Edited by
SVANIBOR PETTAN
and
JEFF TODD TITON

UNIVERSITY PRESS

Oxford University Press is a department of the University of Oxford. It furthers
the University's objective of excellence in research, scholarship, and education
by publishing worldwide. Oxford is a registered trade mark of Oxford University
Press in the UK and certain other countries.

Published in the United States of America by Oxford University Press
198 Madison Avenue, New York, NY 10016, United States of America.

© Oxford University Press 2019

All rights reserved. No part of this publication may be reproduced, stored in
a retrieval system, or transmitted, in any form or by any means, without the
prior permission in writing of Oxford University Press, or as expressly permitted
by law, by license, or under terms agreed with the appropriate reproduction
rights organization. Inquiries concerning reproduction outside the scope of the
above should be sent to the Rights Department, Oxford University Press, at the
address above.

You must not circulate this work in any other form
and you must impose this same condition on any acquirer.

Library of Congress Cataloging-in-Publication Data
Names: Pettan, Svanibor, 1960– | Titon, Jeff Todd, 1943–
Title: De-colonization, heritage, & advocacy : an Oxford handbook of applied
ethnomusicology, volume 2 / edited by Svanibor Pettan and Jeff Todd Titon.
Description: New York, NY : Oxford University Press, [2019] |
Series: Oxford handbooks | Includes bibliographical references and index.
Identifiers: LCCN 2018027980 | ISBN 9780190885731 (pbk.) |
ISBN 9780190885755 (epub)
Subjects: LCSH: Applied ethnomusicology.
Classification: LCC ML3799.2 .D4 2019 | DDC 780.89—dc23
LC record available at https://lccn.loc.gov/2018027980

Contents

List of Figures, Tables, and Box — vii
List of Contributors — ix
About the Companion Website — xi

PART I AN INTRODUCTION TO APPLIED ETHNOMUSICOLOGY

Sections

1. Applied Ethnomusicology: A Descriptive and Historical Account — 3
   JEFF TODD TITON

2. Applied Ethnomusicology in the Global Arena — 30
   SVANIBOR PETTAN

3. An Introduction to the Chapters — 57
   JEFF TODD TITON AND SVANIBOR PETTAN

PART II ADVOCACY

Chapters

1. Advocacy and the Ethnomusicologist: Assessing Capacity, Developing Initiatives, Setting Limits, and Making Sustainable Contributions — 69
   JEFFREY A. SUMMIT

2. Applied Ethnomusicology as an Intercultural Tool: Some Experiences from the Last 25 Years of Minority Research in Austria — 99
   URSULA HEMETEK

3. Being Applied in the Ethnomusicology of Autism — 148
   MICHAEL B. BAKAN

4. Motivations and Methods for Encouraging Artists in Longer Traditions   187
   BRIAN SCHRAG

5. Activist Ethnomusicology and Marginalized Music of South Asia   220
   ZOE C. SHERINIAN

PART III INDIGENOUS PEOPLES

6. Decolonization and Applied Ethnomusicology: "Story-ing" the Personal-Political-Possible in Our Work   253
   ELIZABETH MACKINLAY

7. Andes to Amazon on the River Q'eros: Indigenous Voice in Grassroots Tourism, Safeguarding, and Ownership Projects of the Q'eros and Wachiperi Peoples   272
   HOLLY WISSLER

Index   327

Figures, Tables, and Box

Figures

1.1	Map of Uganda by Dan Cole, GIS Coordinator, Smithsonian National Museum of Natural History	70
1.2	Worship in the Moses synagogue on Nabogoya Hill, Uganda	76
1.3	Photograph of the Peace Kawomera Growers Coop sign	83
2.1	Ruža Nikolić-Lakatos, 1994	111
2.2	Ceija Stojka, 1991	112
2.3	Poster for the event from 1990	116
2.4	Serbian Roma women dancing at the event, 1990	118
2.5	Ševko Pekmezović	123
2.6	From Sağlam 2007:64	131
2.7	Logo of the Saz Association	132
2.8	Mansur Bildik playing the Saz in Amerlinghaus, June 7, 2014	133
2.9	R-Kan	134
4.1	*Ethnomusicology* articles treating ethnolinguistic minority musics	207
4.2	The Create Local Arts Together (CLAT) methodology	209
7.1	The location of the Q'eros Nation in Peru. The Wachiperi region is due north of the Q'eros Nation, in the beginning of the green Amazon section	276
7.2	The location of the Q'eros Nation and the Q'eros River in reference to the Department capital of Cusco and province capital of Paucartambo	276
7.3	Digitized archives returned to the Queros-Wachiperi community. Estela Dariquebe and Manuel Yonaje, front, are the only two elders alive who recorded with Patricia Lyon in 1964 and 1965	278
7.4	Two US tourists with three Q'eros, learning about the Q'eros pinkuyllu flutes	280
7.5	A Q'eros couple sharing music with US tourists from inside an Inca niche	287

7.6	A young US high school student on a National Geographic student group tour in Peru learns a Q'eros song	289
7.7	A Q'eros man gives a "high five" to a US student on a National Geographic student group tour who has sung a Q'eros song with him	290
7.8	Estela Dariquebe, Carmen Jerewa, Manuel Yonaje: The three elders of the Queros-Wachiperi community who remember the traditional songs	302
7.9	Carmen Jerewa, the only active healer and esuwa singer in the community of Queros-Wachiperi	306
7.10	Front cover, Wachiperi CD: *Cantos Wachiperi: Familia linguística Harakbut, Grupo étnico Wachiperi*	312
7.11	Back cover, Wachiperi CD. CD song contents	313
7.12	Manuel Yonaje listens to Patricia J. Lyon's Wachiperi archive recordings	317

Tables

I.1	Comparative Musicology, Folk Music Research, and Ethnomusicology	39
2.1	Ethnic Minority Groups in Austria	106
2.2	Roma in Austria: Major Communities	112
4.1	Number and Integrality of Gbaguru Enactments, Mono Community	135

Box

4.1	Graded health assessment of artistic communication genres	203

Contributors

Michael B. Bakan is Professor of Ethnomusicology and Head of the World Music Ensembles Program at Florida State University, USA. He has published widely on the ethnomusicology of autism, Balinese gamelan music, and world music pedagogy, and serves as series editor for the Routledge Focus on World Music series. His current work aims to advance the epistemological positions of autistic self-advocacy and neurodiversity through musical engagement and ethnography.

Ursula Hemetek is Professor and Head of the Institute of Folk Music Research and Ethnomusicology at the University of Music and the Performing Arts, Vienna, Austria. The main focus of her research is the music of minorities in Austria, and her publications in the fields of Applied ethnomusicology and Music and minorities focus on Roma, Burgenland Croats, and recent immigrant groups. She has been Chairperson of the ICTM Study Group Music and Minorities from 1999 to 2017. Since 2017 she has been Secretary General of the ICTM.

Elizabeth Mackinlay is an Associate Professor in the School of Education at the University of Queensland, Australia, where she teaches Arts Education, Indigenous Education, Qualitative Research Methods, and Women's Studies. She completed her Ph.D. in Ethnomusicology in 1998 at the University of Adelaide and was awarded a second Ph.D. in Education from the University of Queensland in 2003. She is currently the co-editor of the *Australian Journal of Indigenous Education* (AJIE).

Svanibor Pettan is Professor and Chair of the Ethnomusicology Program at the University of Ljubljana, Slovenia. Initiator and first chair of the ICTM Study Group Applied Ethnomusicology and a founding member of the SEM Section on Applied Ethnomusicology, he contributes to the advancement of the field in the global arena with studies in various formats, addressing war-peace continuum, minorities, conflicts, and education. He currently serves as Vice-President of the International Council for Traditional Music and as Chair of its Study Group Music and Minorities.

Brian Schrag is SIL International's Ethnomusicology and Arts Coordinator, and founder of the Center for Excellence in World Arts, Dallas, USA, a graduate program in applied ethnoarts. He has performed sustained ethnomusicological research in the Democratic Republic of Congo and Cameroon, and holds a Ph.D. in Ethnomusicology (UCLA), an M.A. in Intercultural Studies (Wheaton, IL), and a B.S. in Cognitive Sciences (Brown University). He actively promotes artistic creativity for healing and education in communities affected by Huntington's Disease.

Zoe C. Sherinian is Professor of Ethnomusicology at the University of Oklahoma, USA. She has published the book *Tamil Folk Music as Dalit Liberation Theology* (Indiana University Press, 2014), as well as articles on the indigenization of Christianity in *Ethnomusicology, the world of music* and *Women and Music*. She has also produced and directed two documentaries on the changing status of outcaste drummers in India, *This Is a Music: Reclaiming an Untouchable Drum*, and *Sakthi Vibrations* on Dalit women drummers of the Sakthi Folk Cultural Centre.

Jeffrey A. Summit holds an appointment as Research Professor in the Department of Music and Judaic Studies at Tufts University, USA, where he is also Emeritus Jewish Chaplain and Emeritus Neubauer Executive Director of Tufts Hillel. His research focuses on music, identity, and spiritual experience, both in the American Jewish community and with Muslims, Jews, and Christians in Uganda. Since 2002, he has been involved in advocacy projects in Uganda supporting university education, Fair Trade, and interfaith cooperation.

Jeff Todd Titon is Professor of Music, Emeritus, at Brown University, Providence, Rhode Island, USA, where for 27 years he directed their Ph.D. program in ethnomusicology. The author or editor of eight books and numerous essays, he is well known as a pioneer in developing phenomenological and ecological approaches to ethnographic fieldwork, for theorizing and practicing an applied ethnomusicology based in reciprocity and friendship, and for introducing the concepts of cultural and musical sustainability to the fields of folklore and ethnomusicology. His current research on a sound ecology may be tracked at https://sustainablemusic.blogspot.com.

Holly Wissler is an applied ethnomusicologist, documentary filmmaker, tour leader and expert lecturer in Peru for National Geographic, Wilderness Travel, and U.S. university study abroad programs. Her research includes the musical traditions and modernization of the Quechua Q'eros (Andes) and the Harakbut Wachiperi (Amazon). She shares her time between Cusco, Peru and Austin, Texas, where she recently moved for the education of her deaf, adopted son from Q'eros, at the Texas School for the Deaf. She is adjunct lecturer in ethnomusicology at the University of Texas, Austin, USA.

About the Companion Website

www.oup.com/us/ohaev2

Oxford has created a website to accompany *The Oxford Handbook of Applied Ethnomusicology*. Audio recordings and color photographs, which cannot be made available in a book, are provided here. The reader is encouraged to consult this resource in conjunction with the chapters. Examples available online are indicated in the text with Oxford's symbol ⏵.

The list of sound recordings available online is given below:

Sound 7.1. "Wiquntuy" (*pukllay taki*—carnival song). Recording: Holly Wissler, February 2, 2007. Singer: Inocencia Quispe Pinkuyllu: Lucio Chura.

Sound 7.2. "Kapiro" (Welcome song, Great egret). Recording, Holly Wissler, December 10, 2010. Singer: Manuel Yonaje.

Sound 7.3. "Kapiro" (Welcome song, Great egret). Recording, Patricia J. Lyon, July 17, 1965. Singer: Mariano Dariquebe.

DE-COLONIZATION, HERITAGE, AND ADVOCACY

PART I

AN INTRODUCTION TO APPLIED ETHNOMUSICOLOGY

Our Introduction to this volume consists of three sections. Although applied ethnomusicology is practiced now in many regions of the world, it has developed differently in various times and places, just as ethnomusicology itself has. We begin in Section 1 (by Titon) with a focused statement on applied ethnomusicology as it has developed from a single representative area (the United States), and then broaden out in Section 2 (by Pettan) to a global perspective, where a greater plurality of voices and viewpoints may be observed, so that we may end with the understanding that applied ethnomusicology is no single field but is instead an ever-emergent movement, responding differently at various times and places, by means of music-centered interventions, to different cultures, histories, needs, and conditions. Indeed, this volume as a whole offers just such a plurality of voices and viewpoints. In addition to discussing histories and developments in national and global perspectives, particularly in the contexts of the US-based Society for Ethnomusicology (SEM) as well as the UNESCO-affiliated International Council for Traditional Music (ICTM), the co-editors also each offer personal perspectives, based in many years of involvement. Section 3, jointly written by Titon and Pettan, offers an introduction to the chapters that follow.

We wish to thank many people who have made this work possible. Suzanne Ryan, music editor at Oxford University Press, supported this project from the outset and helped us to understand how to shape the volume in conformity with *Handbook* expectations. The anonymous external reviewers read perceptively and made many useful comments and suggestions. For guidance, vision, and support along the path to applied ethnomusicology, Titon would like to thank colleagues and teachers Alan Kagan, Mulford Sibley, Charlotte Heth, David McAllester, Dennis Tedlock, Burt Feintuch, Erma Franklin, Loyal Jones, Elwood Cornett, Kenneth Irby, Maryanne Wolf, Sandy Ives, Archie Green, Bess Lomax Hawes, Daniel Sheehy, and Robert Baron.

Pettan would like to single out Samuel Araújo, Anthony Seeger, and Kjell Skyllstad, three important visionaries in applied ethnomusicology (among many more), who continue to inspire his own thinking and doing. Both editors thank the contributors to this volume, with whom it was a true honor and pleasure to join forces in creating this essentially important *Handbook*.

SECTION 1

APPLIED ETHNOMUSICOLOGY
A Descriptive and Historical Account

JEFF TODD TITON

Ethnomusicology and Applied Ethnomusicology

I like to think of *ethnomusicology* as the study of people making music (Titon, 1989, 1992b: xxi–xxii). People make sounds they call music, and they also make ideas about music. Those ideas form the cultural domain called music. They include what music is and is not; what it does and cannot do; how it is acquired and how it should be transmitted; what value it has; what it should (and should not) be used for; what it has been in the past and what it will be in the future; whether it should be encouraged and supported, or discouraged and repressed; and so forth. Just as music differs among individuals and social groups throughout the world, so do people's ideas about it differ, and this has been so throughout history.

Applied ethnomusicology puts ethnomusicological scholarship, knowledge, and understanding to practical use. That is a very broad definition. More specifically, as it has developed in North America and elsewhere, applied ethnomusicology is best regarded as a music-centered intervention in a particular community, whose purpose is to benefit that community—for example, a social improvement, a musical benefit, a cultural good, an economic advantage, or a combination of these and other benefits. It is music-centered, but above all the intervention is people-centered, for the understanding that drives it toward reciprocity is based in the collaborative partnerships that arise from ethnomusicological fieldwork. Applied ethnomusicology is guided by ethical principles of social responsibility, human rights, and cultural and musical equity. Although some ethnomusicologists regard applied ethnomusicology as a career alternative to academic work—and indeed, it can be—it's not always helpful to make that distinction, because ethnomusicologists who do applied work are employed both inside academic institutions, such as universities and museums, and outside them in government agencies, nongovernmental organizations (NGOs), and client organizations directly. In other words, the place of employment does not determine whether the ethnomusicology has any application outside the world of scholarship. What matters is the work itself: how, where, and why the intervention occurs, and the communities to whom we feel responsible (Titon, 2003; Dirksen, 2012).

Putting ethnomusicological scholarship, knowledge, and understanding to practical use and terming it *applied* implies the usual distinction made in the sciences between pure research, or the pursuit of knowledge for its own sake (as it is often called), and applied research, or knowledge put to practical use. It is possible to minimize this distinction, claiming that the moment a researcher circulates knowledge within a scholarly community it is being put to beneficial use. Classroom teaching is of course another kind of use. Besides, the phrase knowledge for its own sake appears oxymoronic, for in what sense can knowledge possibly be for its own sake if knowledge cannot logically be an agent or a self? If all ethnomusicological knowledge is put to use in one way or another, then the term applied ethnomusicology is redundant. All of this may be so, but for strategic reasons the editors of this volume find the term useful, in order to highlight a certain kind of activity and distinguish an ethnomusicology based in social responsibility where knowledge is intended for beneficial use in communities outside the academic world from an ethnomusicology which is meant to increase and improve the storehouse of knowledge about music and circulate it among scholars. In the absence of this distinction, as I will argue later (see below, "Applied Ethnomusicology in the United States: A Brief History"), applied ethnomusicology has been marginalized or ignored in the definitions and histories of our field that circulate among ethnomusicologists. Indeed, examination of ethnomusicology curricula reveals very few, if any, courses devoted to applied work at the doctoral level. The Ph.D. is a research degree, after all, and the chief criterion for career advancement in the university remains research that enjoys a high intellectual reputation among scholars. Fortunately, however, a sense of social responsibility motivates an increasing number of ethnomusicologists, employed inside and outside the academic world, who find ways to integrate it into their scholarly research, and to apply it in the public arena. Readers who wish to know more about my personal involvement with, and views on, applied ethnomusicology are invited to consult Titon 2003 and various entries on applied ethnomusicology on my blog at http://sustainablemusic.blogspot.com.

This volume is not meant as a "how-to" handbook, like the *Girl Scout Handbook*. Rather, in keeping with the other Oxford Handbooks in this series, it offers a sampling of current scholarship related to its subject, with contributions from some leading exponents. Applied ethnomusicology is a field of practice and theory, rather than a discipline with a bounded subject and an established, universally agreed-upon methodology. A branch of the academic discipline of ethnomusicology, its scope is still expanding. While its practitioners are in broad agreement over putting ethnomusicological knowledge to use rather than simply pursuing it as an end in itself, we differ in emphasis, whether in definition, method, or purpose (Harrison, 2012). Readers may look here for a variety of subjects, approaches and models.

Applied Ethnomusicology in Contemporary North America: A Brief Overview

What kinds of activities are applied ethnomusicologists involved in? Where, typically, do we intervene in the public arena? The co-editors of this volume, one active in North America, the other in Europe, have determined to write about these activities in the areas they know best. As I am most familiar with activities in the United States, and the professional organization based there (the *Society for Ethnomusicology*, or SEM), what follows in my part of this Introduction highlights US-based applied ethnomusicology. I will discuss the history (and prehistory) of applied ethnomusicology, and its reception, in the United States since the late 1800s. But before sketching that history, I describe applied ethnomusicology as it is practiced today. What are applied ethnomusicologists doing now? What are our goals, and how are we positioned within the larger world both within and outside the academy?

First, we are involved in promoting traditional music, dance, and other cultural expressions in order to benefit artists, traditions, and communities. Whether undertaken by ethnomusicologists acting primarily on their own behalf, or whether supported by cultural organizations, these *cultural policy interventions* are among the oldest types of applied ethnomusicology and remain one of the most common, particularly as directed toward minority, immigrant, and otherwise underserved populations within developed nations, and among indigenous peoples throughout the world. Sometimes, but not always, these musics are considered threatened or even endangered. Lately, sustainability has become the generally accepted policy goal, whether the musics are endangered or not (see Schippers, Chapter 4, and Titon, Chapter 5, in Volume 1). Cultural trauma has often been an important motivating factor, particularly when cultural renewal appears important in the face of political and economic stress (see Haskell, Chapter 6 in Volume 1). Examples of these interventions include the settlement schools in the southern Appalachian mountains, begun more than a century ago to promote the arts and crafts of mountain folk culture; the immigrant folk music and dance programs for children and adults in large cities such as New York and Chicago, which involved settlement schools and included festivals as well as adult recreation groups and additions to the public school curriculum; national radio broadcasts undertaken by Alan Lomax shortly before World War II to bring the songs and stories of ordinary citizens into media circulation; regional and national festivals such as the Smithsonian Folklife Festival, begun in the 1960s; policymaking and granting agencies that promote community arts, such as historical societies, arts councils, and the National Endowments; and NGOs devoted to expanding the creative economy through musical heritage and cultural tourism, sometimes with a view to recovering from ecological disasters such as hurricanes, urban blight, and mountaintop removal. In the twenty-first century, UNESCO has become the major international force in cultural policy, with its treaties encouraging the preservation of what it calls intangible cultural heritage. The United States has not signed these treaties, but outside the United States many ethnomusicologists are involved with UNESCO activities and indeed, some North American ethnomusicologists participated in the planning and ongoing review stages. Ethnomusicologists have worked as consultants, arts administrators, ethnographic fieldworkers, festival presenters, radio and television producers, podcasters and internet site developers, educators, facilitators, mediators, writers, expert witnesses, and in various other capacities formulating and administering cultural policies whose purpose is sociocultural, economic, and musical benefit. Ethnomusicologists also have been among those theorizing cultural policy interventions, and have contributed to a growing critical literature evaluating these practices. Many of the chapters in this volume comprise a part of this ongoing scholarship concerning applied ethnomusicology.

Another area of practice is *advocacy*, either on behalf of particular music-makers or a music community as a whole. Rather than adopting the role of the neutral, objective, scientific observer gathering information, the applied ethnomusicologist assumes the role of a partisan, working in partnership toward goals that are mutually understood and agreed upon. Indeed, the most successful advocacy usually arises after ethnomusicologists have visited and listened to the musicians articulate their concerns and what they would like to achieve. Seldom has partnership worked when the ethnomusicologist plays the role of expert and imposes solutions to problems perceived from a distance, or fails to understand the musical community's perspective. Advocacy includes grant-writing on behalf of individuals and communities; writing promotional and press materials; acting as an agent to arrange performances; facilitating community self-documentation initiatives; repatriation of recordings and musical artifacts from museums and archives; political lobbying for arts spaces; facilitating community arts education projects; researching the history of musical traditions for the community; acting as an intermediary between cultural insiders and outsiders; long-term planning for the sustainability of community music cultures; and in general working in partnership and on behalf of musicians and their communities. Advocacy usually arises from relationships developed over time, when an ethnomusicologist is attracted to particular musicians or music cultures, visits them for research purposes and returns, and determines to make a commitment that goes beyond mere study. Academic ethnomusicologists undertaking long-term fieldwork in a community are well-positioned for this, but while an increasing number do become advocates, some prefer to remain neutral observers.

A third area of practice involves *education*. Often educators themselves, applied ethnomusicologists work with other educators designing curricula, and to bring musicians into the schools to demonstrate, teach, and perform; they also facilitate visits to performance spaces where youngsters may observe and participate in music-making activities. Music education once prepared youth to participate mainly in the culture of classical music, or as US academics call it these days, Western art music. As cultural pluralism and multicultural initiatives in North American schools gained traction in the last third of the twentieth century, musical pluralism increased, introducing popular music, jazz, and the music and dance of ethnic communities to the school curricula. Ethnomusicologists have been active in making musical activities more inclusive, fostering interest in local musical artists and traditions, particularly from newly arrived cultural and ethnic groups. In this way, music is viewed as a way to increase intercultural understanding.

Other areas of contemporary practice include *peace and conflict resolution; medicine; law and the music industry; libraries, museums, and sound archives; journalism;* and *environmental sound activism and ecojustice.* Peace-related applications are more frequent outside North America, but work of this sort has been done in Canada in disputes between First Nations communities and the Canadian government, while music has been an important part of labor and civil rights movements in the United States since the nineteenth century. Among the projects of medical ethnomusicology are HIV-AIDS work in Africa, therapeutic work with post-traumatic stress survivors, and music within the autism community. Legal applications have involved ethnomusicologists testifying as expert witnesses, particularly in music copyright infringement cases, and work on copyright and intellectual property issues as the question "who owns culture" becomes increasingly important when money is to be made and cases of exploitation have been documented. Ethnomusicologists have served as advisors to the World Intellectual Property Organization (WIPO), a UNESCO-sponsored group attempting to arrive at laws for protecting intellectual property rights in the international arena. Ethnomusicologists are contributing to ecological studies of the soundscape, and of the effects of environmental noise on physiological and psychological health. We are involved in political action opposing sound pollution, such as noise from ocean vessels and military activities that affect whales, dolphins, and other sea mammals. Applied ethnomusicologists are contributing to the new discipline of ecomusicology, which involves music and sound in a time of environmental crisis. Journalists educated in ethnomusicology bring to world music a broadly informed historical and geographical perspective. Some are writing for newspapers, magazines, and online publications; many are active in promoting music, and some are performing musicians ourselves. Ethnomusicologists working in the music industry serve as consultants, ethnographers, technical assistants, and producers. Many libraries, museums, universities, and other institutions maintain sound archives where archivists with ethnomusicological training offer expertise in acquisition, cataloging, grant-writing, preservation, and outreach.

Since the 1990s, when applied ethnomusicology became a recognizable force within ethnomusicology, other names have been advanced to describe some of the work that applied ethnomusicologists do; but they ought not to be confused with applied ethnomusicology, which is the covering term.[1] *Public-sector ethnomusicology* describes applied ethnomusicology that is practiced by people employed by public-sector, taxpayer-funded (i.e., government) institutions such as (in the United States) the Library of Congress, the Smithsonian Institution, the National Endowment for the Arts, and state arts councils; and whose efforts are directed to the public at large while often targeted at particular communities within it. By definition, "public-sector ethnomusicology" is unable to include applied ethnomusicology as practiced by those who work in the private sector, in NGOs such as museums, historical societies, foundations, and various non-profit organizations, even when part of their funding comes from government grants; nor does it describe the work of applied ethnomusicologists in corporations and client organizations. *Public ethnomusicology* is a better name for this activity, insofar as it focuses on applications in the public arena. But both terms, public sector and public, neglect the private sphere and perpetuate an unhelpful distinction between academia and the world outside of colleges and universities. As I have pointed out, applied ethnomusicology is practiced by those employed inside the academic world as well as outside of it. Ethnomusicology appears to be in danger of replicating the same terminological virus that has infected American folklore studies since the 1980s, one which American Folklore Society President Barbara Kirshenblatt-Gimblett labeled a "mistaken dichotomy" (Kirshenblatt-Gimblett, 1988).

APPLIED ETHNOMUSICOLOGY: BEING, KNOWING, AND DOING

Some ethnomusicologists are attracted to applied work, and others not so much. Most ethnomusicologists, I've observed, do share certain characteristics, however. Sound and music are immensely important to the way we orient ourselves. As humans, we are beings "in the world" through all of our senses, but we are particularly aware of vibrations that come to us as sound. Epistemologically, we feel that knowing sound—and knowing by means of sound—is essential to being human in the world and is one of the most important avenues through which to understand the human condition. Certainly it is our special avenue. Where we diverge, somewhat, is in what we *do* as a result of this ontological and epistemological orientation. Some of us are most interested in pursuing and increasing knowledge about sound and music in the world, the music of the world's peoples. This is the usual end of scholarship. Scholars feel a special responsibility to present, discuss, debate, and circulate this knowledge among colleagues and students in the institutional world of universities and professional associations of ethnomusicologists. Others, those of us who practice applied ethnomusicology, also feel a responsibility to help put this knowledge to practical use in the public arena; and so either in addition to our research, scholarship, and teaching within the university world, or instead of it, we also involve ourselves in interventions into musical communities, for public benefit.

Some 45 years ago Mantle Hood wrote a textbook about the nature of ethnomusicology, but instead of titling it *Ethnomusicology* he named it *The Ethnomusicologist* (Hood, 1971). In the Introduction he described an ideal ethnomusicologist's background, education, skills and aptitudes, and personality. It was an unusual emphasis for a graduate textbook in ethnomusicology, but then this was an unusual book, often written in the first person, and to some extent reflecting, I think, the California social and intellectual atmosphere of the 1960s that had also produced public figures like Stewart Brand and Jerry Brown. Although the influence of personality on an ethnomusicologist's accomplishments is not often written about, it is sometimes discussed among ethnomusicologists, especially when we reflect on ethnographic fieldwork, that rite of passage in which ethnomusicologists (like their counterparts in cultural anthropology) traditionally travel to a different, and sometimes strange, culture and while there, try to learn something of the musical universe among that group of people. It is difficult, sometimes alienating, even psychologically traumatic, work (Wengle, 1988); and ethnomusicologists tend to think that certain personality types are better able to accomplish it than others. Applied ethnomusicologists like to interact with our field subjects, not just observe them. We feel a desire to give something back in exchange for what we are learning, and this impulse leads us not only to research but to work directly for the benefit of those we visit. And so although most ethnomusicologists are in the world ontologically and epistemologically in similar ways, we differ somewhat over what we should be doing with those ways of being and knowing. It should go without saying that applied ethnomusicologists engage in research and contribute to the growth of knowledge. Our Ph.D.s are research degrees, after all, and many of us have made substantial scholarly contributions to the flow of knowledge inside academia. But we also feel a social responsibility to put that knowledge to use in the public arena.

APPLIED ETHNOMUSICOLOGY IN THE UNITED STATES: A BRIEF HISTORY

As the co-editors worked on this volume and saw it through an eight-year period of invitations, proposals, abstracts, essays, reviews, revisions, and yet more reviews and more revisions, it became increasingly and unsettlingly clear that many US contributors thought of their work within a local and national context but knew relatively little about the history, ideas, and accomplishments of applied ethnomusicologists living outside the United States. Non-US contributors were similarly knowledgeable about applied work in their spheres of activity outside North America, but generally unaware of the history, projects, scholarship, and cultural policies generated by applied ethnomusicology in North America. Ideas that had been theorized, practiced, and thoroughly critiqued in some localities were being introduced in others as if they were newly discovered. More than once, contributors seemed to be reinventing wheels. Many whose work would benefit from an exchange of ideas with others involved in similar projects elsewhere were not taking advantage of that possibility. Although we believe that the reasons for this insularity have more to do with institutional histories and geography than with any serious divergence over assumptions, approach, and goals, one of the happy consequences of this volume, we hope, will be to increase the dialogue among practitioners of applied ethnomusicology no matter where they work, so that each becomes aware of the ways in which similar problems have been faced, and solutions attempted, elsewhere, while problems and issues that had not even occurred to some will become apparent after reading about the work of others. Another consequence of this insularity, however, was that it became impossible to sketch a unified history and description of applied ethnomusicology apart from those considerations. For that reason, in this section I construct a history of applied ethnomusicology in the United States, related to the growth of ethnomusicology and its professional organization, SEM, founded in 1955. (Svanibor Pettan writes in Section 2 of this Introduction about the communities of applied ethnomusicologists associated with the International Council on Traditional Music [ICTM], and its earlier incarnation, the International Folk Music Council [IFMC, founded in 1947].) In doing so, I draw on a graduate seminar in the history of ethnomusicological thought which I led at Brown University from 1988 until 2013. Reflexivity, postcolonial ethnomusicology, efforts to sustain musical genres and cultures, collaborative ethnography and advocacy, tourism and the creative economy, archival stewardship and repatriation of field recordings, applications to medicine and to peace and conflict resolution, proper roles for government in the arts, the place of world music in education—these are not new themes in our field, but the timing of their entrances, their reception, and their use in applied work has not been uniform among the North American, European, Asian, African, Australian, and Latin American communities of applied ethnomusicologists.

Strictly speaking, the history of ethnomusicology began in 1950, when Jaap Kunst invented the term and it entered scholarly discourse (Kunst, 1950). I prefer to think of the pre-1950 period as ethnomusicology's prehistory, paying particular attention to the two disciplines, comparative musicology and cultural anthropology, that combined in the 1950s as ethnomusicology.[2] I find prototypes of US applied ethnomusicology among nineteenth-century ethnologists and folklorists whose field research in music exhibited both social responsibility and collaborative involvement with musical communities for their benefit. Music was an integral part of early folklore and anthropology, not an afterthought. From the very beginning, scholars writing for the *American Anthropologist* and the *Journal of American Folklore* showed much interest in people making music. The second issue of the former contained an essay by Washington Matthews (1843–1905) on a Navajo sung prayer (Matthews, 1888), for example, while the inaugural issue of the latter featured an article on Kwakiutl music and dance by Franz Boas (1858–1942), the most influential North American anthropologist of his generation (Boas, 1888). Boas's article described some of the group's music, stories, and their ideas and behavior in relation to them; it contained musical transcriptions, and mentioned his 1886 music collecting trip with the German comparative musicologist and music psychologist Carl Stumpf among the Bella Coola. Nothing in Boas's article might be considered applied ethnomusicology per se, but Boas undertook a public anthropology project of enormous import in the early twentieth century when he opposed so-called scientific racism and helped establish the idea that differences in human behavior result from learned cultural, rather than fixed biological, traits.

Matthews's work was aided by a deeply collaborative relationship in which he underwent Native rituals and may have married a Hidatsa woman. Collaborative relationships in which the parties work toward mutually agreed-upon goals became a hallmark of applied ethnomusicology, but their roots may be found in people like Matthews, as well as Alice Cunningham Fletcher (1838–1923), whose collaborative work moved more clearly in the direction of social and economic benefits that would be recognized today as applied ethnomusicology. Fletcher, who became President of both the American Anthropological Association and the American Folklore Society, as well as Vice President of the American Association for the Advancement of Science, lived with the Sioux in 1881, and collaborated with an Omaha, Frances La Flesche, whom she took into her household from 1890 on. Falling ill with a severe case of rheumatoid arthritis in 1883, she was nursed back to health by her Native American friends, who sang to her while she lay recovering. Then, she wrote, "the sweetness, the beauty and meaning of these songs were revealed to me" (Fletcher, 1994: 8). Like the others, Fletcher undertook ethnographic studies of Native music; but she also worked tirelessly on behalf of Native American education, integration, and advancement into mainstream culture.

"Giving back" is the usual term North American ethnomusicologists employ to identify this reciprocity, which has taken various forms over the decades. However, Fletcher's efforts at aiding Native Americans are characterized today as attempts to Americanize them, a "grievous error in the administration of Native American lands and peoples" according to a Smithsonian Institution author (Smithsonian: Fletcher). Ethnomusicologists consider it unfortunate that the Omaha songs she collected were published with Western harmonization, added to them by the musician John Comfort Fillmore, who convinced Fletcher that these harmonies were implicit in the Omaha melodies (Fletcher, 1994). Nonetheless, Fletcher may be understood in her time as a progressive. The principal alternative to Americanization (or Christianization), after all, had for nearly three centuries been genocide. And prominent American composers such as Edward MacDowell were quoting, transforming, and harmonizing Native American melodies in their musical compositions.

Daniel Sheehy and Anthony Seeger trace the history of twentieth-century pioneers in applied ethnomusicology, such as Robert Winslow Gordon, Alan Lomax, and Charles Seeger (Sheehy, 1992; Seeger, 2006). In terming them applied ethnomusicologists, Seeger, Sheehy, and others combine ethnomusicology's historical and pre-historical periods. Certainly, these ancestors would have been called applied ethnomusicologists if ethnomusicology proper had come into being prior to 1950. To some extent their work was related to that of early anthropologists such as A. L. Kroeber and others on endangered Native American languages. The Lomaxes' folk music collections were meant for the general public, to supply a kind of people's alternative to the art music that was being taught in the public schools. Alan Lomax insisted that the treasure trove of folk music should be made accessible through media production, which in the 1940s and 1950s meant radio programs—he produced dozens of them for national broadcast. He issued an appeal for "cultural equity" that articulated many of the principles under which he had been operating for decades (Lomax, 1972). Lomax's "Appeal" may be the single most often-cited document in the literature of US applied ethnomusicology. Charles Seeger, Anthony Seeger's grandfather, had issued a call in 1939 for an applied musicology that would follow from government involvement in the arts, a vision in some ways similar to the situation in China today (Seeger, 2006: 227–228; also see Zhang, Chapter 6 of Volume 3). Seeger and his wife Ruth Crawford Seeger, John and Alan Lomax, Herbert Halpert, Zora Neale Hurston, and others were involved in efforts to encourage folk music (as the authentic popular music of a democratic society) during the Roosevelt administration. These activities, of course, diminished greatly as the United States concentrated during the 1940s on mobilization for World War II. But Sheehy concludes that "there is a tradition of applied thought and purpose that should be included in the history of ethnomusicology," as well as "an evolving sense of strategy and techniques for action that has flowed through this thought and that demands our attention as ethnomusicologists" (Sheehy, 1992: 329). Anthony Seeger entitled his 2006 essay "Lost Lineages" in the history of ethnomusicology and, like Sheehy, called for a more inclusive history of the field.

The usual historical accounts of ethnomusicology in the United States are not so inclusive: applied ethnomusicology is treated either as a peripheral activity or, more often, ignored entirely. These mainstream accounts trace ethnomusicology's roots to comparative musicology, a scientific project of the European Enlightenment. They do not pay much attention to its roots in folklore and cultural anthropology. In 1885 Guido Adler defined comparative musicology as "the comparison of the musical works . . . of the various peoples of the earth for ethnographical purposes, and the classification of them according to their various forms" (Haydon, 1941: 117). Comparative musicology began in the latter part of the nineteenth century with the systematization of music knowledge, which proceeded with the measurable, classificatory, and comparative procedures borrowed from philology, embryology, and other sciences, generating various hypotheses concerning origins, growth, diffusion, and function. Aided by the recording phonograph and efforts of various music collectors, it included the comparative work on the musical scales of various nations accomplished by the Englishman Alexander Ellis, and the research of the German Carl Stumpf and others in music psychology (or psychophysical science, as it was then called). Comparative musicology was further developed as a research discipline in early twentieth-century Berlin by Stumpf's younger colleague Erich von Hornbostel, Curt Sachs, and others, with related scholarship accomplished by Béla Bartok in Hungary, Constantin Brailliou in Rumania, and others in the fields of comparative musical folklore and the sociology of music.

Comparative musicology arrived in the United States in 1925 in the person of George Herzog, who had been von Hornbostel's assistant in Berlin. He went on to study anthropology with Franz Boas at Columbia University, specializing in "primitive music," as it was then called. Herzog received his doctorate in 1931 under Boas's supervision and pursued an academic career at Yale, Columbia, and Indiana University that lasted until the mid-1950s. He was recognized during this period as the leading authority on "primitive music." Among his students were two of the founders of SEM, David McAllester and Willard Rhodes. Bruno Nettl, who has written knowledgeably about Herzog's contributions to comparative musicology, was another of his students (Nettl and Bohlman, 1991: 270–272; Nettl, 2002: 90–92; Nettl, 2010: 168). Herzog's writings exhibited an empirical, scientific method that required large amounts of reliable data, a high standard to which he held himself and others. "All evidence," he wrote, "points to the wisdom of dispensing with sweeping theoretical schemes and of inquiring in each case into the specific historical processes that have molded the culture and musical style of a nation or tribe.... So little is actually known ... that the main attention of this field [of comparative musicology] is devoted to increasing that little, and collecting more material before it all disappears under the impact of Western civilization" (Herzog, 1936: 3). He had learned the importance of fieldwork and data-gathering from his teacher Boas, and he insisted on that, as well as musical transcription and analysis, from his students. His methods added Boas-styled ethnographic research to the comparative analysis that characterized the work of Horbostel and the Berlin school.

A useful summary of comparative musicology, with due attention to Herzog's prominence in the United States, appeared in Glen Haydon's graduate-level textbook, *Introduction to Musicology* (Haydon, 1941). As outlined there, its purpose was to increase knowledge of the music of the world's peoples. Academic research was the means to that end. The work of numerous comparative musicologists, chiefly European, was described, and their most important publications referenced. But comparative musicology soon underwent a facelift. Historical accounts date this to Jaap Kunst's book *Ethno-Musicology* (Kunst, 1950, and two subsequent editions), which defined *ethnomusicology* as the study of "all tribal and folk music and every kind of non-Western art music. Besides, it studies as well the sociological aspects of music . . . " (ibid., 1950: 1). Although he is usually credited with inventing the term *ethnomusicology*, Kunst's argument for the name change rested chiefly on redundancy of the word "comparative." All good science, he argued, is comparative in nature; disciplines like linguistics and embryology had, after all, dropped the adjective for the time being. His argument was persuasive, and some comparative musicologists began to adopt the new name, while others who wished to place more emphasis on the cultural study of music and less on musical analysis welcomed the name change and saw opportunity in it. However, comparative musicology remained the ancestral predecessor for Kunst and in later US historical accounts of the discipline, chiefly by Bruno Nettl (1956, 1964, 1983, 2002, 2005, 2010) as well as others. For nearly 60 years these historical accounts have informed generations of ethnomusicology professors and graduate students, in the United States and elsewhere. Despite increased theoretical sophistication and a growing recognition of historical relativism (e.g., Nettl and Bohlman, eds., 1991; Nettl, 2010; Rice, 2014), different subject emphases by other authors (e.g., Hood, 1971; Merriam, 1964), and an enlarged cast of characters (McLean, 2006), these mainstream histories continue to construct ethnomusicology as a research discipline almost exclusively centered in the academic world. Applied ethnomusicology seldom appears; when it does, it usually is treated with some reservations. As long as comparative musicology remained ethnomusicology's central occupation, applied work would be marginal at best.

The founding of the Society for Ethnomusicology (SEM) in 1955 not only provided an opportunity for a new emphasis on the cultural study of music, but might also have moved applied ethnomusicology to a more central position. Why it did not do so, at a time when applied anthropology was becoming important within US cultural anthropology, is an interesting question. In large part, as this brief history will show, the answer has to do with the founding generation's desire to establish and expand ethnomusicology as an academic discipline, on a firm institutional footing, throughout the university world. In so doing, they missed an opportunity to integrate applied work into the agenda of the new Society. It was left for the next generation to do so.

The early period of SEM was, predictably, taken up with debate over the direction of the discipline. In its first 15 years or so, the SEM journal, *Ethnomusicology*, was filled with essays by many leading practitioners who attempted to define the discipline and influence its course. Research in ethnomusicology's first two decades (ca. 1950–1975) has been characterized as falling broadly into two approaches, one musicological and the other anthropological (Kerman, 1986: 155–181). This is an oversimplification, but it is useful in highlighting the legacies of Hornbostel and Herzog, which in SEM could be seen in the work of Herzog's former colleague Kolinski, William Malm, George List, Mantle Hood, and Nettl, among others. Their focus was on collecting, recording, transcribing, describing, classifying, analyzing, and comparing music in order to increase the music knowledge-base and to test theories concerning musical distribution, diffusion, and acculturation. Like Herzog, most were interested also in the ethnographic study of cultural contexts for music ("music in culture") and in comparing and contrasting music's functions within cultures. Unless one thinks of the polymath Seeger as a comparativist, these comparative musicologists were not represented among the four SEM founders; but their work was prominent in monographs and in *Ethnomusicology*, where they advanced their scholarship and their view of what ethnomusicology ought to be. They also played a major role in establishing ethnomusicology as an academic discipline at the graduate level in US universities during the first 20 years of SEM.

On the other side of the debate over the future of ethnomusicology were the anthropologists, dance ethnologists, folklorists, and various other scholars who shared an interest in music and had been attracted to the new field. Most prominent among these were the anthropologists Alan Merriam and David McAllester, both among the four founders of SEM. Herzog was noticeably absent from SEM's origins, and it is worth asking why. Nettl, who writes movingly and generously about Herzog, observed that Herzog already was behaving erratically in 1952 (he would be hospitalized from the mid-1950s onward, with occasional time off, until his death in 1983, for what we would now call a bipolar disorder) and attributes his absence to this (Nettl, 2002: 90–92; Nettl, 2010: 168; Nettl and Bohlman, 1991: 271–272). No doubt this is correct; but it appears that the founders also wished to escape Herzog's dominance over the field. McAllester reported that as far as he knew, he was the only student ever to complete the doctorate under Herzog's supervision. "The campus was littered with the bodies of failed Herzog students," McAllester said. Herzog's habit was to demonstrate to them time after time that they could not meet his standards. "He never failed them in so many words," McAllester continued, "but they had a very hard time ever getting an appointment with him, and when they finally did, it was all at such a high level that they felt sort of defeated. If they brought in a transcription, it was so bad that he went over it note by note to show them and said, now see if you can't, now that you've had this practice, do better next time. Then a month or so later, when they caught up with him again, then the same thing would happen again." Rhodes was one of the dropouts, but he was already a full professor at Columbia and did not need the degree; yet it remained a sore point with him and his friend McAllester both. Even before Herzog moved from Columbia to Indiana University in 1948, he had been showing signs of the mental instability that would institutionalize him (Memorial Resolution, 1983). Herzog was Nettl's dissertation supervisor at Indiana, but before Nettl could complete his doctorate, Herzog's erratic behavior forced him to move to a different supervisor. "Bruno studied with him [Herzog] when he went out to Indiana, and he [Nettl] had a professor for a father, and so he had a strong position," McAllester said. (Paul Nettl, Bruno's father, was a professor of musicology at Indiana University.) "And he [Nettl] demanded another teacher, and he finished his Ph.D. with Carl Voegelin, the linguist. He left Herzog, but most of us couldn't do that. We were with Herzog and it was do or die, and many died" (McAllester, 1989).

No wonder then, given McAllester's and Rhodes's opinion of him, that Herzog was not invited into the inner circle of SEM founders. At that time they may have been less aware of Herzog's illness and decline than Nettl and the others who worked with Herzog at Indiana. But that must be only part of the answer. The other part is that McAllester, Merriam, Rhodes, and Seeger wanted to take a new direction, to move away from comparative musicology and Boasian ethnography, and toward an ethnomusicology that would make room not only for a greater variety of authoritative voices but also for more emphasis on the cultural study of music. Reaching out to scholars throughout the world, in 1953 the four founders initiated an ethnomusicology *Newsletter*, and two years later they founded the Society for Ethnomusicology (SEM), designed to foster communication and research in the field. SEM immediately began publishing a journal, *Ethnomusicology*, which since its inception has served as the flagship research periodical for the discipline. It is worth pausing for a moment to examine what the founders themselves thought they were up to. Nettl, reminiscing about this early period, the name change from "comparative musicology" to "ethnomusicology," and the founding of SEM, recalls that he (and others, he thinks) regarded these events more as a "revival" of a great scholarly tradition (comparative musicology, which had been all but eliminated in Europe during the Nazi era) than as a revolution (Nettl, 2010: 160–162). Inclined toward his teacher Herzog's understanding of that tradition, Nettl's subject position is understandable. Still a graduate student at the time and not directly involved as a founder, he had nevertheless set his course and was already a major stakeholder in the new field. His memoirs (Nettl, 2002, 2010, 2013) of this transitional period are both charming and invaluable, filled with information unavailable elsewhere and required reading for anyone interested in the history of ethnomusicology. In these memoirs, he tries to deconstruct the "myth" of SEM's "grand entrance," as he puts it, arguing that its historical significance and the importance of the four founders has been overrated (Nettl, 2010: 160–165). In retrospect, it is apparent that comparative musicology continued to exert a strong influence upon ethnomusicology during its first few decades (ca. 1950–1980). But the new Society, the new name, and its founders' orientation toward anthropology is a historical fact that signaled a significant and enduring new direction for the field.

Let me try to reconstruct something of that significance as I believe it to have appeared to the founders at the time. (In so doing, I rely in part on my conversations with Rhodes, Merriam, Seeger, and especially McAllester about that period.) McAllester recalled that after Herzog was finally confined to a mental hospital, he could no longer exercise his former control over degrees, grants, and publications in the field. "He became so ill that he had to be in an institution, and then the lid was off and the Society [SEM] could be established" (McAllester, 1989). For the four founders, SEM represented a move away from comparative musicology, not simply as an escape from Herzog's iron grip, but in establishing a new interdisciplinary field: ethnomusicology. The founders resisted efforts from other Societies who tried to dissuade them from starting a new Society. The American Musicological Society sent representatives to their early meetings and "announced that we should not be a splinter group, but that we should be part of the American Musicological Society.... And we said, if we joined them, the AMS, there were a whole bunch of people that would not be any longer members. We had folklorists, anthropologists, ethnologists, acousticians, physicists... and they would have dropped out if we had become a part of the American Musicological Society." These same scholars likewise would have left SEM had they allied themselves with the IFMC, McAllester reported. "Maud Karpeles came and pleaded with us to become a wing of the International Folk Music Council.... Alan Merriam particularly, well, Charlie Seeger too, they were both very insistent that it not get into the hands of... the International Folk Music [Council]. So when we started the society, they [the IFMC] soon got wind of it, and they were very upset because they had their American branch and they were afraid we would simply split their society and draw membership away from them.... There were scholars among them, great scholars among them, but they were not anthropologically oriented. And it just happened by the way we operated, that the Society for Ethnomusicology began with an anthropological orientation" (McAllester, 1989). Nettl agreed: "The beginning of the SEM was deeply rooted in the anthropological background of its most influential leaders" (Nettl, 2010: 143).

McAllester recalled the excitement that accompanied the founding of SEM, along with the possibilities of new directions for the Society. For Merriam even more than for McAllester, that direction was to be cultural anthropology. Eventually he termed this direction "the anthropology of music" rather than "comparative musicology," and he lobbied hard for the study of music, not in culture, but *as* culture, a phrase ("music as culture") that Merriam referenced to his earlier "unpublished thoughts" (Merriam, 1977: 204). According to Merriam, music was not something that existed within a cultural context; it *was* culture in the anthropological sense itself, with its own domain of ideas, behavior, and sonic dimension. Obtaining a full professorship in anthropology at Indiana University in 1962, Merriam was not only a founder but a forceful presence in SEM from the very beginning until his untimely death in an airplane crash in 1980. His area interests were in indigenous musics primarily, Native American and African. A former jazz musician, he had little use for the study of folk music, and even less for bi-musicality, about which more shortly. When I taught a summer session in Indiana's Folklore Institute in 1977, he invited me to his home a number of times. He had just remarried, and was in an expansive mood. Relevant for this historical sketch is the attitude he expressed toward the IFMC. He affirmed that the founders had refused Maud Karpeles's invitation to join the International Folk Music Council rather than form their own Society. Nettl attributed Merriam's reasons for objecting to the IFMC to "his perception of the IFMC as specifically interested in music alone, the notion that folk-music scholars were interested in only a small segment of the music of any society; and the idea that the IFMC included a substantial practical component, that is, was in large measure a society of folksingers and dancers" (Nettl, 2010: 143). Merriam's views had evolved since then, for in 1977 he told me the IFMC as a group was insufficiently objective and scientific about music as a human phenomenon. If they had been, they would have been concerned with all music, not mainly the oldest layers of music in what were then regarded as folk societies (Redfield, 1947). And if they had been, they would not have been so concerned with authenticity and so worried about salvaging this music for archival preservation; or worse yet, reviving it for a sophisticated urban audience. Merriam took some pleasure in noting that Indiana University's Folklore Institute did not share this attitude toward musical revivalism; indeed, Richard Dorson, the head of the Institute, had coined the term "fakelore" to describe it, and on the advice of George List, the senior ethnomusicologist in the Folklore Institute, Dorson would not permit amateur folk musicians in their doctoral program to undertake music research unless they had had sufficient formal training in Western music theory and history to be admitted to ethnomusicology courses. As Indiana was one of only a very few universities in the US granting doctoral degrees in folklore, the amount of academic research in US folk music during the Dorson-List-Merriam era was severely diminished as a consequence. For Merriam, ethnomusicology was revolutionary insofar as it elevated anthropology to a position of equality with musicology in birthing the new offspring, ethnomusicology. The *ethno-* prefix (derived from the Greek *ethnos* [= people with a common culture]) firmly established it as a new discipline that was properly part of "the scientific study of man," as anthropology had long been defined. Merriam assiduously pursued this goal, which he called "sciencing about music" (Merriam, 1964: 25 et passim).

With SEM established on the promise of interdisciplinarity and new directions, particularly from anthropology, one might have expected that the new organization would have been hospitable to applied ethnomusicology. Anthropologists had by then started putting their knowledge to use in solving social problems. John Van Willigen dates the rise of a socially committed applied or "action" anthropology to 1945, although he notes that anthropologists had for decades previously taken on community consultantship roles (van Willigen, 2002). But this exciting, albeit controversial, development in anthropology did not cross over into SEM with any success until decades later. The reasons, in retrospect, are not entirely surprising. To establish ethnomusicology within the most secure of institutional bases, that is, within universities, it was necessary to position it as a research science, aiming to increase knowledge of the music of the world's peoples. Musicological and anthropological ethnomusicologists might disagree over the discipline's emphasis, but they agreed that scholarship and the production of knowledge were its goals. Applications of that research in the public arena might be well and good, but the pursuit of knowledge for its own sake had always been valued most highly in university settings, where it could be protected from outside forces. In 1950 ethnomusicology itself was a fringe discipline in the United States, with only a few courses being offered (sometimes in anthropology departments, sometimes music) and only a few professors available to advise doctoral dissertations. For ethnomusicology to expand inside the university world, professors must succeed in establishing courses, programs (especially graduate programs), tenure tracks, and recognition of the discipline as a legitimate academic pursuit. The proven strategy to advance the discipline in the university world would be through research, emphasizing that study of the music of the world's peoples would add to the store of knowledge about human behavior and achievement. Research "for its own sake" was then, and remains, regarded in the academy as more elegant, of higher and "purer" disinterested purpose than research driven by applications. In the arts and humanities, where contemplation of the pure aesthetic object was required for philosophy, literary criticism, and art history, disinterested acts of scholarship were experienced as pleasurable in themselves. Eventually, one could hope, every music department, every music school or conservatory, and every anthropology department would have at least one ethnomusicologist doing research and offering music courses with a worldwide scope; and some would have more than one and would establish graduate programs training future generations of ethnomusicologists as the discipline would expand. Professionalization of ethnomusicology as a research discipline, and with that a need to distance it from well-meaning amateurs who also engaged in music research, was a second reason. Applied work might be done by those who lacked the proper scientific attitude and scholarly training to conduct credible research: missionaries, for example, who had historically put music to use in attempting to convert indigenous peoples, or amateur collectors who became partisans on behalf of those whose music they recorded. I believe that a third reason was the distrust, among this generation of scholars who came of age during or soon after World War II, of social engineering, whether for political, cultural, or musical ends. Applied research put to practical use in musical or cultural interventions, despite intended benefits, was something Americans might well oppose, particularly given the uses to which music had been put during the Nazi regime, and was still being put in the Soviet sphere. Many in the previous generation of US music scholars had been born in Europe and had fled to North America to escape Nazi persecution and establish a musical scholarship inside a university world where they would be free from political interference. I do not mean to suggest that a cabal of ethnomusicology professors drew up such a plan, but rather that they were inclined by personality and training to move in that direction. Partly as a result, in its first two decades, ethnomusicology became more firmly established as a scholarly discipline; but applied ethnomusicology languished inside the US academic world.

Merriam was perhaps the first US ethnomusicologist to recognize an applied ethnomusicology by that name, although he did not favor it. The phase "applied ethnomusicology" did not appear in the SEM *Newsletter* or journal until Merriam's 1963 review of Henry Weman's *African Music and the Church in Africa*. Merriam wrote that this book is "perhaps most accurately described as a study in applied ethnomusicology, for his principal concern is how African music can be used . . . " in missionary work (Merriam, 1963b: 135). Merriam expanded on his comments a year later in *The Anthropology of Music*, and it is worth looking at them in detail:

> . . . the ultimate aim of the study of man. . . involves the question of whether one is searching for knowledge for its own sake, or is attempting to provide solutions for practical applied problems. Ethnomusicology has seldom been used in the same manner as applied or action anthropology, and ethnomusicologists have only rarely felt called upon to help solve problems in manipulating the destinies of people, but some such studies have been made [here he references Weman's book] and it is quite conceivable that this may in the future be of increased concern. The difficulty of an applied study is that it focuses the attention of the investigator upon a single problem which may cause or force him to ignore others of equal interest, and it is also difficult to avoid outside control over the research project. Although this problem is not yet of primary concern, it will surely shape the kinds of studies carried out if it does draw the increased attention of ethnomusicologists.
>
> (Merriam, 1964: 42–43)

Here, as elsewhere, Merriam privileges "knowledge for its own sake." In criticizing applied work for its narrow focus, Merriam is appealing to the idea that ethnomusicology should study music as a whole; but "outside control" may be viewed as a threat to academic freedom, while the phrase "manipulating the destinies of people" expresses that distrust of and distaste for the political and cultural interventions of applied anthropology and, by extension, of applied ethnomusicology.

Several books and articles critique recent interventions, especially those resulting from UNESCO initiatives to preserve intangible cultural heritage (e.g., Weintraub and Yung, 2009). But this tradition of critique may be traced to Merriam's "white knight" label for those ethnomusicologists who feel called to "function as knights in shining armor riding to the defense of non-Western music" (Merriam, 1963a: 207). Skepticism toward applied ethnomusicology is also evident in Bruno Nettl's histories and descriptions of the field. Nettl, more than anyone else among the founding generation of SEM, shouldered the responsibility to construct a history of ethnomusicology, something which he has come to call his "elephant" (Nettl, 2010). The sole active survivor of his generation of ethnomusicologists, Nettl early on assumed the mantle of spokesperson for the discipline, and today he is recognized in the United States and elsewhere as its elder statesman. As intellectual history is his central concern, he devotes relatively little attention to applied ethnomusicology. His most influential book, *The Study of Ethnomusicology*, treats applied ethnomusicology within the context of applied anthropology: "In the course of the 1950s there developed a concept and a subdiscipline, 'applied anthropology,' whose task it was to use anthropological insight to help solve social problems, particularly those occasioned by rapid culture change in the wake of modernization and Westernization." Applied anthropologists also were consulted in attempts to solve economic problems such as third-world poverty. They advised government organizations such as the United States Agency for International Development (USAID), on interventions involving democratization, agricultural modernization, and economic development. Rapid social change and cultural upheaval was the result of the intervention, not the original problem to be solved. No wonder then, as Nettl continues, that although "Anthropologists wanted to help [they] frequently ended up offending the local population and doing what was perceived as harmful. As a result, in the late 1960s and early 1970s they were widely attacked for doing work of no relevance to social problems, of mixing in local politics, of spying. Ethnomusicologists shared in this criticism. . . ." Here, applied ethnomusicologists' efforts to conserve traditional music and culture are conflated with applied anthropologists' efforts meant to aid in the modernization of traditional culture. The implication is that, like applied anthropologists, applied ethnomusicologists were criticized as offensive, harmful, and irrelevant; and that they barged into local politics and were accused of being spies. But if this critique of anthro-colonialism is accurate about interventions meant to bring about modernization and development, it does not follow that it applies to interventions by applied ethnomusicologists meant to conserve traditional music. Nettl then balances the critique with a somewhat more positive view:

> the picture [of applied anthropology and ethnomusicology] is not entirely negative. Some societies are happy to have outsiders come, appreciate their efforts, their respect for the traditions, and their help in restoring vigor to rapidly disappearing musics. Persian and Indian music masters are proud to have Western scholars as students, for it raises their prestige locally and legitimizes their traditional art in the face of modernizing doubters. Even so, there is often the feeling that members of the society itself, given the right training, equipment, and time, could do it better.
>
> (Nettl, 1983: 297; repeated in the 2nd edition, 2005: 206)

Nettl points out that some ethnomusicologists "espouse fieldwork in which informants become collaborators, the members of a community being studied in effect becoming co-collaborators" (ibid.). Yet Nettl's deep unease with applied work as social engineering is embedded in the tone and weight of his discussion and in the examples he offers; and it is apparent where he thinks the majority of ethnomusicologists stand. For the first edition of this book (1983) this was a correct assessment, but by the second edition (2005) it was not. Indeed, in a recent interview he acknowledged applied ethnomusicology's considerable appeal to a new generation (Fouce, 2014: 1).[3]

A few ethnomusicologists in SEM's founding generation were involved in applied projects during the 1960s and 1970s, yet they did not call it applied ethnomusicology. No doubt they thought of these as proper activities for an ethnomusicologist, but to my knowledge they did not think of them as part of a subfield where research was directed toward the public interest. Some, most prominently SEM founder David McAllester, took an advocacy role in educating music teachers and broadening the kindergarten-through-high school curricula to include examples of the musics of the world's peoples. McAllester worked through the Music Educators' National Conference to accomplish this goal, and he advised several graduate students in the Wesleyan University world music program who went in this direction, among them Patricia Shehan Campbell (see her Chapter 3, coauthored with Lee Higgins, in Volume 3). Another prominent ethnomusicologist in the founding generation, Mantle Hood, undertook applied ethnomusicology projects in Indonesia. He related the story of his successful intervention to revive Javanese gamelan gong-making (for the large gong *ageng*), which had nearly gone extinct. However, he also reported that his intervention resulted in some unintended, negative consequences. He offered another example, when he was called on for suggestions to improve gamelan educational practice—what innovations would he recommend? But here he stepped back from applied ethnomusicology and refused to interfere, thinking that Western influence would not be good for the tradition (Hood, 1971: 358–371). His major work on ethnomusicology ends with a section on cultural exchange through music and the arts as part of a program to further international understanding—putting ethnomusicological knowledge to practical use for a clear and intended social benefit.

Thus it could be fairly said that SEM's founding generation concentrated their US efforts in two areas: first, on research in order to increase knowledge about music and to circulate it among scholars; and second, to secure an institutional base for ethnomusicology within the academic world. In the latter, they were more successful in the music divisions of the universities and colleges (variously called music departments, schools of music, conservatories, and the like) than in anthropology departments. Growth within music divisions allied the discipline more closely with musicology than anthropology, and although the SEM founders envisioned a broadly interdisciplinary field with a new emphasis on the cultural study of music—and achieved this at SEM conferences and to some extent in the SEM journal, *Ethnomusicology*—the institutional growth of the discipline favored the musicologically oriented scholars.

Ironically, however, it was not by positioning ethnomusicology as a research science that institutional growth was achieved; rather, in the last half of the twentieth century ethnomusicology benefited from a combination of external circumstances that the founding generation did not foresee. The most important of these were, first, the meteoric rise in the popularity of world music among the general public, and especially the young, which began in the 1960s. Second was the reversal, in US cultural mythology, from the idea that the nation was a melting pot that produced a single American type, to the acceptance of cultural diversity and pluralism, which in the field of education broke the Eurocentric hold on curricula and opened it to a variety of minority voices in the humanities: literature, fine arts, music, and history. Youth cultures became deeply involved in alternative musics, including folk music, blues, and bluegrass. World music began to enjoy widespread popularity, as George Harrison of the Beatles studied sitar in India, and Hindustani musicians Ali Akbar Khan and Ravi Shankar went on extended annual tours throughout the United States. Recording companies such as Nonesuch released world music recordings and targeted both indigenous as well as Asian art musics to an appreciative public. Young men and women turned to world music as one of many paths toward personal growth. Fueled by the rising popularity of world music, master musicians from Ghana, North and South India, the Arab world, China, Japan, and Indonesia soon were in residence as world music performance ensemble directors at American colleges and universities where ethnomusicologists were already teaching. Performance was attracting students into the field. Mantle Hood, director of the Ethnomusicology Institute at UCLA, spearheaded this movement, advocating on behalf of what he called bi-musicality. Just as serious study of a foreign language could turn a person bilingual, so serious study of a foreign music could make one bi-musical and impart a knowledge of that music that was otherwise unavailable. Some senior ethnomusicologists tempered their enthusiasm for world music performance ensembles, however, and for decades they were conspicuously absent at the University of Illinois and Indiana University. Nonetheless, the possibility that world music might be learned intrigued many, and some went on to enroll in graduate programs in ethnomusicology, resulting in more degrees, professors, and programs. By 1970 it was possible to study ethnomusicology and obtain the doctorate by studying with Hood at UCLA, Fredric Lieberman at Brown, George List and Merriam at Indiana, Nettl at Illinois, Robert Garfias at Washington, William Malm at Michigan, and McAllester at Wesleyan, among other universities. Moreover, those with doctoral training in ethnomusicology had begun teaching at other colleges and universities, and SEM's US membership had increased.

Diversification and expansion of the US college and university music curriculum created a demand for professors who could teach the new courses. Within music divisions, this meant the end of the near-complete domination of Western art music (or classical music, as the American public calls it). Now popular music, jazz, and the music of the world's peoples took their place among the course offerings. Gradually, ethnomusicologists began to realize that they could take a proactive role and convince university administrators that one way to accomplish their goal of affirmative action toward so-called American minority groups (something which ethnomusicologists by and large supported) was through greater diversity of music offerings, which would also mean more ethnomusicology hires. As programs and departments were established in African American studies, Native American studies, Asian American studies, Hispanic American studies, and the like, it became apparent that the music of American minorities, along with world music, had an important role to play in the expanded curricula. Of course, ethnomusicologists were far from the only ones to benefit from diversity, cultural pluralism, and affirmative action in the academic world; but while the popularity of world music has ebbed and flowed since the 1960s, the movement toward greater cultural diversity within US higher education has been persistent.

The folk music revival, rising popularity of world music, and the positive value now attached to ethnic roots and cultural pluralism brought about a renewed emphasis in applied ethnomusicology outside the academic world before it had much impact inside it. Because Alan Lomax embodied this public work in applied ethnomusicology—not only as a collector, writer, and promoter, but also as an advocate for cultural democracy and musical pluralism—it is instructive to ponder his encounter with none other than George Herzog, who also believed in the value of musical diversity and had devoted his life to the study of folk and "primitive" music. Herzog, as noted, embodied comparative musicology in the United States during the 1930s and 1940s. After Lomax had been "Assistant in Charge" of the Archive of American Folk Song at the Library of Congress for several years—field-collecting, acquiring from others, and curating recordings—he decided to move his base of operations, from February through June of 1939, to Manhattan to obtain "more systematic academic training in anthropology and in the anthropological approach to primitive and folk music." He hoped to study with Herzog and other anthropologists at Columbia, and also "to study music with private instructors" (Cohen, 2010: 115). A recently published collection of Lomax's correspondence reveals the encounter with Herzog—from Lomax's viewpoint, of course—to have been less than successful. Herzog would not let Lomax into his course, insisting that he must take his two courses in sequence—primitive music (offered in the fall) followed by folk music (in the spring). Herzog would not budge from the requirement. To Harold Spivacke, his supervisor at the Library of Congress, Lomax then wrote, "I met a very much surprised Dr. Herzog at Columbia this morning, a Dr. Herzog who told me that I had made a great mistake in coming to school to take his course this term, that I should have come next term, should have come next year and for a whole year. Such a neurotic little academic man you never saw before" (Cohen, 2010: 121). Although Lomax had a marvelous ear, outstanding musical taste, and broad knowledge of folk music, he had little formal musical education and could be regarded as a well-meaning amateur in search of professional training. In some scientific disciplines, such as ornithology and astronomy, serious work by amateur researchers is highly valued; and in the early history of science, the majority of natural historians and natural philosophers were amateurs and proud of it. But Herzog was wary of amateur music research. Their confrontation, exacerbated by their prickly personalities and strong convictions, can be understood as a sign of incompatibility between public and academic ethnomusicologies in an earlier era; today, as mentioned earlier, more practitioners of applied ethnomusicology are employed within academia than outside it.

Indeed, the growth of US applied ethnomusicology from the 1960s through the 1980s owed much to Alan Lomax's continuing influence, his call for cultural equity, the work of public folklorists, and the establishment of government institutions that supported cultural pluralism within the arts. At the federal level were the Office of Folklife Studies at the Smithsonian Institution, the Folk Arts Division of the National Endowment for the Arts, and the Archive of Folk Culture at the Library of Congress, enlarged from the former Archive of American Folk Song, which Lomax had directed, and under the aegis of a new Library unit, the American Folklife Center. Regional, state, and, in some cases, city arts councils also were established, funded in part by the National Endowment for the Arts, and by the end of the 1980s most of the state arts councils employed at least one folklorist and a few employed ethnomusicologists (see Murphy, Chapter 5 of Volume 3). Folklore in the United States, while conservative in the academic world, enjoyed a tradition of populist activism outside it. Each of these government agencies employed scholars as consultants, and some employed them as arts and humanities administrators; thus, a large public outreach and concern for the health of expressive culture within various US communities was put in place, with a growing number of ethnomusicologists involved in public folklore, most often as consultants, but sometimes as advocates and collaborators, doing applied work. Several ethnomusicologists worked as presenters at folk festivals, their prior fieldwork having identified and documented some of the musicians who performed there. Music was the most prominent among the arts singled out by public folklorists for identification, documentation, and presentation. As arts administrators, ethnomusicologists were employed by the Smithsonian Institution (Thomas Vennum, Charlotte Heth) and by the Folk Arts Division of the National Endowment for the Arts (NEA; Daniel Sheehy), which also hired numerous ethnomusicologists as consultants to sit on panels recommending funding for various community music projects as well as for apprenticeships and heritage awards (see Titon, Chapter 5 of Volume 1). Bess Lomax Hawes held an informal session at the SEM conference most years during the 1980s to inform ethnomusicologists of the opportunities for submitting applied ethnomusicology project proposals to the NEA. This activity, known in the 1970s and 1980s as public-sector folklore, in the 1990s became known simply as "public folklore," and influenced the course of applied ethnomusicology in the United States profoundly.

Academic ethnomusicologists involved in public folklore thus began to think of their work as applied ethnomusicology, but SEM remained chiefly an organization devoted to communicating research among scholars. It was not until most of the founding generation aged and gradually relinquished leadership that applied ethnomusicology was able to enter SEM in a significant way. But it was not merely a changing of the generations. A significant change within academia resulted from the growing critique of science, fomented by post-structuralist and critical cultural theory, and culminating in the so-called "science wars" of the 1980s. North American graduate students in ethnomusicology during this period—beginning in the late 1960s—could not help being affected, as were cultural anthropologists and folklorists. The result, particularly among those attracted to the study of music as culture, was a turn in ethnomusicology from science toward cultural critique, from the musical object to the musical experience, from analysis to interpretation, from explanation to understanding. As a result, US ethnomusicology took a humanistic turn, and the cultural study of music moved to the forefront until, by the end of the 1980s, ethnomusicology had assimilated the humanistic cultural anthropology of Clifford Geertz, Dennis Tedlock, James Clifford, George Marcus, Vincent Crapanzano, Paul Rabinow, and others, a far cry from the empirical anthropology Herzog had championed. Much of this ethnomusicological humanism eventually achieved theoretical expression in the "new fieldwork" (Barz and Cooley, 1996) of reflexivity, reciprocity, and advocacy. Meanwhile, the scientific ethnomusicologists were in gradual retreat. A review of the essays in *Ethnomusicology* since about 1976 shows the balance point moving in the direction of music as culture rather than as form and structure. In 2010 the musicological ethnomusicologists came together outside SEM to form their own scholarly association (Analytical Approaches to World Music) with its own journal.[4]

Ethnomusicology's humanistic turn led a growing number of North American ethnomusicologists toward applied ethnomusicology in one form or another—advocating on behalf of individual musicians, musical communities, and musical life in particular places. The new fieldwork had become experience-centered, with ethnomusicological monographs such as those by Berliner (1978) and Keil (1979) reflecting this first-person turn to reflexivity. Kenneth Gourlay's 1982 essay in SEM's journal, "Towards a Humanizing Ethnomusicology," offered a theoretical basis for the new direction, along with a strongly worded critique of Merriam's insistence on science (Gourlay, 1982). In that same issue of *Ethnomusicology*, Charles Keil's essay, "Applied Ethnomusicology and a Rebirth of Music from the Spirit of Tragedy," charted a path toward work that "can make a difference" through "an insistence on putting music into play wherever people are resisting their oppression" (Keil, 1982: 407). Keil's 1982 essay caught the spirit of the postcolonialism that was central to cultural critique in the new anthropology, and to critical theory in cultural studies. And because applied ethnomusicology did not become a movement until the era of decolonization, it could (and did) oppose colonialism, orientalism, and other manifestations of the arrogance of Western power, while answering (if not avoiding) the critiques of colonialism that were being (and that continue to be) leveled at applied anthropology. Meanwhile, an ever-increasing number of US ethnomusicologists were becoming involved in public folklore and were realizing that there was much good work to be done for music in the public arena.

A humanized ethnomusicology thus made it possible for a resurgence of a postcolonial applied ethnomusicology, manifesting itself not only in a new fieldwork based in reciprocity leading to advocacy, but also through institutional gains within SEM. Applied ethnomusicology went mainstream within SEM during the 1990s. As the program chair for the 1989 SEM conference, I invited colleagues from my years in the early 1980s as a consultant for the NEA Folk Arts Division to present papers on a pre-planned panel. Entitled "From Perspective to Practice in 'Applied Ethnomusicology,'" the panel included the following presenters and papers: Robert Garfias, "What an Ethnomusicologist Can Do in Public Sector Arts"; Daniel Sheehy, "Applied Ethnomusicology as a State of Mind"; Charlotte Heth, "Getting It Right and Passing It On: The Ethnomusicologist and Cultural Transmission"; and Bess Lomax Hawes, "Practice Makes Perfect: Lessons in Active Ethnomusicology." When in 1990 I became editor of *Ethnomusicology*, this panel formed the starting point for a special issue entitled "Ethnomusicology and the Public Interest," which featured articles by Daniel Sheehy, Bess Lomax Hawes, Martha Ellen Davis, and Anthony Seeger. This was the first time that applied ethnomusicology was featured in the SEM journal. In my introductory article for that special issue, I wrote that ethnomusicology in the public interest "is work whose immediate end is not research and the flow of knowledge inside intellectual communities but, rather, practical action in the world outside of archives and universities" and that "as a way of knowing and doing, fieldwork [which is constitutive of ethnomusicology] at its best is based on a model of friendship between people rather than on a model involving antagonism, surveillance, the observation of physical objects, or the contemplation of abstract ideas" (Titon, 1992a: 315, 321). Sheehy's article there began the process of constructing an alternative history for ethnomusicology in the United States, one in which applied work was more central (Sheehy, 1992). Hawes was invited to give the plenary Seeger Lecture at the 1993 SEM conference, and this autobiographical talk, meant in part to attract listeners to applied work as a calling, was published two years later in *Ethnomusicology* (Hawes, 1995). In 1998 Keil, continuing in the vein of postcolonial critique, called in the SEM journal for an "applied sociomusicology" that, by reclaiming participatory music-making "for the vast majority," would help engender a revolution in consciousness that would overturn the global corporate capitalist world order and reverse the coming eco-catastrophe as we move toward "sustainable futures" (Keil, 1998: 304).

At the 1998 SEM Conference, Doris Dyen and Martha Ellen Davis convened a meeting to assess interest in proposing a standing Committee on Applied Ethnomusicology to the SEM Board. Until that meeting, a single name for this activity had not yet risen to the surface; among those in circulation then were "applied," "active," "action," "practice," "public," and "public sector" (Titon, 1992a: 320–321). As applied ethnomusicologists themselves, with experience in the public sector and in the academic world, Davis and Dyen felt the time was opportune for organizing something more formal to bring together those with common interests in working for the benefit of musical communities in the public arena. Thirty-eight hopeful founders (the editors of this volume among them) attended, their proposal was accepted by the SEM Board, and the Committee was established, with a variety of definitions of applied ethnomusicology. In 2000, Dyen and Davis, who had taken on the role of chairs of the Committee, appointed a deputy chair, Tom Van Buren, and successfully petitioned the Board to recognize the group as the Applied Ethnomusicology Section. Dyen and Davis stood aside in 2002 while appointing co-chairs Ric Alviso and Miriam Gerberg to join Van Buren, who stepped down in 2004 in favor of Mark Puryear. Alviso was succeeded in 2008 by Jeff Todd Titon, Gerberg in 2009 by Kathleen Noss Van Buren, Puryear in 2010 by Maureen Loughran, Noss Van Buren in 2014 by Michael Bakan, Loughran in 2015 by Erica Haskell, and Haskell in 2018 by Klisala Harrison.

During the Committee and Section's first decade, the co-chairs worked to make the group a comfortable space within SEM for ethnomusicologists employed outside of the academic world. To that end, they organized practical panels on non-academic careers for ethnomusicologists, such as the "Ethnomusicologists at Work" series, organized by Gerberg; and on strategies for survival both inside and outside official institutions. Co-chairs Gerberg, Puryear, and Alviso established Section prizes for outstanding presentations at SEM, and awards for travel grants to the conference. In the new millennium, as applied ethnomusicology has become increasingly popular among graduate students and welcomed inside academic institutions, the Section has become an SEM meeting-place and platform for applied ethnomusicologists based both within and outside academia. Most recently, the Section has sponsored panels involving themes such as music and politics, community advocacy, activism and "giving back," conflict resolution, ethics, repatriation of artifacts from archives and museums, medicine, the environment, and social justice. It also sponsors presentations from guests who do not normally attend the SEM conferences but who have worked in applied ethnomusicology either independently or in extra-academic institutions. For example, at the 2011 conference, Debora Kodish, public folklorist and director of the Philadelphia Folklore Project, led a Section-sponsored discussion among traditional music and dance activists and community scholar-practitioners from the African-American and Asian-American communities in Philadelphia, showcasing a model for ethnomusicologists seeking strategies for work in community-based institutions. With in excess of 300 members, Applied Ethnomusicology is now one of the largest and most active among the SEM Sections, exceeded in membership only by the student and the popular music Sections.

As might be expected of a practical endeavor, theorization of applied ethnomusicology lagged behind practice, but recent years have witnessed an increasing number of publications and events centered on applied ethnomusicology itself. These included an international conference on applied ethnomusicology organized by Erica Haskell and Maureen Loughran, at Brown University (Invested in Community, 2003), a special issue of *Folklore Forum* devoted to applied ethnomusicology (Fenn, 2003), a section devoted to applied ethnomusicology in an issue of *Ethnomusicology Review* (2012), and a book of essays, *Applied Ethnomusicology: Historical and Contemporary Approaches* (Harrison, Mackinlay, and Pettan, 2010). Rebecca Dirksen authored an excellent overview of contemporary practice, with an emphasis on work by US-based ethnomusicologists, while Timothy Rice's book-length "very short introduction" to the discipline devotes the last two of nine chapters to what is in effect applied ethnomusicology (Dirksen, 2012; Rice, 2014). This *Oxford Handbook,* first published in a one-volume clothbound edition in 2015, continued in this vein, offering a cross-section of contemporary international work in the field. In 2017, one entire day's programming of the annual SEM conference was devoted to public, public-sector, and applied ethnomusicology. In response to the continued use of those three terms (public, public sector, and applied), Klisala Harrison argued that "applied" was the covering term, particularly in the international context; and that "public" and "public sector" were best understood as sub-areas of "applied" that made sense only in certain national contexts (Harrison, 2016).

Concluding this sketch of applied ethnomusicology in the United States, I do not mean to dismiss entirely the critique that applied ethnomusicology may be used for undesirable ends. Knowledge is not innocent; cultural information has a long history of being put to use for military purposes and colonial conquest. Music used in the service of a social or musical benefit may turn out to have negative consequences, or what looks like a benefit to one political entity may be a harm to another. Merriam's charge that applied ethnomusicologists are engaged in "manipulating people's destinies" is one way of looking at missionary work, for example, and it is a fact that missionaries have put their knowledge of music to use for that purpose for many centuries. Today, faith-based organizations such as SIL put ethnomusicological knowledge to use in aiding local artists in indigenous communities, with the goal of a "better future: one of justice, peace, joy, physical safety, social continuity and spiritual wholeness" (SIL). Other forces are intervening: corporations, governments, technology, the law, and so forth. Social responsibility requires social justice, cultural equity, and decolonization. I believe there is no self-correcting "invisible hand" in the marketplace or anywhere else that would permit scholars the luxury of research without social responsibility. Nor would scholars be well advised to accumulate knowledge and then supply it to those who in their ignorance would put it to use.

SEM had been slow to adopt a more active role, but recognition of the need for the organization to enter the larger political sphere has gradually come. For many years, SEM took the position that while ethnomusicologists were of course free to express their personal political views, the organization itself must not take a public political stand. But in 1976 the SEM *Newsletter* editor refused to print an employment advertisement from a university representing a government that practiced apartheid, an early harbinger of change. Not long afterward, SEM began endorsing resolutions supporting the rights of scholars detained by governments for political reasons, and the rights of musicians to travel freely internationally. It has passed position statements on rights and discrimination, copyright ownership and sound recordings, and ethical considerations. Finally, in 2007, in response to a request from the SEM Ethics Committee, the SEM Board of Directors approved a "Position Statement against the Use of Music as Torture." Arising in response to numerous reports of music as part of the torture arsenal employed by US military and intelligence agencies and their allies against suspected terrorist detainees, it reads in part that the Society for Ethnomusicology "calls for full disclosure of US government-sanctioned and funded programs that design the means of delivering music as torture; condemns the use of music as an instrument of torture; and demands that the US government and its agencies cease using music as an instrument of physical and psychological torture" (SEM Torture). The position statement on music as torture was a significant step in SEM's evolution. It recognizes that ethnomusicologists are citizens of the world with social responsibilities, and that our professional organization has not only the right but also the duty to represent the profession's ethical beliefs and act upon them.

During the second decade of the twenty-first century, the SEM leadership's recognition of the ethnomusicologist's social responsibility continued to grow, fueled by increased interest in applied ethnomusicology among graduate students, many of whom were contemplating careers outside the academic world. At the University of Limerick, Ireland, in the same year that the clothbound, one-volume edition of this *Oxford Handbook of Applied Ethnomusicology* was published (2015), SEM and ICTM sponsored a joint, three-day Forum on the subject of an activist, community-engaged ethnomusicology, attended by more than 100 ethnomusicologists from all over the world, at which the editors of this volume were among the keynote speakers.[5] A book of essays from that Forum is in preparation under the editorship of forum conveners

Beverley Diamond and Salwa El Shawan Castelo-Branco; upon publication it will move both SEM and ICTM yet further towards *Transforming Ethnomusicology* (forthcoming) in an applied direction.

Notes

1. Its recognition was signaled in 1992 when the Journal of the Society for Ethnomusicology devoted a special issue to the subject (*Ethnomusicology* 36[2]).
2. In Kunst's definition ethnomusicology was chiefly a new name for the discipline of comparative musicology. But as we shall soon see, US cultural anthropologists interested in music saw opportunity in the new name, founded the international Society for Ethnomusicology in 1955, and were prominent among its leaders. Thus by 1955 ethnomusicology could be described as a new and interdisciplinary field, not just a new name for an older academic discipline.
3. In a 2013 interview he characterized as one of four "new, or newish developments in ethnomusicology" a "widespread concern with the need to do things that benefit the peoples whose music and musical culture are studied" (Nettl, 2014: 1).
4. In the new millennium, science is making a small comeback as music theory and comparative studies are applied in these analytical approaches to structural features of world musics. Science is manifest also in a growing interest among ethnomusicologists in neuroscience and music psychology, and questions concerning music and human evolution.
5. The Forum was titled Transforming Ethnomusicological Practice Through Activism and Community Engagement, and was held in Limerick, Ireland, September 13–16, 2015. Further information about it may be found at https://www.ictmusic.org/joint-sem-ictm-forum-2015.

SECTION 2

APPLIED ETHNOMUSICOLOGY IN THE GLOBAL ARENA

SVANIBOR PETTAN

An Introductory Vignette

In 1975, a documentary film about hunting, *Ultime grida dalla savana* (internationally known as *Savage Man Savage Beast*) was released. The authors intended to document the phenomenon of hunting in different spatial and cultural contexts. The viewers can see not only animals hunting animals and humans hunting animals, but also animals hunting humans, and finally, humans hunting humans. The scenes in which lions eat a tourist and in which humans mutilate the bodies of caught humans were received with particular controversy. The filmmakers Antonio Climati and Mario Morra were filming all the scenes with the clear attitude of detached observers, documenting the multifaceted footage in the domain of their professional interest and showing no intention whatsoever to intervene. The basic symbolic standpoint of this film brings up a number of useful questions concerning the attitudes in the field of ethnomusicology in its both temporal and spatial contexts, and highlights the stance of intervention in positioning applied ethnomusicology.[1]

The stance of the above-mentioned filmmakers reflects the attitude prevalent in the ethnomusicological mainstream within the past decades, which can be summarized in the following way: studying music as it is, not as a researcher or anybody else would want it to be. I vividly recall an example from my doctoral studies at the University of Maryland Baltimore County, in which the professor pointed out a music producer of an African music CD, who insisted on removal of those parts from the musical instrument that were responsible for the production of a buzzing sound. The producer's opinion was that the recording without them would be more pleasing to the ears of international audiences, which would consequently increase the profit expected from the final product. Of course, such an uninformed and disrespectful intervention into the aesthetics of the musicians invoked laughter and criticism among the students, with no need for further discussion. The question, which I considered essential, that is, whether "those who know" (us, the ethnomusicologists) would actually consider making a step beyond the level of an academic debate and try to intervene, by providing the ignorant producer who misused his power over the musicians with arguments against his action, was left unanswered.

The two cases (the film and the CD producer), extreme as they are, raise at least two useful points:

a. The decision whether to intervene or not has moral implications.
b. In order to be successful, intervention has to be based on knowledge, understanding, and skills.

What Is Applied Ethnomusicology, and What Isn't It?

As will be discussed later, definitions may vary according to the parameters such as time, place, research tradition, and individual preference, but the essence is captured in the wording created and accepted at the 39th World Conference of the International Council for Traditional Music (ICTM) in Vienna in 2007, suggesting that "[a]pplied ethnomusicology is the approach guided by principles of social responsibility, which extends the usual academic goal of broadening and deepening knowledge and understanding toward solving concrete problems and toward working both inside and beyond typical academic contexts." Characterization of the ICTM Study Group on Applied Ethnomusicology that follows provides further clarification, suggesting that it "advocates the use of ethnomusicological knowledge in influencing social interaction and course of cultural change."

The introduction to the book *Applied Ethnomusicology: Historical and Contemporary Approaches* (Harrison, Mackinlay, and Pettan, 2010) analyzes this definition part by part and also addresses three common misconceptions about applied ethnomusicology, which are worth mentioning in this context:

1. Applied ethnomusicology does *not* stand in opposition to the academic domain, but should be viewed as its extension and complement.[2]
2. Applied ethnomusicology is *not* an opposition to the theoretical (philosophical, intellectual) domain, but its extension and complement.[3]
3. Applied ethnomusicology is *not* an opposition to ethnographic, artistic, and scientific research, but their extension and complement.[4]

The introductory article to the above-mentioned volume ends with a quotation of Michael Birenbaum Quintero: "Apply your ethnomusicology or someone else will apply it for you," which once again points to intervention as a key notion.

There is a rich myriad of opinions about applied ethnomusicology among ethnomusicologists worldwide, from those who claim that all ethnomusicology is in fact applied, to those who feel that applied ethnomusicology does not enjoy necessary respect within the academic discipline and therefore should not be discussed at all. It is easy to agree with Daniel Sheehy's belief that "all ethnomusicologists have at one time or another been applied ethnomusicologists" (Sheehy, 1992: 323). But "applied ethnomusicology as a *conscious practice*," says Sheehy, "begins with a sense of purpose, a purpose larger than the advancement of knowledge about the music of the world's peoples" (ibid.). This is why I started my part of this Introduction with the crucial question of *intervention*, or in other words, with the conscious decision-making of a researcher whether or not to step beyond the mere study of the selected phenomenon and affect the researched circumstances. It is the sense of purpose, rather than any specific topic, that defines applied ethnomusicology. There are "sensitive" topics, such as, for instance, the roles of music in the Israeli/Palestinian divide, in which the author of the book (for whatever reason) does not mention applied ethnomusicology (see Brinner, 2009); and there are seemingly "neutral" topics, for instance the lullabies in Slovenia, which are from their initial conceptualization framed as "applied" by the author (see Juvančič, 2010).

There are many more or less known individuals, organizations, projects, and publications known for promoting the use of music for the betterment of human condition. Their work, though inspiring, if not rooted in ethnomusicological research should not be considered "applied ethnomusicology." Venezuelan musician, activist, economist, and politician José Antonio Abreu and his El Sistema, Argentinian/Israeli/German pianist and conductor Daniel Barenboim and his West-Eastern Divan Orchestra, Irish musicians and activists Bob Geldof (Live Aid) and Bono (ONE Campaign), Musicians Without Borders, Young at Heart, Studio MC Pavarotti, most articles in the journals such as *Music and Arts in Action* and *Sounds in Europe* are just a few examples, among many more.

Some ethnomusicologists express concern about the power imbalance in projects that fit within the realm of applied ethnomusicology (e.g., Hofman, 2010). The title of my first conference paper on the topic, presented in 1995, started exactly with the same notion: "Ethnomusicologist as a Power Holder?" The sentence with the question mark looks even more bizarre in the light of Deborah Wong's reminder that "[e]thnomusicology is marginalized in most music departments because its radical relativism challenges logocentric thinking about music" (2013: 348). In my conference presentation, based on the work with Bosnian refugees in Norway (see below), I addressed the issue of power share with the participants in, to the extent possible, equal, horizontal terms. The (later) article by Samuel Araújo and members of the Grupo Musicultura (2006), inspired by Paolo Freire's dialogical pedagogy (1970), is a good example of the same intention. There is, however, the other side of the coin, which should not be overlooked. If a certain kind of knowledge and/or access to power holders in a society for the benefit of the people in need is the comparative advantage of an ethnomusicologist, and there is a consensus between the interlocutors and the ethnomusicologist that he or she should use it, I can hardly think of counterarguments. This is how Anthony Seeger benefited the Suyá community in Brazil and Ursula Hemetek the Roma people in Austria. In Harris M. Berger's words, one should be aware of the dual nature of power:

> Power is, in one sense, the power to act, the ability to bring forth events in the world. But because our action is always social—always something we achieve because of and with others, past, present, future—the potential for domination is inherent, even ripe, in the entirety of social life, and even the most mundane, equitable, or convivial practice is informed by larger social contexts and the legacies of domination that they entail. This is as true of practices of music making, teaching, research or public sector work as it is of any other kind of activity. Seeing the social life of music as a domain of coordinated practice that is inherently, rather than contingently, political is one way of coming to terms with these difficult issues.
>
> (Berger, 2014: 319).

A Personal Stance

Just as Salwa El-Shawan Castelo-Branco did in her Epilogue to the seminal volume *Music and Conflict* (O'Connell and Castelo-Branco, 2010), let me add to this Introduction a personal stance that should define my own position.

In my opinion, every scholar should be free to decide whether to make a step beyond the usual goal of deepening and broadening knowledge, understanding and skills, and consciously intervene into the human and cultural environment of his or her research interest. While doing fieldwork in the 1980s on the East African islands of Zanzibar and Pemba for my B.A. thesis (University of Zagreb, Croatia) and in Egypt for my M.A. thesis (University of Ljubljana, Slovenia), my clear intention was to affect the self-focused folk music research in what was Yugoslavia at the time and to relate it to the much larger international community of ethnomusicologists, which I was learning about mainly from the periodicals (*Yearbook for Traditional Music, Ethnomusicology, the world of music*). My goal was clearly not the mere scholarly work based on the data from elsewhere in the world, but the conscious intervention into the essence of the discipline as it was understood in my home country at that time.

Between my B.A. and M.A. studies, I was obliged to serve for a year in the Yugoslav People's Army. Following my research interests, I asked the military authorities in Croatia to be sent to serve in the multicultural city of Prizren in far-away Kosovo, which was the most politically unstable part of what was Yugoslavia in the early 1980s. After becoming the instructor for cultural affairs, I came to the position not only to conduct fieldwork (by using a military tape recorder), but also to take it a step further: to bring regularly together youngsters from different ethnic communities and fellow soldiers into a choir. Obviously, research was beneficial to the work with the choir, and contacts established through the choir activities had a positive impact on my research.

Following the end of my doctoral studies (University of Maryland) in 1992, I was faced with the dilemma of whether to try to find a position in the safety of American academia or to return to my disintegrating, war-torn country. I decided once again to cross the boundary of intervention and use my capacities not only to study "music and war at home," but also to explore whether my knowledge, understanding, and skills could in any way confront the growing hatred and help reducing the suffering of the people affected by the war. My interlocutors in Croatia were highly unusual for any type of ethnomusicological inquiry known to me at that time: they included refugees and internally displaced people, soldiers, people in shelters, representatives of nongovernmental organizations (NGOs), radio editors, producers and sellers of music cassettes under both official and black market circumstances, members of the diasporas, and nonetheless musicians—amateur and professional, representatives of diverse musical genres and with diverse political orientations. Popular music was at the forefront, but my research encompassed folk and art music, as well. What was the essence of my intervention beyond the limits of research? My ethnomusicology students in both Zagreb and Ljubljana received assignments to work on joint performances with refugees in refugee camps in order to develop a sense of compassion and togetherness, and their seminar projects—for instance, one about music in various local religious communities at the time of political calls for unification (one ethnicity, one religion, one language, one territory)—clearly aimed for more than a mere broadening and deepening of knowledge.

Invited to teach for a term at the University of Oslo in Norway in the mid-1990s, I took the opportunity to implement a project, together with my senior host Professor Kjell Skyllstad. A few years earlier he envisioned and carried out a project named *The Resonant Community* (Skyllstad, 1993), the first case in my experience that had all elements of an applied ethnomusicology project. In the period from 1989 to 1992 music of various origins (African, Asian, European, and Latin American) had been successfully used in some elementary schools in Norway in order to foster "interracial understanding." Included and affected by this project were the teachers, pupils, and their parents, for whom teaching kits were created; some of the best musicians from four continents shared their arts with them. The evaluated and confirmed impact of *The Resonant Community* inspired us to put together the Azra project, an innovative proactive attempt, with the focus on Bosnian refugee musicians and Norwegian music students, which has been already presented elsewhere (e.g., Pettan, 1996; Skyllstad, 1997; Pettan, 2010), and thus not need to be described here. Therefore, I will dedicate just a few words to its methodological aspects.

I believe the Azra project fits into what Sheehy refers to as "conscious practice" and "sense of purpose." It is a "horizontal" (not "top-down") project, driven by the clear wish for intervention by well-intended scholars and their collaborators who together, in Angosino's words, "had a concern for using their knowledge for the betterment of the human condition" (Angrosino, 1990: 106). The goals of the project were as follows: (1)

strengthening Bosnian cultural identity among the refugees from Bosnia-Herzegovina in Norway, and (2) stimulating mutually beneficial cross-cultural communication between the Bosnians and the Norwegians involved. The project was envisioned as a triangle consisting of three principal domains: research, education, and music-making. Its realization was carried on in four stages: (1) recognition of the problem and definition of the goals and basic strategies; (2) collection and analysis of data, plus refinement of the strategies; (3) intervention; and (4) evaluation of the results.

Work on this project made me aware of two distinctive types of mediation, which I termed *indirect* and *direct*. *Indirect mediation* means that the scholar gives the results of his or her research to those in a position to apply them. *Direct mediation* means that scholar himself or herself actively participates in the application of scholarly knowledge, understanding, and skills. Skyllstad and I used both categories in the Azra project. While mediating indirectly through conference papers, lectures, articles, and interviews, using the synthesis of empirical fieldwork and relevant literature to encourage other people to act, we reached the limits with no insight into the consequences of our involvement. Direct mediation proved to be more useful and far-reaching. For instance, within the Azra project, Skyllstad and I were able to shape its goals and contents, observe its flow and modify it when needed, and evaluate all its stages, including the final results.

My series of publications in different formats (books, articles, CD-ROM, film), accompanied by proactive lectures and picture exhibitions—all dedicated to Roma people, largely silenced victims of the war in Kosovo in the 1990s—can be seen as yet another application of ethnomusicological knowledge, understanding, and skills. The publications include those with scholarly rigor and those aimed at communication with general audiences (more in Pettan, 2010). One of the professional involvements that I highly value, but have never written an article about, is my role in the advisory committee at the Slovenian annual state review titled "Let's sing, let's play musical instruments, let's dance" for children and youngsters with special needs.

To summarize, like many other fellow ethnomusicologists, I am involved in projects of public interest. Not everything I do in ethnomusicology has an applied extension. In my invited lectures on applied ethnomusicology, I often encourage scholars in the audience to think of research that goes beyond the broadening and deepening of knowledge in the direction of benefiting the people they study. Some become inspired, while others simply do not want to think in these terms. And it is right to be so. For me, this is the clear line between ethnomusicology and applied ethnomusicology.

"Applied" in Other Disciplines

It is a common practice that scientific and scholarly disciplines have their applied domains. To mention just some, there are applied mathematics, applied physics, applied biology, applied geography, applied sociology, applied anthropology, and then (surprisingly seldom) applied musicology, partly substituted by the category of applied music. If hydrology, for instance, is the study of water and encompasses "the interrelationships of geologic materials and processes of water" (Fetter, 2001: 3), then "applied hydrogeologists are problem solvers and decision makers. They identify a problem, define the data needs, design a field program for collection of data, propose alternative solutions to the problem, and implement the preferred solutions" (ibid.: 11). Applied sociology refers to "any use of the sociological perspective and/or its tools in the understanding of, intervention in, and/or enhancement human social life" (Price and Steele, 2004), while applied anthropology refers to "any use of anthropological knowledge to influence social interaction, to maintain or change social institutions, or to direct the course of cultural change" (Spradley and McCurdy, 2000: 355).

Curiously, neither the International Musicological Society nor the American Musicological Society have sections focused on applied musicology. UCLA musicologist Elisabeth Le Guin points out that the reason might be that "in the institutional structure of the discipline's most prestigious academic society,[5] a stigma lingers around the idea of 'putting music to use,' as the SEM describes applied ethnomusicology: a ghost of the old idea, coeval in its origins with my undergraduates' obdurately antiverbal Romanticism, that music should amount to something more than its use-value" (LeGuin, 2012).

A recent book with applied musicology in its title refers to "using zygonic theory to inform music education, therapy, and psychology research" (Ockelford, 2013). According to *The Oxford Companion to Music*, applied music is an American term for a study course in performance, as opposed to theory.

It is worth inquiring about the independent scientific and scholarly societies that have the adjective "applied" in their names, which implies that they have already answered the "ultimate aim" in Merriam's terms, that is, whether "one is searching out knowledge for its own sake, or is attempting to provide solutions to practical applied problems" (Merriam, 1964: 42–43) in favor of the latter. In general, "applied societies" are international and are far from being small outfits of the main disciplinary bodies; some count their members in the thousands.[6] Although the aims of these societies are defined in the disciplinarily determined ways, the great majority of them make clear that they promote the outcomes of their disciplines with the intention that the public benefits from their efforts.[7] This is particularly clearly emphasized by the Society for Applied Anthropology, active since 1941, whose "unifying factor is a commitment to making an impact on the quality of life in the world" (www.sfaa.net).

A Brief Worldwide Overview

It is quite fascinating to observe engaged scholarship within the Australian ethnomusicological realm, from Catherine Ellis (1985) to the studies of Grace Koch (2013), Catherine Grant (2014), Huib Schippers and Catherine Grant (2016), Aaron Corn, Muriel Swijghuisen Reigersberg, Sally Treloyn and several others. High ethical stands and participatory work promoted by the research institutions focused on indigenous people of Australia, such as Australian Institute of Aboriginal and Torres Strait Islander Studies (AIATSIS), as well as the active/activist involvement in Aboriginal rights issue by several leading Australian ethnomusicologists, provide inspiring lessons for applied ethnomusicologists worldwide (see Newsome, 2008). The articles by Elizabeth Mackinlay in this volume of the *Handbook*, and by Dan Bendrups and Huib Schippers in Volume 1 make a strong Australian contribution to the applied work with the Aborigines, other minorities, and carriers of music cultures in various parts of the globe.

"The practice of ethnomusicology has been central in the professional lives of ethnomusicologists in Southeast Asia," claims Tan Sooi Beng in her article about activism in Southeast Asian ethnomusicology, pointing to a project of empowerment of youth in Penang, Malaysia, to revitalize traditions and bridge cultural barriers (2008: 69). For her, and for many colleagues elsewhere in Asia, to be an ethnomusicologist means not only involvement in scholarly activities such as teaching, documenting, publishing, and organizing conferences, but also application of the ethnomusicological knowledge toward solving particular cultural problems "so as to bring about change in their respective societies" (ibid.: 70). Terada Yoshitaka provides yet another good example of sensitive work in various formats (e.g., 2005, 2008, 2010, 2011), and so do Weiya Lin, Pamela Onishi, Mayco Santaella and several others. Tan Sooi Beng in Volume 1 of the *Handbook* and Zhang Boyu in Volume 3 present Asian views and approaches from within, while Zoe Sherinian in this volume, Joshua Pilzer in Volume 1 and John Morgan O'Connell in Volume 3 complement them from outside, covering at least some other parts of the world's largest continent.

Practical aspects of ethnomusicology are very much present in Africa, too, from indigenous teaching approaches to music education, preservation of cultural roots, building of musical instruments, to diverse uses of music against xenophobia and prejudices related to HIV/AIDS. The works of Daniel Avorgbedor (1992), Angela Impey (2002), Bernhard Bleibinger (2010), Kathleen Van Burren (2010), along with Andrew Tracey, David Dargie, Diane Thram and Patricia Opondo, to mention just a few, point to a rich diversity of approaches. In this volume, Jeffrey Summitt and Brian Schrag provide their own views and experiences in applied ethnomusicology in Africa.

South America is certainly the site of some of the major ongoing developments in applied ethnomusicology. This is the case thanks to two extraordinary thinkers in the field, Brazilian Samuel Araújo and US-based Anthony Seeger, whose particularly important work and scholarly formation is related to Brazil. Araújo intends "to highlight the political substance and epistemological consequences of new research contexts and roles as one area with potentially ground-breaking contributions toward the emergence of a more balanced social world, i.e. one in which knowledge will hopefully emerge from a truly horizontal, intercultural dialogue and not through top-to-bottom neo-colonial systems of validation" (Araújo, 2008: 14). Seeger's work could justifiably be discussed in any geographic context, as his articles and keynote addresses resound on all continents (2006, 2008). In this volume, Holly Wissler demonstrates how applied ethnomusicological projects affect two South American communities, one in the Andes, and the other in the Amazon.

Following Daniel Sheehy (1992) and Anthony Seeger (2006), Maureen Loughran (2008) noted that some leading ethnomusicologists in the North American context, such as Alan P. Merriam (1964), Mantle Hood (1971), and Bruno Nettl (1964, 1983) largely ignored the work of applied ethnomusicologists while presenting the major developments within the discipline.[8] The co-editor of this volume, Jeff Todd Titon, has presented in Section 1 of this Introduction the history of ethnomusicology in North America from his perspective, as he lived and lives it, adding previously unknown aspects and enriching the general understanding of the discipline. Besides him, several other authors in the *Handbook* refer to various extents to applied ethnomusicology in the North American contexts, including Jeffrey Summitt and Michael Bakan in this volume, Klisala Harrison in Volume 1, and Susan Oehler Herrick, Patricia Shehan Campbell, Clifford Murphy and Alan Williams in Volume 3.

My own firsthand experiences are largely linked to Europe, where I was born and where I live and practice ethnomusicology. This is why the following section will be about Europe. The authors linked in various ways to Europe in the *Handbook* include Ursula Hemetek in this volume, Klisala Harrison, Erica Haskell and Britta Sweers in Volume 1, and Lee Higgins and Dan Lundberg in Volume 3.

Some European Views: Ethnomusicologies

The fact that there is no single, ultimate definition of ethnomusicology suggests that we may consider the coexistence of ethnomusicologies, not only in different parts of the world, but also within a single, no matter how small, location. For instance, while I may find the definition proposed by my US colleague Jeff Todd Titon ("the study of people making music") acceptable, my Slovenian colleague, folklorist Marko Terseglav, defines it very differently, as "a discipline, researching spontaneous folk vocal and instrumental music, its characteristics and development" (Terseglav, 2004: 124).

In a sharp contrast to Vienna in neighboring Austria, which figures as one of the two cradles of comparative musicology[9] and is at the same time home to the lasting legacy of folk music research, ethnomusicology in Slovenia is rooted exclusively in folk music research. Table I.1 points to the major distinctions between the two and relates them to the current ethnomusicological mainstream.[10]

In an article, in which she compares the features of comparative musicology and folk music research in Vienna in the early twentieth century, Ursula Hemetek points to some other important distinctions, for instance, recording with phonograph by the former and notation by ear by the latter; music as text with no context versus music as text with context; interdisciplinarity related mainly to natural sciences versus interdisciplinarity related mainly to humanities; and (particularly important in this context) the association of comparative musicology with the academia-based "ivory tower" versus folk music research's "highly motivated volunteers outside academia" and application of (research) results (Hemetek, 2009: 62).

The multitude of languages and nation-state ideologies affected research within the European space differently than in North America and Australia. By far, not all of

Table I.1. Comparative Musicology, Folk Music Research, and Ethnomusicology

	Comparative Musicology	Folk Music Research	Ethnomusicology
When?	1885–1950s	From late 18th century	From 1950s
What?	Musics of "primitive peoples" and "high Oriental cultures"	Peasant music	People making music
How?	"Armchair"	Collecting; fieldwork (short-term)	Fieldwork (long-term)
Who?	"Other" people	"Own" people	Any people
Where?	Elsewhere	Within own ethnic/national realm	Anywhere
Why?	Knowledge	National duty	Understanding

the European countries came under the umbrella of comparative musicology, but all contributed to the legacy of folk music research. Distinctive developments of the discipline in politically, geographically, historically, demographically, economically, linguistically, religiously, and nevertheless culturally diverse national contexts within Europe inspired studies that testify primarily about the specifics of European ethnomusicologies; put together, they enable comparisons and insights into common features. Interestingly, with a few exceptions (e.g., Clausen, Hemetek, and Saether, 2009; Ling, 1999), Europe was encompassed as a whole primarily by ethnomusicologists from North America (e.g., in Bohlman, 1996, 2004; Rice, Porter, and Goertzen, 2000). Some authors discussed them within the theoretical frame of nationalism (e.g., Bohlman, 2011), some pointed to the shared developmental periods (e.g., Elschek, 1991); yet others inverted the historical trends by placing those seen in Europe a century ago as the inferior Others (Roma and Jews; comp. Wallaschek, 1893) to the forefront of contemporary Europe by naming them "transnational ethnic groups" (Rice, Porter, and Goertzen, 2000).

In the post–Cold War Europe of the 1990s, national ethnomusicologies received considerable attention, including those of Denmark (Koudal et al., 1993), Finland (Moisala et al., 1994), Latvia (Boiko, 1994), Italy (Giuriati, 1995), Spain (Marti, 1997), Croatia (Pettan et al., 1998), and many more. This research trend continued in the 2000s, as reflected in the symposium on National Ethnomusicologies: The European Perspective (Cardiff University, 2007) and the plenary roundtable under the same name at the ICTM World Conference (Vienna, 2007), both organized by one of the authors in Volume 3 of this *Handbook*, John Morgan O'Connell, and in subsequent studies.[11]

Let us now take a closer look at the micro-plan of Croatia and Slovenia, since 1992 two neighboring independent European countries, which spent the period of the formation of ethnomusicology first as the parts of the multiethnic Austro-Hungarian Empire (1867–1918), and then as the constituent parts of what later became known as Yugoslavia. As in many other parts of Europe, ethnomusicology in Croatia and Slovenia grew from the national awakening of the nineteenth century and the sense of importance of a nation's "own" folk song for the creation and affirmation of national identity. The characteristic procedure, through the first half of the twentieth century, included extensive fieldwork, notation and analysis of the collected songs, publishing collections, and writing syntheses based on the analysis of collected materials. The aim was to define specific national features, different from those of the neighboring peoples, which would in turn provide the basis for the development of national culture. In Croatia, the key figures, such as Franjo Kuhač (1834–1911) and Božidar Širola (1889–1956), were musicians, to whom the novelties in the field of comparative musicology were known. Kuhač was interested in collecting and writing about folk songs of South Slavs (not exclusively Croats), comparing their features with those of non-Slavs (Germans, Italians, Turks). Širola, himself a composer, even earned a doctorate under the mentorship of comparative musicologist Robert Lach in Vienna, and used comparative methodological procedures in dealing with Croatian folk music. In the Slovenian cultural space, at about the same time, the initiative was taken by two widely trained linguists with Viennese doctorates and an interest in ethnology: Karel Štrekelj (1859–1912) and Matija Murko (1861–1952). Just like their predecessors, as far back as the late eighteenth century, they focused primarily on language in the folk songs. In contrast to Štrekelj's emphasis on Slovenian repertoire, Murko did research (with phonograph), for example, of sung epic poetry in Bosnia, as well.

The next generations of principal researchers included Vinko Žganec (1890–1976) and Jerko Bezić (1929–2010) in Croatia, and France Marolt (1891–1952) and Zmaga Kumer (1924–2008) in Slovenia. Žganec, doctor of law and musician, and Marolt, himself a musician, were typical representatives of folk music research in a cultural historic sense, who institutionalized the discipline in Croatia and Slovenia, respectively. Kumer and Bezić earned their doctorates within the discipline. In contrast to Kumer, who became one of Europe's best and latest representatives of the folk music research domain, Bezić was systematically broadening the scope of ethnomusicology in Croatia by opening the space for research of urban music phenomena and in general of influences from abroad. Thanks to the interaction with his multidisciplinary institutional colleagues in Zagreb, influenced by both American (e.g., Alan Dundes, Dan Ben Amos) and Russian (Kiril Chistov) folklorists, he defined the subject of ethnomusicology as the so-called "folklore music," referring to musical communication in small groups (more in Marošević, 1998). The next (current) generation of ethnomusicologists in both countries is actively involved in what can be called mainstream ethnomusicology.

Within what was Yugoslavia, practically each constituent republic had its own "school of ethnomusicology," with unquestionable commonalities, but also distinctive features. Each of these "schools" was thematically focused primarily on the material from within its own political unit and its own people in the ethnic sense. While the folk music research paradigm was the unquestionable basis, each "school" had a different stance toward the developments of ethnomusicology elsewhere and used the results of the "mainstream" at different paces.

Aware of the discrepancy caused by the lack of comparative musicology at home and even more by the lack of their own interest in studying the Others, Serbian ethnomusicologists decided to translate, with a considerable delay, two books rooted in comparative musicology. The translation of Fritz Bose's *Musikalische*

Völkerkunde (1953) was published in 1975, and Curt Sachs's *The Rise of Music in the Ancient World East and West* (1943) as late as 1980 (Saks, 1980).[12] These books became a window to "folk music from other parts of the world" for generations of students of ethnomusicology in Serbia. The translation of John Blacking's *How Musical Is Man?* (1973) was intended to be a contribution to/from the Sarajevo "school" in Bosnia-Herzegovina (Bleking, 1992).[13] In Slovenia, the translations include Curt Sachs's *Eine Weltgeschichte des Tanzes* (1933) in 1996, Roberto Leydi's *L'altra musica* (1991) in 1995, and Alan P. Merriam's *The Anthropology of Music* (1964) in 2000. The other "schools" felt self-sufficient and did not translate any foreign books with a wider scope of the discipline.

According to Bohlman, "Folk music and folk song as objects have not disappeared from the practices of European musicians and scholars, but have instead provided them with complex ways of connecting tradition to modernity, and of emblematizing the past in the present" (1996: 106). Elschek suggests that in this process, "cooperation with anthropology and ethnology has been more successful than with historical musicology" (1991: 101).

Applied Ethnomusicologies

One could argue whether various colonial expositions and other showcases involving comparative musicologists should be identified as a part of the early history of applied ethnomusicology and to what extent comparative musicology in general contributed to the "public sector" of the discipline.[14] At the same time, it is clear that the other branch of European ethnomusicology—folk music research—was throughout the previous century linked to the applied domain. The principal goal of many folk music researchers, that of protection of their national heritage, implied practical application of their findings. Besides scholarly procedures that usually included field research, transcription, analysis, archiving, and publication, they often actively engaged in the popularization of folk music and dance. Important channels for this were state-sponsored folklore ensembles in Eastern Europe and less formalized revival ensembles in Western Europe. Ethnomusicologists assumed various roles in these processes: providing the ensembles with musics and dances collected in the field, writing musical arrangements and/or choreographies, singing, playing instruments and/or dancing, leading the ensembles, and touring with them.

An increasing influx of immigrants in Western Europe in the second half of the twentieth century gradually raised interest in their musical cultures among ethnomusicologists. In addition to important studies on immigrant musics (e.g., Ronström, 1991) and cultural policies (Baumann, 1991), several ethnomusicologists, particularly in Sweden, became involved in applied projects such as the *Ethno* camp for young musicians in Falun and music-making within the ensembles such as the *Orientexpressen*.[15] In Norway, Kjell Skyllstad initiated the earlier-mentioned three-year project named *The Resonant Community* in several elementary schools in the Oslo area in 1989, bringing together ethnomusicology and music education in paving the way to better appreciation between Norwegians and the immigrants from Africa, Asia, and Latin America through their respective musics (Skyllstad, 1993). Multicultural education, which in the United States "grew out of the ferment of the civil rights movement of the 1960s" (Banks and McGee Banks, 2001: 5), gradually became recognized and also debated in Europe. Krister Malm was actively involved in two relevant events in the 1990s: the European Music Council's conference Aspects on Music and Multiculturalism in Falun in 1995 (Malm et al., 1995)[16] and in the first world conference on music and censorship in Copenhagen in 1998, where the organization Freemuse was established (Korpe and Reitov, 1998). Ursula Hemetek was beginning applied work with various minorities in Austria (Hemetek, 1996), which would later lead to official political recognition of the Romani people in Austria (Hemetek, 2006). My applied work with refugees from Bosnia-Herzegovina in Norway, Croatia, and Slovenia, with the internally displaced victims of the war in Croatia, and with Romani victims of the war in Kosovo has been presented earlier.

In 2003 Italian ethnomusicologists organized the ninth international seminar in ethnomusicology in Venice, titled Applied Ethnomusicology: Perspectives and Problems. While recognizing that "setting up museums, service within administration of colonial empires, organization of concerts, divulgence by means of publication of writings and recordings". . . were part of the professional profile of comparative musicologists at the beginnings of the 20th century, they also noticed recent "significant developments" and pointed to issues such as intercultural education, music in relation to diaspora, immigration, and refugees, "spectacularization" of traditional music, and cultural cooperation projects.[17] One of the curiosities of this seminar is the absence of folk music research.

The further conference-related developments of applied ethnomusicology in Europe are largely linked to the framework of the International Council for Traditional Music (ICTM). They will be systematically presented later in this text.

Let us now, just as in the previous section, turn our attention to the micro-plan of Croatia and Slovenia in order to discuss the stances of the most representative Croatian and Slovenian researchers toward application. Certainly, the publication of national folk song collections was not the final aim of the researchers. Either the early musically trained researchers themselves or other musicians harmonized (e.g., Kuhač) or otherwise "improved" the songs in order to create nationally distinctive art music. Marolt was known for arranging the collected songs for his acclaimed choir and for adjusting the collected dances for the staged performances by his own and other folklore ensembles. Application was somehow seen as a natural extension of research by many of these early ethnomusicologists. In fact, Jerko Bezić in Croatia and Zmaga Kumer in Slovenia were the first ones who restrained from applications, trying "to affirm ethnomusicology as an autonomous discipline based on fieldwork, theorizing, evidence and debate, detaching it from requisite utilitarity" (the original quotation is referring to Bezić only; Ceribašić, 2004: 6).[18] Today's ethnomusicologists in both countries complement their research activities by serving in juries at the reviews of folklore performances at local, regional, and national levels; serving in the organization of festivals, symposia, and other discipline-related events; Croatians are involved in the UNESCO's Intangible Cultural Heritage agendas.

Staff at the research institutes in both Zagreb and Ljubljana comprises specialists in several disciplines, including ethnochoreologists. Inspired by the developments in applied ethnomusicology, at least one researcher, Tvrtko Zebec, theorizes about applied ethnochoreology (Zebec, 2007). Joško Ćaleta, an ethnomusicologist in Zagreb, in whose work research and performing applications are closely intertwined, claims that applied activities are often paying his research activities (interview, July 14, 2014), which is a meaningful point to be taken into consideration.

This section ends with a complementing view from the other side of Europe, from the United Kingdom. In the words of Kathleen Van Buren, "Ethnomusicologists need to think more deeply about how to serve others, not just ourselves, through our work. This means listening to people within communities where we live and work, allowing their perspectives to help guide our choice of our topics and activities, trying to collaborate and respond to their needs when we can, and empowering them rather than ourselves" (2010: 219).

The International Council for Traditional Music

Perhaps the most efficient access to applied ethnomusicology in the global arena is through the principal international association of ethnomusicologists, which is the International Council for Traditional Music (ICTM), with current representation in more than 120 countries and regions on all continents. The association was established in London in 1947 under the name International Folk Music Council (IFMC). We should keep in mind that the establishment of IFMC precedes Kunst's book *Musicologica: A Study of the Nature of Ethno-musicology, Its Problems, Methods, and Representative Personalities* (1950) and the wide acceptance of the term *ethnomusicology* that followed.[19] It was an era of comparative musicology and folk music research paradigms, which were affecting each other in various ways and to various extents in various places.

IFMC's roots are clearly in the folk music research paradigm, which is evident from the following description:

> In her capacity as Honourable Secretary of the International (Advisory) Folk Dance Council, Maud Karpeles (1885–1976) organized the International Conference on Folk Song and Folk Dance, held at the Belgian Institute in London, 22–27 September 1947. Delegates from twenty-eight countries participated, mostly appointed by the governments of their respective nations, as well as a UNESCO representative. . . . On the afternoon of Monday, 22 September 1947, the Vice Chairman of the conference,

Stuart Wilson (1889–1966), proposed "that an International Folk Music Council be formed."

(www.ictmusic.org; see also Karpeles, 1971).

The article in which Karpeles offered her reflections on the 21 years of existence of the IFMC says a lot about its intellectual climate, including the sentences "In all parts of the world the traditional practice of folk music is disappearing—gradually in some regions and rapidly in others—and if we are to save our musical heritage for the benefit of our own and future generations, it is necessary to act quickly. Collecting activities are, of course, being carried on, but these must be intensified if precious material is not to be lost. As the saying goes, 'It is later than we think'" (Karpeles, 1971: 29). The attitudes of this kind were later largely discredited in the mainstream of the discipline as "salvage ethnomusicology," pointing to "romanticism, paternalism, and hegemony" (see also Grant, 2014: 80). Cultural relativism and the absence of value judgments became, at different paces in different parts of the world, the *sine qua non* of modern ethnomusicology.[20]

The objectives of IFMC were the following: (1) to assist in the preservation, dissemination, and practice of the folk music of all countries; (2) to further the comparative study of folk music; and (3) to promote understanding and friendship between nations through the common interest of folk music.[21] What matters particularly from the point of view of applied ethnomusicology, besides the applied overtones in the presented objectives, is the envisioned work of the newly established Council. The list of proposals included "the holding of conferences and festivals; the publication of a catalogue of recordings, bibliographies, a manual for collectors, and an international collection of folk songs; the promotion of national and international archives; the institution of a general method of dance notations; and the development of a guide to the classification of folk tunes" (Karpeles, 1971: 17). In the course of 1950s and 1960s, IFMC indeed published several catalogues, bibliographies, dictionaries, manuals, collections, statements, and songbooks. In order to accomplish these aims, the structure of IFMC included not only National Committees, but also the Radio Committee, Folk Dance Committee, and more, the names being subject to change from time to time.

The intention of the IFMC in the post–World War II years was to bring together composers, researchers, and other specialists interested in folk music and dance into a truly international association; even the intention to be related to UNESCO was there from the very inception of the Council. Maud Karpeles's principal source of inspiration was Cecil Sharp, the founding father of the folklore revival in England in the beginning of the twentieth century. Within the newly established Council she became secretary under the presidency of Ralph Vaughan Williams, renowned art music composer and English folk song collector. Members of the first Executive Board likewise included various specialists—by far, not all of them researchers—each from a different country. While referring to legacies of the previous editors, the new editor of the *Yearbook of the IFMC*, Bruno Nettl, noted their determination to "present scholarship of the highest quality and to exhibit samples of what was emanating from research carried on in all parts of the world" and that "[s]cholars from the many nations and cultures of the world do not always think, study, and write in the same style, and the editor of an international publication must tread the thin line between rigid standardization and chaotic diversity" (Nettl, 1974: 7). He intended to broaden the coverage of research to those parts of the world that had not been represented in the *Yearbook* and its predecessor the *Journal of IFMC* thus far.

A particularly important shift was the change of the name of the Council after more than three decades of its existence, strongly argued within a heated discussion by the new Secretary General Dieter Christensen at the 26th World Conference in Seoul, Republic of Korea, in 1981. Erich Stockmann recalls the consequences of this change: "It worked like magic and opened up doors in regions where the word 'folk music' had a somewhat pejorative ring" (Stockmann, 1988: 8).[22] The immediate result was new members in countries on all continents (see also H. M., 1983: 3).

The current official presentation of ICTM ends up with the sentence significant for this Introduction: "By means of its wide international representation and the activities of its Study Groups, the International Council for Traditional Music acts as a bond among peoples of different cultures and thus serves the peace of humankind." The year 1947 marked the start of both the Council and the Cold War period. Until the end of the Cold War in 1991, ICTM was actively involved in crossing the political, administrative, economic, lingual, cultural, and other boundaries set by the two military alliances, while also including in its framework those countries that proclaimed themselves "neutral" and "nonaligned." The Council authorities, including the Presidents, were from any of these politically delineated territories, and the World Conferences, Study Group Symposia, and Colloquia were intentionally taking place in all four of them (NATO, the Warsaw Pact, Neutral, Nonaligned).

Let me document this practice with two extraordinary examples.[23] The first of them takes us to a symposium on Traditional Music in Asian Countries, organized as a joint venture with the International Music Council in 1983. The symposium took place in Pyongyang, DPR Korea, and was attended by scholars from Afghanistan, China, India, Indonesia, Japan, DPR Korea, Mongolia, Pakistan, Papua New Guinea, the Philippines, the USSR, and PR Yemen. The second example refers to the 28th World Conference, hosted jointly by Stockholm (Sweden) and Helsinki (Finland). Its closing ceremony took place on the other side of the Iron Curtain, in Leningrad (USSR; today's St. Petersburg in Russia). The older members of the Council are aware of this legacy and for a good reason proud of it.

Out of the total of 44 World Conferences, 18 took place outside Europe: two in Africa (Ghana, South Africa), seven in Asia (Israel, Republic of Korea, Hong Kong, Japan, twice in China, Kazakhstan), five in North America (three in the US, two in Canada), one in Central America (Jamaica), two in South America (Brazil), and one in Australia. Of those taking place in Europe, four took place in the countries on the Eastern side of the Iron Curtain (Romania, Czechoslovakia, Hungary, German Democratic Republic), one in the nonaligned Yugoslavia, and six in the neutral countries Switzerland, Austria (three times), Finland and Sweden (jointly), and Ireland. The sites of smaller-size IFMC/

ICTM gatherings, such as the Colloquia, Symposia of the Study Groups, and from 2015 on also Fora, point to the inclusion of many more countries from the world's political spectrum (e.g., Cuba, Oman, Vietnam). Serving as a communicational channel across any boundaries continues to be the conscious strategy of the Council, which justifies the view that the Council itself is a project in applied ethnomusicology. The ongoing enlargement of the ICTM World Network is a part of the same frame of thought.

The International Council for Traditional Music and Applied Ethnomusicology

Despite its international aspirations, IFMC was for a long time considered a primarily European association. Europe was the place of its foundation and residence, and Europe was home to most of its members, conferences,[24] and publications[25]—even "folk music" in its name was largely seen as a European marker. As suggested earlier, the name change from "folk" (IFMC) to "traditional" (ICTM) broadened the acceptability of the Council worldwide in the 1980s. The current frame of interests within the ICTM clearly exceeds "traditional" music, but the name of the Council remains the same, for better or worse.[26]

Search for the first mention of applied ethnomusicology in any ICTM context led to the 27th World Conference in 1983 in New York, where Ghanaian ethnomusicologist Daniel Avorgbedor presented a paper titled "The Effects of Rural-Urban Migration on a Village Musical Culture: Some Implications for Applied Ethnomusicology."[27] The next instance took place six years later, at the 30th World Conference in 1989 in Schladming (Austria), where German ethnomusicologist Artur Simon presented his paper "The Borneo Music Documentation Project (Northern Nigeria). Aspects of Documentation, Field Research in Africa, and Applied Ethnomusicology."

The author of the first mention of applied ethnomusicology in the *Bulletin of the ICTM* was John Baily. In his report on the UK National Committee, he included the following, published in April 1988:

> Members of ICTM UK have a particular interest in music in the multi- (or inter-) cultural school curriculum, and we have established a sub-committee to look into the question of teaching resources available in the UK. . . . With the same objectives we are represented on the UK Council for Music Education and Training, which is in the process of setting up a standing committee to look into the place of non-Western music in our education system. . . . Ethnomusicologists, like all other academics in contemporary Britain, have to look to their "performance indicators"; and seek to justify their existence, in part, through this form of applied ethnomusicology.

The next instances were my report on ethnomusicology in Croatia (*Bulletin of the ICTM* #90 from April 1997), in which applied ethnomusicology was related to organization of folklore festivals and amateur musical life; and Cynthia Tse Kimberlin's and Pirkko Moisala's "In Memoriam" (*Bulletin of the ICTM* #91 from October 1997), where they indicated applied ethnomusicology as one of the areas of interests of Marcia Herndon.

The first article with applied ethnomusicology in its title published in the *Yearbook for Traditional Music* was authored by the Austrian scholar Ursula Hemetek: "Applied Ethnomusicology in the Process of the Political Recognition of a Minority: A Case Study of the Austrian Roma" (*Yearbook for Traditional Music*, vol. 38, 2006). The next major development was the special section, with a group of eight authors, on Music and Poverty, put together by the Finish/Canadian ethnomusicologist Klisala Harrison (*Yearbook for Traditional Music*, vol. 45, 2013). One should of course be aware that the lack of the wording "applied ethnomusicology" does not imply the absence of the articles relevant for the current discussion in the earlier years, with Angela Impey's 2002 essay "Culture, Conservation and Community Reconstruction: Explorations in Advocacy Ethnomusicology and Action Research in Northern KwaZulu" serving as a convincing evidence.

As far as the ICTM scholarly gatherings are concerned, the 15th Colloquium, titled *Discord: Identifying Conflict within Music, Resolving Conflict Through Music*, organized by John Morgan O'Connell in Limerick, Ireland, in 2004 can be interpreted as anticipation of what is to follow. Although music and conflict make a suitable ethnomusicological topic and applied ethnomusicology was not particularly emphasized in the colloquium documents, several presentations pointed to "ethnomusicology as an approach to conflict resolution." The articles developed from this event form the representative ethnomusicological volume on music and conflict (O'Connell and Castelo-Branco, 2010).

The 38th World Conference of the ICTM that took place in Sheffield, England, in 2005 featured applied ethnomusicology and ethnochoreology as one of the themes, pointing to "situations in which scholars put their knowledge and understanding to creative use to stimulate concern and awareness about the people they study."[28] Presenters were invited to consider issues of advocacy, canonicity, musical literacy, cultural property rights, cultural imperialism, majority-minority relations, application of technologies such as the internet and their effects on music and dance. One plenary session explicitly featured applied ethnomusicology,[29] and yet another plenary session considered it among the other subjects.[30]

A symposium titled Ethnomusicology and Ethnochoreology in Education: Issues in Applied Scholarship took place in Ljubljana, Slovenia, in 2006. The members of the ICTM's Executive Board, who came to Ljubljana for their regular annual meeting, and the other invited scholars presented and evaluated their immediate experiences and visions of the efficient transfer of scholarly knowledge into educational domains. Presentations from contexts around the globe discussed modalities of connections between theory and practice, methods of promoting, teaching, and learning of traditional music and dance, and the strategies of preparing textbooks, recordings, and other materials for various stages of educational processes (see the report by Kovačič and Šivic, 2007).

The ICTM's 39th World Conference in Vienna in 2007 featured two important events: a double panel, The Politics of Applied Ethnomusicology: New Perspectives, with six participants, each from a different continent,[31] and a meeting at which 44 members agreed to establish a study group with a focus on applied ethnomusicology.[32] Following the adoption of the definition and mission statement, the Study Group on Applied Ethnomusicology was approved at the Executive Board's meeting in Vienna on July 12, 2007.

The next year, in 2008, Ljubljana hosted the first symposium of the newly established Study Group on Applied Ethnomusicology, which was well attended by scholars from all continents. Anthony Seeger delivered the keynote address. This event featured the history of the idea and understandings of applied ethnomusicology in worldwide contexts; presentation and evaluation of individual projects, with an emphasis on theory and method; and applied ethnomusicology in situations of conflict. It is worth mentioning the use of the Native American "talking circles" as one of the means of communication within this Study Group.

The international intentions of the Study Group continued at the symposia in Hanoi, Vietnam (2010), Nicosia, Cyprus (2012), East London—Hogsback—Grahamstown, South Africa (2014), Cape Breton, Canada (2016), and Beijing, China (2018).[33]

Thematic frames of the symposia are trustworthy indicators of the dynamics of the Study Group and, to a smaller extent, of the interests of local organizers. In Hanoi, where the joint symposium with the Study Group on Music and Minorities took place, the emphasis was on definitions and approaches to applied work in various geographical contexts; on proactive roles that ethnomusicology can play in contributing to the sustainability of performing arts through archiving, disseminating, contributing to policies, understanding socioeconomic factors, developing audiences and markets, and empowering communities to forge their own futures; and on performing arts in building peace, negotiating power relationships, and strengthening identities through formal and informal education. Note that the use of the term "performing arts" is a manner of paying respect to the perspective, which is widely shared in Southeast Asia.

The symposium in Nicosia featured applied ethnomusicology in the contexts of social activism, censorship, and state control; in relation to various types of disability, pointing to human rights and the making of disability politics and including disability research, special education, and music therapy; and in relation to diverse social configurations of conflict, including interpersonal and intergroup, interethnic, interreligious, and interclass, with emphasis on the divided island of Cyprus.

The symposium on three locations in South Africa opened up the question of institutions, usually associated with formal and informal rules, procedures, and norms, from schools and festivals to large international bodies such as UNESCO, including instituting and institutionalization issues; and the question of media and their social, political, and cultural impacts on applied work.

The symposium in Cape Breton related music to labor and exchange, opening the floor for socio-economic agendas. Intangible cultural heritage was linked to sustainable development and tourism. Pedagogical issues found their place next to research networking at the time of intensified migrations, and methodological agendas with emphasis on collaboration and criticality.

The symposium in Beijing called for the attention to power structures that affect musical practices and their carriers, to formal and informal learning, and to reflections on how we approach cultural sustainability and on the methods we use. This was a joint symposium with the new ICTM Study Group on Music, Education and Social Inclusion.

As far as the publications related to ICTM are concerned, four of them are at disposal to the readers. First, the earlier mentioned double panel that took place at the ICTM World Conference in Vienna in 2007 inspired the creation of the thematic issue of the *Muzikološki zbornik/Musicological Annual*, 46(2), entirely dedicated to applied ethnomusicology (Pettan, 2008).[34] Five ethnomusicologists reflect on their experiences linked to Brazil, Australia, the United States, Malaysia, and former Yugoslavia; the volume also serves as a Festschrift on the 80th birthday of the aforementioned Norwegian scholar Kjell Skyllstad, an important early thinker in applied ethnomusicology.

The second edited volume resulted from the inaugural Study Group's symposium in Ljubljana and is titled *Applied Ethnomusicology: Historical and Contemporary Approaches* (Harrison, Mackinlay, and Pettan, 2010). Its 13 essays, by authors from Africa, Australia, Europe, and North America, are widely used and quoted, in this volume as well, so no additional presentation is needed here.

The third is a special thematic section on Music and Poverty in the *Yearbook for Traditional Music* 45 (Harrison, 2013). Its seven articles address various aspects of this important and largely neglected problem in the diverse contexts of Brazil, Canada, Haiti, India, Nepal, and USA.

The fourth publication is the Finnish journal *COLLeGIUM*. Its volume 21 is entirely dedicated to the theme Applied Ethnomusicology in Institutional Policy and Practice (Harrison, 2016). Based on some of the best presentations from the Study Group Symposia in 2010, 2012, and 2014, the volume features case studies from Australia, China, Germany, the Seychelles, South Africa, United Kingdom, United States, and Zimbabwe.

Individual Views

How else could ICTM contribute to better comprehension of the emerging field? By means of its wide international representation, it can provide us with the perspectives from different geographic and cultural environments. The answers to my five essential questions were provided by five ethnomusicologists, each from a different continent.[35] Some of them are more inclined to applied ethnomusicology than the others, but together, they provide a useful global myriad of perspectives about the field. I asked for anonymous, individual views, therefore they are indicated as "A view from Australia," "A view from Asia," and so on.

1. How would you define applied ethnomusicology, or at least what is its essence in your opinion?

>A view from Australia: The application of ethnomusicological method and theory to addressing practical issues.
>
>A view from Asia: If we define applied ethnomusicology as research activities with social conscience and political involvement, I think whatever we do as ethnomusicologists should be applied ethnomusicology at least in some ways.
>
>A view from South America: I can only see a matter of degree in its definition, acknowledging an aspect, which is inherent to any research, namely its potential to be applied to different purposes. However, in most of what has been termed as such in the humanities one finds embedded ideals of social justice and equity, sometimes of reparation and/or reconciliation, all of which are also subject to different and even contradictory perspectives.
>
>A view from Africa: Generally, how our practical work in the field is applied in an academic environment. Music is not taught in an European or abstract way, that is, by explaining music with words, but holistically, by doing—listening, imitating, and playing. Based on that experience we teach African music theory practically on instruments. It is much more appropriate and easier for people to understand musical concepts doing it that way.
>
>A view from Europe: I do not subscribe to the term "applied ethnomusicology," although I understand why it is necessary. I think the engagement of scholars with the communities they work with should be/is a given.

2. Have you done any project(s) that would fit into your notion of applied ethnomusicology?

>Australia: Preparing indigenous people's land claim is the obvious example, that is, applying knowledge of their musical culture to demonstrate rights over land using an indigenous conceptual system. I was one of three researchers (with an anthropologist and a linguist) who prepared one of the largest such claims. During the hearing of the case (by a Supreme Court judge) songs and dances were performed to demonstrate ownership of the land according to their own system of land ownership.
>
>Asia: Following what I mentioned above, I would like to think all my projects are within the realm of applied ethnomusicology.
>
>South America: They have ranged from short-term documentation projects related to safeguarding and revitalizing traditions perceived to be vanishing to long-term horizontal collaborations with grassroot organizations, forming research groups working on music and social justice among residents of areas affected by patterns of injustice and inequity.
>
>Africa: We also understand applied ethnomusicology as offering of our expertise to people in order to develop a musical environment. This can be in form of

workshops, teaching in schools, music projects, community outreach, and curriculum development, which takes the background of people and local needs into consideration. In our current curriculum African music components are compulsory. We just brought new streams and modules to respond to local needs; for instance the course Basic Music Literacy for students from villages who have problems with music theory and music literacy, and the streams Music Technologies and Production and Music and Arts Administration. The two streams aim at providing students with practical skills which make them more employable, and which enable them to start their own business within the music industry. We hope that these two new streams will in the future help to improve the musical infrastructure in the region.

Europe: I was involved in the application of projects to the UNESCO representative list of Intangible Cultural Heritage and served on an advisory committee to the Ministry of Culture on ICH matters. For over 20 years, I also promoted the founding of a national sound archive. Finally, I consider the publication of an encyclopedia—an all-encompassing research project with a wide outreach among musicians, cultural politicians and scholars—as "applied ethnomusicology."

3. Is the distinction between "academic" and "applied" work present in your working environment? If so, how is the "applied" domain valued compared to the "academic" one?

Australia: When I worked at the institute it was required of researchers to demonstrate the benefit of the proposed research to the community. This resulted in a blending of scholarly and applied research. Later, when I was working in the university environment, there was much more emphasis on scholarship for its own sake, and the application of research results was not highly valued.

Asia: There are theorists so to speak who are mainly concerned with the refinement of theoretical explorations. I respect such endeavors as long as they have applicable dimension. The "applied" domain has been treated unfairly as activities conducted by less qualified/serious scholars, partly because of the narrow definition of the "academic" domain, but also due to the inability on the part of "applied" ethnomusicologists to advance a new vision of theory construction.

South America: No.

Africa: A distinction between academic and applied work is still there (for instance when you have to teach different research methodologies or history of ethnomusicology), but the boundaries are quite blurred. A lot of our academic research is based on applied work and—as explained earlier—theory is thought practically (which is the direct application of knowledge obtained in the field).

Europe: I try to avoid making this distinction. But, in my institution we have many projects that can be classified as applied: museum expositions, digitization, community work, projects in schools, etc. I would say 40% applied.

4. Is the "applied" domain present in your teaching curricula?

Australia: I always tried to show the relationship between applied and theoretical ethnomusicology.
Asia: Whenever I teach I emphasize the importance of socially engaged research activities.
South America: Yes, in the obligatory bibliographies of both undergraduate and graduate courses as well as in systematic outreach and research programs.
Africa: We do not offer a degree program or specific modules on applied ethnomusicology. Yet, as already explained, indigenous music is compulsory, theory is taught practically, and articles on applied ethnomusicology are discussed in class. Thus, although not formalized in terms of specific modules, applied ethnomusicology is a reality here.
Europe: In my seminars, I discuss researchers' social responsibilities and the many spheres of ethnomusicological work. But, we do not have a course on "applied ethnomusicology."

5. Do you know of any university offering a course in applied ethnomusicology or applied ethnochoreology?

Australia: No.
Asia: There may be, but not that I know of.
South America: No, but I know several universities that offer opportunities to both graduate and undergraduate students to engage in applied research in the sense I outlined before, as well as portions of their curricular components devoted to applied approaches.
Africa: This is a tricky question. Applied approaches differ from institution to institution, and the motives and conditions are hardly comparable. Unlike other universities in the country, our Music Department had hardly any resources. We had to build up from zero, which means that applied ethnomusicology was a necessity and therefore a reality. At another university, applied ethnomusicology was simply understood as building up an African ensemble. Elsewhere, there was some teaching of indigenous instruments, but not applied ethnomusicology in our understanding. At Kwazulu Natal you find a completely different situation with Patricia Opondo, who is a very focused and an internationally trained academic. Applied ethnomusicology is officially part of the curriculum.
Europe: No.

What can we make of the replies of these five ethnomusicologists? All of them are well established as professionals and work in either university or research institute settings. Their representativeness is balanced in terms of geography and gender, as well, but none of them belongs to a young generation of scholars, which is seeking for more radical solutions, such as active involvement in applied projects as a part of the study curricula. At this point I would like to add that a course in applied ethnomusicology, which counts to the obligatory master level courses, exists since 2012 at the Department of Musicology of the University of Ljubljana.

The International Council for Traditional Music and the Society for Ethnomusicology

In contrast to the eight years younger Society for Ethnomusicology (SEM), which is defined as "a U.S.-based organization with an international membership" (www.ethnomusicology.org), IFMC/ICTM was envisioned in international terms in all respects. Its Secretariat moves its base periodically from one country to another; it has so far been based in the United Kingdom, Denmark, Canada, the United States, Australia, and Slovenia. Both past and current membership figures suggest that SEM, which is the US National Committee of ICTM, is larger than ICTM, but also that the single country with the largest number of members in ICTM is the United States. The two societies have distinctive intellectual histories and the resulting theoretical and methodological paradigms. In words of Dieter Christensen,

> SEM and ICTM are both unique in their roles, and they complement each other; SEM as the regional organization in North America that represents the interests of professional, academic ethnomusicologists in the USA and Canada, and at the same time serves the field of ethnomusicology world-wide through its publications; and the ICTM as the international organization in the domain of traditional music including ethnomusicology that serves scholarship with an emphasis on the mutual recognition and understanding of diverse inquiring minds.
>
> (Christensen, 1988:17).

IFMC/ICTM cherished various languages in its scholarly publications until 1985, when the last article so far in a language other than English was published in the *Yearbook for Traditional Music*. From 2006 on, the *Yearbook*'s general editor Don Niles reintroduced the practice of adding abstracts in native languages of those people who are the principal subjects of the articles. This practice was originally introduced in the 1980s, following Yoshihiko Tokumaru's proposal.

Jeff Todd Titon has described in Section 1 of this Introduction how the four founders of SEM, led by Alan P. Merriam, rejected Maud Karpeles's invitation to join IFMC and instead decided to keep SEM as an independent society. IFMC reported about the new society in the following manner in its 11th *Bulletin* from 1957: "On November 18th, 1955, at the 54th Annual Meeting of the American Anthropological Association in Boston, the Society for Ethnomusicology was founded for the purpose of establishing communication among persons in primitive, folk, and oriental music, and for furthering research and scholarship in these fields. The Society plans to continue publication of the

Ethno-Musicology Newsletter three times yearly, to meet annually in conjunction with societies of anthropologists, folklorists and musicologists, and to engage in other activities of benefit to members" (Anon., 1957: 6).

According to Erich Stockmann, one of the Presidents of the Council, Maud Karpeles was sensitive to occasional criticisms and used to ask him anxiously several times in the course of the 1950s: "Are we really not 'scientific' enough? She knew my answer" (Stockman, 1988: 5). Dieter Christensen, Secretary General of the Council for 20 years, noted that the "American issue" and the "scientific issue" were clearly related (Christensen, 1988: 14).

There are several important connections between the two societies that should be mentioned here. At the inauguration of IFMC in 1947, seven US "correspondents" were identified, among them Curt Sachs, Percy Grainger, and Alan Lomax. The "Liaison officer" (single national representative) of the United States in the IFMC for 10 years (1952–1962) was Charles Seeger, one of the SEM's founding fathers. Following Seeger's mandate, the United States was uninterruptedly represented in the IFMC/ICTM by the "National Committee" until 1999, starting with Charles Haywood and ending with Ricardo Trimillos. After a five-year break, Timothy Rice, then the SEM President, re-established the connection and SEM became officially recognized as the ICTM's US National Committee.

The first SEM President, Willard Rhodes, later became ICTM's fourth President, while councillor in the first SEM nomenclature Bruno Nettl later served in a variety of roles in both societies, as did (and still do) many other scholars, from the United States and from the other countries.

It is appropriate to complete this section of the Introduction by pointing to a joint Forum, that took place in September 2015 in Limerick, bringing together the two major ethnomusicological associations—ICTM and SEM—around the theme of importance for applied ethnomusicology: Transforming Ethnomusicological Praxis through Activism and Community Engagement. This historical event, the first such collaboration between ICTM and SEM, was co-chaired by the SEM President Beverley Diamond and the ICTM President Salwa El-Shawan Castelo-Branco.

> The Forum will focus on ethnomusicological praxis and collaborative strategies in different international contexts and political situations. While there is now a long history in ethnomusicology of initiatives that have sought to address problems of inequality, disparity and oppression, and a shorter history pertaining to such matters as health and environmental change, the symposium will focus, not on the problems per se, but on the methodologies that could best enable our work to have greater social impact. We are interested in critically assessing and finding strategies and best practices of collaboration, communication and policy formulation.
>
> (from the Call for papers)

This joint event convincingly testifies about the current intellectual climate in both major associations of ethnomusicologists, which is very much in tune with the ideas presented in the *Handbook*.

Notes

1. Controversy over the genre of exploitation documentary, so-called *mondo films* such as this one, suggesting that the genuine documentary footage is sometimes mixed with staged sequences, does not impact the film's symbolic standpoint.
2. The practitioners are scholars whose professional positioning may vary from universities and other schools, research institutes, archives, museums, media, and nongovernmental organizations, to freelance status.
3. Applied ethnomusicology is about how musical practice can inform relevant theory, and about how theory can inform musical practice. Knowledge of data, theories, and methods of ethnomusicology, as much as ethical concerns, are essential.
4. There is a need for increased critical reflection on political agendas, moral philosophies, and ideologies of applied ethnomusicology projects, as well as on the role of personal agency in applied ethnomusicological work.
5. Here she refers to the American Musicological Society.
6. For instance, the Society for Applied Spectroscopy, founded in 1958, has more than 2,000 members worldwide.
7. The aim of the Society for Applied Microbiology is to advance for the benefit of the public the science of microbiology in its application to the environment, human and animal health, agriculture and industry. The aim of the Society for Applied Philosophy is to promote philosophical study and research that has a direct bearing on areas of practical concern, such as law, politics, economics, science, technology, medicine, and education.
8. Timothy Rice's book *Ethnomusicology: A Very Short Introduction*, to the opposite, ends with the chapter titled "Public Service" and points to the fact that "[e]thnomusicologists are increasingly asking themselves the question 'Ethnomusicology for what purpose?'" (2014: 120). It is my hope that this *Handbook* will encourage ethnomusicologists to seek answers to this question, both inside themselves and in the world that surrounds them.
9. The other being Berlin.
10. For some useful current views on comparative musicology, see Schneider (2006), thematic issue of the Polish journal *Muzyka* 1 (2009), and the website http://www.compmus.org.
11. By scholars such as Naila Ceribašić, Marija Dumnić, Adriana Helbig, Ana Hofman, Jelena Jovanović, Ivona Opetčeska Tatarčevska, Selena Rakočević, Velika Stojkova Serafimovska, Jasmina Talam, Ljerka Vidić Rasmussen and Dave Wilson.
12. In case of Sachs, the German version titled *Die Musik der Alten Welt in Ost und West* (1968) served as the source for translation.
13. The translator Ljerka Vidić Rasmussen used to study there under the mentorship of Blacking's former doctoral student Ankica Petrović. Petrović was widely regarded the first representative of "mainstream ethnomusicology" in what was Yugoslavia. Introduction of new disciplinary paradigms met many obstacles in the intellectual environment rooted in the strong folk music research school established by Cvjetko Rihtman.
14. This section uses parts of one of my earlier articles (Pettan, 2008) and provides updates.
15. For instance, Dan Lundberg, Owe Ronström.
16. The proceedings contain articles by Kristof Tamas, Max Peter Baumann, Mark Slobin, and Krister Malm.
17. This seminar took place just a month prior to the conference *Invested in Community: Ethnomusicology and Musical Advocacy*, which took place at Brown University in Providence, Rhode Island, featuring "applied ethnomusicologists (who) work as musical

and cultural advocates, using skills and knowledge gained within academia to serve the public at large. They help communities identify, document, preserve, develop, present and celebrate the musical traditions they hold dear."

18. This does not count for their institutional colleagues, who continued to supply the arrangements for musicians and choreographies for the dancers in folklore ensembles.
19. The Ukrainian/Soviet folk music researcher Kliment Kvitka (1880–1953) proposed and described the term as early as 1928 (see Lukanyuk, 2006). Interestingly, the second, enlarged edition of Kunst's book was published in 1955 under the auspices of IFMC.
20. See Chapter 2 by Harrison in Volume 1 of the *Handbook*, calling for a reconsideration of this issue.
21. The third objective clearly referred to "recognition of the painful fact that the Second World War had created deep rifts between nations and peoples" (Stockmann, 1988: 2).
22. Paul Rovsing Olsen, the Council's President at that time, provided the following comment: ". . . we hope to have found a name which, much better than the original one, explains what our Council stands for in the world of scholarship—and in the world of international organizations. The IFMC has been concerned, from its beginnings, with all kinds of traditional music, not only with 'folk music.' This has not always been understood by outsiders" (Rovsing Olsen, 1981: 2).
23. Don Niles and Krister Malm respectfully shared the details of these events with me.
24. The first IFMC conference took place in Basel, Switzerland, in 1948.
25. The first issue of the *Journal of the International Folk Music Council* (predecessor of the *Yearbook of the International Folk Music Council* from 1969 and of the *Yearbook of the International Council for Traditional Music* from 1981) was published in 1949. The other publication was the *Bulletin of the International Folk Music Council*, starting in 1948.
26. In the forthcoming part of this section I gratefully acknowledge the assistance of ICTM's Executive Assistant Carlos Yoder.
27. A later version was published in 1992 in the journal *African Music*.
28. Applied ethnomusicology (and ethnochoreology) became one of the conference themes 22 years after Avorgbedor first mentioned it in his ICTM conference paper.
29. *Applied Ethnomusicology and Studies on Music and Minorities—The Convergence of Theory and Practice* with Ursula Hemetek, John O'Connell, Adelaida Reyes, and Stephen Wild.
30. Including war and revitalization in Croatia of the 1990s and early 2000s. The session was organized by Naila Ceribašić.
31. Organized by Samuel Araújo (South America) and me (Europe); the other panelists were Maureen Loughran (North America), Jennifer Newsome (Australia), Patricia Opondo (Africa), and Tan Sooi Beng (Asia).
32. I initiated the Study Group and became its first Chair; Klisala Harrison became Vice-Chair, and Eric Martin Usner became Secretary. As I became Secretary General of ICTM in 2011, Klisala Harrison assumed the duties of the Study Group's Chair, Samuel Araújo became Vice-Chair, and Britta Sweers became Secretary. In 2019, Huib Schippers serves as Chair, Adriana Helbig as Vice-Chair, and Weiya Lin as Secretary.
33. The Symposia were hosted by Svanibor Pettan, Le Van Toan, Panicos Giorgoudes, Bernhard Bleibinger, Marcia Ostashewski, and Zhang Boyu, respectively.
34. Scholarly journal, published by the Department of Musicology of the University of Ljubljana. It is available at (http://revije.ff.uni-lj.si/MuzikoloskiZbornik/issue/archive).
35. Section 1 of the Introduction, by co-editor Jeff Todd Titon, covers North America, so I did not include it here.

SECTION 3

AN INTRODUCTION TO THE CHAPTERS

JEFF TODD TITON AND SVANIBOR PETTAN

IN the Introduction we have identified several activities of contemporary applied ethnomusicologists. The chapters in this volume illustrate a range of these. Two of the authors discuss cultural policy interventions through UNESCO's initiatives in safeguarding intangible cultural heritage: Wissler (Chapter 7, Peru) and Hemetek (Chapter 2, Austria). The mixed record of success is leading applied ethnomusicologists to agree that the best outcomes occur in small-scale projects resulting from long-term partnerships and mutual goals. Local and regional cultural differences require that policies adapt to varying conditions. Top-down, bureaucratic solutions are apt to be less successful and more likely to have negative consequences. Such best practices have characterized most, if not all, successful applied ethnomusicology projects, whether cultural policy interventions or not.

Advocacy for social justice underpins the majority of the contributions to this volume. Merriam's "white knight" critique of ethnomusicologists who feel it is their duty to champion the music and music-cultures they research mocked the impulse to sound the trumpet for musical justice, but it is social justice that characterizes much applied work today, while musical and cultural equity is understood as a given. Bakan's Chapter 3 reveals how music may become part of an agenda for social justice among autistic youth. He proposes an ethnographic model of disability as a potential alternative and complement to the existing social and medical models, arguing in turn that the ethnographic and relativistic tenets of applied ethnomusicology hold the potential to effectively promote neurodiversity and autism acceptance. Summit's Chapter 1 shows how musical activism can become peace activism based on economic cooperation. He asks what happens when our experiences in the field conjoin with ethical, moral, and religious imperatives to pursue social justice and give back to the people with whom we work. His chapter addresses issues and offers a framework for ethnomusicologists to consider when moved to partner with the people whose music we study, who so generously help us and sometimes become our teachers and our friends. Chapter 4 by Schrag and Chapter 7 by Wissler reveal how musical advocacy can bring about mutual social and political benefits. Schrag urges ethnomusicologists to re-engage with practitioners of multigenerational artistic traditions among ethnolinguistic minorities. Many of these art forms are at risk because of globalized communication. He guides arts-in-culture scholars through an approach anchored to event analysis and relationships, leaning toward enactments of traditional genres rather than liminal fusions. He offers practical tools that communities may use in their steps toward more lively artistic futures. Wissler shows that collaborative applied ethnomusicology projects based in shared experience and executed in small groups are just as valid and often are more effective than large-scale organizational projects. Two case studies show how grassroots approaches support the effectiveness of indigenous voice and representation in regard to the uses of traditional music in tourism, safeguarding, and music ownership via CD production. Sherinian, in Chapter 5, shows advocacy's potential as a revolutionary political force that can not only aid the politically oppressed but also re-center marginalized musics within ethnomusicology itself. Using phenomenological methods and dialogical processes from two case studies of Tamil Dalit (former outcaste or untouchable) folk music from her fieldwork and ethnographic filmmaking in India, Sherinian argues that engagement with the meaning and value of marginalized South Asian music forces us to recognize and deconstruct local hegemonies of musical style and ethnomusicology's contributions to the perpetuation of them, not only in fieldwork, but also in teaching content and academic/community programming. She examines methods (including filmmaking and participant activism) to approach contexts where the oppressed use music to assert identity and cultural politics of revaluation against local hierarchies of musical value that contribute to Dalit Action Theory: that is, politicized agency of the oppressed asserted through the arts, necessitating an activist ethnographic methodology focused on collaboration, dialogue, and reciprocity. Transformation often accompanies advocacy, not just musical, social, and political but also personal, as Bakan's and Summit's chapters reveal.

Education is also a concern for applied ethnomusicologists. Although the topic is treated more fully in Volume 3, in the present volume Summit (Chapter 1) describes an educational initiative in a Jewish community in Uganda that is characterized by long-term reciprocity, contrasting it with failed projects that resulted from well-meaning but short-term visits and superficial understandings. Hemetek and Mackinlay (Chapters 2 and 6) also recognize the activist aspect of education.

Peace, conflict resolution, and cooperation among peoples is another area that appeals to the contributors in this volume and the others in the *Handbook*. Summit (Chapter 1) discusses how he helped promote the work of an Ugandan Fair Trade coffee cooperative that brought together Jewish, Christian, and Muslim growers in an interfaith operation in common cause. Important aspects of conflict management are imbedded in the study provided in Chapter 2 by Hemetek (with focus on three distinctive minority cases).

Medical ethnomusicology, in which ethnomusicologists ally themselves with health-related therapeutic interventions, has a separate *Handbook* in the Oxford series, which readers are advised to consult. The name is a formation derived from the subfield of medical anthropology, considered a branch of applied anthropology. Given its established identity and a growing literature of its own, the editors have not emphasized it in this volume; nevertheless, Bakan's work in the area of music and autism (Chapter 3) exemplifies applied ethnomusicologists' work in the area of health and well-being.

What should be the approaches in applied ethnomusicology to the pertinent issues rooted in colonial history and attitudes? Contributors such as Sherinian (Chapter 5) and Mackinlay (Chapter 6) remind us that work under postcolonial circumstances still requires immense sensitivity from the researcher. This notion is particularly emphasized in Mackinlay's chapter, based on her work with the indigenous people of Australia, in which the distinctive form of presentation contributes to the strength of her discourse.

Finally, sustainability is a theme that unites most of the chapters in this and the other two volumes that comprise the *Handbook*. Musical, and sometimes also cultural, sustainability is a goal of many arts policy initiatives today. It is often one of the ends of advocacy, and has long been one of the chief reasons for music education. For example, advocacy based on cultural equity and musical rights moves toward sustainability and a kind of musical justice as well as social justice. However, sustainability depends on individuals as well as on institutions; and here the applied ethnomusicologist can act as instigator. Wissler (Chapter 7) and Summit (Chapter 1) exemplify ways in which initiatives by individual applied ethnomusicologists have made a significant difference in helping to sustain musical and cultural traditions.

References

Angrosino, Michael V. (1990). *The Essentials of Anthropology*. Piscataway, NJ: Research and Educational Association.

Anon. (1957). "Society for Ethnomusicology." *Bulletin of the IFMC* 11: 6.

Araújo, Samuel. (2008). "From Neutrality to Praxis: The Shifting Politics of Ethnomusicology in the Contemporary World." *Muzikološki zbornik/Musicological Annual* 44(1): 13–30.

Araújo, Samuel. (2009). "Ethnomusicologists Researching Towns They Live in: Theoretical and Methodological Queries for a Renewed Discipline." *Muzikologija* 9: 33–50.

Araújo, Samuel. (2010). "Sound Praxis: Music, Politics, and Violence in Brazil." In *Music and Conflict*, edited by John Morgan O'Connell and Salwa El-Shawan Castelo-Branco, pp. 217–231. Urbana-Champaign: University of Illinois Press.

Araújo, Samuel, and members of the Grupo Musicultura. (2006). "Conflict and Violence as Theoretical Tools in Present-Day Ethnomusicology: Notes on a Dialogic Ethnography of Sound Practices in Rio de Janeiro." *Ethnomusicology* 50(2): 287–313.

Avorgbedor, Daniel. (1992). "The Impact of Rural-Urban Migration on a Village Music Culture: Some Implications for Applied Ethnomusicology." *African Music* 7(2): 45–57.

Banks, James A., and Cherry A. McGee Banks. (2001). *Multicultural Education: Issues & Perspectives*. New York: John Willey & Sons.

Barz, Gregory F., and Timothy J. Cooley, eds. (1996). *Shadows in the Field: New Perspectives for Fieldwork in Ethnomusicology*. New York: Oxford University Press.
Baumann, Max Peter, ed. (1991). *Music in the Dialogue of Cultures. Traditional Music and Cultural Policy*. Wilhelmshaven: Florian Noetzel Verlag.
Berger, Harris M. (2014). "New Directions for Ethnomusicological Research into the Politics of Music and Culture: Issues, Projects, and Programs." *Ethnomusicology* 58(2): 315–320.
Berliner, Paul. (1978). *The Soul of Mbira*. Chicago: University of Chicago Press.
Blacking, John. (1973). *How Musical Is Man?* Seattle: University of Washington Press.
Bleibinger, Bernhard. (2010). "Solving Conflicts: Applied Ethnomusicology at the Music Department of the University of Fort Hare, South Africa, and in the Context of IMOHP." In *Applied Ethnomusicology: Historical and Contemporary Approaches*, edited by Klisala Harrison, Elizabeth Mackinlay, and Svanibor Pettan, pp. 36–50. Cambridge: Cambridge Scholars.
Bleking, Džon. (1992). *Pojam muzikalnosti*. Beograd: Nolit.
Boas, Franz. (1888). "On Certain Songs and Dances of the Kwakiutl of British Columbia." *Journal of American Folklore* 1(1): 49–64.
Bohlman, Philip V. (1988). "Traditional Music and Cultural Identity: Persistent Paradigm in the History of Ethnomusicology." *Yearbook for Traditional Music* 20: 26–42.
Bohlman, Philip V. (1996). *Central European Folk Music*. New York: Garland.
Bohlman, Philip V. (2004). *The Music of European Nationalism: Cultural Identity and Modern History*. Santa Barbara, CA: ABC-CLIO.
Bohlman, Philip V. (2011). *Focus: Music, Nationalism, and the Making of the New Europe*. New York: Routledge.
Boiko, Martin. (1994). "Latvian Ethnomusicology: Past and Present." *Yearbook for Traditional Music* 26: 47–65.
Bose, Fritz. (1953). *Musikalische Völkerkunde*. Freiburg in Breislau: Atlantis.
Bose, Fritz. (1975). *Etnomuzikologija*. Belgrade: Univerzitet umetnosti u Beogradu.
Brinner, Benjamin. (2009). *Playing across a Divide: Israeli-Palestinian Musical Encounters*. Oxford: Oxford University Press.
Castelo-Branco, Salwa El-Shawan, ed. (2010). *Enciclopédia da Música em Portugal no Século XX*. Lisbon: Círculo de Leitores/Campo das LEtras.
Ceribašić, Naila. (2004). "Double Standards: Negotiating the Place for Ethnomusicologists in Croatia." Conference paper.
Christensen, Dieter. (1988). "The International Folk Music Council and the Americans: On the Effects of Stereotypes on the Institutionalization of Ethnomusicology." *Yearbook for Traditional Music* 20: 11–18.
Clausen, Bernd, Ursula Hemetek, Eva Saether, eds. (2009). *Music in Motion: Diversity and Dialogue in Europe*. New Brunswick, NJ, and London: Transaction Publishers.
Climati, Antonio, and Mario Morra. (1975). *Ultime grida dalla savanna* (film). Rome: Titanus.
Cohen, Ronald D., ed. (2010). *Alan Lomax, Assistant in Charge: The Library of Congress Letters, 1935–1945*. Jackson, MS: University of Mississippi Press.
Diamond, Beverley, and Salwa El Shawan Castelo-Branco, eds. (forthcoming). *Transforming Ethnomusicology*. New York: Oxford University Press.
Dirksen, Rebecca. (2012). "Reconsidering Theory and Practice in Ethnomusicology: Applying, Advocating and Engaging Beyond Academia." *Ethnomusicology Review* 17. http://ethnomusicologyreview.ucla.edu/journal/volume/17/piece/602 (accessed July 1, 2014).
Ellis, Catherine. (1985). *Aboriginal Music: Education for Living. Cross-cultural Experiences from South Australia*. St. Lucia: University of Queensland Press.

Elschek, Oskar. (1991). "Ideas, Principles, Motivations, and Results in Eastern European Folk-Music Research." In *Comparative Musicology and Anthropology of Music*. edited by B. Nettl and P. Bohlman, pp. 91–111. Chicago: University of Chicago Press.
Fenn, John, ed. (2003). *Folklore Forum (Special issue on applied ethnomusicology)* 34(1–2): 119–131.
Fetter, C. V. (2001). *Applied Hydrogeology*. Upper Saddle River, NJ: Prentice-Hall.
Fletcher, Alice C., with the assistance of Frances La Flesche. (1994 [1893]). *A Study of Omaha Indian Music*. Lincoln, NE: Bison Books.
Freire, Paulo. (1970). *Pedagogy of the Oppressed*. New York: Herder and Herder.
Grant, Catherine. (2014). *Music Endangerment: How Language Maintenance Can Help*. Oxford: Oxford University Press.
Giuriati, Giovanni. (1995). "Italian Ethnomusicology." *Yearbook for Traditional Music* 27: 104–131.
Gourlay, Kenneth. (1982). "Towards a Humanizing Ethnomusicology." *Ethnomusicology* 26(3): 411–420.
H. M. (Hahn, Man-young). (1983). "Preface." *Yearbook for Traditional Music* 15: 3.
Harrison, Klisala. (2012). "Epistemologies of Applied Ethnomusicology." *Ethnomusicology* 56(3): 505–529.
Harrison, Klisala. (2013). "Music, Health, and Socio-Economic Status: A Perspective on Urban Poverty in Canada." *Yearbook for Traditional Music* 45: 58–73.
Harrison, Klisala, ed. (2016). *Applied Ethnomusicology in Institutional Policy and Practice* (Thematic volume). *COLLeGIUM* 21.
Harrison, Klisala. (2017). "Why Applied Ethnomusicology?" COLLeGIUM 21:1–17. https://helda.helsinki.fi/bitstream/handle/10138/167843/Collegium%20Vol%2021%20Introduction.pdf?sequence=1.
Harrison, Klisala, Elizabeth Mackinlay, and Svanibor Pettan, eds. (2010). *Applied Ethnomusicology: Historical and Contemporary Approaches*. Newcastle upon Tyne, UK: Cambridge Scholars Publishing.
Hawes, Bess Lomax. (1995). "Reminiscences and Exhortations: Growing Up in American Folk Music." *Ethnomusicology* 39(2): 179–192.
Haydon, Glen. (1941). *Introduction to Musicology*. New York: Prentice-Hall.
Hemetek, Ursula, ed. (1996). *Echo der Vielfalt/Echoes of Diversity. Traditionelle Musik von Minderheiten—ethnischen Gruppen/Traditional Music of Ethnic Groups—Minorities*. Vienna: Böhlau Verlag.
Hemetek, Ursula. (2006). "Applied Ethnomusicology in the Process of the Political Recognition of a Minority: A Case Study of the Austrian Roma." *Yearbook for Traditional Music* 38: 35–57.
Hemetek, Ursula. (2009). "The Past and the Present: Ethnomusicology in Vienna. Some Considerations." *Muzyka* 1(212): 57–68.
Herzog, George. (1936). "Primitive Music." *Bulletin of the American Musicological Society* 1: 2–3.
Hofman, Ana. (2010). "Maintaining the Distance, Othering the Subaltern: Rethinking Ethnomusicologists' Engagement in Advocacy and Social Justice." In *Applied Ethnomusicology: Historical and Contemporary Approaches*, edited by Klisala Harrison, Elizabeth Mackinlay, and Svanibor Pettan, pp. 22–35. Cambridge: Cambridge Scholars.
Hood, Mantle. (1971). *The Ethnomusicologist*. New York: McGraw-Hill.
Impey, Angela. (2002). "Culture, Conservation and Community Reconstruction: Explorations in Advocacy Ethnomusicology and Action Research in Northern KwaZulu." *Yearbook for Traditional Music* 34: 9–24.
Invested in Community: Ethnomusicology and Musical Advocacy. (2003). Conference on Applied Ethnomusicology, Brown University, March 8–9. Videotapes of presentations

by applied ethnomusicologists and community scholars from Europe, the United States, and Native North America may be viewed at http://library.brown.edu/cds/invested_in_community/.

Jordan, Judith V. (2001). "A Relational-Cultural Model: Healing Through Mutual Empathy." *Bulletin of the Menninger Clinic* 65: 92–103.

Juvančič, Katarina. (2010). "Singing from the Dark: Applied Ethnomusicology and the Study of Lullabies." In *Applied Ethnomusicology: Historical and Contemporary Approaches*, edited by Klisala Harrison, Elizabeth Mackinlay, and Svanibor Pettan, pp. 116–132. Cambridge: Cambridge Scholars.

Karpeles, Maud. (1971). "The International Folk Music Council: Twenty-One Years." *Yearbook of the International Folk Music Council* 1: 14–32.

Keil, Charles. (1979). *Tiv Song*. Chicago: University of Chicago Press.

Keil, Charles. (1982). "Applied Ethnomusicology and a Rebirth of Music from the Spirit of Tragedy." *Ethnomusicology* 26(3): 407–411.

Keil, Charles. (1998). "Applied Sociomusicology and Performance Studies." *Ethnomusicology* 42(2): 303–312.

Kerman, Joseph. (1986). *Contemplating Music: Challenges to Musicology*. Cambridge, MA: Harvard University Press.

Kirshenblatt-Gimblett, Barbara. (1988). "Mistaken Dichotomies." *Journal of American Folklore* 101(400): 140–155.

Koch, Grace. (2013). *We Have the Song, So We Have the Land: Song and Ceremony as Proof of Ownership in Aboriginal and Torres Strait Islander Land Claims*. Canberra: Australian Institute of Aboriginal and Torres Strait Islander Studies, Research Discussion Paper No. 33.

Korpe, Maria, and Ole Reitov, eds. (1998). *1st World Conference on Music and Censorship*. Copenhagen: Freemuse.

Koudal, Jens Henrik, et al. (1993). "[Three articles by different authors (Koudal, Torp and Giurchescu, Hauser) on selected ethnomusicological issues in Denmark]." *Yearbook for Traditional Music* 25: 100–147.

Kovačič, Mojca, and Urša Šivic. (2007). "Ethnomusicology and Ethnochoreology in Education: Issues in Applied Scholarship, Ljubljana, September 21–25, 2006." *Bulletin of the International Council for Traditional Music* 110 (April): 67–69.

Kunst, Jaap. (1950). *Musicologica: A Study of the Nature of Ethno-musicology, Its Problems, Methods, and Representative Personalities*. The Hague: Martinus Nijhoff.

LeGuin, Elisabeth. (2012). "Applied Ethnomusicology and Musicology." *Ethnomusicology Review* 17. http://ethnomusicologyreview.ucla.edu/journal/volume/17/piece/599.

Leydi, Roberto. (1991). *L'altra musica*. Giunti: Ricordi.

Leydi, Roberto. (1995). *Druga godba: Etnomuzikologija*. Ljubljana: Studia Humanitatis.

Ling, Jan. (1999). *A History of European Folk Music*. Rochester, NY: University of Rochester Press.

Lomax, Alan. (1972). "Appeal for Cultural Equity." *the world of music* 14(2): 3–17.

Loughran, Maureen. (2008). "But what if they call the police—Applied Ethnomusicology and Urban Activism in the United States." *Muzikološki zbornik/Musicological Annual* 44(1): 51–67.

Lukanyuk, Bohdan. (2006). "Do Istorii termina etnomuzikologija" (On the History of the Term Ethnomusicology). *Visnyk Lviv Univ.* 37: 257–275.

Malm, Krister, et al. (1995). *Aspects on Music and Multiculturalism*. Stockholm: The Royal Swedish Academy of Music.

Marošević, Grozdana. (1998). "The Encounter Between Folklore Studies and Anthropology in Croatian Ethnomusicology." *the world of music* 40(3): 51–82.
Marti, Josep. (1997). "Folk Music Studies and Ethnomusicology in Spain." *Yearbook for Traditional Music* 29: 107–140.
Matthews, Washington. (1888). "The Prayer of a Navajo Shaman." *American Anthropologist*, 1(2): 148–171.
McAllester, David. (1989). Unpublished videotape of seminar at Brown University, transcribed by Lisa Lawson. Accessible from the author, and from the American Folklife Center, Archive of Folk Culture, Library of Congress, Washington, DC.
McLean, Mervyn. (2006). *Pioneers of Ethnomusicology*. Mamaroneck, NY: Aeon Books.
Merriam, Alan. (1963a). Review of Henry Weman, "African Music and the Church in Africa." *Ethnomusicology* 7(2): 135.
Merriam, Alan. (1963b). "Purposes of Ethnomusicology: An Anthropological View." *Ethnomusicology* 7(3): 207.
Merriam, Alan. (1964). *The Anthropology of Music*. Evanston, IL: Northwestern University Press.
Merriam, Alan. (1977). "Definitions of 'Comparative Musicology' and 'Ethnomusicology': An Historical-Theoretical Perspective." *Ethnomusicology* 21(2):189–204.
Merriam, Alan. (2000). *Antropologija glasbe*. Ljubljana: Znanstveno in publicistično središče.
Moisala, Pirkko, ed. (1994). "Ethnomusicology in Finland (eight articles by different authors)." *Ethnomusicology* 38(3): 399–422.
Nettl, Bruno. (1956). *Music in Primitive Culture*. Cambridge, MA: Harvard University Press.
Nettl, Bruno. (1964). *Theory and Method in Ethnomusicology*. Glencoe, IL: The Free Press.
Nettl, Bruno. (1974). "Editor's Preface." *Yearbook of the International Folk Music Council* 6: 7–8.
Nettl, Bruno. (1983). *The Study of Ethnomusicology: Twenty-nine Issues and Concepts*. Urbana: University of Illinois Press.
Nettl, Bruno. (1988). "The IFMC/ICTM and the Development of Ethnomusicology in the United States." *Yearbook for Traditional Music* 20: 19–25.
Nettl, Bruno. (2002). *Encounters in Ethnomusicology: A Memoir*. Warren, MI: Harmonie Park Press.
Nettl, Bruno. (2005). *The Study of Ethnomusicology: Thirty-one Issues and Concepts*. New edition. Urbana: University of Illinois Press.
Nettl, Bruno. (2006). "We're on the Map: Reflections on SEM in 1955 and 2005." *Journal of the Society for Ethnomusicology* 50(2): 179–189.
Nettl, Bruno. (2010). *Nettl's Elephant: On the History of Ethnomusicology*. Urbana: University of Illinois Press.
Nettl, Bruno. (2013). *Becoming an Ethnomusicologist: A Miscellany of Influences*. Lanham, MD: Scarecrow Press.
Nettl, Bruno. (2014). "Fifty Years of Changes and Challenges in the Ethnomusicological Field." Interview by Héctor Fouce. *El oído pensante* 2(1): 1–11. http://ppct.caicyt.gov.ar/index.php/oidopensante (accessed March 16, 2014).
Nettl, Bruno, and Philip V. Bohlman, eds. (1991). *Comparative Musicology and Anthropology of Music*. Chicago: University of Chicago Press.
Newsome, Jennifer. (2008). "From Researched to Centrestage: A Case Study." *Muzikološki zbornik/Musicological Annual* 44(1): 31–49.
Ockelford, Adam. (2013). *Using Zygonic Theory to Inform Music Education, Therapy, and Psychology Research*. New York: Oxford University Press.

O'Connell, John Morgan, and Salwa El-Shawan Castelo-Branco. (2010). *Music and Conflict*. Urbana: University of Illinois Press.

Pettan, Svanibor. (1996). "Making the Refugee Experience Different: *Azra* and the Bosnians in Norway." In *War, Exile, Everyday Life: Cultural Perspectives*, edited by Renata Jambrešić Kirin and Maja Povrzanović, pp. 245–255. Zagreb: Institute of Ethnology and Folklore Research.

Pettan, Svanibor, guest ed. (1998). *the world of music* 40(3) (*Music and Music Research in Croatia*). Berlin: Verlag für Wissenschaft und Bildung.

Pettan, Svanibor. (2008). "Applied Ethnomusicology and Empowerment Strategies: Views from across the Atlantic." *Muzikološki zbornik/Musicological Annual* 44(1): 85–99.

Pettan, Svanibor. (2010). "Music in War, Music for Peace: Experiences in Applied Ethnomusicology." In *Music and Conflict*, edited by John Morgan O'Connell and Salwa El-Shawan Castelo-Branco, pp. 177–192. Urbana-Champaign: University of Illinois Press.

Price, Jammie, and Steve Steele. (2004). *Applied Sociology—Terms, Topics, Tools and Tasks*. Boston: Ceenage Learning.

Rakočević, Selena. (2015). "Ethnochoreology as an Interdiscipline in a Postdisciplinary Era: A Historiography of Dance Scholarship in Serbia." *Yearbook for Traditional Music* 47: 27–44.

Redfield, Robert. (1947). "The Folk Society." *American Journal of Sociology* 52(4): 293–308.

Rice, Timothy. (2014). *Ethnomusicology: A Very Short Introduction*. New York: Oxford University Press.

Rice, Timothy, James Porter, and Chris Goertzen, eds. (2000). *Garland Encyclopaedia of World Music*, Vol. 8: *Europe*. London: Routledge.

Ronström, Owe. (1991). "Folklor: Staged Folk Music and Folk Dance Performances of Yugoslavs in Stockholm." *Yearbook for Traditional Music* 23: 69–77.

Rovsing Olsen, Poul. (1981). "Summing Up the Conference." *Bulletin of the International Council for Traditional Music* 59: 2.

Sachs, Curt. (1933). *Eine Weltgeschichte des Tanzes*. Berlin: Dietrich Reimer/Ernst Vohsen.

Sachs, Curt. (1943). *The Rise of Music in the Ancient World East and West*. New York: Norton.

Sachs, Curt. (1968). *Die Musik der Alten Welt in Ost und West*. Berlin: Akademie-Verlag.

Sachs, Curt. (1997). *Svetovna zgodovina plesa*. Ljubljana: Znanstveno in publicistično središče.

Saks, Kurt. (1980). *Muzika starog sveta*. Belgrade: Univerzitet umetnosti u Beogradu.

Schippers, Huib, and Catherine Grant, eds. (2016). *Sustainable Futures for Music Cultures: An Ecological Perspective*. New York: Oxford University Press.

Schneider, Albrecht. (2006). "Comparative and Systematic Musicology in Relation to Ethnomusicology: A Historical and Methodological Survey." *Ethnomusicology* 50(2): 236–258.

Seeger, Anthony. (1992). "Ethnomusicology and Music Law." *Ethnomusicology*, 36(3): 345–359.

Seeger, Anthony. (2006). "Lost Lineages and Neglected Peers: Ethnomusicologists outside Academia." *Ethnomusicology* 50(2): 215–235.

Seeger, Anthony. (2008). "Theories Forged in the Crucible of Action: The Joys, Dangers, and Potentials of Advocacy and Fieldwork." In *Shadows in the Field: New Perspectives for Fieldwork in Ethnomusicology*, edited by Gregory Barz and Timothy J. Cooley, pp. 271–288. Oxford: Oxford University Press.

SEM Torture. Society for Ethnomusicology Position Statement on Torture. http://www.ethnomusicology.org/?PS_Torture (accessed July 1, 2014).

Sheehy, Daniel. (1992). "A Few Notions about Philosophy and Strategy in Applied Ethnomusicology." *Ethnomusicology* 36(3): 323–336.

SIL. SIL International is a US-based, international Christian missionary organization. Formerly the Summer Institute of Linguistics. http://www.sil.org/arts-ethnomusicology (accessed July 1, 2014).

Skyllstad, Kjell. (1993). *The Resonant Community. Fostering Interracial Understanding Through Music*. Oslo: University of Oslo.
Skyllstad, Kjell. (1997). "Music in Conflict Management—A Multicultural Approach." *International Journal of Music Education* 29: 73–80.
Smithsonian: Fletcher. Foreword to "Camping with the Sioux: The Fieldwork Diary of Alice Cunningham Fletcher." Smithsonian Institution, Department of Anthropology. Online exhibit at http://anthropology.si.edu/naa/exhibits/fletcher/foreword.htm (accessed July 1, 2014).
Spradley, James, and David W. McCurdy, eds. (2000). *Conformity and Conflict: Readings in Cultural Anthropology*. Boston: Allyn and Bacon.
Stockmann, Erich. (1988). "The International Folk Music Council / International Council for Traditional Music—Forty Years." *Yearbook for Traditional Music* 20: 1–10.
Tan, Sooi Beng. (2008). "Activism in Southeast Asian Ethnomusicology: Empowering Youths to Revitalize Traditions and Bridge Cultural Barriers." *Muzikološki zbornik/Musicological Annual* 44(1): 69–83.
Terada, Yoshitaka. (2005). *Drumming out a Message: Eisa and the Okinawan Diaspora in Japan* (documentary film).
Terada, Yoshitaka. (2008). "Angry Drummers and Buraku Identity: The Ikari Taiko Group in Osaka, Japan." In *The Human World and Musical Diversity: Proceedings from the Fourth Meeting of the ICTM Study Group 'Music and Minorities' in Varna, Bulgaria 2006*, edited by Rosemary Statelova, Angela Rodel, Lozanka Peycheva, Ivanka Vlaeva, and Ventsislav Dimov, pp. 309–315, 401. Sofia: Bulgarian Academy of Science, Institute of Art Studies.
Terada, Yoshitaka, (2010). *Angry Drummers: A Taiko Group from Osaka, Japan* (film).
Terada, Yoshitaka, (2011). "Rooted as Banyan Trees: Eisa and the Okinawan Diaspora in Japan." In *Ethnomusicological Encounters with Music and Musicians: Essays in Honor of Robert Garfias*, edited by Timothy Rice, pp. 233–247. Surrey, UK: Ashgate.
Terseglav, Marko. (2004). "Etnomuzikologija." In *Slovenski etnološki leksikon*. Ljubljana: Mladinska knjiga.
Titon, Jeff Todd. (1984). *Worlds of Music: An Introduction to the Music of the World's Peoples*. New York: Schirmer Books.
Titon, Jeff Todd. (1989). "Ethnomusicology as the Study of People Making Music." Paper delivered at the annual conference of the Society for Ethnomusicology, Northeast Chapter, Hartford, CT, April 22.
Titon, Jeff Todd. (1992a). "Music, the Public Interest, and the Practice of Ethnomusicology." *Ethnomusicology* 36(2): 315–322.
Titon, Jeff Todd. (1992b). "Preface." In *Worlds of Music*, general editor Jeff Todd Titon. New York: Schirmer Books.
Titon, Jeff Todd. (2003). "A Conversation with Jeff Todd Titon." Edited and conducted by John Fenn. Special issue on applied ethnomusicology. *Folklore Forum* 34(1–2): 119–131.
Titon, Jeff Todd. (2009a). "Economy, Ecology and Music: An Introduction." *the world of music* 51(1): 5–16.
Titon, Jeff Todd. (2009b). "Music and Sustainability: An Ecological Viewpoint." *the world of music* 51(1): 119–138.
Van Buren, Kathleen J. (2010). "Applied Ethnomusicology and HIV and AIDS: Responsibility, Ability and Action." *Ethnomusicology* 54(2): 202–223.
Van Willigen, John. (2002). *Applied Anthropology* (3rd ed.). New York: Praeger.
Wallaschek, Richard. (1893). *Primitive Musik. An Inquiry Into the Origin and Development of Music, Songs, Instruments, Dances and Pantomimes of Savage Races*. London: Longmans, Green and Co.

Weintraub, Andrew, and Bell Yung, eds. (2009). *Music and Cultural Rights*. Urbana: University of Illinois Press.

Wengle, John. (1988). *Ethnographers in the Field: The Psychology of Research*. Tuscaloosa: University of Alabama Press.

Wong, Deborah. (2014). "Sound, Silence, Music: Power." *Ethnomusicology* 58(2): 347–353.

Yung, Bell. (2009). "UNESCO and China's *Qin* Music in the Twenty-first Century." In *Music and Cultural Rights*, edited by Andrew Weintraub and Bell Yung, pp. 140–168. Urbana: University of Illinois Press.

Zebec, Tvrtko. (2007). "Experiences and Dilemmas of Applied Ethnochoreology." *Narodna umjetnost* 44(1): 7–25.

PART II
ADVOCACY

CHAPTER 1

ADVOCACY AND THE ETHNOMUSICOLOGIST

Assessing Capacity, Developing Initiatives, Setting Limits, and Making Sustainable Contributions

JEFFREY A. SUMMIT

INTRODUCTION

WHILE we are drawn intellectually to our research, what happens when our experiences in the field conjoin with ethical, moral, and religious imperatives to pursue social justice and give back to the people with whom we work? In this article, I address a set of issues and offer a project framework that ethnomusicologists might consider when we are moved to partner with the people whose music we study, who so generously help us and sometimes become our teachers and our friends. Many ethnomusicologists have made the decision that the role of scholar and the role of advocate are not mutually exclusive. However, the success of advocacy projects depends on a thoughtful negotiation between these roles. I believe that the model James Clifford suggests for participant observation can be helpful for those of us who have chosen to assume multiple roles in the communities in which we conduct our research. He describes participant observation as "tacking between the 'inside' and the 'outside' of events on the one hand grasping the sense of specific occurrences and gestures empathetically, on the other stepping back to situate these meanings in wider contexts" (1988: 34). When deciding how, and if, to become involved in an advocacy initiative, I believe it is important for the ethnomusicologist to "tack back" and ask a series of questions: How do we assess our motivation and personal capacity when deciding if, and how, to engage in advocacy? How can we ensure that our advocacy makes a real contribution? With limited time and resources—and often unlimited need—how do we determine the personal, financial, and psychological limits to advocacy? How do we evaluate if, and how, our advocacy projects are sustainable? I explore these questions below in a way that is meant to be both personal and practical.

For the past 13 years, I have been involved in two advocacy projects in Uganda. In the first, I am raising funds, and working with community leadership, to support more than 20 students from the Abayudaya (Jewish) community outside Mbale (see Figure 1.1) studying in local colleges and universities. In the second project, I've been promoting the work of a Jewish, Christian, and Muslim Fair Trade coffee cooperative that is dedicated to building and promoting interfaith cooperation. In both projects, the music I have studied and recorded, and the CDs I have produced for Smithsonian Folkways Recordings, undergird my advocacy work. From my experience, I present a number of scenarios that problematize our advocacy efforts and suggest points for consideration when we come to see ourselves as "partners in a common cause" with members of the communities in which we conduct research (Titon, 2003).[1]

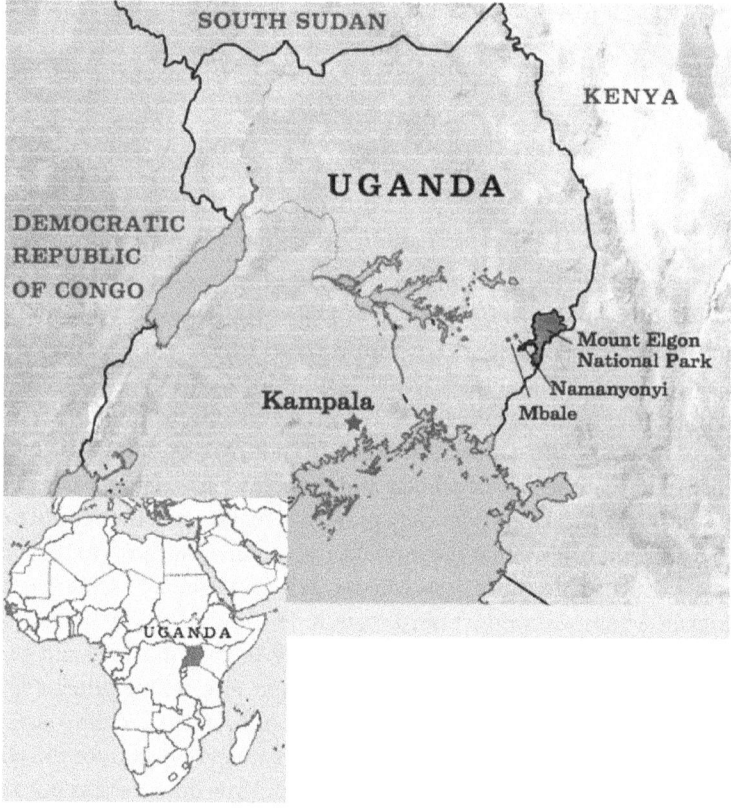

FIGURE 1.1 Map of Uganda by Dan Cole, GIS Coordinator, Smithsonian National Museum of Natural History, in ©2012 *Delicious Peace: Coffee, Music & Interfaith Harmony in Uganda* (SFW CD 50417).

(Map courtesy of Smithsonian Folkways Recordings)

Personal Motivation

I was brought into advocacy work through a convergence of influences: my own spiritual tradition, my experience with service learning, the influence of colleagues who have engaged in advocacy, and the stated values—and support—of my university. In my own religious tradition, I have been influenced by the field of relational ethics and most profoundly by Martin Buber's construction of the I-Thou relationship, an approach that sees our very existence as based on encounter (1970). Rabbinic traditions of social justice, with an emphasis on *tikkun olam* (our responsibility to "repair the world," Hebrew), have influenced me as well.[2] For example, the Talmud weighed the balance of action and learning in life. In the second century C.E., Rabbi Akiva and Rabbi Tarfon argued about the relationship between study and action. The core of their disagreement was framed by this question: What is more important, study or righteous action? If you could only focus on one area, should you concentrate on becoming educated or doing good deeds? Rabbi Tarfon answered, saying that action is greater. But Rabbi Akiva countered his argument and stressed that if you had to choose between the two, it was study that was the greater value (Babylonian Talmud, Tractate *Kiddushin* 40b). For a society that cared deeply about ethical action and social justice, this seems like a strange decision. Should not doing righteous action be paramount? But the rabbinic tradition supported Rabbi Akiba's decision and interpreted it in this way: If you only focused on doing good deeds, that might never lead you to become an educated person. But if you immersed yourself deeply in learning, your studies *had* to lead you to act ethically, to raise a moral voice, to be committed to repairing what was broken in the world. It was inconceivable to the rabbis in the Talmud that education would not lead to right action. That view has shaped my own understanding of the purpose of education: education that connects teaching and research to advocacy; education that thoughtfully examines what constitutes effective activism; education that is committed to a university having an impact for good in our world.

Even as we respect the religious and spiritual beliefs of the people whose music we study, I am very aware that the phrase "religious values" is itself a can of worms. I have found that my academic colleagues rarely reference or discuss their own spiritual beliefs. "Religion" gets painted with a wide brush in the university and is more often associated with narrow sectarian views than with a deep respect for the other. While my religious tradition has influenced my approach to advocacy, I situate myself in dynamic opposition to a legacy of colonialism and a history where religion has often been used as a means of political manipulation, economic oppression, violent homophobia, and cultural devastation for subaltern people in East Africa and beyond.

Of course, one does not have to be motivated by a specific religious tradition to engage in advocacy. In his examination of the role of the "engaged university" and ethnomusicology in the United States, Eric Martin Usner writes, "I am in higher education to make a difference" (2010: 76). He speaks about how the music itself is a witness of something profound—"call it beauty, community or a sense of shared humanity; call it God." Usner discusses how an engagement with the music nurtures understanding and compassion for being human, and from that vantage point, asks how to turn that understanding "into real world acts." So, too, when Daniel Sheehy discusses the philosophy and strategic approaches to problems inherent in applied ethnomusicology, he begins his analysis from the assumption of interpersonal responsibility and connection. He asks, what ethnomusicologist has "never gone out of his or her way to act for the benefit of an informant or a community they have studied?" Sheehy states that applied ethnomusicology begins with a sense of larger purpose, "first to see opportunities for a better life for others through the use of music knowledge and then immediately to begin devising cultural strategies to achieve those ends" (1992: 323, 324). The fact that he does not place this commitment to social justice in a specific religious tradition does not make it any less grounded or powerful.

The fact that I see a confluence between my own spiritual imperatives and current directions in applied ethnomusicology deepens my commitment to engage in advocacy. When Jeff Todd Titon introduces and frames the special issue of *Ethnomusicology* that he edited on "Music and the Public Interest," he describes this approach as work that "involves and empowers music-makers and music-cultures in collaborative projects" and results in "practical action in the world" (1992: 315). Titon emphasizes that the nature of this practical action is relational, shaping our approach to ethnographic fieldwork as well. When he writes that "fieldwork at its best is based on a model of friendship between people rather than on a model involving antagonism, surveillance, the observation of physical objects, or the contemplation of abstract ideas" (1992: 321), Titon is describing the essence of fieldwork, in the language of Martin Buber, as an I-Thou, rather than an I-It relationship.

So, too, when Kay Shelemay stresses the importance of ethnography "predicated on negotiated relationships" (2008: 153), she is teaching that with relationship comes responsibility. Shelemay's perspectives developed from her experience doing fieldwork with Jews of Syrian descent who live in Brooklyn, New York. She examines the role of the ethnomusicologist "who, while seeking to document the transmission process, becomes a part of it" (2008: 141), moving the researcher into a reciprocal stance in relation to the people whose music one studies. Such directions in applied ethnomusicology have expanded how researchers understand and define reciprocity. In 2007, the International Council for Traditional Music established a study group devoted to applied ethnomusicology and sponsored a series of conferences. In the volume on applied ethnomusicology that developed from their work, Ana Hofman considers ethnomusicologists' engagement in advocacy and social justice, reassessing the role of reciprocity in ethnographic fieldwork. She examines this new ethnomusicological epistemology, with its understanding that the researcher "constructs reality together with social subjects" who become active partners and interlocutors, and calls for a re-evaluation of our responsibilities to the people whose music we study. She writes, "This approach includes the presumption of respect, equality and reciprocity among the research participants" (2010: 23). As I consider the interplay between these three areas, I have come to believe that reciprocity is a way to evidence my respect for the people whose music I study. It is also a way to address equality in a world where my privilege impacts my relationship with the women and men who have become my friends, teachers, and partners over the years that I have worked in Uganda.

Lessons from Service Learning

As a chaplain at our university, I have been involved in social justice and service learning during my years at Tufts. My approach in developing advocacy projects in Uganda was also shaped by my interactions with Tufts students, and with the local organizations where they were volunteering while doing service learning in the Boston community. In their book *The Unheard Voices: Community Organizations and Service Learning*, Randy Stoecker and Elizabeth Tryon examine the service learning relationship from the perspective of the local agencies and projects that accept and work with student volunteers. Successful service experiences depend on repositioning the relationship, from "top-down"—where university students decide on service projects they will bring to local communities to "bottom-up"—where the communities play a key role in directing and shaping the students' experience. Listening to the "unheard voices" of the agencies and the people being served was essential in building successful partnerships. Rather than viewing service learning as a linear cause-and-effect process, Stoecker and Tryon suggest that it be viewed as a dialectic organizational process in which feedback from the local community shapes the strategies and actions of those engaged in service (2009: 7; also see Usner, 2010: 81–86).

Over the years, a number of key issues continually emerged in our discussions with students who were working with community organizations both locally and internationally. It was essential that students did not conceive projects in a social and organizational vacuum but rather in thoughtful collaboration with local agencies and communities. Even while doing direct service, it was important to consider larger dynamics impacting systemic social and economic change. We also found it essential to include broader education on the root causes of the issues we addressed through service initiatives, as well as integrating a commitment to sustainability for the programs we developed with a community. I have found this multi-tiered approach essential in developing service projects, as I discuss later in this chapter when I describe the CASES methodology.

I have also been influenced and inspired by colleagues' applied work as they engage in advocacy. Current epistemological approaches in ethnomusicology have, as examined in the work of Ana Hofman and many others, "destabilized the dichotomy between the "theoretical" and the "activist" (2010: 23). Many ethnomusicologists have decided that the role of scholar and the role of advocate are not mutually exclusive and made profound contributions to the communities they have studied. To name only a few, I would reference Anthony Seeger's collaboration with the Suyá in Brazil to preserve and promote their culture (1987), Steven Feld's work with the Kaluli in Papua New Guinea to prevent deforestation in the rain forests (1982, 1991), and Kay Kaufman Shelemay's dedication to the transmission of *pizmomim* (paraliturgical hymns) and community advocacy with Jews of Syrian descent in New York (2008). Jeff Todd Titon's broad contributions to our understanding of the ways that ethnomusicologists can contribute to cultural sustainability, social activism, community education, and cultural policy have helped me understand that a commitment to research and a commitment to advocacy can be mutually enhancing, rather than mutually exclusive (2003). Gregory Barz and Judah M. Cohen's focus on the role of music and the arts in providing education, hope, and healing for victims of HIV/AIDS in Africa presents a range of examples of ethnomusicologists engaged in effective advocacy (2011). These scholars, and many others, have provided carefully conceived, community-grounded models that have inspired my own advocacy work in Uganda.

I am also fortunate to work at a university whose mission stresses the importance of active citizenship. As explained on the website of the Jonathan M. Tisch College of Citizenship and Public Service of Tufts University, "An active citizen is a person who understands the obligation and undertakes the responsibility to improve community conditions, build healthier communities, and address social problems. He or she understands and believes in the democratic ideals of participation and the need to incorporate the voice, perspective, and contributions of every member of the community."[3] True to their mission, Tufts University has been supportive of my work in Uganda over the years, writing about my projects in university publications, mounting a major exhibition of my work with music, photography, and material culture in the university's art gallery, and hosting coffee farmers from Peace Kawomera coffee cooperative to teach about their success developing this economic venture to address interfaith conflict and promote community development.

I write about personal motivation at some length because I've found that a process of self-reflection, ideally one that cultivates humility and problematizes the efficacy of social justice work, is a good first step for anyone engaging in advocacy or direct service. I have used Monsignor Ivan Illich's address "To Hell with Good Intentions" to good effect with our undergraduate students. In this challenging talk, Illich, a cultural critic, philosopher, and religious leader, speaks to North American volunteers about to embark on a service trip to Mexico in 1968 and pleads with these privileged volunteers from North America to recognize their "inability,... powerlessness and incapacity" to do the "good" which they intend to do during short-term service.[4] Ideally, a process of self-reflection helps disavow activists of grandiose ideas, inspires humility, and focuses on the ways the advocate will be changed more than the ways he or she will change others. A clear understanding of the personal importance and self-motivation for advocacy is especially important in the academy, where faculty's involvement in this work is often not recognized or rewarded by additional compensation, valued substantially toward tenure, or granted academic prestige. For all its rewards, advocacy is messy work. We swim against strong currents of economic and social injustice. Self-reflection is essential initial preparation before we commit and jump in.

Assessing Capacity and Conceptualizing a Project

After understanding our personal motivation, the next step toward effective advocacy is assessing our capacity to contribute to a community. It often feels like we barely have enough time for our research, writing, and teaching, and it is a personal choice whether or not an ethnomusicologist invests time and energy in developing, implementing, and sustaining an advocacy project. In East Africa, many factors make any advocacy work feel daunting—unlimited need, a colonial legacy of imposed social and economic structures to "better" society, complicated histories of inter-family and inter-community jealousy and rivalry. I have often found myself repeating the dictum "no good deed goes unpunished" as I approach a difficult challenge or roadblock in one of the projects in which I am engaged.

Once a researcher decides that he or she wants to develop an advocacy project, the first step is to conduct a personal assessment: In addition to our research skills and academic training, what talents, experience and personal commitments do we bring to the communities with whom we work? What resources at our universities can be helpful as we assess the opportunities and risks inherent in advocacy projects? Often an answer is clear, and a skill can have an immediate impact. In Uganda, I worked with a recording engineer who was also an electrician. During down times in our recording, John rewired the community's primary school building. Other projects are easy and short term: Teenagers in the Abayudaya community had formed a music group and wanted to record a number of hip-hop songs they had written to forefront the community's new generation of musicians. They lacked the funding to record in a local studio. I spent an afternoon recording them on my equipment and burned copies of a demo CD so that they could promote their music both locally and send it to international visitors who had expressed interest in their efforts. Quick, one-shot projects can make a contribution, but projects with long-term impact demand greater planning.

I started working with the Abayudaya (Jewish people) in Uganda in 2000. This community of approximately 1,000 people living in villages surrounding Mbale in Eastern Uganda are practicing Jews (Figure 1.2). Many members scrupulously follow Jewish ritual, observe the laws of the Sabbath, celebrate Jewish holidays, keep kosher, and pray in Hebrew. There are other communities of indigenous Africans who claim Jewish lineage, such as the Beta Yisrael of Ethiopia or the Lemba of South Africa and Zimbabwe. The Abayudaya do not; they self-converted to Judaism in 1919. Moved by their belief in the truth of the Torah, the Five Books of Moses, the Abayudaya developed their Jewish practice and liturgy in the process of separating themselves from Christian missionary activity and British political rule. Their founder, Semei Kakungulu, a powerful Ganda leader, considered Christianity and Islam and then, according to community elders, asserted, "Why should I follow the shoots when I can have the root?" Since the community's initial self-conversion and through the difficult period of Idi Amin's rule,

FIGURE 1.2 Worship in the Moses synagogue on Nabogoya Hill, Uganda.

(Photo by Richard Sobol)

the Abayudaya have been distinguished by their commitment to following mainstream Jewish practice, an approach that has been amplified since their increased contact with Jews from North America and Israel beginning in the mid-1990s. Approximately half of the community went through a *halakhic* (Jewish legal, Hebrew) conversion in 2002 by a visiting *beit din* (rabbinic court, Hebrew) from Judaism's Conservative Movement.

In the course of my time with the community, it became clear that the Abayudaya's needs in health, welfare, and education were substantial. Since their self-conversion to Judaism in the 1920s, the community did not attend local missionary schools, where conversion to Christianity was required for admission. Desiring to maintain their Judaism, the majority of the community had forgone secular education and had remained subsistence farmers. One nongovernmental organization (NGO) in particular, Kulanu (All of Us, Hebrew), was a model of thoughtful advocacy and was working with the community to support primary and secondary school education, to secure sources for clean water, and to explore sustainable economic models to develop indigenous crafts to sell to the Jewish community in North America. But how could I contribute in a meaningful way and give back appropriately to the community for their generosity and hospitality?

As an ethnomusicologist, I first worked to fulfill what we consider basic reciprocal requirements: I worked with local leaders and musicians to determine an appropriate level of compensation for the musicians I recorded. I made copies of my recordings and interviews for the community. I negotiated an agreement with the Abayudaya leadership counsel that directed royalties from my recordings, video, and writing back to the community. But still, it felt like there was more to do. After speaking at length with a broad range of people in the community, and with faculty colleagues at Tufts who work in the area of international development, I chose one tightly focused project that seemed doable. Two members of the community had been accepted to local colleges but did not have the funds to pay tuition. At that point, I assessed my capacity as an advocate. I do a lot of fundraising in my role as executive director of Tufts Hillel and have developed relationships with wealthy donors who are committed to social justice and engaged in many projects in the Jewish community. It costs approximately $3,000 a year for a student to attend university—a bargain when compared to Tufts but far beyond the reach of a farmer in Eastern Uganda. But raising $6,000 a year for four years felt possible. I dedicated all the profits from my Smithsonian Folkways Recordings CD to a fund for university education, and I committed to raising the balance of tuition funds to support university education for these two students studying in Uganda.

Over the years, I have found that the path of social justice and community service with the Abayudaya was littered with the skeletons of unsuccessful advocacy initiatives. Students and other visitors from North America feel empowered by a culture of activism fostered by their high schools, universities, and religious communities. They jump in quickly to initiate social justice projects. Jews from North America visit the community for several days and are transfixed and inspired by their experiences with this Jewish community in Africa. In most cases, the passion and commitment of these individuals were not tempered by a fuller understanding of community needs and the experience necessary to implement a successful project. I learned this quickly on my second research trip to the community: Boxes of school textbooks from the United States languished in a corner of the Semei Kakungulu primary school building. A teacher from New England had run a textbook drive in his community and shipped these books to the Abayudaya. Unfortunately, he did not discuss what books were used in the curriculum with the school's teachers and headmaster and they could not be integrated into the teachers' lesson plans. But even more, the school had no money to build bookshelves for the books, and the roof of the school leaked during the rainy season. Wet books mildewed in their cardboard shipping boxes. In another project, a large weaving loom was locked in a mud brick building. Hopeful supporters had sent the loom, thinking that the community could develop an industry weaving and selling *taleisim*, Jewish prayer shawls. But this type of weaving was not an indigenous craft, and there were neither people to train community members nor much enthusiasm for a complicated craft project that felt foreign to the community. In another project, two well-meaning university students were able to have 12 laptop computers donated to the community. They carried the laptops to Uganda, and for six weeks, they conducted workshops with high school students to train them in basic computer skills. The program was well received by the high school students that summer, but the organizers did not work with the school's administrators or with community leadership to ensure that the computer education project was sustainable. After the organizers left, the computers were sold off, one by one, to pay for more pressing community needs. I have come to understand that the success of any advocacy project depends on carefully conceived initiatives, determined with local communities, with thoughtful attention to the dynamics of on-the-ground implementation and sustainability.

The CASES Methodology

I was part of a team working to develop a set of standards for social justice and community service work for International Hillel. We later refined this approach working in partnership with the NGO "Repair the World."[5] The CASES methodology grew out of our shared experience and involves five components that I believe are essential to consider when developing advocacy initiatives: *c*ommunity partnerships, *a*dvocacy/*a*ctivism, direct *s*ervice, *e*ducation, and *s*ustainability. I discuss each component in greater detail in the following sections.

Community Partnerships

Advocacy projects must be planned in thoughtful partnership with community organizations, leadership, and the people who will hopefully benefit from the project. Simply put, you cannot plan advocacy by yourself. Community activists and leaders represent important entry points for advocacy projects. It is also helpful to assess the agendas that local leaders bring to the table. The dynamics of community leadership often disenfranchise segments of a community, and broader discussions with community members are essential as one plans an initiative. Our professional training as ethnomusicologists positions us well when building community partnerships. Eric Martin Usner examines community service learning (CSL) and the "third revolution" in higher education in the United States—a renewed emphasis on active citizenship and civic participation—and stresses the value and applicability of our fieldwork training for the ethnographer about to engage in effective service. Participant observation, an understanding of the ethics and logistics of negotiating entry into a community, interview techniques, methods for reflecting on work in the field such as field notes, the ability to deal with culture shock and ethnocentrism, experience and theory for problematizing differences and diversity—all are essential skills necessary for developing community partnerships that position an advocacy project for success (2010: 89).

Our skills as researchers also help us examine the history and success of past and current projects, whether initiated by the community themselves or outside activists. It is essential to determine how these initiatives are funded, who is implementing them, and if community members see them as successful. Community members or leaders who administer projects in conjunction with outside agencies often have privileged access to resources, and it is important to understand how funding changes the dynamics of power and privilege in a community. Even a modest project can infuse a local community with more cash than a family makes in a year. It is important to conduct preliminary research to understand a community's basic economics, the cost of local services, and market dynamics in order to understand the potential impact when new resources are brought into a village or town. As such, maintaining transparent communication is important so that community members understand how and where funds are allocated and who controls the flow of resources.

When I was working on these projects in Uganda, I was watched carefully during every interaction that involved money. When I was recording various music groups of coffee farmers of the Peace Kawomera Fair Trade Coffee Cooperative, I first had long discussions with the elected leadership of the cooperative, and with local musicians, to determine fair compensation for the groups that I recorded. But the leadership felt that it was just as important to determine how the cash was presented to the groups. It was essential that the performers knew that the money was distributed equitably. After each performance, in a small ceremony, I thanked the performers and publicly announced the amount I was presenting to the group, handing the money to the group's leaders in the presence of all assembled. In my experience, nothing foments community discord and division as quickly as the perception of misappropriation of funds or unfair distribution of resources. Providing compensation to these musicians is only one example; I work to maintain this level of transparency in the larger advocacy projects in which I am engaged as well.

In a successful partnership, the advocate works in collaboration with the community to establish a shared vision and to set common goals to address community needs. Good community partnerships also have to be built on an advocate's realistic appraisal of how much time and energy one can commit to a project. By our nature, advocates are positive and enthusiastic about the success we hope to achieve. It is better to under-promise and over-deliver.

My first and foremost partnership in the Abayudaya university scholarship program is with the community itself. I work on the principle that while I am contributing to the Abayudaya's educational vision, community leaders must direct and run this project. All the money I raise is sent to the elected Abayudaya leadership council, which includes women and youth representation. I do my best to make sure that my e-mail communication is transparent, copying in a broad representation of respected community leaders when I wire tuition funds or address issues. The local council administers and distributes the funds. While I am often approached by individual students for funding, I try to avoid dealing with individuals at all costs. So, too, when donors approach me and say they want to "adopt" a student, I do my best to discourage individual donor-student connections and encourage people to fund the larger project. Funding individual students invariably leads to personal requests for money, "end-runs" around community leadership, and then to jealousy and community discord. I feel conflicted because the "adoption" approach might generate more funds, but my experience has led me to believe that this will hurt the project in the long run.

Other Partnerships

At the same time that I was working to partner with the leadership of the community, I had a number of decisions to make in regard to my relationship with NGOs that were already working on a range of projects with the Abayudaya. I had tremendous respect for Kulanu, the primary organization that was engaged with the community when I began my research in 2000. I spoke to and met with a number of their leaders, both to learn about their current projects and to have a deeper sense of the history, challenges, and success of past advocacy projects with the community. I wanted to make sure not to duplicate their efforts or work at cross-purposes. In addition, NGOs often compete for donors, and I wanted to make sure that my projects would not be competitive with their important initiatives in nutrition for schoolchildren and primary and secondary education. But I struggled with a larger issue: Should I conceive of my university education initiative as a separate project, or should I try to have Kulanu integrate it into their existing projects? Should I simply raise funds to send to them, rather than working directly with the community? On the positive side, having an existing NGO run and administer the project might make it easier for me: I would not have to deal directly with the community, be concerned with the details of fund transfers, or negotiate the logistics and priorities of the project with the Abayudaya leadership. Besides, I trusted this NGO, they had integrity and evidenced a strong on-the-ground understanding of the needs of the community. On the other hand, I wanted to be more in control of the substantial funds that I was raising and felt that I could engage donors in a deeper way if they were working directly in a project. I also valued my direct connection with the community's leadership and with the students benefiting from the program. This advocacy work brought me into community discussions that strengthened my connections with members and taught me a lot about the community's goals and priorities. In addition, I had experience conceptualizing and implementing community programs. I decided to run the project myself but maintain active connections with Kulanu, apprising them of the funds I was raising and the direction of the project. This partnership has been respectful and productive, and I often call on their leadership to discuss complicated problems and seek their advice and counsel.

When writing about ethnomusicology's responses and responsibilities to endangered music cultures, Klisala Harrison and Svanibor Pettan report that the International Council for Traditional Music's study group on applied ethnomusicology stressed that it was important to approach applied work with "a willingness to place oneself in positions of vulnerability, discomfort and sometimes even subservience, embracing unfamiliar and sometimes counterintuitive approaches to appreciate process and outcomes" (2010: 7). This has applicability to advocacy projects as well. I encountered this when the community leadership decided not to fund the education of a student who was engaged to a Christian woman. An explicit goal of the college scholarship program was to strengthen the Abayudaya, and the leadership saw intermarriage as a threat to community continuity. Leaders expressed that if the partner of the student was willing to convert, funding would continue, but if not, they did not want to support a student who they feared would leave the community. While I understood and respected the leadership's role in making this decision, a number of funders of the project thought that this approach was exclusionary and, just as their liberal synagogues in the United States welcomed non-Jewish partners without insisting that they convert, so, too, the Abayudaya should exercise a similar policy. This issue became contentious when the student began to email donors directly, hoping to apply pressure on the community leadership. It was uncomfortable to become involved in the negotiations between the donors and leadership. My role became that of an educator, speaking with the donors about the challenges that the community faced to maintain their Judaism and why imposing their values on the community could undermine the success of the project in the long run. I also spoke to the community leadership to explain the donors' perspectives, stressing that such policy decisions had to be made locally. In the end, the community leadership negotiated a solution with the student that enabled him to continue receiving funding while his fiancée studied for conversion.

Advocacy and Activism

I often use a story from the book of Genesis to illustrate the difference between thoughtful advocacy and activism that focuses on a direct fix to social and economic problems. I say, "Imagine that you were an activist during the time that the Jews were slaves under Pharaoh. It was decreed that all the first-born baby boys would be killed. So imagine you are standing by the banks of the Nile and a drowning baby floats by! What do you do? Of course, you jump in and pull out the baby! You revive the child, give the child something to eat and drink! You've done something immediate and important. Now, *that's* effective activism. But then another baby floats by and another and another and at some point, you have to walk up stream and see who's throwing babies into the river, and why, and what it would take to stop them. That's advocacy."

Focused activism addresses immediate pressing needs. I was fortunate that other NGOs, and a few synagogue groups from the United States, were concentrating on health and welfare with the Abayudaya community. Malaria impacted many community members, and during the time of my early research in Uganda, several elders succumbed to the disease. Kulanu was working on a program to obtain and deploy mosquito nets throughout the community and to organize educational programming about malaria prevention and treatment. They were also raising funds to provide nutritious food for children in their primary school. The fact that other organizations and individuals were working on immediate issues of health and welfare freed me to consider a project that could contribute to community development from within.

Ideally, the advocate is committed to work toward systemic change. Before I began the university education project, I engaged in a broad series of discussions to learn of the community's vision for their future. I spoke with students in the high school, women's groups, community leaders, and members living in more isolated villages who often felt ignored and cut off from aid projects that helped those in the community's center.

Many of the first songs I recorded were written by high school students and stressed the importance of education. Students sang of their commitment to education and the importance of completing their studies. The community also modified local Bagisu circumcision songs and added lyrics such as "You need to go to school before you obtain leadership positions" ("Maimuna," track 18, Summit, 2003). High school students wore T-shirts with the motto "Education is the key to our success." This focus led me, in consultation with the community's leadership, to concentrate on university education and providing opportunities for the community youth who hoped to study law, medicine, engineering, tourist services, education, accounting, and other professions. Since the beginning of the project, the university graduates have contributed substantially to the community. Several received their degrees in education and have become teachers and administrators in the Abayudaya's primary and secondary schools. A student trained in medicine staffed a local clinic. An engineer built houses, as well as a hotel that is used by visitors to the community. Another community member who received a degree in hotel management runs this community guesthouse. A student who received his degree in tourist services organizes tours of the community and local area. While this university education project often feels like a long-term investment, there are positive ways that it is impacting the economic strength, health, and daily welfare of the community.

I have also been influenced by the work of John Paul Lederach in the area of peace building and conflict transformation. Lederach recounts his understanding of the power of music for transformation with a reference to the familiar story that he describes as "the fairy tale of the Pied Piper." After the town's elders go back on their promise to pay the Piper for ridding the town of rats, the Piper plays his flute, and all the children follow him away from town. Lederach says that when he first heard the story as a boy, its moral seemed clear: "when you give a promise, you had best keep your word." But he recounts that when he revisited the story four generations later, he saw a different lesson: the power of the musician, the flutist, "to move a town, address an evil and move the powerful to accountability" (2005: 152). I have experienced this power in the course of my advocacy work with the Abayudaya. Muyamba Eria, the chairman of the Abayudaya's Board of Directors, recently wrote to me from Mbale, reporting that over the years, this project has enabled more than 40 community members to earn bachelor's degrees in different academic disciplines. While I play a role as an advocate, the project's success is grounded in the community's music. Both the community and I were thrilled when the CD received a Grammy nomination for best traditional world music album. With Smithsonian Folkways Recordings support, we managed to have three members of the community attend the awards celebration in Los Angeles. This popular recognition generated both revenue and publicity that directly helped the university tuition project. Ultimately, the community's music redressed a colonialist legacy that prevented these Jews from receiving an education, as they refused to attend missionary schools that require conversion for admission.

As ethnomusicologists, we can also use our position and skills to leverage the impact of a community's music. Svanibor Pettan describes "advocate ethnomusicology" as "any use of ethnomusicological knowledge by the ethnomusicologist to increase the power of self-determination for a particular cultural group" (2010: 16; also see Spradley and McCurty, 2000: 422; Pettan, 2008: 90). This was the nature of my work with the Peace Kawomera (Delicious Peace) Fair Trade Coffee cooperative outside Mbale (Figure 1.3). I saw the genesis of this interfaith coffee cooperative up close. J. J. Keki was one of the community leaders and prominent musicians whom I recorded and interviewed for my work on the Abayudaya CD. His vision for the cooperative grew out of seeing what can happen when religious conflict leads to violence. On his first trip to the United States for a lecture tour in 2001, he stayed at our home in Boston early in September before traveling to New York City. He was on his way to meet a friend who was going to show him the city from atop the World Trade Center and was actually walking up to the entrance when American Airlines Flight 11 hit the North Tower. When J. J. learned that the terrorists had been motivated by religious beliefs, he said, "I think we should begin something. We have coffee. Maybe we make a co-op of Jews, Muslims, and Christians, and then we can teach the world how to work together." When he returned to Uganda, he walked from village to village, asking his Jewish, Christian, and Muslim neighbors if they would be willing to form a Fair Trade coffee cooperative, saying, "Use whatever you have to create peace. If you have a body, use your body to bring peace, not to cause chaos. If you have music, use your music to create peace. We are using coffee to bring peace to the world." With the involvement of Laura Wetzler of Kulanu, they established a relationship with the Thanksgiving Coffee Company to buy and market their coffee. Coffee farmers compose songs to stress the positive benefits of interfaith cooperation,

FIGURE 1.3 Photograph of the Peace Kawomera Growers Coop sign.

(Photo by Richard Sobol)

the transformative impact of Fair Trade prices and to encourage their neighbors to join the coffee cooperative.

For example, in the song, "Educate our Children," the Balitwegomba Choir sings in Lugisu about the economic benefits of Fair Trade and the impact this business model has on community education (track 15, Summit, 2012).[6] In rural Uganda, the government pays special attention to the role of women in national development, and there are many women's clubs and organizations. It is common for these clubs to have choirs as one of their activities. This women's choir composed this song in the style of the Bagisu. This instrumental accompaniment is called *luwempele*, which refers to two sticks played on a wooden block. Selected lyrics are below.

> We are facing many problems.
> We look to Fair Trade to educate our children.
> We have cultivated coffee in order to educate our children.
> We look to Fair Trade and ask for a better price when we cultivate coffee,
> All members of Peace Kawomera, let us rejoice!
> God Almighty, thank you!
> Our children are going to school now!
> Thank you, Fair Trade!
> All these ladies are grateful!

In this next song, the Akuseka Takuwa Kongo Group sings in Lugwere, "Let All Religions Come Together" (track 10, Summit, 2012). Their lead singer, Saban Nabutta, is a master at improvising lyrics for special occasions, such as weddings, graduations, political gatherings, and celebrations to introduce a bride and groom to each other's families. He sings in the traditional lyric-heavy style of the Bagwere, built around the lead singer's vocal improvisation for the occasion at hand. The *akadongo* (lamellaphone), also called *kongo*, is played throughout Uganda. In this ensemble, we also hear the *endingigdi* (one-string tube fiddle) and *nsasi* (shaker). Selected lyrics are below.

> All religions, let us come together.

So that we can succeed in this world.

> I am telling all religious leaders that God is the one who created us all.
> Our grandparents are Adam and Eve.
> We have the same ancestors. Let us not segregate each other: it destroys the world.

> Let us come together so we can overcome these troubles and promote development.

Many factors drew me to my research and recording with this coffee cooperative. I knew many of the Jewish coffee farmers from my work with the Abayudaya, and I was interested in the musical traditions of their Christian and Muslim neighbors. On a deeper level, I was personally inspired by one man's response to the tragedy of

9/11. At a time when the world was becoming more insular and xenophobic, J. J. Keki and the farmers of the cooperative were sharing a broad vision of peace and interfaith cooperation.

In his book *The Moral Imagination*, Lederach addresses the question "How do we transcend the cycles of violence that bewitch our human community while still living in them?" and states, "Transcending violence is forged by the capacity to generate, mobilize, and build the moral imagination" (2005: 5). He goes on to explain that "the moral imagination requires the capacity to imagine ourselves in a web of relationships that includes our enemies; the ability to sustain a paradoxical curiosity that embraces complexity without reliance on dualistic polarity; the fundamental belief in and pursuit of the creative act; and the acceptance of the inherent risk of stepping into the mystery of the unknown that lies beyond the far too familiar landscape of violence." I was drawn to J. J. Keki's audacity—and to the courage and commitment of the farmers—as they worked and sang together across religious, ethnic, and language boundaries to model a vision of interfaith cooperation. As I watched J. J. Keki encourage his Jewish, Christian, and Muslim neighbors to join the coffee cooperative, his work fired my own moral imagination. I asked, how was I positioned to contribute to the success of this work? In the volume of *Ethnomusicology* that addresses music in the public interest, Daniel Sheehy writes about how we can empower community members to become musical activists (1992). But for me, this worked in the other direction. When I saw that the coffee farmers were engaged in musical activism, to draw more members to the cooperative and increase the profits realized through Fair Trade, to teach a vision of interfaith harmony, then I realized that I, too, could use my skills to be a musical activist for their community. Their music moved me to become a partner in a common cause.

I felt inspired by this project, but I also believe that an advocate must be dispassionate in accessing the integrity of community projects. I hoped the peace that the Peace Kawomera coffee cooperative was creating was real. I know how challenging interfaith cooperation can be. In my work as a chaplain at Tufts, I have been involved in Jewish, Christian, and Muslim interfaith work over the years. I was eager to explore the impact that Keki's cooperative had on neighboring communities. Was their cooperation creating peace, or was it just a clever way to market Fair Trade coffee? Through scores of interviews and participation with the members of the cooperative, it became clear that this venture was changing attitudes and impacting the level of day-to-day social and economic cooperation among these religious communities. Many of the coffee farmers have taken the mission, and message, of the interfaith cooperative to heart. It is common to hear these farmers speak about the importance of separate religions coming together and becoming "one person." They model this in the leadership structure of their cooperative, in their social interaction, and in the music that farmers are writing to convey the importance of peace, cooperation, and economic justice. To date, more than 1,000 farmers have joined the Peace Kawomera coffee cooperative. When these Jewish, Christian, and Muslim farmers stress the importance of interfaith harmony, write songs, and sing together, their music embodies the performance of peace.

While Peace Kawomera has established a viable model of economic and interfaith cooperation, the success of the venture rests on the cooperative's ability to sell coffee. I realized that a CD of their music and a video that told their story to a larger audience in the United States and Europe could both impact sales and present a viable model for interethnic and inter-religious economic cooperation. My first conversations were with the leadership of the cooperative: Did they want their story presented more broadly? Would this help the success of the cooperative? The chairman, secretary manager, and treasurer all stressed that they were telling the story of the cooperative every way they could: in local newspapers, to reporters, and to visitors committed to Fair Trade who visited Mbale. J. J. Keki was also scheduling a lecture tour to the United States and Europe. They were enthusiastic about a CD that would present the songs that the farmers were composing. Smithsonian Folkways Recordings also had a historical commitment to the role of music in social and economic justice dating back to Woody Guthrie and Pete Seeger and were positive about the value of the project. The Thanksgiving Coffee Company in California, which markets their coffee, also saw value in the music's ability to tell the larger story of the cooperative and connect their consumers to the lives and economic challenges faced by these coffee farmers. I spoke at length with Ben Corey-Moran, President of Thanksgiving Coffee Company, who stressed the power of Fair Trade to bring a healing and empowering connection to the people who produce items that we value in our lives. Of course, he wanted to sell coffee: this was the vehicle he was using to improve the economic situation of these farmers. But he believed that sharing the community's music brought us more deeply into the lives of these farmers. He believed that once we understood the role that these men and women played in providing us with a product that we valued, how could we not want to use our purchasing power, habits, and daily practice in a way that gives life to the values we hold dear to our hearts: relationships, connection, quality, justice? Together, the components of this advocacy project involved recording the cooperative's music, working with community members to translate their songs, contextualizing the impact of Fair Trade on the farmers' lives, and facilitating the connection between the Thanksgiving Coffee Company and Smithsonian Folkways Recordings.

In her discussion of the ethical dilemmas that arise when a researcher imposes his or her values onto the people in a research setting, Ana Hofman cautions that unintended consequences can arise when one engages in advocacy (2010: 28). I was conscious of this during my research and promotion of the coffee cooperative. There were extremist groups, hostile toward interfaith work in East Africa, that might target the cooperative, or specifically the Jewish community. But the community was clear that they wanted more publicity for their work, and they welcomed a reporter from Al Jazeera who produced a news segment about the cooperative. When I asked if they were concerned that publicity might make them a target for violence, they explained that they believed deeply in the importance of their interfaith model and understood the risks involved in interethnic and interfaith work.

Advocacy work with subaltern cultures that have a legacy of colonialism must be placed in a historical context where European efforts to "help" local communities by bettering their economic and cultural situations have subjugated and oppressed local people (Hofman, 2010: 25). I am conscious that the dynamics of race, class, and privilege that provide me access to distribute the community's music internationally and raise funds to support a university education project also position me in an unequal power dynamic with the community. Ana Hofman emphases that the very act of recording, writing about, and portraying people's work is an act of domination and subjugation that maintains a power dynamic over people who are not representing themselves. While a careful definition of roles in a negotiated partnership can mitigate this situation, the dynamic stands. When a leader of the Abayudaya community wished to attend rabbinic school in the United States, to achieve the status of rabbinic ordination and increase the community's connection to world Jewry, I used my contacts and connections to help him achieve that goal. I was using my power at the community's request, but my academic credentials and professional access to the North American Jewish community clearly placed me in an unequal power dynamic with the community.

I would also observe that digital technology is beginning to level this playing field a bit. The Abayudaya work strategically with a wide range of academics, activists, journalists, funders, and friends. It is becoming easier for them to produce and market their own music. They increasingly exercise their own agency in determining how, when, and where to present themselves and their music culture (Summit, 2008: 322). I also have come to understand how many members of the Abayudaya have in turn empowered me as an ethnomusicologist, through their trust, generous time, and willingness to work together on a range of my academic projects.

Service

Direct service addresses pressing, unmet community needs: collecting and distributing food for the homeless, staffing shelters for abused women, tutoring grade-school children, and providing SAT prep for disadvantaged high school students applying to college. For many volunteers in university settings, direct service is the most common form of community volunteering. The indicators of success for direct service include demonstrating that the service has a positive impact on communities and the individuals served. Volunteers ideally work in collaboration with community members to determine that the outcomes are valued and deemed effective by those in the community. Direct service opportunities must be carefully matched with volunteers' skills, interest, and availability. Much of the success of direct service projects depends on logistical details: managing volunteers' schedules and transportation, and matching these with community members' genuine needs. Even when community needs are great, it is common for direct service projects to recruit volunteers and not have sufficient work, or viable time blocks, to take advantage of volunteers' schedules.

In the course of my work in Uganda, I have participated in occasional direct service: teaching in the community's secondary school and meeting with university students to discuss career direction and plans. There never feels like there is enough time, and I choose to focus that time on my research. After self-assessment, I have decided that my value is greater as an advocate.

While direct service addresses specific community needs, I believe that its value goes beyond that. Of course, as ethnomusicologists, we work to develop this deep cultural understanding through our fieldwork. Direct service can also provide opportunities for this close contact with members of a community. Spending time in people's homes, teaching in a school, and being a resource during times of unexpected difficulty ideally strengthen relationships and bring us into deeper contact with members of a community. When I am raising money for the Abayudaya scholarship program from overstretched business people and professionals in Boston, often someone will look at pictures of the Abayudaya living in mud-brick homes, or carrying water in jerrycans, and say, "These people are so poor!" My response is shaped by my direct experience with the community. An understanding of the richness of a community's cultural and religious life, a connection to close family structures, a different appreciation of the rhythm of days, months, and years in an agricultural community all help to problematize simple dichotomies such as rich versus poor or advantaged versus disadvantaged.

Education

Ideally, an effective initiative includes a commitment to both learn and teach about the deeper social, economic, and historical contexts in which advocacy occurs. In both of my advocacy projects in Uganda, the music has been a core component of these aspects of education. While my research and recording of the Abayudaya's music eventually focused on their liturgical and paraliturgical traditions, I first recorded many songs that stressed the importance of education and community development. In the villages, important societal issues are commonly addressed through music. In his book on the role of music in HIV/AIDS education in Uganda, Gregory Barz discusses the "purposeful" nature of music and entertainment, and details the role of music in education, communication, and community outreach (2006, 2007). These songs reflected the Abayudaya's community values and priorities that arose from their own strategic discussions about projects that would benefit their community. When their high school students sang about their commitment to education, punctuated with the chorus "We shan't give up," I trusted the music. I was also concerned that my research and recordings would open the community to more ethno-tourism from Jewish communities abroad. I wanted to make sure that the Abayudaya sought or would welcome such contact. In fact, they sang of their isolation and their desire to connect to the international Jewish community. Their songs, together with extended discussions with their leadership, helped me determine the direction of my advocacy projects. Similarly, when working with the Peace Kawomera Fair Trade coffee cooperative, their music helped define my agenda as an advocate. The farmers sang about the importance of expanding the cooperative as a way to expand their market. They also sang about the impact of Fair Trade prices on community health and education. In discussions with the cooperative's leadership, they stressed that if I could share these sentiments more broadly, I would help the work of the cooperative and have an impact on the farmers' livelihoods.

After determining that these projects were line in community desires and values, I set out to learn more about sustainable aid and advocacy in Africa. Here, I turned to the resources of our university. I contacted a number of colleagues at Tufts Friedman School of Nutrition Science and Policy and in the Medical School who had been involved in aid projects in Africa. I also spoke with a number of my former students who had worked in the Peace Corps. I posed a series of questions in regard to the educational initiative I was considering. In their experience, what projects worked, and which were doomed to failure? Was it possible to continue a project remotely after you returned home? How might one avoid the dangers and pitfalls when large sums of money were directed toward community projects? These discussions were extremely valuable as I conceptualized the education project and considered how to partner with community leadership and the NGOs already working in the community.

From my experience directing local service projects with undergraduate students, I knew that it was important to structure time for self-reflection on my involvement in this initiative. When I led sessions for students who were doing local community service projects, I began to speak more personally about my nascent work in Uganda and reflect on the problems and issues that I was facing. This process was helpful in thinking through and focusing my concerns. A number of my graduate students had experience in international service, and their reflections were especially helpful. In addition, I put together an informal board of advisors for this project, composed of colleagues and friends with international service experience and good common sense. I stressed that I needed friends who would be honest and would help me identify the mistakes I was making, what problems I was overlooking, and the issues that lay ahead. This help from colleagues and friends was invaluable as I launched the education project.

The music also plays an essential role in my lectures and presentations on the Abayudaya community. The Smithsonian Folkways Recordings CD enjoyed commercial success, and I have been invited to lecture around the country in Jewish settings, at synagogues, schools, and community centers. I conclude my lectures with a description of the challenges and issues that the community is currently confronting, and I describe the impact of the university education project. I tell the stories of a few of the university students and mention how much it costs for a student to attend university in Uganda for a year. I ask if anyone is interested in the project and invite them to speak with me after the lecture. I am often approached by potential funders. So, too, a number of synagogues have taken on this project as one of their social justice initiatives. I build my presentation around my recordings of the Abayudaya's liturgical and paraliturgical music. On one level, I do this because I love to challenge stereotypes and show that Jews are more diverse—culturally, racially, economically—than many in the North American Jewish community assume. On another level, playing the community's religious music is a boundary-leveling strategy, a servable bridge, viscerally connecting to potential funders. Vojko Veršnik explores and applies the image of a bridge to both "connect and divide" groups of people in an ongoing cultural and educational exchange between

Slovenia and Thailand and the musical interaction between younger singers and elderly pensioners in Slovenia. In both of these cases, Veršnik examines "the potential of music as a connecting tool within the realm of applied ethnomusicology" (2010: 135; Summit, 2000: 140–142). So, too, I find that the Abayudaya's liturgical music works as an effective connector, a boundary-leveling strategy with Jewish visitors from North America, one that has helped bring financial support to the community. Many North American Jews want to know if these Africans are really Jewish, and my recordings of the Abayudaya singing familiar liturgy in Hebrew set to rest questions of authenticity and establish a bond of peoplehood.

I spoke to one woman active in her Conservative congregation who visited the community in 2009. She said, "There I was in Uganda, but I felt so at home in the service! We really are one people." It should be obvious that the lives of a Ugandan subsistence farmer and an upper middle-class American business woman have less, rather than more, in common. Yet these shared liturgical traditions undergird a powerful sense of peoplehood felt by both communities when these Jews meet. When this woman returned to Boston, she became actively engaged in raising money to support the Abayudaya university education project.

When I speak about the work of the Peace Kawomera Fair Trade coffee cooperative, I share the music that the farmers have written to educate their neighbors to the benefits of fair trade and interfaith cooperation. Coffee farmers singing about Fair Trade and economic justice has a deeper impact than a display in the local supermarket. Potential consumers and retailers are drawn into the story of the cooperative and often focus on the issue of Fair Trade with a new interest and intensity.

Sustainability

How do we assess our long-term responsibility after we begin an advocacy project with a community? Are we obligated to be involved until we change the focus or location of our research? Are we obligated to be involved forever? While one can become enthusiastic about beginning an advocacy project, it is essential to develop a plan to ensure that an initiative is sustainable over time.

It is natural to defer what feels like a distant problem when a project is just beginning, but it is important to discuss strategies for an initiative's sustainability in the early stages of the project's development. One should try to anticipate possible changes in community needs, organizational leadership, and related infrastructure. With the Abayudaya education project, it was essential to consider donor engagement and retention, as well as strategies to identify and involve new donors. For me, one of the most challenging aspects of the project has been managing the program's growth and the community's expectation to send increasing numbers of students to colleges and universities.

Certain advocacy projects can be designed so that they ultimately revert to community management and control. In certain ways, the Abayudaya education project has aspects of this approach. The community hopes to develop an educated, professional class that will provide a base for economic growth and development. Realistically, this is a long-term solution at best. For example, this program has trained a number of teachers who now work in the community's primary and secondary schools, but their pay is much too low to send their own children to college. It is conceivable that larger community projects, such as a health center the community is developing in Mbale, could generate greater funds and provide a sustainable source of revenue. Together with the leadership of the community, I am about to begin an assessment of the impact of the scholarship program on individuals, families, and the community as a whole.

A few years after I started the university education project, the two students completed their studies. One student became the headmaster of the community's primary school and the second student completed his degree in engineering. But with the possibility of a college education, more students worked hard, hoping to attend college. Now there are 20 students supported by this project, and the tuition bill for last term was about $25,000. It is inspiring to spend time with these students as they realize their dream of attending local colleges and universities. Yet, I am losing sleep as I struggle to raise $50,000 a year for this project. I have managed to engage a few major donors, and while this has made the fundraising a bit easier, at the moment too many eggs are in one basket. When one of the major donors wished to decrease her contribution, I met with her and together we developed a four-year plan for a gradual funding decrease that would give me the opportunity to develop and enlist new substantial donors. Together with a small group of volunteers, I developed a donor retention plan. Once or twice a year, I ask the students funded by the program to write a brief report on their studies and email that to me. I edit their stories into an update and share that with our donors. On my last trip to Uganda, I solicited a member of our research team to make a short video for current and potential donors in which the students spoke about their studies and career plans. I have increased my fundraising efforts, reaching out more actively to local synagogues. The students' success is inspiring, but I struggle to keep the program sustainably within my fundraising capacity. I am deeply committed to this project, but in many ways, it is now more than I bargained for.

Defining Limits and Managing Expectations

One of the important resources that we need to preserve and sustain is our own energy and commitment to an advocacy project. Over-commitment seems to define our lives in academia, and it is essential to determine how much time and effort we can devote to an advocacy project before frustration sets in and we abandon our efforts. For those of us who do research in locations where needs are great, we simply must learn how to manage expectations and determine when "no" is the appropriate answer.

For the first 10 years of the project, the funding and the number of qualifying students grew at approximately the same pace. It became more challenging when the resources for the project began to plateau and more and more students from the community were motivated by the opportunity to attend university. I did a careful assessment of my capacity to raise more funds and decided that I needed to cap the amount I was able to raise at $50,000 a year. However, the elected leadership council of the community, who administered the funds, did not want to turn away qualified students. For several years, they decided to fund all the students who were accepted to local colleges and universities, distributing less money to each of them. Individual students began to email me and complain that it was difficult it was for them to succeed in their studies if they did not have enough funding for food and lodging. After discussions with the leadership council, they decided to reduce the number of students so that they could provide adequate stipends for living expenses in addition to tuition.

It is challenging to manage the growth of this program. More students have been passing the entrance examinations for university, and this year the leadership council sent me proposed expenses for the project that exceeded the maximum I felt that I was able to raise. I went back to our lead donors and discussed the growth of the program. While the funders were committed to the project, they did not feel they were able to increase their donations. It was painful to have to say no, but I told the leadership council that I had to maintain funding at the stated level. The leaders were disappointed but decided that they would establish a waiting list, and when students graduated, new students would be accepted. This was a difficult decision for me. I knew a number of the rising students personally but felt I did not have the capacity to grow the project indefinitely.

The Difficulty in Setting Limits

Even when we carefully define the scope and direction of a project, members of the local community can harbor different expectations. I had been clear with the community leadership that the focus of this project was to provide university education for Abayudaya students studying in Uganda. However, one of the women in the community had a dream to pursue a master's degree in education in the United States after successfully graduating from university in Kampala. She had carefully prepared for our meeting and detailed why, and how, pursuing her degree in Boston would be helpful to her and to the community. At the end of her presentation, she requested that I raise the funds to support her graduate studies in Boston. I considered her request carefully, and it is difficult to convey how painful it was to answer "no." While it seemed possible to raise $3,000 a year to support a student's education in Uganda, it felt beyond my capacity to raise $30,000 a year for one student and provide the logistical and personal support necessary for a student studying in a graduate program in the United States. I spoke at length with her about applying for graduate scholarships and other possible options, but tears rolled down her face as I told her I simply was not willing to take on this large project.

Success Creates More Expectations

A successful project will create more expectations within a community. When I produced the CD of the music of the Jewish, Christian, and Muslim coffee farmers of the Peace Kawomera cooperative, I explained to their leadership that I thought the greatest contribution of the project would be to widely publicize their story, and that, in turn, would increase coffee sales. This was of specific value because even through Thanksgiving Coffee Company committed to buying the farmers' full production at the advantageous Fair Trade price, their coffee was marketed in two ways. All the coffee that could be sold under the Delicious Peace label generated an addition premium of $1 a package. The rest of the coffee was blended with other Fair Trade coffees and sold in various mixes. The cooperative could realize substantial profits if their brand sold a higher volume of coffee.

At the same time, I decided to donate all of my profits from CD sales to fund educational initiatives for children of members of the cooperative. This amounts to 10% of the cost of each CD. The majority of the sales are digital downloads, which cost less than a physical CD and thus generate less profit. While I had explained this in detail to the cooperative, J. J. Keki's expectations were shaped by the commercial success of the Abayudaya CD and the subsequent growth of the Abayudaya education project. Shortly after the Delicious Peace CD was released, the cooperative leadership emailed me to say that they had many students waiting to go to university and asked, when would I be able to wire the funds? It was difficult to have to tell them that if we wanted to think about a university education project, the funds generated from the CD would only be a small part of that budget. Even though I had tried to be transparent when I detailed how the recording project could be helpful for the community, the success of the other education project had created high expectations among members of the cooperative.

THE IMPACT OF ADVOCACY ON OUR RESEARCH

My involvement in these advocacy projects has impacted my research in a number of ways. While I feel ethically and religiously obligated to this project, I am afraid that I spend too much precious time on fundraising, organization, and lecturing—time that should be devoted to my research and writing. On the other hand, this advocacy has led to a deep level of trust and connection with the community and has opened doors to further research. When I began my work on the music of the coffee farmers in the Peace Kawomera cooperative, I was known in the community. When we signed an agreement that profits from a CD, book, or film would be fairly directed back to the cooperative, the negotiations were fairly simple. I have established a reputation with this community, and they knew I was not going to cut and run. It is also helpful that people are very responsive to me when I am doing research. Every day that I am in Uganda, I get a lot of work done.

In my role as rabbi and executive director of Tufts Hillel, I co-directed a five-campus project in which we received significant funding from the academic affairs section of the Department of Homeland Security to establish Jewish, Christian, and Muslim dialogue groups and education on campus. I allocated part of that funding to bring the leadership of the cooperative from Uganda to Tufts University so that we could learn from their example and experience, a move that enriched and complicated my research. I have set my sights on doing a larger project with video and a traveling museum exhibit that will bring this story to a broader public. This has made the project move more slowly as I work to secure larger funding. While I have some connections at Starbucks, I have been hesitant to bring the project to them. While they are a major buyer of Fair Trade coffee, the company is not fully committed to Fair Trade. I am afraid such an alliance might co-opt this project and challenge its integrity. At the same time, such a connection might provide a much larger audience for an important story of economic justice and interfaith cooperation.

My research on the ground with coffee farmers has also given me a more nuanced perspective on the Fair Trade movement. I've learned that Fair Trade is great for farmers when the coffee market is low and during inevitable fluctuations in the market. But right now, the coffee market is high and large companies are offering farmers $.20 or $.30 a pound more than the Fair Trade price for their coffee. In the balance, I am a supporter of Fair Trade, but I need to be careful how and where I share my perspectives so as not to undermine the work of this, and other, Fair Trade cooperatives. I also want my research on coffee and Fair Trade to be seen in a larger context than in promoting the work of a specific cooperative and marketing a specific coffee. In the liner notes to the Delicious Peace CD I state, "While this recording highlights the music and impact of a particular Fair Trade cooperative, I believe that supporting Fair Trade in general is an effective way for consumers to bring fairer compensation to the men and women who produce products that we value and use in our daily lives" (Summit, 2012: 24, liner notes).

The Reciprocal Impact of Advocacy

When I work with students engaged in service learning in Boston, I find it important to stress that they might be the ones changed more profoundly than the people with whom they are working. Like many, I was deeply impacted by the 9/11 bombings of the World Trade Center in New York. When J. J. Keki founded Peace Kawomera as a response to those attacks, I was inspired by his work. I am moved as I listen to Saban Nabutta, of the Akuseka Takuwa Kongo Group, sing "Friends, let us be united so we can be as one!" ("Let All Religions Come Together," track 10, Summit, 2012). Many of the coffee farmers have taken the mission, and message, of this interfaith cooperative to heart. When he found out that I was from America, the lead singer of the Mbiko Aisa Farmers Embaire Group, Katerega Alamanzani, gently lectured me, "I am sorry to mention it about the United States and Afghanistan, but why do you fight there? What is the problem? Come up with a resolution. Regardless of tribe, color or religion, be one person!" My research with the musicians in the cooperative moved me to deepen and expand my own efforts to promote Jewish, Muslim, and Christian dialogue on campus.

In his introduction to a collection of self-reflective essays on the subject of American Jewish ethnography, Jack Kugelmass discusses the researcher's need to reconcile interests that are "purely scientific" with "the personal quest" for authenticity and community. He states that this approach to research speaks to "the ethnotherapeutic value, the search for wholeness, that ethnography can bring to bear in postmodern society" (1988: 1,2). This sense of connectedness has had profound, and occasionally unexpected, effects on me in the course of engaging in community advocacy.

Over the years, I have tried to maintain a certain emotional distance from these projects. I gloss over the moving emails that I periodically receive from the students thanking me for my efforts. I am extremely uncomfortable when some students call me their "father." Yet, when I returned to Uganda last summer, I was greeted by the first woman in the community to receive a university degree, shortly after she completed her education at Makerere University. I had known her since she was 12 years old, and I had seen her suffer through bouts of malaria in Uganda. This woman had stayed at our home in Boston when she visited the United States. I understood the dedication she had shown to her studies over the years. When she thanked me for raising the funds for her tuition, totally to my surprise, I burst into tears, caught off guard and overwhelmed by the impact of the project on this individual. I am familiar with the verse in the book of Proverbs that states "Charity (righteous action) saves one from death" (10: 2) but I simply had never understood the power and meaning of the concept as I wrote a check to the United Way or planned a project from the comfort of my office at Tufts. While advocacy is often understood as a means to impact the other, in unexpected ways, it is the advocate who is transformed by this work.

Conclusion

I have been deeply influenced by the work of the rabbi and philosopher Abraham Joshua Heschel, who taught that spiritual traditions begin "with a consciousness that something is asked of us." That understanding led Heschel to "pray with his feet" as he marched with Dr. Martin Luther King in Selma. I often ask, what is asked of me as I work with these communities in Uganda? In a society that puts tremendous stress on the individual, I struggle to think in terms of "we" rather than "I." As I do my work, I try to keep in mind the words of a poem by Adrienne Rich ("In Those Years," 1995):

> In those years, people will say, we lost track
> of the meaning of we, of you
> we found ourselves
> reduced to I. . . .

It took me a long time to find my voice and to learn how to say "I" but that feels like the first step in a longer journey. I would not downplay the challenges or complications of advocacy, but in my experience, I feel that the spirit is enriched by thoughtfully engaging in this work and systematically putting into practice what it means to say "we."

Notes

1. Jeff Todd Titon. "Closing Address" at the conference "Invested in Community: Ethnomusicology and Musical Advocacy," Brown University, 2003. http://dl.lib.brown.edu/invested_in_community/index.html.
2. For a discussion of the meaning and historical development of the term *tikkun olam*, see Jane Kanarek, "What Does Tikkun Olam Actually Mean?" in *Righteous Indignation: A Jewish Call for Justice* (Woodstock, VT: Jewish Lights Publishing, 2008), and Earl Schwartz, "Tz'dakah, Tikkun Olam, and the Educational Pitfalls of Loose Talk," *Conservative Judaism* 63(1) (2011): 3–24.
3. http://activecitizen.tufts.edu/z-misc/tufts-students-are-active-citizens/
4. http://www.swaraj.org/illich_hell.htm
5. Adapted from: "Making the CASE," a section of "Moving From Band-Aid Solutions to Systematic Change: A Service-Learning 'How-To' Manual for Hillel Foundations" (Hillel: The Foundation for Jewish Campus Life, 2001).
6. For liner notes, full lyric transcriptions and translations, see http://media.smithsonianfolkways.org/liner_notes/smithsonian_folkways/SFW50417.pdf.

References

Barz, Gregory. (2006). *Singing for Life: HIV/AIDS and Music in Uganda*. New York: Routledge.
Barz, Gregory. (2007). Singing for Life: Songs of Hope, Healing, and HIV/AIDS in Uganda. Recorded, produced, and annotated. Various artists. Smithsonian Folkways Recordings SFW CD 40537.
Barz, Gregory, and Judah M. Cohen, eds. (2011). *The Culture of Aids in Africa: Hope and Healing Through Music and the Arts*. New York: Oxford University Press.
Buber, Martin. (1970). *I and Thou: A New Translation with a Prologue "I and You" and Notes by Walter Kaufman*. New York: Charles Scribner's Sons.
Clifford, James. (1988). *The Predicament of Culture: Twentieth-Century Ethnography, Literature and Art*. Cambridge, MA: Harvard University Press.
Feld, Steven. (1991). Voices of the Rainforest. Audio cassette, RACS 0173, Ryko.
Feld, Steven. (1982). *Sound and Sentiment: Birds, Weeping, Poetics, and Song in Kaluli Expression*. Philadelphia: University of Pennsylvania Press.
Harrison, Klisala, and Svanibor Pettan. (2010). "Introduction." In *Applied Ethnomusicology: Historical and Contemporary Approaches*, edited by Klisala Harrison, Elizabeth Mackinlay, and Svanibor Pettan, pp. 1–20. Newcastle upon Tyne, UK: Cambridge Scholars Publishing.
Heschel, Abraham Joshua. (1983 [1955]). *God in Search of Man: A Philosophy of Judaism*. New York: Farrar, Straus and Giroux.
Hofman, Ana. (2010). "Maintaining the Distance, Othering the Subaltern: Rethinking Ethnomusicologists' Engagement in Advocacy and Social Justice." In *Applied*

Ethnomusicology: Historical and Contemporary Approaches, edited by Klisala Harrison, Elizabeth Mackinlay, and Svanibor Pettan, pp. 22–35. Newcastle upon Tyne, UK: Cambridge Scholars Publishing.

Kanarek, Jane. (2008). "What Does Tikkun Olam Actually Mean?" In *Righteous Indignation: A Jewish Call for Justice*, edited by Or N. Rose, Jo Ellen Green Kaiser, and Margie Klein, pp. 15–22. Woodstock, VT: Jewish Lights Publishing.

Kugelmass, Jack, ed. (1968). *Between Two Worlds: Ethnographic Essays on American Jewry*. Ithaca, NY; London: Cornell University Press.

Lederach, Jean Paul. (2005). *The Moral Imagination: The Art and Soul of Building Peace*. New York: Oxford University Press.

Pettan, Svanibor. (2008). "Applied Ethnomusicology and Empowerment Strategies: Views from across the Atlantic." *Muzikološki zbornik/Musicological Annual* 44(1): 85–99.

Rich, Adrienne. (1995). "In Those Years." In *Dark Fields of the Republic: Poems 1991–1995*. New York: W. W. Norton & Company.

Seeger, Anthony. (1987). *Why Suyá Sing: A Musical Anthropology of an Amazonian People*. Cambridge: Cambridge University Press.

Sheehy, Daniel. (1992). "A Few Notions about Philosophy and Strategy in Applied Ethnomusicology." *Ethnomusicology* 36(3): 323–336.

Shelemay, Kay Kaufman. (2008). "The Ethnomusicologist, Ethnographic Method, and the Transmission of Tradition." In *Shadows in the Field: New Perspectives for Fieldwork in Ethnomusicology* (2nd ed.), edited by Gregory Barz and Timothy J. Cooley, pp. 141–156. New York: Oxford University Press.

Spradley, J. P., and D. W. McCurdy, eds. *Conformity and Conflict: Readings in Cultural Anthropology* (12th ed.). Boston: Pearson Allyn and Bacon, 2000.

Stoecker, Randy, and Elizabeth A. Tryon, eds., with Amy Hilgendorf. (2009). *The Unheard Voices: Community Organizing and Service Learning*. Philadelphia: Temple University Press.

Summit, Jeffrey A. (2000). *The Lord's Song in a Strange Land: Music and Identity in Contemporary Jewish Worship*. New York: Oxford University Press, 2000.

Summit, Jeffrey A. (2003). Abayudaya: Music from the Jewish People of Uganda. Recorded, compiled, and annotated. Various artists. Smithsonian Folkways Recordings SFW CD 40504.

Summit, Jeffrey A. (2008). "Music and the Construction of Identity among the Abayudaya (Jewish people) of Uganda." In *The Garland Handbook of African Music* (2nd ed.), edited by Ruth M. Stone, pp. 312–324. New York: Routledge.

Summit, Jeffrey A. (2012). Delicious Peace: Coffee, Music and Interfaith Harmony in Uganda. Produced, compiled and annotated. CD and video. Smithsonian Folkways Recordings, SFW CD 50417.

Schwartz, Earl. (2011). "Tz'dakah, Tikkun Olam, and the Educational Pitfalls of Loose Talk." *Conservative Judaism* 63(1): 3–24.

Titon, Jeff Todd. (1992). "Introduction: Music, the Public Interest, and the Practice of Ethnomusicology." *Ethnomusicology* 36(3); 315–322.

Titon, Jeff Todd. (2003). "Closing Address." Delivered at the conference "Invested in Community: Ethnomusicology and Musical Advocacy," Brown University. http://dl.lib.brown.edu/invested_in_community/index.html.

Titon, Jeff Todd, with John Fenn. (2003). "A Conversation with Jeff Todd Titon." *Folklore Forum* 34(1–2): 119–131.

Usner, Eric Martin. (2010). "United States Ethnomusicology and the Engaged University." In *Applied Ethnomusicology: Historical and Contemporary Approaches*, edited by Klisala

Harrison, Elizabeth Mackinlay, and Svanibor Pettan, pp. 76–95. Newcastle upon Tyne, UK: Cambridge Scholars Publishing.

Veršnik, Vojko. (2010). "Solid as Stone and Bone: Song as a Bridge Between Cultures and Generations." In *Applied Ethnomusicology: Historical and Contemporary Approaches*, edited by Klisala Harrison, Elizabeth Mackinlay, and Svanibor Pettan, pp. 76–95. Newcastle upon Tyne, UK: Cambridge Scholars Publishing.

CHAPTER 2

APPLIED ETHNOMUSICOLOGY AS AN INTERCULTURAL TOOL
Some Experiences from the Last 25 Years of Minority Research in Austria

URSULA HEMETEK

THE discipline of ethnomusicology should definitely, by its very nature, have great potential to be used as a tool of intercultural mediation. Manifold are the approaches and publications in modern ethnomusicology to underline this aspect, such as the book *Music in Motion* (Clausen/Hemetek/Saether, 2009). I interpret applied ethnomusicology according to Maureen Loughran: "as a philosophical approach to the study of music in culture with social responsibility and social justice as guiding principles" (2008: 52). Intercultural mediation can be one aspect in this much broader concept. Minority research, on the other hand, is very much connected to applied ethnomusicology (see Hemetek, 2006; Pettan, 2008). This is the point of departure for this chapter, which is based on research activities in ethnomusicology focusing on the intercultural potential of music and some possible applications of this potential in the course of minority studies.[1] As this work is the outcome of a long-term engagement, it also enables me to reflect critically on the role of the fieldworker with respect to active/passive, interventionalist/non-interventionalist stances. The question will be raised as to how far the "partnership model of fieldwork" suggested by Ian Russell (2006) covers part of the task of applied ethnomusicology in connection with discriminated groups and intercultural mediation.

THEORETICAL BACKGROUND

Music and Minorities and Applied Ethnomusicology

The history of ethnomusicology, a discipline that is said to have been founded by Guido Adler in Vienna as "comparative musicology" with the aim of comparing different music cultures, shows some a priori intercultural potential. This potential was not always visible or emphasized in the long history of the discipline, but this is not the focus of this chapter. For my topic, it is important to theorize especially one aspect that is specifically connected to applied ethnomusicology: music and minorities.

Minorities, being exotic on the one hand, and underprivileged and discriminated against on the other, seem to be a central theme throughout the history of ethnomusicology. They were subject to ethnomusicological research very early on. Alice Cunningham Fletcher (1838–1923) was one of the pioneers doing fieldwork with Native Americans—a research topic that was located "on her doorstep." She is also recognized as a pioneering anthropologist who advocated for both Indian reform and Indian education. One of her statements, quoted in Temkin (1988) illustrates her approach, which already seems to be connected to application of her findings: "Living with my Indian friends ... I found I was a stranger in my native land. As time went on, the outward aspect of nature remained the same, but change was wrought in me. I learned to hear the echoes of a time when every living thing even the sky had a voice. The voice devoutly heard by the ancient people of America I desired to make audible to others" (as quoted in Temkin, 1988: 99).

In Europe it was mostly the Jews and the Roma who were identified as exotic (see Schachiner, 2008), but within the tradition of European folk music research there was no room for serious research on minorities, except if they were seen as an extension of the nation. There are manifold examples of such approaches, for example the German *Sprachinselforschung* (see Kuhn, 1934) or research on the Burgenland Croats by Franjo Kuhač (1878–1881), among many others.[2]

One important precondition for establishing research on minorities in ethnomusicology in the modern sense—neither exotic nor nationalistic—was the recognition of heterogeneity, which is closely connected with urban areas as a field of research. Adelaida Reyes sees a clear connection between the concepts of research on minorities and those of urban ethnomusicology because

> in a scholarly realm built on presumptions of cultural homogeneity, there was no room for minorities. These require a minimal pair—at least two groups of unequal power and most likely culturally distinct, both parts of a single social organism. Homogeneity does not admit of such disparate components.... The conditions that spawn minorities—complexity, heterogeneity, and non-insularity—are "native" not to simple societies but to cities and complex societies.
>
> (Reyes, 2007: 22)

Adelaida Reyes was one of the pioneers of these ideas; as early as 1979 she had published an article on the topic, although in a sociological journal (Reyes-Schramm, 1979), especially focusing on definitions of minorities, which is of course crucial to the entire discourse.

One scholarly conference that pointed toward a new thinking about minorities and ethnomusicology in Europe was a conference in Zagreb in 1985. Pettan (2012) writes about it:

To the best of my knowledge, the first ethnomusicological conference world-wide with the key words "music" and "minorities" took place twenty-seven years ago in Zagreb. The key person, the representative of the hosting institution—*Zavod za istraživanje folklora Instituta za filologiju i folkloristiku* (currently Institute of Ethnology and Folklore Research)—was Jerko Bezić. Those whom he invited to take part in this historical conference included his colleagues from Yugoslavia, from the neighboring countries (Austria, Hungary, Italy) and from Germany. Besides his programmatic contribution and those with a focus on institutional (Haid), fieldwork (Walcher [replaced by Hemetek]) and individual strategies (Tari), specific repertoires (Bašić), and comparisons of musical features (Boljunčić, Fracile, Habenicht), most of the participants reported either about their own minority national group (e.g. Starec on Italians in Istria, Sheholli on Albanians in Kosovo, Kmet on Slovaks in Yugoslavia, Logar on Slovenes in Austrian Carinthia, Strajnar on Slovenes abroad) or a minority group within their own territorial contexts (e.g. Pietsch on Croats in Austrian Burgenland, Petrović on Sephardic Jews in Bosnia and Herzegovina, Gojković on Romanies in Yugoslavia, Kovalcsik on Romanies in Eastern Europe). Most presenters tried to point out interethnic connections" (Pettan, 2012: 450).

There was a publication following that conference (Bezić, 1985).

I was privileged to attend the conference, which was my first international conference ever, being a young Ph.D. student with no international experience, and what I remember best was the personality of Jerko Bezić, who was the most integrative figure of the entire event. Given the lack of professional interpreting, he actually did all that himself, being fluent in Serbo-Croatian, Slovenian, Italian, English, and German. He actually accomplished a great deal of intercultural communication by acting this way.

This conference inspired the later foundation of the International Council for Traditional Music (ICTM) Study Group on Music and Minorities in 1997.[3] From the beginning, it seemed to be very important to define the word *minority* for the purposes of the Study Group. Definitions are manifold and very much depend on the respective political situation.

The definition that was and still is used by the ICTM Study Group on Music and Minorities is the following: "Minorities = groups of people distinguishable from the dominant group for cultural, ethnic, social, religious, or economic reasons."

The definition was the result of intense discussion, of course, and it proved to be a key problem. It was suggested that discrimination be made the common denominator, which de facto is the case, because all minorities, however we define them, have this in common: there are some markers of "difference" with regard to the dominant society (language, habits, citizenship, outward appearance, religion, sexual orientation, and so on), and they face discrimination in one way or another. But to use "discrimination" in the definition would at that time have been too political for an international organization like the ICTM. So, finally, the discussions resulted in using the phrase "dominant group," also in order to include the manifold different approaches from colleagues all over the world.

The discussions taking place in the surroundings of this Study Group seem to be important, as they mirror scholarly discourses and thus provide a theoretical framework for the definition of who are the consultants with or for whom we work, the people we study. I would like to quote here from the first publication of the Study Group from 2001, which shows the discourse at that time:

> The discussion process reveals the wide range of interests and scholarly traditions with regard to minorities. The complexity of the topic itself calls for a variety of approaches and interdisciplinary connections. That minorities are defined in relation to majorities is unavoidable, but their relationship can be seen from different points of view. Is it primarily a relationship of power or a relationship of culture, of social circumstances, of ethnicity, religion, or economics? Sociologists tend to define it as power relationship, which has its effects on cultural processes, the majority requiring conformity and penalizing deviation . . . . [Reiterer 1996]. On the other hand, especially in music, this deviation from the mainstream can also be instrumentalized by and integrated into the majority's culture. Mark Slobin argues in his article *Four Reasons Why We Have No Musical Minorities in the United States* that dividing lines begin to disappear due to new identity constructions, and the outcome can be seen in musical production as well as in instrumentalizing musical styles in connection to political events (comp. Slobin 1995).
>
> (Hemetek, 2001a: 21)

Some of Bruno Nettl's ideas from 1992 were very useful as well. He saw growing interest in the study of the music of minorities in modern ethnomusicology. "In particular, the fate of musics removed from their original home such as African-American, overseas Indian, European and Asian immigrants in the Americas, European and Middle Eastern repertoires in Israel have come to be of special interest" (Nettl, 1992: 380). He sees this interest as being mainly connected with two research concepts: urban ethnomusicology on the one hand—cities being multicultural centers—and long-term studies on the transfer of cultural systems into new surroundings (Nettl, 1992: 380). In addition, he sees a new attitude in ethnomusicology that pays special attention to minorities: "Ethnomusicologists increasingly have recognized that a society may be divided musically along various lines, and scholars have therefore begun to concentrate on the repertoires and musical behaviour of segments of a population. Whereas they once looked at small samples of the songs of a tribe with the assumption that these examples signified a homogenous repertory, they have since come to study linguistic, religious and ethnic minorities" (Nettl, 1992: 380).

While speaking of "linguistic, religious and ethnic minorities," with regard to the sociopolitical circumstances in the United States and in Western European countries, Nettl refers mainly to migrant communities. No doubt, migrant communities were and are a particularly emphasized subject in the Study Group. In the words of Adelaida Reyes,

Migration creates one of the largest, if not the largest, human groups out of which minorities emerge. What migrants bring with them as capital for building new lives in resettlement depends on what they had in the old life, the manner of their departure and the reasons for it, what as a consequence they leave behind and what they take with them. How they deploy this capital depends on their vision of the present and the future, but it is a vision encumbered in their particular past. The lives they create in resettlement are shaped by all these, but not by these alone. For once in a new environment, they must interact with a host society, most likely a dominant one, within which, as minorities, they must now accommodate themselves.

(Reyes, 2001: 38–39)

"The capital for building new lives" is not limited to ethnicity, ethnic tradition, or traditional culture. One of the key words in our discussions that came up in this context is *identity*. It is very common and has different connotations, such as ethnic, national, individual, collective, multiple, and cultural identity, among others. "Music, Dance and Identity in Minority Cultures" was one of the themes of the Study Group meeting in Ljubljana, and most papers concentrated on that. It is a fact that music and dance can obviously play an important role in the identity construction of minority cultures, and they could be interpreted as collective to a certain extent. But from the very beginning of our discussions, there were voices that rejected that way of interpreting the musical phenomena of immigrants, like Eva Fock in her study of young descendants of immigrants in Denmark, stating that,

in the eyes of the majority, symbolic collective identities overshadow the much more complex and vulnerable individual identities of the youngsters. Without looking beyond what is served on a silver plate by media or public politics, the old stereotypes of "ethnic" and "traditional" youngsters as strangers in a modern world are maintained. In reality, the individual way of combining a clear personal preference with the ability to adapt to constantly changing demands, is typical for these youngsters.

(Fock, 1999: 75)

In the meantime, the discourses within the Study Group have added new aspects, although the definition of the term *minority* has not been changed. The Study Group has followed the arguments raised by Eva Fock—collective identity as such is under discussion. Hybridity seems to be a new important aspect as well, and power relations are very much discussed. The topic "Race, Class and Gender" has been added, and the Study Group Symposium in 2014 in Osaka, Japan, included sexual minorities as one of the themes for the first time (see www.ictmusic.org/group/music-and-minorities).

Concerning applied ethnomusicology, there are to be found several approaches throughout the history of the Study Group. In a conference publication of 2004, the topic was explicitly raised. "Minorities are very often groups of people who are discriminated against in one way or other" (Hemetek (2004: 50). Martin Stokes says: "When we are looking at the way in which ethnicities and identities are put into play in musical performance, we should not forget that music is one of the less innocent ways in which dominant categories are enforced and resisted" (1997: 8). "Ethnomusicologists, seeing and realizing that minorities are often in the weaker position in these power relations when working with a group, very often feel the need for some action that crosses the borderlines of our discipline" (Hemetek, 2004: 50–51).

At the World Conference of the ICTM in Sheffield in 2005, the Study Group organized a panel called "Applied Ethnomusicology and Studies on Music and Minorities: The Convergence of Theory and Practice." The relevance of applied ethnomusicology to the study of music and minorities, and vice versa, and what constitutes this relevance were explored. One follow-up of this panel was an article in the ICTM Yearbook (Hemetek, 2006).

After the ICTM Study Group on Applied Ethnomusicology had been founded in 2007, a very successful joint meeting of the two Study Groups was organized in Hanoi in 2010, which again manifested the interrelatedness of the two approaches in ethnomusicology.

Having outlined the development of music and minorities studies in connection to applied ethnomusicology by using the example of the Study Group, I will now give a political and historical background of the geographical and sociopolitical context of the following case studies. As we always deal with music in its social function, it goes without saying that the context is important. It is even more important in connection with applied ethnomusicology, because application requires a well-founded knowledge of the political and social circumstances of the people we work with in order to achieve some benefit for their situation.

The Austrian Minority Situation: Historical and Political Background

Austria is the result or remainder of the Austro-Hungarian monarchy (1867–1918), which was a multinational country with many languages and cultures, including Czech, Slovakian, Ukrainian, Croatian, Polish, Hungarian, Slovenian, and Jewish, as well as Roma, cultures.

Austria did not have overseas colonies and was not confronted with overseas immigration, as the United Kingdom, France, Portugal, and the Netherlands were, as a result of colonialism. Austria was formed by migration, but it was first of all an inland migration, within the Austro-Hungarian monarchy. During the last 50 years, however, there has been massive immigration from eastern and southern Europe. In the 1960s Austria needed migrant workers and thus began the immigration of Yugoslavian and Turkish people.

Due to its location as a Western country on the border of several former communist states, there were also several waves of refugees from Hungary in 1956 (the "Hungarian uprising" against the Soviets ended up in violent restoration of the regime), from Czechoslovakia in 1968 (the so called "Prague spring" challenging Soviet control, which ended up in Soviet invasion), from Poland in 1981 (declaration of martial law following the "Polish crisis" challenging Soviet control), and from Bosnia in 1992 (see later discussion in this chapter).

The inland migration during the monarchy and the reduction of the territory after World War I resulted in the existence of so-called "autochthonous" ethnic minorities, those who have been living in a certain region for a hundred years or more. They are citizens of Austria and have been granted certain rights. They are also recognized as an ethnic group (*Volksgruppe*). The term *Volksgruppe* has only existed in Austria as a political category since 1976, due to the so-called *Volksgruppengesetz* (Ethnic Groups Act), and it includes only ethnic minorities with a distinct culture and language that have lived in Austria for at least three generations, thereby granting them certain rights. This law does not include immigrants of recent years, who therefore remain without such rights. Table 2.1 provides an overview on ethnic minority groups in Austria.

According to the latest census in Austria in 2011, the numbers of foreigners in Austria are as follows (see Statistik Austria, 2011: 35):

Austrian population total: 8,404,252
Foreigners: 1,452,591 (that is, 17.3%)

According to countries of origin (including Austrian citizens born in the respective country):

Germany: 220,330[4]
Serbia/Montenegro/Kosovo: 208,809
Turkey: 184,815
Bosnia and Herzegovina: 131,128
Croatia: 69,654
Romania: 68,142
Poland: 59,753
Czech Republic: 45,213
Hungary: 41,348
Italy: 29,447
Russia: 27,149
Slovakia: 26,079
Macedonia: 23,127
Other groups: less than 20,000.

The division into "ethnic groups" and immigrants seems to be outmoded in times of globalization and EU integration. Among other reasons that have to do with history, there is one to be found in Austria's political self-definition: Austria does not want to be seen as a country of immigration, although de facto it is. Immigration is seen as more of a threat than as a necessity. Xenophobia is stirred up by some political parties that

Table 2.1. Ethnic Minority Groups in Austria

Ethnic Groups*	In Their Territory since
Slovenes in Styria	6th century†
Slovenes in Carinthia	9th century
Hungarians in Burgenland	10th century
Roma in Austria	15th century
Croats in the Burgenland	16th century
Czechs in Vienna	19th century
Slovakians in Vienna	19th century
Hungarians in Vienna	20th century‡
Foreigners: Immigrants and Refugees (Largest Groups)	**In Austria since**
From former Yugoslavia	1960 onward
From Turkey	1960 onward
From Czechoslovakia	1968
From Poland	1981
From Bosnia	1992

* There are other groups in Austria that would be considered to be minorities, like the Jenische, the Trentinians in Vorarlberg, and, of course, the Jewish population. Jenische and Trentinians are not mentioned because, although ethnically defined, they are not recognized as *Volksgruppe*. The Jewish have officially denied any ethnic definitions, due to the Nazi ideology defining Jews as a "race." The Jewish population in Austria suffers from a long history of discrimination; during the Nazi holocaust a high percentage of the Austrian Jewish community was murdered. The Jewish community in Austria today is very heterogeneous; there are different religious groups, ranging from very orthodox to liberal, and they are still exposed to racism.

† The Slovenes in Styria only have been recognized in 2003 as part of the Slovenian *Volksgruppe*.

‡ The Hungarians in Vienna—mostly refugees from 1956—were recognized as part of the Hungarian *Volksgruppe* in 1992.

look for scapegoats in times of economic recession. And these are found in the form of immigrants.

Immigrants in Austria are discriminated against on several levels. There is the labor market, housing, and structural discrimination by the law, not to mention having to face everyday racism. It is very difficult for them to obtain Austrian citizenship. The integration process—which I define by referring to Bauböck (2001: 14) as a "process of reciprocal adjustment between an already existing group and a settling group"—is not at all satisfactory. The reactions of immigrants themselves are to be found in different strategies, which are between—but also include—two extremes: One is withdrawal into the ghetto, the other is assimilation. In the case of withdrawal, immigrants limit private social contact to members of their own nationality, and find their niches in which to survive. This is of course understandable, but it does not lead to a successful integration process. But even in the case of assimilation, which I would define as the complete abandonment of ethnic markers like language and customs, there still is discrimination because of the visibility of "otherness" by skin color, accent, or a person's name. The majority—the dominant group—reacts to the challenges of immigration not by adjustment but rather by rejection, thereby hindering the integration process.

I have tried to argue the reasons for this Austrian peculiarity of the division into ethnic groups and immigrant minorities in Austria. Nevertheless, it seems somehow paradoxical. In the meantime, a third generation of immigrants is living in Austria. They were born here, have hardly any contact with the homeland of their grandparents, but are still considered immigrants, or are referred to using the now-common expression "people with immigrant backgrounds."

All these groups are considered as minorities mainly for ethnic or religious reasons. But of course there are social and economic reasons as well, because certain immigrant groups are to be found in the lower social segment. There are other groups that would also be included in a minority definition that derives from power relations and makes discrimination the common denominator: for example, gay, lesbian, and transgender persons, as well as disabled persons.

All these groups have representative nongovernmental organizations (NGOs) and are more or less influential and more or less successful. The NGO minority scene is very diverse in Austria, and it is important to underscore that within all of the groups there is no homogeneity, neither in a political, ethnic, or social sense, nor in terms of political representation.

One NGO in Austria, Initiative Minderheiten (Initiative Minorities), is and has been very important for music and minority studies. It is one of the very few minority NGOs in Austria that does not want to "represent" one or more minority groups, but tries to act as a platform for a broad range of different groups. The mission statement says the following:

> Since 1991, Initiative Minderheiten has been advocating and contributing towards creating a society that acknowledges and affords equal treatment and equal rights to minorities in their individual life concepts regardless of their ethnic, social or religious affiliation, sexual orientation or dis/ability. A society can only be considered to have acknowledged minority rights if it facilitates and supports different life concepts in a fair and equal manner. Initiative Minderheiten works towards creating minority alliances.
>
> Initiative Minderheiten defines a minority as people who experience discrimination based on their ethnic, social or religious affiliation, sexual orientation or dis/ability. Politically, discrimination means excluding certain people from certain rights; socially, it means experiencing prejudices and exclusions. In Austria, legally recognized ethnic groups are also considered minorities, as well as migrants and refugees, lesbians, gays and transgenders, and people with dis/abilities. This

definition is not based on a group's number of members, but rather on their lack of power in comparison to that of the hegemonic majority.

(www.initiative.minderheiten.at)

The means by which Initiative Minderheiten wants to reach these goals are based on intellectual capacities and use traditional as well as internet media. It carries out applied research projects, exhibitions, art projects, and other smaller projects that are usually received very well by the public. Initiative Minorities does not do social work.

Ethnomusicology was involved in some of their research as well as art projects from the very beginning. The theoretical discussions within this organization influenced minority studies in Austria to a certain extent. This is especially important because in Initiative Minderheiten, minorities function as researchers, not as "objects" of research. The application of results is intended, as the goal is combating discrimination, as well as structural improvement of the minority situation. This can serve as a model for applied ethnomusicology in minority studies and definitely influenced ethnomusicology research methods in Austria.

In all of the following case studies, the political sense of responsibility was the guiding principle of the research and action; they also have been chosen in order to show that sometimes it is hard to draw a line between political activism and research.

Applied Ethnomusicology in Specific Minority Contexts: Roma, Bosnian Refugees, Immigrants from Turkey

All three groups, as minorities in the Austrian context, face discrimination in one way or another. There are different strategies of applied ethnomusicology (see Pettan, 2008; Sheehy, 1992) involved in each of the cases, due to different sociopolitical circumstances. The three cases have also been chosen due to their chronological nature, thereby showing a certain development of awareness and discourse level in ethnomusicology, due to the fact that neither the term *applied ethnomusicology* nor a theory of it were available in 1989, when the engagement started. I hope to broaden the theoretical and methodological scope of applied ethnomusicology by analyzing the strategies involved in each of the cases.

Here is a short survey of the three case studies: In the process of the political recognition of Roma in Austria (initiated in 1989 and the following years), their traditional music and its presentation in public contributed to proving that a group of people who had been discriminated against and who formerly were seen merely as a social minority were in fact an ethnic one, with a distinct cultural heritage of their own. Several research projects by Austrian scholars on Roma music formed the basis for activities in the broadly conceived field of applied ethnomusicology, yielding work in the areas of intercultural mediation, political activism, public promotion, and education. Public promotion of "ethnic" music was my main approach in 1990 and subsequently. Many of the former activities seem to be very outmoded today. Times and contexts have changed significantly, and a shift from "ethnic representation" to "intercultural encounters" (for example, in a Roma music school in Vienna) is noticeable.

The example of the engagement with the Bosnian community was limited to the time of the civil war in the former Yugoslavia and afterward (1994–2000). From 1992 onward, about 100,000 Bosnian refugees came to Austria due to the policy of "ethnic cleansing" by the Serbian as well as the Croatian army in Bosnia. They were merely seen as "poor" people by Austrians, and were associated with blood and tears. Many Bosnian intellectuals were in Austria at that time, among them many musicians. They were very unhappy with this public image and wanted to react by showing their potential. Ethnomusicology could function as a kind of midwife in documenting and presenting in public the cultural treasures that the refugees had brought with them. The genre *Sevdalinka* was chosen to represent the Bosnian intercultural heritage by the musicians themselves and by researchers. A program involving music and literature was presented to ethnically mixed audiences, and this enabled intercultural encounter to a certain extent. It was an activity that was necessary at a certain time due to political circumstances, initiated by the wishes of a community.

From my experiences with the different communities of immigrants from Turkey in Vienna from 2003 onward, I have learned to be very careful with the label "ethnic" in music. The approximately 200,000 immigrants from Turkey in Austria are as manifold in their cultural expressions as the majority Austrians. In practice, "ethnic" music is just one of many music styles. Politically, immigrants from Turkey are the most discriminated group in Austria today due to rising Islamophobia and the xenophobic public discourses of most political parties in Austria. Ethnomusicological strategies to fight discrimination must take into account the fact that many musicians from the Turkish community do not want to be labeled according to their ethnic roots. Here, ethnomusicology has to advocate more on the level of opinion-leading via expertise in different majority institutions (involving music education, for example).

In a critical analysis of some former activities in Austria, I will draw attention to the fact that applied work can have side effects that are quite unintentional and can only be noticed from a historical distance. This is only possible in long-term studies. What was intended in all three cases was to transform the research results into contexts where they might function as an intercultural tool, which was more or less successful, by using the methods of applied ethnomusicology for the benefit of the people we study. These contexts include political interventions, feeding-back models, public promotion, and strategies of influencing public discourse.

The Case of the Roma: Political Recognition and Ethnicity, or Political Intervention and the Invention of Ethnicity

Europe invented the "Gypsy." This is the somewhat modified title of a book published in 2011/2013: *Europa erfindet die Zigeuner* (Europe Invents the Gypsies), written by

Klaus Michael Bogdal from the perspective of comparative literature. His primary sources are literary documents, and by analyzing these and other historical sources—always written by non-Roma—he shows how, from the fifteenth century onward, the myth of the "Gypsy" was constructed by non-Roma. It is an analysis of how non-Roma dealt with Roma, and it clearly shows the dichotomy within the construct: on the one hand, Roma were rejected, even hated and discriminated against, while on the other hand, Gypsy romanticism arose. This romanticism was strongly connected to music. It is evidence for the invention of the narrative that was constructed without any participation of Roma themselves. The answers to the question of how it is possible that a group of people can be reviled and their music adored at the same time are mostly to be found in these narratives. Music connected to Roma was constructed as a positive stereotype, and Gypsies were and still are thought to be the most gifted musicians in many societies. This is also due to the fact that Roma sometimes participate in their own stereotypification—mostly because stereotypes sell in the music business, a fact that Carol Silverman stresses in her recent book *Romani Routes. Cultural Politics and Balkan Music in Diaspora* (Silverman, 2012).

The invented myth of a people who have no home and are constantly on the move has many consequences: one is that Gypsies are not considered to belong to any nation-state, and are always located on the margins of societies. In 1988 there was severe discrimination against Roma in Austrian society. The prevailing opinion among the majority society was that they were a group of people who steal, who wander about somewhere in the woods, who do not work, and who are mainly criminals.

There was very little reliable information publicly available at that time. My first encounter was actually a documentary on Austrian TV that was titled *Ihr werdet uns nie verstehen* (You will never understand us). This statement, as well as the entire documentary, aroused my curiosity. I have written about that process elsewhere (see Hemetek, 2006); here is a quotation from that publication:

> The title of the film was a quote of one Sinto (one of the Roma groups living in Austria, see below) in the film, and he really meant what he said: that we as *gañe*, as non-Roma, could never understand the Roma, because we were so different from each other. But at the same time it was the film's aim to make *gañe* understand—at least a little bit—who Roma are and how they live, because this was the first well founded information, the first serious documentary on the life of Roma in Austria there ever broadcast as far as I know. This film explained a lot about Roma in Austria, about their view of life, their living conditions and their history. A social and cultural dichotomy was emphasised with Roma on one side versus *gañe* on the other. There was a beautiful song at the end of the film which touched me deeply although I did not know anything about the music, its language or meaning. The film conveyed the following message to me and new thoughts started working in my mind: There is a people, living in my country, who are severely discriminated against, who are somehow mysterious, telling me "I would never understand them." This was fascinating music completely unknown in public at that time, and I learned that the singer of the moving song lived in Vienna, only a short distance from my home.

(Hemetek, 2006: 39–40) (Figure 2.1)

FIGURE 2.1 Ruža Nikolić-Lakatos, 1994.

(Photo by Birgit Karner Archive of the Institute of Folk Music
Research and Ethnomusicology)

After I had started to make contacts in 1989 in order to learn something about the Roma and their music, the first singer I spoke to and interviewed was the Lovari (one of the Roma groups, see below) woman Ceija Stojka (Figure 2.2). Ceija, who had survived the Nazi concentration camps, told me about her life, about her experience of prejudice and racism, and how Roma had to hide their ethnic identity to escape this discrimination. In spite of that, Ceija Stojka had decided to write a book about her experiences, and for the first time in Austria, in 1988, there was a Romani publicly outing her ethnic background (Stojka, 1988). My first interviews with her were about what music meant in her life and even what it had meant in the concentration camps (see Hemetek/Heinschink, 1992).

One of the findings of the research was that Roma in Austria are by no means a homogenous group, but are very diverse in terms of their history, their cultural identity, and what they considered to be "their" music (see Table 2.2).

I do not want to repeat what I have written elsewhere, but briefly, the social and cultural, especially musical, identification is very diverse; there is not just one "Romani culture," one "Romani music," but many different ones. The language, Romani, exists in many different variants, and some groups do not even speak it any more. The different Roma groups have been influenced by different cultural traditions, due to different locations of their stay before they came to Austria. Therefore, due

FIGURE 2.2 Ceija Stojka, 1991.
(Photo by Gerhard Maurer Archive of the Institute of Folk Music Research and Ethnomusicology)

Table 2.2. Roma in Austria: Major Communities

Name	In Austria since	Coming from
Burgenland Roma	15th century	Hungary
Lovari	1900/1956	Slovakia, Hungary
Sinti	19th century	Bohemia, Germany
Kalderara	1965	Serbia
Gurbeti	1965	Serbia
Arlije	1965	Macedonia, Kosovo

to their specific history, the social structure of Roma is very different from that of other minorities. But in spite of all this, the movement of political and cultural self-representation of the Roma had begun in Austria, coinciding with the beginning of ethnomusicological research. The political aim was to be recognized as a so-called *Volksgruppe* (see earlier discussion). To acquire this legal designation, it is necessary to prove their ethnicity, to prove that Roma in Austria were an ethnic group. Now this was a new approach, a least in the public perception, because Roma were seen as a social problem, and not as a group with a distinct cultural tradition, although they were viewed by the general public as somehow racially defined and different. But the ascribed identity markers were rather bad habits, such as stealing. In 1955, when certain rights for ethnic groups were defined in the constitution, nobody would have thought of Roma; nor were they considered in 1976, when the *Volkgruppengesetz* as the legal instrument for these matters had been implemented. This ignorance reminds one of National Socialism, when the argument for killing and deporting Roma was their status of being so-called antisocial elements and criminals. Even after World War II, Roma who had been deported to concentration camps were denied compensation based on the argument that they had been arrested and deported as criminals. The first official argument to deny their recognition as a *Volksgruppe* came in 1990 when Austrian Prime Minister Franz Vranitzky said that he did not see any "cultural markers" that indicated an ethnic tradition, which was necessary for their recognition. This entire matter is influenced by the history and ideology that underlie the idea of the European nation-state. Nation-states in Europe from the nineteenth century onward were defined by ethnic criteria, and the nation was—and still is—seen as something of value. National identity is expressed in "national" cultural practices. Whereas all the other ethnic groups in Austria can claim some kind of "national" tradition, deriving from their "homeland," the Roma lack these, because they have no common homeland, and the different groups have entered the territory from various neighboring countries. They have no common cultural tradition in the sense of a "national culture"—apart from, to a certain extent, the Romani language. But it was necessary to provide evidence for their ethnic tradition, and the Roma wanted to do this (see Hemetek, 2006). So this was the political agenda of the Romani political movement when ethnomusicology became involved by making first recordings and interviews.

What was intended in fieldwork was what Ian Russell called the "partnership model of fieldwork" (Russell, 2006) in an article about his long-term study of carol singing in the Sheffield region. Russell writes:

> The present research is firmly set in the "home" world (Stoeltje, 1999, 160–161), where reciprocity is manifested through implicit obligation, and at times by negotiation. I see it as a process that develops hand-in-hand with the building of relationships and growth of mutual trust over an extended period of time (Georges and Jones, 1980). Humanity and friendship become paramount and the researcher and his or her associates, partners, or consultants build relationships that are both interactive and balanced (Hood, 1971, 222; Titon, 1995, 288). The common interest in the musical traditions becomes a shared interest, as the distinctions between insider and outsider become transcended or tend to disappear altogether. This process is understood as a partnership (Myers, 1993, 12–13), with the responsibility for the integrity of the relationship lying firmly with the fieldworker.
>
> (Russell, 2006: 16)

The aspect of where research is located seems to very important. If the fieldwork is based "at home," and the consultants also live in the same country, geographically very close, experiences concerning the environment, the economic and political system, and so on, are shared. Consultants are well informed about research activities, and friendships develop out of mutual interests and long-term engagement. Thus it was easier to apply ethnomusicological results for the "benefit" of the Roma in Austria.

The Invention of Roma Ethnicity?

There is a long tradition in European folk music research which is very close to a setting that Timothy Cooley describes beautifully in his "musical ethnography of a specific Tatra Mountain region called Podhale" (a region in southern Poland) (Cooley, 2005). At the beginning of his book he offers a striking image that is programmatic for all that follows: a monument from 1903, with a bust of Dr. Tytus Chałubiński, a renowned physician from Warsaw, who in the late nineteenth century set up a sanatorium in Zakopane and actively promoted tourism in the Tatras. Chałubiński organized guided tours, and the guides involved were locals, the so-called Górale (highlanders), who also provided music and dance for tourists. Jan Krzeptowski-Sabała, the doctor's preferred mountain guide, is seated at the base of the monument in Górale in traditional costume, a folk violin in his left hand, a bow in his right. The intellectual with urban background and the "indigenous," prototypical, old-world Górale symbolize the forces that until then had shaped cultural practices in Podhale. One product of that process was the "invention of Górale ethnicity," according to Cooley (2005).

Inspired by rising nationalism, along with the invention of the nation-state in the eighteenth and nineteenth centuries, folk music researchers throughout Europe tried to provide evidence of their national heritage by collecting authentic folk music. And they tried to prove its uniqueness and differences from the music of other nations. They were always intellectuals from urban centers who went to the countryside, to the rural areas that were so "pure, untouched by civilization, so authentic and romantic." The people there were to a certain extent "exotic" and their music making seemed "untouched by the pollution of urban influences, of modernity, of change" (see Cooley, 2005: 5). Of course, all these seemingly untouched musics had always been subject to changes. The folk music researchers intended to safeguard this national heritage by writing it down or using other media for documentation.

There is an ideological aspect as well. Researchers convinced musicians that they were the pillars of national music tradition and that they should cherish that heritage. Musicians might have been astonished about that interest, but as these collectors were intellectuals and from a higher social class, were dedicated to their work, and proved to be *aficionados*, they were respected. The musicians might have obtained the feeling that their everyday music making had an additional quality besides its primary function in the community. This quality was underscored by the successful promotion activities of the researchers. They founded choirs and folklore groups in the urban centers to cultivate the heritage, they organized stage presentations and tours for the musicians, and they established institutions that promoted the music as well as research on and collections of this music. The development of tourism is an important aspect as well. The financial benefit obtained by the musicians themselves proved to be a very convincing argument, and they acted according to expectations. They saw their own musical practice from a new perspective, and the appreciation of certain aspects of their music making changed their own attitude toward it. The outsiders' judgment changed the insiders' attitude. What before had been everyday musical life now became a "traditional heritage" of special value.

Actually, the assumptions made here can be proven by many examples. Austrian examples include researchers such as Josef Pommer (1845–1918) or Konrad Mautner (1880–1924), urban intellectuals who discovered and promoted Alpine music, and by doing so invented what was probably not ethnicity, but at least a tradition.

All this seems to be long ago, but I ask myself if it is really so different from the first ethnomusicological approaches in Austria to Roma, including my own. The similarities might not be striking at first sight, but while thinking about this chapter and rereading Cooley's book, it came to my mind that there might be some. Ethnomusicologists present "their" musicians in public performances. The intellectual ethnomusicologist presents the—let us say—"authentic, prototypical" musician to an audience that probably hears this kind of music for the first time. The way this music is presented and the additional information that is given by the ethnomusicologist influence its perception and reception. This way of presentation also influences the musicians themselves. I would ask to what extent ethnomusicological activities have contributed to an invention of Roma ethnicity and Roma tradition.

The Croatian ethnomusicologist Naila Ceribašić says, "Scholars are nonetheless involved in the reproduction of their research subjects," and she continues by turning to the field of applied ethnomusicology: "Scholars are unavoidably implicated in their research subjects, understanding and respect are inscribed in the foundations of ethnomusicology, interest is inevitably translated into valuation, and consequently scholarly work is, willy-nilly, a kind of applied work as well" (Ceribašić, 2007: 4–5).

Two aspects of applied ethnomusicology seem to be important here (as categorized by Daniel Sheehy, 1992): developing new frameworks for musical performance, and feeding back musical models to the communities that created them (Sheehy, 1992). Naila Ceribašić is, like many other colleagues in Eastern Europe, constantly involved in festival productions of traditional music. To a certain extent, these are new frameworks for musical performance. And the feeding back of musical models also occurs constantly via the production of various media by ethnomusicologists.

Public Performance as a Promotion Model

The first presentation of Romani culture in Austria in 1990 was called "Exceptional Gypsies" (Figure 2.3). The entire presentation was meant as a counterpoint to prejudices and as support for Roma political activities. The only Austrian Roma organization at that time—*Roma Verein zur Förderung von Zigeunern*—was involved in its preparation, although it was actually two non-Roma intellectuals and one Roma artist who did the job: Mozes Heinschink, a linguist and expert in Romani

FIGURE 2.3 Poster for the event from 1990.

culture, Ilija Jovanović, a Romani poet, and me, an ethnomusicologist. The program consisted of different aspects of Romani culture: music, painting, literature, and film. The whole event lasted a month, for three evenings a week. The exhibition of paintings by Karl Stojka provided a background for film presentations followed by discussions, Romani literature with music, concerts, and a political podium discussion. The location was a gallery-pub of Vienna's alternative scene, and there was free admission to all events. Additionally, we had a book exhibition and other informational material. The diversity of Romani culture was presented by choosing four Romani groups: Lovari, Sinti, Burgenland Roma, and Kalderaš-Serbian Roma. Mostly the participants were Roma performers and artists living in Austria, but there were also some artists from abroad, including Mateo Maximoff from France and the ensemble Kalyi jag from Hungary.

The title "Exceptional Gypsies" obviously stemmed from the sociopolitical situation of the time concerning Roma, based on clichés and ignorance. The organizers felt that they had to use the word "Gypsy" (*Zigeuner* in German), although it was pejorative; if they had used Roma instead, nobody would have known what the event was about. The subject of the poster again is a cliché—a dancing Gypsy girl—and was created on the basis of an ethnological photograph by Czech researcher Eva Davidová. It was about how non-Roma see the Gypsies; it was the external perspective of an ethnic group meant to attract non-Roma.

It would be by no means politically correct or appropriate to advertise a Roma event in such a way today in Austria, and probably it was not at that time either. Austrian media covered the event very positively in general, but I do remember one article that criticized exoticism in particular, and of course this critique was correct.

The posters of the events that followed over the years were somewhat different and politically more correct. This was also due to the fact that in the meantime the Vienna-based Roma organization Romano Centro had been founded (in 1991) and took over responsibility for the content of the events. What had not changed was the ethnomusicological approach. In the organizing team, I was mainly responsible for the music. What links the outcome to the above-mentioned folk music research tradition is that it was the aim to present what was thought to be the "real," the "authentic" Roma music—music from internal musical practice that had not been performed for non-Roma before. One evening there was a presentation of the musical traditions of Serbian Roma. It was supposed to be spontaneous, and it was a kind of simulation of a wedding meal; pork was served, and there was a lot of dancing as well. Some Roma women were dressed very traditionally (Figure 2.4), and upon my request they did present some of the "old" songs. On the other hand, the musicians—a wedding *orkestra*—played music as they always did, a mix of melodies that appealed to the public and that were modern: El Condor Pasa, or the film music from *Dr. Zhivago*, along with many Serbian dance tunes.

The Lovari contribution was jazz for the opening of the event: Harri Stojka, the best-known Lovari musician at that time, felt no need to present any "ethnic" roots and played jazz standards. But his aunt Ceija Stojka, on the other hand, did present some of the rich vocal Lovari tradition, songs that she had sung to me before, during interviews, and that I asked her to present in public for the first time.

The process with the Burgenland Roma was similar. In preparation for the event there were negotiations with the consultants regarding what to present to the public. The outcome was a few songs in Romani, sung by Gisela Horvath, accompanied by the well-known Hungarian Gypsy music ensemble. This was also the first time that Burgenland Roma sang in Romani in public for a non-Roma audience. This Roma music from internal practice was very attractive for the non-Roma audience, and the presentations were successful.

One aspect of this event was a display of ethnicity for the first time for a non-Roma public in Austria. Ethnomusicology was in search of "authentic" musical material, and to a certain extent this did contribute to the invention of one aspect of Roma ethnicity—invention not in the sense of creating something that was not there before,

FIGURE 2.4 Serbian Roma women dancing at the event, 1990.

(Photo by Newald)

but in the sense of finding a new performance context and new meaning for the music. Applied ethnomusicology contributed to a process of identity construction in the outward self-identification of Roma, by using "otherness" as a trademark. It was the exotic element that was attractive. This happened in close cooperation with the musicians; they themselves thought that it was a good way to perform that "otherness" in order to make non-Roma understand something and to build bridges. Roma musicians have followed this road since then to a certain extent. Harri Stojka, the jazz musician who only presented jazz standards in 1990, has shown growing interest in "ethnic roots" and has produced CDs including traditional Lovari songs since then (for example, *Gitan Coeur* in 2000, or *Gypsy Soul/Garude apsa* in 2005; see www.harristojka.at); we now find Kalderaš weddings scenes in modern theater productions of Serbian Roma, like in *Liebesforschung* (see www.initiative.minderheiten.at), presented in 2007.

What is most striking is the development of Ruža Nikolić-Lakatos, a Romni (Roma woman) from the Lovari group with a huge repertory of traditional songs (see Figure 2.1). She was and is very much appreciated among her group for her singing abilities. She was absent in the 1990 presentation, because she refused to perform. She thought that her songs in the Lovari tradition were not meant for non-Roma. She was talked into changing her mind, and she became one of the most popular Roma singers in Austria. She performs old and new Lovari songs for non-Roma and she is appreciated for her "authenticity" and for presenting some "traditional heritage" of Romani culture. That is why in 2011 the Lovari songs have even been inscribed into the National Inventory of Intangible Cultural Heritage upon Ruža's application.[5] The UNESCO website describes them in the following way:

> Songs are an important part of the Lovara's cultural tradition. The history behind the name of this Roma group leads us back to their former occupation as "horse traders" (*Lovara*). Their songs are mostly about the family and community, yet the role of the individual and the former ways of life of the Lovara are also mirrored in them. These songs are like a reservoir for their language, as they contain phrases and metaphors typical of the Lovara, which have now (almost) become extinct in everyday life. The songs of the Lovara encompass two main genres: the slow, lyrical song and the dance song. Thanks to outstanding singers, such as Mongo Stojka, Ceija Stojka and the applicant Ruzsa Nikolic-Lakatos, new songs are continuously added to the repertoire.
> (http://immaterielleskulturerbe.unesco.at/cgi-bin/unesco/element.pl?eid=77&lang=en)

Of course this inscription has a political component. The Austrian UNESCO Inventory contains 62 elements (2013). We find very disparate elements, for example the *Landler* of the Innviertel, the Sword Dance of Dürrnberg, Classical Horsemanship and the High School of the Spanish Riding School, the Ötztal dialect, as well as "Roman"—the language of the Romani people of Burgenland. That minority expressions included in this list are extraordinary compared to the inventories of other states. It indicates that Austria sees the cultural expression of minorities as an outstanding part of Austria's culture, like all the other elements on the list. Maybe this is a first step toward inscribing Lovari culture into the cultural and collective memory[6] of Austria. So the change from the times when the prime minister could not see any "cultural markers," thus denying the Roma recognition as a *Volksgruppe*, seems to be quite remarkable.

The preconditions were the recognition of the Roma as an ethnic group, which finally happened in 1993, although the appointment of the consultative body that realized the actual implementation did not occur until 1995.

Although I looked very critically upon these activities in the past, there is evidence that applied ethnomusicology as an intercultural tool was to a certain extent successful. The public presentations themselves served as kind of mediation, because the audiences were mostly non-Roma and obviously wanted to learn something about Roma. As there was hardly any information available in public, the programs served as a tool to reduce prejudices and provide firsthand information to a certain extent. This was the beginning, and today the situation is quite different. Much has been published in ethnomusicology and other fields of research, and many Roma authors and artists in fine arts, film, and music are active in Austria. Researchers still are mostly non-Roma, although this also begins to change. There are now a few Roma in academia, and some of them are also politically active, for example in the above-mentioned NGO Romano Centro. The foundation of this NGO in 1991 was actually stimulated by *Ausnahmsweise Zigeuner*, because the need to have political representation in Vienna became obvious through this cultural presentation. Public interest, as well as cultural representation, was the stimulus for the foundation. Romano Centro has in the meantime become the best informed and most active Roma NGO, among many others that have since been founded in Austria. Its activities are manifold. The empowerment of Roma through political and educational approaches is on the agenda, as well as raising awareness of discrimination mechanisms in the majority society—historical and contemporary. In connection with music, there is an extraordinary initiative: In 2012 the Vienna Gypsy Music School was established by Romano Centro. It is still in a nascent state, but the main goals have been set. The school is open to Roma and non-Roma and tries to transmit some of the many different Roma music styles that are to be found in Vienna. The teaching methods will also draw from these traditions, which is quite a challenge because the models of transmission in Romani tradition and in Austrian music schools are as far apart as can be. But the students are also offered Western music theory in order to provide familiarity with the Austrian model of institutional music teaching. I do hope it will succeed, because for me it is a very convincing symbol of empowerment in the form of the institutionalization of intercultural mediation in music (for further information, see www.romano.centro.org).

The Bosnian Refugees: Sevdalinke as a Means of Relocation, or Nostalgia as a Tool for Indirect Intervention

In research, there are different ways to deal with war and exile scenarios connected to the civil war in the former Yugoslavia. Among many, let me just mention the book *War, Exile, Everyday Life: Cultural Perspectives*, which gives excellent examples. Svanibor Pettan's refugee project of applied ethnomusicology in Norway *Azra*—analyzed in this book—is very well known among ethnomusicologists as a model (Pettan, 1996). There are other approaches that include pedagogic activities, such as in refugee camps with children (see Pesek, 2009). I would call these "direct" interventions, as both have a clear target of integration. Additionally, Pesek's approach is very close to humanitarian work.

In the Austrian project presented here, a different strategy is involved. Having neither the infrastructure nor the framework nor the abilities to do something similar to the above-mentioned projects, this project was started with the main ethnomusicological method—fieldwork—and from that, a model was developed that I would call "indirect" intervention.

Bosnian refugees were forced migrants. The reason for migration is important for the relationship people have with their native country. Adelaida Reyes calls for attention to be given to this phenomenon, because it has consequences: "In studies of migrant minorities, the majority is automatically assumed to be the host society. But when the minorities under study are forced migrants, another majority forces itself into the picture. I call this a 'shadow majority' " (Reyes, 2001: 39).

Around 75,000 Bosnian refugees from the civil war in the former Yugoslavia, most of them Muslim Bosniaks, have been integrated in Austria since 1992. Integration does not mean that they have the status of Austrians; most of them still hold Bosnian citizenship. For many of the refugees, Austria seemed the best option because, due to working immigration since the 1960s, there were already a certain number of Bosnians resident there, and there were some family connections. Many Bosnian intellectuals fled to Vienna because they thought it would be a city that would give them an opportunity to survive intellectually. The memories of the Austro Hungarian monarchy and Vienna as a cultural and intellectual center for the Balkans seemed to play a role as well. Many of them were actually disappointed.

Some of the refugees came in organized transports to Austria and could not choose where to go, and so many people who formerly lived in rural areas were transferred to cities, and the other way around. Most of them could not speak German and found themselves in living conditions that were absolutely new to them.

The research activities began in 1994. From the very beginning there was probably an applied aspect of this research, because of personal involvement, which is very often a stimulus for application of results. Also influential were the activities of several NGOs that shared the regret of the disintegration of the former Yugoslavia and tried to argue and take political action to highlight the strong bonds between the different ethnicities, the obvious family ties between them, and the absurdity of neighbors shooting at each other. They were clearly opposed to the war and the violation of human rights. One organization was called Dialog, and many intellectuals from the former Yugoslavia were part of it.

The research fellow at the Institute was a Bosnian ethnomusicologist, a refugee herself, who was deeply involved, mentally and physically, in the refugee and war scenario. Sofija Bajrektarević came to our institute in 1994. She was a refugee from the city of Banja Luka, which was controlled by Bosnian Serb forces, while her husband Anis Bajrektarević was from Sarajevo and had a Muslim Bosniak ethnic background. Their ethnically mixed marriage was the reason for their flight. Sofija had given birth to a son in Austria. She had studied ethnomusicology in Sarajevo with Ankica Petrović and was trying to find an opportunity to use her scholarly knowledge in the new surroundings. As our institute had already established a focus on music and minorities in 1990 with the projects on Roma research, this seemed to be a fitting new challenge. We managed to get funding for two projects about the documentation of musical activities of war refugees from Bosnia and Herzegovina in Austria. Sofija's intention was to show that interethnic exchanges had been a fact for a long time in her country, especially in the field of traditional music. This approach was partly due to her own musical socialization, but also due to her ethnomusicological research in Bosnia. It seemed to be a very interesting proposition to investigate whether this was still the case in Austria in the Bosnian community. Sofija felt that this multicultural Bosnian musical soundscape was endangered by the war. One CD production by Ankica Petrović and Ted Levin suggested this in its title: *Bosnia: Echoes from an*

Endangered World; this served as a model and as a point of departure for our research in Austria. Most of the recordings published on the CD stem from a fieldwork trip of the authors during the years 1984–1985. The war was a strong motivation to publish it. Ted Levin writes in his introduction: "The musical voices presented on this recording have for the most part been silenced. Some of the performers have died, at least one has been wounded and one taken prisoner, the rest are scattered amidst the carnage of the War, their fate unknown, and unknowable" (Levin, 1993). The royalties from the sale of the CD were donated to charitable organizations involved in humanitarian aid in Bosnia.

The musical world that we were encountering among the Bosnian community in Austria was still alive, contrary to the "silenced voices" from the CD. And these voices wanted to be heard.

"When I Sing My Thoughts Fly to Bosnia"

The *sevdalinka* genre proved to be a musical symbol of this endangered world during the field research. Among the refugees there were also traditional singers. Their music, especially the *sevdalinke*—traditional Bosnian urban love songs—obtained a new significance for them and for the whole community in migration (see Bajrektarević and Hemetek, 1996; Hemetek and Bajrektarević, 2000). They used it, as Martin Stokes calls it "to relocate" themselves (see below).

The quotation "When I sing my thoughts fly to Bosnia" is from Ševko Pekmezović, one of these singers (Figure 2.5). He comes from Kozluk, a small village near the Serbian border, where the entire Muslim Bosniak community (1,200 people out of 1,500) were forced to leave by the Serbian authorities in 1992. This happened often during the war and was cynically called "ethnic cleansing." What was formerly a multiethnic country was to be transformed into a monoethnic one by forcing people to leave or by killing or deporting them. The people from Kozluk fortunately stayed alive. By chance, all of them were transferred to Austria and achieved refugee status. Almost no one spoke German. They were taken care of by different NGO organizations in different parts of Austria. Most of them stayed in Austria and integrated themselves into Austrian society to a certain extent; some of them have Austrian citizenship by now. *Sevdalinke* very often deal with unfulfilled love, but also with concrete places or historical incidents. For a long time these songs have been associated with Bosnia; they were *the* form of Bosnian musical expression in general and people identified with them greatly, even before the war. During and after the war these songs were mainly associated with the Muslim Bosniak population of Bosnia, due to the "oriental" melismatic melodic structure and their emergence during Ottoman rule. Before the war, *sevdalinke* used to have an interethnic quality because there were *sevdalinke* in many towns, and Muslim, Croatian, Serbian, and other ethnicities in Bosnia all practiced *sevdalinke*. Therefore many of the refugees in Austria chose that genre for their musical identification.

Another reason might be that there really are very specific places mentioned in them, places that people had been to and that they liked. So for them these songs symbolized their former home and functioned as a means of "relocation" (Stokes, 1997). Here is one example, sung by Ševko Pekmezović.

FIGURE 2.5 Ševko Pekmezović.
(Photo by Rudolf Pietsch, Archive of the Institute of Folk Music Research and Ethnomusicology)

Dunjaluče
Ševko Pekmezović: Voc.; Himzo Tulić: Saz
Recording: December 14, 1995, Gerlinde Haid, cultural presentation in Vienna
1. *Dunjaluče, golem ti si,*
Sarajevo, seir ti si
Baščaršijo, gani ti si
haj, a Vratniče, gazil ti si.
2. *Oj, Bistriče, strmen ti si*
Ćemaluso, duga ti si,
Latinluče, ravan ti si,
Haj, Bezistane, mračan ti si.
3. *Tašlihane, širok ti si,*
lijepa Maro, lijepa ti si,
dosta si me napojila,
haj, od dušmana zaklonila.
Oh World, Oh People
1. Oh world, oh people, how great you are
Sarajevo, you're so beautiful
Baščaršija*, you're so rich,

ahay, but you Vratnik*, you're gorgeous.
2. Oy, Bistrik*, you are so steep,
Ćemaluša**, you're so long,
Latinluk*, you are so flat,
ahay, you Bezistan***, you're dark.
3. Tašlihan*, you're so wide,
pretty Mara, you're so beautiful
you made me drunk enough,
ahay, you sheltered me from my foes.
* Baščaršija, Vratnik, Bistrik, Latinluk, Tašlihan:
the famous parts of ancient Sarajevo's downtown
** Ćemaluša: the former main street of Sarajevo
*** Bezistan: the Turkish-style marketplace under a single roof

(from Bajrektarević and Hemetek, 1996: 61)

The three verses documented here manifest the special quality reflected in the city of Sarajevo. This is very concrete, although it is based on the past, but these texts make it clear why Ševko says that when he sings he has the feeling of a film being shown in his head and he can see everything he sings about. He did sing *sevdalinke* before he came to Austria, but now he sings them to remember home in the situation of displacement. Ševko also started to present these songs to an Austrian public, in order to make Austrians understand that Bosnia is not only a country of war but also of culture.

This was actually the moment when the research work became applied work. Before that, we had documented his repertory, which was huge (about 300 different *sevdalinke*). There had always been the option of a publication, but it was still in the planning stage. Ševko liked the recording sessions. He usually came to the institute, because his housing conditions did not permit recording in his apartment. In order to be able to sing as an expression of enjoying himself, he usually brought some food and drink to simulate a "real" Bosnian evening. After a while, Ševko spoke about presenting his songs to an Austrian public. He had done so already on two occasions by including his songs in events that featured other contributions as well. He wanted to go on working with a format that would be dedicated to Bosnian music alone. Together with Ševko and other musicians whom we had met during the research, we developed a format of a cultural presentation, which in another article I labeled as an "informative strategy of intercultural encounter" in the context of minorities. One principle of this type of presentation is to let the majority participate and to try to make listeners understand the differences and similarities (Hemetek, 2001b). It was called a "Bosnian evening" and was first presented to the public on December 15, 1995, coinciding with the ratification of the Dayton agreement. It consists mainly of *sevdalinke*, several types of which are sung by different performers, none of whom had performed in public in Bosnia. The program was structured in such a way that we tried to create an atmosphere in which performers and audience were both actively involved. We did this by using a specific performance concept with no clear distinction between stage and audience, by singing two songs together as part of the program (the texts and translations were passed around), and by avoiding amplification. The audience and the performers should feel as if they were part of a Bosnian gathering. There were pieces of music as well as pieces of literature, in German as well as in Bosnian, and the similarities as well as differences between the two cultures were pointed out. The bilingual concept was important, because Austrians as well as Bosnians were always meant to be in the audience.

Here is one example from the program. The lyrics of the following song were actually written by the German poet Heinrich Heine. It was translated into Bosnian by an unknown author and it became one of the best known *sevdalinke* in Bosnia. We used it in the program because of its German roots, because of its contents, which characterize the atmosphere in Bosnia in the nineteenth century, and because our singer Ševko Pekmezović liked to sing it very much. His performance gives an impression to the Austrian audience of the musical parameters of *sevdalinke*.

Kraj tanana šadrvana

Ševko Pekmezović: vocal.; Himzo Tulić: saz
Recording: December 14, 1995, by Gerlinde Haid at the premiere of our program in Vienna
Transcription: Sofija Bajrektarević
Text
   Kraj tanana šadravana,
   đe žubori voda živa,
   šetala se svakog dana,
   sultanova šćerka mila.
   Svakog dana jedno ropče,
   stajalo kraj šadrvana,
   kako vrijeme prolazilo,
   sve je ropče blijeđe bilo.

Zapita ga jednog dana,
sultanova šćerka mila:
"Kazuj momče odakle si,
iz plemena kojeg li si!?"
"Ja se zovem El-Muhamed,
iz plemena starih Azra,
što za ljubav život gube,
i umiru kada ljube."
German original version by Heinrich Heine:
DER ASRA
Täglich ging die wunderschöne
Sultanstochter auf und nieder
Um die Abendzeit am Springbrunnen
Wo die weißen Wasser plätschern.
Täglich stand der junge Sklave
Um die Abendzeit am Springbrunnen
Wo die weißen Wasser plätschern;
Täglich ward er bleich und bleicher.
Eines Abends trat die Fürstin
Auf ihn zu mit raschen Worten:
Deinen Namen will ich wissen,
Deine Heimat, deine Sippschaft!
Und der Sklave sprach: ich heiße
Mohamet, ich bin aus Yemmen,
Und mein Stamm sind jene Asra,
Welche sterben, wenn sie lieben.
English Translation:
By the subtle Sadrvan[7],
where the lively water hums,
daily was the promenade,
by the Sultan's daughter dear.
Every day one youthful slave,
was standing nearby.
So, as time passed by,
the youngster grew ever more pale.
He was asked one day,
by the Sultan's daughter dear;
"Tell me, youngster, where are you from,
and to which tribe do you belong!?"
"My name is El-Muhammed,
of the old Azra tribes,
who are prepared, in the name of love,
to sacrifice their very lives,
and die when they kiss."

(Bajrektarević and Hemetek, 1996: 63–64)

This program was invited to some festivals, was presented in Austrian villages to aid the integration of Bosnian refugees, and even was invited abroad by a Bosnian organization in Reutlingen, Germany. As a follow-up, some of the musicians were featured in TV documentaries and were invited to other festivals. But this only lasted up to a certain point in time. After the political consolidation in Bosnia and the integration of the Bosnian refugees in Austria, or their repatriation (a few cases), our program fell into oblivion. It did not seem to be needed any longer. *Sevdalinke* have other connotations today; they are very much used for the construction of "national" identity in Bosnia, and in Austria they have become part of the world music scene as well as the disco scene in various cross-over experiments.[8] Ševko still sings "his" traditional *sevdalinke*, but no longer in public.

In the case of this project, it is difficult to evaluate the results of indirect intervention. There were no political consequences, as in the case of the Roma; whether there have been any individual effects is difficult to judge, although I think public awareness of the musical abilities of the singers involved had a positive effect on them and probably helped them to cope with their difficult situation. Again, the whole project had a lot to do with the "partnership model of fieldwork." The researchers were personally involved, and the consultants wanted to obtain the attention of the public. This went hand in hand with intercultural mediation. *Sevdalinke* served as a tool to improve the understanding of the cultural background of the Bosnian refugees among the Austrian majority. And we produced material that can be used in different areas: recordings, videos, photos, texts, and publications. Two students from our university who were refugees themselves wrote their master's theses on the topic of *sevdalinka*, using part of our material (see Kovinjalo, 2007; Rešidbegović, 2002). We accumulated quite a lot of literature on the topic, and our institute is now known for its expertise in this field; in many cases we served as mediators in school projects.

Our research culminated in several publications, one of which is now viewed as a historical document: the CD *Sevdah in Vienna* (Bajrektarević and Hemetek, 1996, with extensive notes in three languages). Some people are very happy when they find it, as it signifies nostalgia to them. University students of Bosnian origin like to discover their roots by using our archive. What we definitely achieved was the documentation of the musical expressions of an endangered world at a certain time, sensing the need that appeared under the given circumstances.

Challenging "Ethnicity": Immigrants from Turkey in Vienna

This section deals with research activities that focused on the urban area. The results come from research projects during the years 2005–2010, which means from a much later time period than the two case studies above. This reveals a shift of research interests within the institute, from research on certain groups with somehow defined constructed identities to the urban area, which is by nature in itself diverse, not only ethnically. The method of applying the results has also changed to a certain extent.

The Construction of Place, Ethnicity, and Identity Through Music in Diaspora

"Amongst the countless ways in which we 'relocate' ourselves, music undoubtedly has a vital role to play. The musical event, from collective dances to the act of putting a cassette or CD into a machine, evokes and organizes collective memories and present experiences of place with an intensity, power and simplicity unmatched by any other social activity. The 'places' constructed through music involve notions of difference and social boundary" (Stokes, 1997: 3). What Martin Stokes says here is, of course, not only true for immigrants; it works for the dominant group as well. But especially in the situation of migration, when a person experiences dislocation, insecurity, constant challenge, unfamiliarity, and discrimination, it might become more meaningful and more important to "relocate" oneself by means of music. Stokes's argument goes further when he says, "I would argue that music is socially meaningful, not entirely but largely because it provides means by which people recognize identities and places, and the boundaries which separate them" (Stokes, 1997: 5).

My findings do confirm these theses, and I quote them because they say a great deal about the motivation behind the music making of immigrants. I would also argue that they say a lot about what kind of music these immigrant groups practice.

I am far from proposing any essentialist interpretation, because music is what any social group considers it to be, and music styles per se do not represent any denoted ethnicity. But on the other hand, one cannot deny that ethnicity is represented by music. *Ethnicity* is, of course, a problematic term, and there have been many discussions about it, especially in a discipline that uses the prefix *ethno-* in its designation, like ethnomusicology. Adelaida Reyes argues that it should not to be omitted, but defined it in a way that makes it useful for interdisciplinary approaches. Reyes mentions this in connection with research in the urban area: "Groups labelled ethnic are a social reality and ... they have come to constitute a structural category in urban social organization. It appears, therefore, that we may have to live with the term a while longer" (Reyes-Schramm, 1979: 17). Stokes does not question the term either, but he does question its definition: "Ethnicities are to be understood in terms of the construction, maintenance and negotiation of boundaries, and not of the putative social 'essences' which fill the gaps within them" (Stokes, 1997: 6). I share the opinion of many anthropologists (see Asad, 1973) that the construction of ethnicities can only be understood by including power relations in the analysis. It is very important to consider insiders' and outsiders' positions in constructing ethnicities. In the case of discriminated people, the definition of outsiders very often contributes to their self-definition. The group in power—the dominant group—defines who is "different."

If a group is constantly perceived by others as "different" because of their ethnic background, its members might begin to stress markers of ethnic difference in their self-awareness. This might also happen in music making, and especially in public performance. Therefore performance in diaspora seems to me to be another very important aspect of the whole topic—the more so because performed music is very often the object of documentation by ethnomusicologists, including my own research. Musical performance often functions as a representation of ethnicity, "otherness," and "difference." One recent publication on the topic, the book *Musical Performance in the Diaspora* (Ramnarine, 2007), is very useful in this context because it provides profound insight into possible ways of interpreting the phenomenon of "administering ethnicity" by performance. And it is about "how identity is shaped and constructed through and as a result of performance" (Johnson, 2007: 71).

But of course the concept of diaspora itself is ambivalent and needs critical analysis. We find a critical approach in cultural studies by Ien Ang (2001, 2003), who has argued that the diaspora concept paradoxically maintains the very logic of the state that the concept is meant to critique. She has written:

> While the transnationalism of diasporas is often taken as an implicit point of critique of the territorial boundedness and internally homogenizing perspective of the nation-state, the limits of diaspora lie precisely in its own assumed boundedness, its inevitable tendency to stress its internal coherence and unity, logically set apart from "others." Diaspora formations transgress the boundaries of the nation-state on behalf of a globally dispersed "people" ... but paradoxically this transgression can only be achieved by drawing a boundary around the diaspora.
>
> (Ang, 2003: 142)

In her further arguments she draws the conclusion that, paradoxically, "the politics of diaspora is exclusionary as much as it is inclusionary, just like that of the nation" (Ang, 2003: 144).

Tom Solomon builds on her arguments when approaching the communities from Turkey in Germany and says:

> It is the tendency which Ang identifies to stress the 'internal coherence and unity' of diasporic social formations that makes it possible for people to confidently speak and write about, for example, a 'Turkish diaspora' (about 24,100 hits on Google for this phrase as of 1 March 2008) in popular and academic discourse. The problem emerges when this kind of analytic shorthand begins to take on a life of its own, as if it refers to a coherent thing out there in the real world that one can point to, rather than a useful abstraction for what is actually a complex social formation full of internal tensions and contradictions, with multiple intersecting histories, discourses, and practices. While paying attention to the sounds of diasporic groups as echoes of diversity within their host societies, we should not forget to listen for the voices of diversity within diasporic groups themselves.
>
> (Solomon, 2008: 78)

The attention to "voices of diversity" within a certain immigrant group is an important point of departure for the following findings.

The Urban Area as a Field of Research: Changing Perspectives

Adelaida Reyes, one of the pioneers of urban ethnomusicology, gives a very useful theoretical background to the distinction between music *in the city* and music *of the city* (Reyes, 2007: 17). Whereas "music in the city" means that the city itself is no more than a passive ingredient with no significant role in explanation, "music of the city" requires a theoretical and methodological framework that gives full value to its complexity. The city is included in the research, either as the context or as the object of the study.

Adelaida Reyes sees a clear connection between the concepts of research on minorities and those of urban ethnomusicology: due to immigration the urban area naturally consists of different, diverse groups. She suggests approaching this diversity as a single organism.

The first research projects in our institute on the topic of music and minorities were more in the tradition of the "music in the city" approach. These were ethnographic studies, focused on specific communities. Both of the above-mentioned projects were located partly in the urban area (most of the Roma and Bosnian refugees also live in Vienna), but the city as a complex organism was not their focus. This approach has changed during the last few years, and in two more recent research projects we tried to grasp a little of the general complex reality of immigrants' music making in the city and of the surrounding conditions and economic aspects as well. The first one, called "Music Making of Immigrants in Vienna" (2005–2006) served to a certain extent as a pilot for the second one: "Embedded industries—Immigrant Cultural Entrepreneurs in Vienna" (2007–2009). The latter was an interdisciplinary study in which ethnomusicology was the partner discipline of sociology and ethnology.

The music making of immigrants from Turkey was part of these investigations, and I want to concentrate on this in the following section due to the fact that immigrants from Turkey are the main focus of xenophobia in Austrian society. Approximately 40,000 immigrants with Turkish citizenship reside in Vienna. Figures comparing various immigrant populations show that they are the second-largest group. About another 30,000 have been naturalized, which makes a total of 70,000.

The officially verifiable heterogeneity of the Turkish population derives from different ethnic and religious backgrounds. Turks, Kurds, and a very few Armenians form three main ethnic and religious groups in Vienna that are registered officially as Turkish citizens. The three main religious backgrounds of immigrants from Turkey are Sunni, Alevi, and very few Christian Orthodox (see Figure 2.6; for further information on the Alevi, see, for example, Erol, 2008).

Another significant difference among the immigrants from Turkey in Vienna is social class. Hande Sağlam is of the opinion that social class is more important in determining identity than ethnicity or religion (see Sağlam, 2007). There are immigrants with Anatolian backgrounds, with usually low educational status, as well as intellectuals from Istanbul. Most of these immigrants came to Vienna to work during the 1960s and 1970s. They were reunited with their families after some years and today we find second and third generations of these first immigrants. The intellectuals are mostly students who decided to stay.

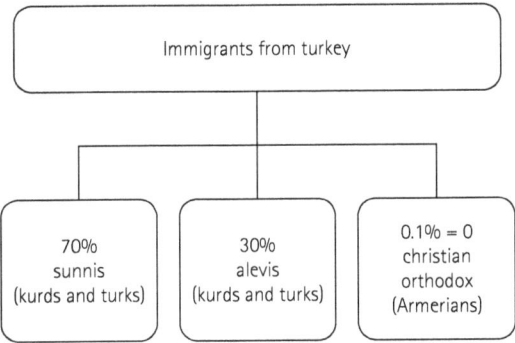

FIGURE 2.6 From Sağlam 2007:64.

In spite of that diversity, there are prejudices among the dominant society against *the* "Turkish immigrant," including the following: that they are backward and conservative, that the women are subordinate, and that they are Islamic fundamentalists—and therefore dangerous and not willing to integrate. These prejudices are not new, but they gained a new intensity after 9/11, when Islamophobia rose extraordinarily, and also after the renewed debate on Turkey joining the European Union (2006–2007). Certain political parties in Austria use xenophobia to collect votes, and we find highly racist posters and slogans before elections, such as *"Wien darf nicht Istanbul werden"* (Vienna must not become Istanbul) or *"Daham statt Islam"* (Home instead of Islam). Usually it is Turkish immigrants, as well as those from Africa, at whom this aggression is aimed.

One can encounter these racist prejudices everywhere, even among Austrian students. One possible ethnomusicological strategy is to do some research on the music of these immigrants in order to have well-founded information to argue against these prejudices.

Via the two research projects on immigrants' music making in Vienna mentioned above, including a focus on immigrants from Turkey, Hande Sağlam, a researcher born in Istanbul, was integrated into the institute's staff. This was extremely important, because her views and approaches added a great deal to the quality of the research. She challenged our former concepts of ethnicity and collectivity by insisting on considering individuality in music making to a much greater extent. She influenced the theories and methods, and also made contacts much easier because of her language abilities.

Studies from Germany on the topic also served as inspiration. In Germany, immigration from Turkey started much earlier than in Austria, and the percentage of immigrants from Turkey is much higher.[9] There is a lively exchange between the diasporic communities from Turkey in Germany and Austria.

We found out that many of the immigrants' organizations are active in fighting discrimination on very different levels. A few try to re-ethnicize and to fundamentalize their people as a reaction to discrimination. The majority try to promote intercultural dialogue on many levels, including teaching and promoting Turkish music.

One of the research strategies was close cooperation with some musicians. The difference from the aforementioned projects is that there was already an infrastructure of very active NGOs, such as the Saz-Verein, an organization founded by Mansur Bildik, a virtuoso of the *saz*, the Anatolian long-necked lute. He is of Kurdish-Anatolian origin, his religion is Alevi,[10] and he migrated from Turkey to Austria for artistic reasons. Mansur Bildik writes:

> In the 1970s my concert tours led me to Europe. By chance I came to Austria. I should have got married to a Turkish girl who lived, however, in Vorarlberg. But I ended up in Vienna. Since 1980 I have been living in this city and since 1990 I have been an Austrian citizen. First of all, it was the music which brought me to Austria: on the occasion of concerts, I was often approached by lovers of Turkish music, as there was a lack of *saz* players in Vienna at that time.
>
> (Bildik and Fuchs, 2008: 23)

Mansur Bildik dedicated his life to teaching the instrument that he appreciates so much. He uses it as a cultural "ambassador," but it is important to note that his main approach is intercultural communication and some of the principles of his religion.

> Non-musical aims like humanity, respect and tolerance play an important role in his life. So does coexistence in music, and in this case he also attaches importance to innovative border crossings beyond traditional Turkish music; this aesthetic coexistence is for him a symbol of social living together. Mansur's *alla turca* interpretations of Mozart (Flosdorf and Marte 2006, 21p.) and performances together with the folk group Hotel Palindrone or with the Austrian pop musician Rainhard Fendrich were exemplary for such crossovers.
>
> (Fuchs 2001, quotation from Bildik and Fuchs, 2008: 26)

Self-organization on the basis of Austrian law means—as we have learned from the Roma case—to found an officially recognized organization (called a *Verein* in Austria; see Figure 2.7). So Mansur took this step in order to realize his visions.

An important step on this way was the founding of the *saz* association 14 years ago, in 1993. The association organises *saz* lessons, workshops and concerts. The lessons

FIGURE 2.7 Logo of the Saz Association.

and periodical student concerts take place in the Amerling-Haus cultural centre. It belongs to the cultural initiative Spittelberg, houses a museum and numerous alternative cultural associations and supports minority cultures. The *saz* association harmonizes with this concept of a socially engaged enthusiasm for cultural diversity.

(Bildik and Fuchs, 2008: 25)

Mansur Bildik (Figure 2.8) continues his activities in the Amerling-Haus. Recently the center was seriously threatened by financial problems. Mansur was engaged in many cultural activities for fundraising and showing solidarity, for example in an event called "Vielfalt statt Monokultur" (Diversity Instead of Monoculture) in June 2014.

It is important to note that from the very beginning, teaching activities were the focus of Mansur Bildik's interest. It is intercultural communication via an instrument that he seeks, and his professional musical ability enables him to use this tool. The applied aspect of our research was to promote Mansur Bildik's activities on the university level and in other institutional contexts. The musical background of Mansur Bildik is traditional music from Turkey, although he crosses musical borders very frequently.

FIGURE 2.8 Mansur Bildik playing the Saz in Amerlinghaus, June 7, 2014.

(Photo by Ursula Hemetek)

FIGURE 2.9 R-Kan.

(from http://profile.myspace.com/December 2006)

But there are other musical activities of immigrants from Turkey that are far from the traditional context.

Wien 10 (Vienna 10)

This is the title of a hip-hop song and refers to the 10th district of Vienna, where many of the Turkish immigrants live. They were part of the mass labor immigration from 1964 onward that followed the initial recruitment of workers by European countries. Now there is a second and even a third generation, and they are still seen as Turkish immigrants, although they were born in Austria.

> R-Kan [Figure 2.9] was born in 1987 in Vienna. He is the youngest son of a Turkish immigrant family. At primary school he was discriminated against because of his immigrant background. At secondary school the situation changed completely because 98% of the pupils were foreigners, and he was chosen as the class representative.
> He started to write his own texts in 2002. Then he left school and was totally lost. Two years later, he changed his life completely and made a new start as a hip-hop singer. His lyrics show us the reality of life of a large part of the second generation and their so-called "public ghetto" in Vienna.
>
> (Sağlam, 2008: 43–44).

In one of his most successful songs he says: "*Ich bin der Junge, den jeder hasste, keine wollte mich featuren, obwohl mein Rap passte*" (I am the guy/that everybody hates/nobody wants to present me/even though my rap fits). This sentence expresses his bicultural existence and its consequences very clearly. The "guy that everybody hates" is not just the protest of a young generation, but clearly points to the racism he faces every day in Vienna.

R-Kan sings only in German. His German is better than his Turkish. In an interview he said that he is not really able to write and sing in Turkish.

Here is one of his most successful songs, "Wien 10!"

Wien 10!, Private Recording by R-Kan in 2007
(from Sağlam, 2008: 44–45)

R-Kan: *Wien 10!*	R-Kan: Vienna 10!
Sprich mein Name richtig, es ist R strich	Say my name correctly, it is R-dash
Ja, ja stich dich	Yes, yes stab yourself
Du kannst mich hassen aber fick dich	You can hate me, but fuck yourself
Wien 10 und meine Jungs, mehr brauch ich nicht	Vienna 10 (district) and my boys, I don't need anything else
Du willst mich dissen aber Junge traust dich nicht	You want to diss me but you don't trust yourself
Auch ohne Weinen fließen meine Tränen	My tears flow even if I don't cry
Ich halte meinen Kopf hoch meinen Rap kann mir keiner nehmen	I keep my head up nobody can take my rap away from me
Ich bin der Junge den jeder hasste	I am the guy that everybody hates
Keine wollte mich featuren obwohl mein Rap passte	Nobody wanted to feature me even though my rap fits
Ich bin weit gekommen, denn ich geh mein Weg	I've achieved a lot because I go my own way
Dersim 62 das ist meine Mentalität	Dersim 62, that's my mentality
Ich weiß woher ich komme, bleib wo ich bin	I know where I come from, I stay where I am
Otto-Probst 7, das ist mein Lebenssinn	Otto-Probst 7 that's the meaning of my life
Wenn ich sterbe, werden mir die Flügel wachsen	When I die, I am going to grow wings
Zu schnell gelebt, ich war schon zu früh erwachsen	Lived too fast, I was grown up too early
R strich Kann, merk dir diesen guten Jungen	R dash Kan, remember this good guy

Wien das ist meine Stadt ich bums aus meine Lunge	Vienna is my city I scream it out of my lungs
Dieses Jahr, dieses Jahr werd ich Star, werd ich Star	This year, this year I'll be a star, I'll be a star
Wien macht mich berühmt ich bin ein guter Junge	Vienna is making me famous, I am a good guy
Es wird hart, es wird hart, ich bleib stark, ich bleib stark	It will be hard it will be hard, I stay strong I stay strong
Wien macht mich berühmt, ich bin ein guter Junge	Vienna is making me famous I am a good guy
Dieses Jahr, dieses Jahr werd ich Star, werd ich Star	This year, this year I'll be a star I'll be a star
Wien macht mich berühmt ich bin ein guter Junge	Vienna is making me famous I am a good guy
Es wird hart, es wird hart ich bleib stark, ich bleib stark	It will be hard, it will be hard I stay strong I stay strong
Wien macht mich berühmt, ich bin ein guter Junge	Vienna is making me famous I am a good guy
Ich hab keine Lehre und auch keine Schule	I don't have an occupation and no school either
Was bringt mir Ehre, Mädchen schauen auf teure Schuhe	What brings me honour, girls look at expensive shoes
Doch ich scheiß darauf und klettre weiter nach oben	But I don't give a fuck about it and I keep climbing upwards
In meiner Nachbarschaft sind die Kids auf Drogen	In my neighborhood the kids are on drugs
Mein Stadt war für mich ein großer Erfolg	My city was a big success for me
In Wien bin (ich) ein Star für das ganze Volk	In Vienna I'm a big star for all the people
Egal welcher Bezirk, jeder liebt mich	Doesn't matter in which district, everybody loves me

(From: Sağlam 2008:44–45)

Musically, this is one style of Turkish hip-hop youth culture, an international phenomenon, common among Turkish immigrants of the second generation in German-speaking countries. Tom Solomon has done extensive research on the genre in Germany. The development in Germany is important for the Austrian scene as well (see Solomon, 2008). The scene is diverse, different languages are used, and different ethnic backgrounds are involved:

> Kurds, Alevis, Germans, and members of other nationalities/ethnic groups have been important in the creation of 'Turkish rap' in Germany. For example, a DJ often credited with popularizing the use of samples and motifs from Turkish folk music on a rap record, DJ Derezon from the (now-defunct) group Islamic Force, is the son of a German mother and a Spanish father (Kaya, 2001: 194). He was born in Kreuzberg, a district in Berlin especially known for having a high concentration of Turkish migrants, but also home to migrants from many other countries. "Turkish rappers" in Germany who do have roots in Turkey may in fact prefer to engage with local multi-ethnic hip-hop communities where German is the *lingua franca*, rather than privilege their "Turkishness," and so, like rappers Kool Savas (whose father is Turkish and mother is German) and Eko Fresh (born in Köln of Turkish parents, grew up in Mönchengladbach near Düsseldorf), rap primarily or only in German, even if they are claimed by others as belonging to the community of "Turkish rappers" in Germany.
>
> (Solomon, 2008: 78–79)

Tom Solomon also points to the fact that a number of "Turkish" rappers in Germany are Kurds but choose to be "Turkish" in their artistic performance. R-Kan actually also has Kurdish roots. His mentioning of "Dersim" is a clear indicator.[11]

Solomon points out that rap music and hip-hop's visual style function as a strategy for cultural intervention, using the "resistant" position associated with this style to make statements about racism and other social problems both in Europe and in Turkey. Rap music and its visual images are a strategy for cultural intervention. There is a "resistant" position associated with this style that makes statements about racism and other social problems (see Solomon, 2008: 85). This image of "Turkish rap," first established in Germany, also is to be noticed in Austria. Actually, this music style obviously fits for expressing protest. There is a very clear message in the mentioned example. The political implication is very clear and outspoken: R-Kan is fighting for his right to be considered as a local, as a citizen of the country that is his birthplace. He fights by singing a song.

These were just two examples within a much broader range of musical activities of immigrants from Turkey in Vienna: from Western classical music (e.g., university students) via all kinds of popular music, world music, and jazz, to Davul and Zurna played at weddings. Likewise, diverse is the self-definition of the human beings who are labeled as Turks by the majority. Why should someone who was born in Vienna, who has never been to Turkey, and who does not even speak the language be considered a Turk? Even Mansur Bildik, who identifies with the musical traditions that he learned in Turkey, feels Viennese and makes use of the musical possibilities of a city that has gained the label of the City of Music due to its musical diversity.

Challenging the Discourses

It is not so easy to clearly identify and categorize applied aspects in this case. And of course it is debatable whether there are any. To my mind, the role of research in humanities is not to find out the "truth," but to add new perspectives and different views to the canon of knowledge. In doing so, we should not avoid taking up clear positions. As Hermann Bausinger says convincingly, "If there are burning problems, hurting, scaring and depressing people and opening up old sores, there is no chance to escape to so-called pure science—you have to make options and say yes or no or you have at least to point to the practical implications of your scientific interests" (Bausinger, 1996: 288).

There are burning problems in Austrian society, and immigrants from Turkey face them very often when confronted by exclusion, racism, and stereotyping, in relation to the employment situation, in housing, on a legal level, and in everyday activities. In the Austrian media we constantly find discourses using ideologically charged terms such as "*Parallelgesellschaft*" (parallel society) and "*Leitkultur*" (dominant/mainstream culture), and the discussion about "integration" tries to suggest that the "Turks" cannot be integrated because they are not willing to, due to their "Islamist" background. They are so different that it would be best to send them "home." These are not only arguments used by the radical right-wing party in Austria; they are also part of the official language of politicians in office. I think it is important to participate in discourses—scholarly and public—in order to clarify some things at least. Our research results suggest that in Vienna there is no such unified category as "the Turks," but rather a population with diverse backgrounds, cultural traditions, and senses of identity, including rural Anatolian as well as urban intellectual. We can also prove that the share of "Islamist" activists is about 2% and that 98% of the population of immigrants from Turkey do not much differ in their approach to religion from most Austrians who are Roman Catholic. In other words, many Muslims and Roman Catholics in Vienna do not live active religious lives. And we can prove that for many people who are labeled "the Turks" there is no other "home" than Austria, because they were born here and do not have stronger ties to any other country. By doing this research and by making the results public, we try to add to discourses and to change attitudes. Of course, our studies are "only" about music. But, as I have tried to argue in this chapter, music is a powerful instrument on many levels concerning minorities. It is important to point toward individual identity constructions that are "hybrid" and "multiple," as we have learned from cultural studies, and it is important to point toward the great potential of individuals who have had the experience of being socialized in more than one culture. Elka Tschernokoscheva puts it this way:

> . . . for me the defining feature of "minority culture" is the fact that it implies more than one perspective (i.e., it is multiperspectival). Minorities are in a position to look at a problem from more than one angle; they know that there is more than one truth. They know that the familiar and the unfamiliar are not diametrically opposed to one another, because one can appear within the other; familiar and foreign elements can merge and may even become inseparable.
>
> (Tschernokoscheva, 2008: 20)

It is debatable whether studies of this kind can have an influence on political reality. I think it is important to find niches of application. In our case it is pedagogy. At our university we teach students of music pedagogy who will become music teachers in their working life. They will face a classroom situation with children of diverse "ethnic" backgrounds, and it is our task to prepare them for this situation.

By conveying to them the results of our studies, we might contradict possible stereotypes in their minds; by providing personal contact with musicians like the aforementioned, we might open up their minds to appreciate musical diversity, and this might enable them to deal respectfully with immigrant children and make use of the great potential that lies in their "multiperspectival" qualities. Although this might seem a small-scale strategy, the preliminary evidence suggests that this research and application venue are profitable in the long term and deserve to be continued and further elaborated.

Conclusions

I have tried to argue in this chapter that there is considerable potential in ethnomusicology, and especially in minority studies, for intercultural communication. Ethnomusicology is suited to working in this way, because music has proven itself to be a powerful instrument of constructing and conveying identities and of "relocation." This potential can be used in applied ethnomusicology.

The three case studies presented in this chapter show three different strategies embedded in their respective sociopolitical circumstances. They also show the development of discourses and methods within the discipline at one specific institution—the Institute of Folk Music Research and Ethnomusicology at the University of Music and Performing Arts Vienna—over a time span of the past 25 years. To a certain extent, they mirror the international discourses in ethnomusicology and minority studies.

The relevance of minority studies in applied ethnomusicology (and vice versa) was another point of departure for this chapter. According to Svanibor Pettan (2008), the growing interest in applied ethnomusicology is often related to exactly those groups of people who are the focus of contemporary ethnomusicologists' research, which he lists as minorities, diasporas, ethnic groups, immigrants, and refugees. This list is based upon the special situation of three states created out of the former Yugoslavia, but is of relevance for Europe as a whole. The common denominator for all these groups of people is that they face a dominant group, and suffer discrimination on different levels. Svanibor Pettan (2008) further argues that applied ethnomusicology has very much to do with the empowerment of such groups. Although the scope of applied ethnomusicology seems to be much broader, in relation to the aforementioned groups of people this is certainly one important aspect of applied work, if not *the* most important one. Therefore the development of the international forum for these discourses in ethnomusicology—the Study Group Music and Minorities within the ICTM—has served as a kind of model.

Ethnomusicology deals with music in a social context, and to my mind we have now arrived at a level of discourse that is characterized by reflection on what we have done in the past, as well as what impact our work has on the people we are dealing with. Ethical considerations have come to the fore within the last decades, as Mark Slobin suggested in 1992: "individual soul-searching must be going on within the discipline constantly." And "[b]y maintaining a continuous discussion of thorny issues and anticipating those to come, ethnomusicology will not solve its ethical problems—since in the nature of human activity this is not a possibility—but will shore up damage done and keep building a framework for future, carefully considered action" (Slobin, 1992: 336). And actually things *have* changed within the discipline since then, if one considers Bartz and Cooley's *Shadows in the Field* (1997), a critical attempt to rethink the role of the researcher in the field. There are many other indicators of these changes, which are convincingly argued in the volume of *Ethnomusicology* (2006: 50, 2) to mark the fiftieth anniversary of SEM, and in many other works. There is a shift in topic and interests in ethnomusicology as well as in methods. Applied ethnomusicology, named as such since 1992, has obviously gained ground within the discipline. Timothy Rice's article "Ethnomusicology in Times of Trouble" (Rice, 2014) emphasizes the important role of ethnomusicology in conflict management.[12] Within this time span, the ICTM Study Group on Music and Minorities and the ICTM Study Group on Applied Ethnomusicology were founded. The emergence of both was grounded in the development of the discipline, but on the other hand had a reciprocal effect on ethnomusicology and international discourses.

Cooperation models between consultants and researchers, as well as different forms of "dialogical knowledge production," seem to have become standards of modern ethnomusicology. The application of results "for the benefit of the people" we work with seems to come quite naturally, also out of the usually very close relationship that develops through fieldwork. The "partnership model of fieldwork" (Russell), including the application of results in presentation and publication, can be noticed frequently. The latter is not new, as it is part of the tradition of European folk music research, but there has been a considerable shift from promoting the musical traditions of "the people" to the "music of individuals."

We have not quite gotten rid of "ethnicity." And it is not likely to happen in the near future. It is an important category in the three case studies presented here. In the case of the Roma, it seems to have been necessary to "invent" something like an essentialist ethnic identity. The development has shown that it was necessary at this stage of political empowerment. Carol Silverman describes this process as "strategic essentialism" in the course of political mobilization of the Roma and interprets it in the following way: "So we may understand the symbols of the Romani rights movement as historically placed responses to marginality" (Silverman, 2012: 54).

I have tried to critically analyze the role of ethnomusicology in this process. In the case of the Bosnian refugees, one song genre symbolized not ethnicity as such, but rather the common musical heritage of people with different ethnic backgrounds who had shared social and national identities. It was the war that destroyed these shared identities. So the song genre of *sevdalinka* served as a symbolic expression of a vanished world and as a means to survive in the situation of being refugees. Applied ethnomusicology served as a vehicle to promote this "nostalgia" to the Austrian majority in order to build bridges and to improve mutual understanding.

In the third case, ethnicity is a category that is very problematic. We know from the discourses in cultural studies that identities are multiple and hybrid. Stuart Hall (1994) states that not only identities, but even all modern nations, are culturally hybrid, which is of course true from a certain perspective, but definitely not from the perspective of Austrian politicians. For immigrants from Turkey it seems especially important to raise the awareness of the possibility of individual choice in defining identity, because public discourse labels them ethnically and one-dimensionally. Although there is already a third generation living in Austria, they are still referred to as "Turks," especially in media discourses and also in the speeches of politicians. The image of the "Islamist Turk" who does not want to integrate him- or herself into Austrian society is portrayed as a "problem." In this case, application means, first of all, drawing attention to the music-making of immigrants from Turkey by making it into a topic of research, and second, challenging the public discourse by conveying a differentiated view based on research and not on prejudices. Changing public attitudes is not easy, and ethnomusicology does not have the power to do it immediately. It is more of a small-scale approach, by organizing symposiums and podium discussions, by promoting individual musicians, and by teaching students who will later be music teachers faced with children from immigrant backgrounds in their classrooms.

My concluding quotation, which is from a time long ago but still valid, shows that the influential ethnomusicologist John Blacking had already thought about the application of results guided by social responsibility. And it also shows that although the discipline has changed considerably since then, we are still fighting the same problems:

> Intolerance and ignorance are not very far apart. And both seem to me to be among the roots of trouble in the world today. I had always thought that I might make it my life work to deal with the intolerance, relying on the work of others for the fight against ignorance. It now seems to me that I might be able to play a small, but more worthwhile part in the struggle against ignorance.
> (John Blacking, quoted from Byron, 1995: 5)

Notes

1. All of the research on which this article is based has been conducted at the Institute of Folk Music Research and Ethnomusicology at the University of Music and Performing Arts Vienna. Since 1990 there has been a research focus on music and minorities at the Institute in research, teaching, and publications. The major research projects conducted during recent years were the following.
   1990–1992: "Traditional Music of Minorities in Austria"
   1993–1995: "Traditional Music of the Roma in Austria"
   1995–2000: "Music of Bosnians in Austria"
   2005–2006: "Music Making of Immigrants in Vienna"
   2007–2009: Project partner in "Embedded Industries—Immigrant Cultural Entrepreneurs in Vienna"

Field research projects concerning immigrants in Salzburg (2004), in Innsbruck (2005), in Vorarlberg (2009), and concerning the music of Slovenes in Styria (1999–2001) 2009–2010: Bi-Musicality and Intercultural Dialogue.
2. More details on this topic, see Hemetek (2007).
3. About the development of the Study Group on Music and Minorities in detail, see Pettan (2012). The first symposium was held in Ljubljana in 2000 and since then symposia were organized every two years. The publications of the Study Group, all edited volumes, are: Pettan, Reyes, and Komavec (2001); Hemetek, Lechleitner, Naroditskaya, and Czekanowska (2004); Ceribašić and Haskell (2006); Statelova, Rodel, Peycheva, Vlaeva, and Dimov (2008); Jurková and Bidgood (2009); Hemetek (2012) Hemetek, Marks, Reyes (2014).
4. The group of Germans in Austria cannot be considered a minority in the sense of suffering from discrimination. Due to the common German language and the rather privileged professional positions of a high percentage of Germans in Austria, they do not have similar problems to the other immigrant groups.
5. The creation of a National Inventory of Intangible Cultural Heritage in Austria, as well as its continuous updating, are tasks that Austria agreed upon when it ratified the UNESCO Convention for the Safeguarding of the Intangible Cultural Heritage in 2009. To explain what this means in Austria, I quote the UNESCO website:

"Intangible cultural heritage comprises the practices, representations, expressions, knowledge, skills as well as the instruments, objects, artefacts and cultural spaces associated therewith, that communities, groups and, in some cases, individuals recognize as part of their cultural heritage. The intangible cultural heritage consists of five overlapping areas:

- Oral traditions and expressions, including language as a vehicle of intangible cultural heritage
- Performing arts
- Social practices, rituals and festive events
- Knowledge and practices concerning nature and the universe
- Traditional craftsmanship.

This intangible cultural heritage, transmitted from generation to generation, is constantly recreated by communities and groups, providing them with a sense of identity and continuity." (http://immaterielleskulturerbe.unesco.at/en/)
6. For discussion of the terms, see Assmann (1999).
7. Šadrvan: a Turkish wooden fountain, usually placed in squares.
8. This statement is not based on follow-up research but only on results from constant observations of the scene in Vienna.
9. Germany always was the main target country of Turkish immigrants in Europe, housing about 60% of the Turkish emigrant population, followed by France (6.3%), the Netherlands (4.8%) and Austria (3.8%).
10. Alevism is a religious belief based on ancient Turkish beliefs. It is a liberal and mystic form of Islam in which music, especially the instrument *saz*, is highly appreciated.
11. Dersim is the Kurdish (Zaza) name of a province in Anatolia that was formerly called Tunceli. There is a specific history connected to the place that includes the "Dersim Rebellion," also known as "Dersim massacre" from 1934. Many immigrants in Austria come from there, and their ethnic background is Kurdish. Therefore "Dersim" can be used as a metaphor in a song, which will be understood by insiders.

12. Many of the other works that seem to be important for that development connected to my field of research have been quoted throughout the article, representing only a very personal selection, of course.

References

Adler, Guido. (1885). "Umfang, Methode und Ziel der Musikwissenschaft." In *Vierteljahresschrift für Musikwissenschaft* 1: 5–20.

Ang, Ien. (2001). *On Not Speaking Chinese: Living Between Asia and the West*. London: Routledge.

Ang, Ien. (2003). "Together-in-Difference: Beyond Diaspora, into Hybridity." *Asian Studies Review* 27(2): 141–154.

Asad, Talal, ed. (1973). *Anthropology and the Colonial Encounter*. New York: Humanities Press.

Assmann, Aleida. (1999). *Erinnerungsräume: Formen und Wandlungen des kulturellen Gedächtnisses*. Munich: Verlag C. H. Beck.

Bajrektarević, Sofija, and Ursula Hemetek. (1996). *Sevdah in Wien, u Beču, in Vienna. Bosnische Musik*. (Tondokumente zur Volksmusik in Österreich, Vol. 5). Vienna: Institut für Volksmusikforschung an der Universität für Musik und darstellende Kunst.

Barz, Gregory F., and Timothy J. Cooley, eds. (1997). *Shadows in the Field: New Perspectives for Fieldwork in Ethnomusicology*. New York: Oxford University Press.

Bauböck, Rainer. (2001). "Gleichheit, Vielfalt, Zusammenhalt—Grundsätze für die Integration von Einwanderern." In *Wege zur Integration* (Bd. 4 der Publikationsreihe des Bundesministeriums für Bildung, Wissenschaft und Kultur zum Forschungsschwerpunkt Fremdenfeindlichkeit), pp. 11–45. Klagenfurt: Drava.

Bausinger, Hermann. (1996). "Concluding Remarks." In *War, Exile, Everyday Life. Cultural Perspectives*, edited by Renata Jambrešić Kirin and Maja Povrzanović, pp. 287–291. Zagreb: Institute of Ethnology and Folklore Research.

Bezić, Jerko, ed. (1985). *Glazbeno stvaralaštvo narodnosti (narodnih manjina) i etničkih grupa [Traditional Music of Ethnic Groups—Minorities]*. Zagreb: Institute of Folk Art.

Bildik, Mansur, and Bernhard Fuchs. (2008). "Imparting Turkish Music in Vienna from 1984–2007." In *Music from Turkey in the Diaspora* (klanglese 5), edited by Ursula Hemetek and Hande Sağlam, pp. 21–36. Vienna: Institut für Volksmusikforschung und Ethnomusikologie.

Bogdal, Klaus-Michael. (2013 [2011]). *Europa erfindet die Zigeuner. Eine Geschichte von Faszination und Verachtung*. Berlin: Suhrkamp Verlag.

Byron, Reginald, ed. (1995). "The Ethnomusicology of John Blacking." In *Music, Culture, Experience: Selected Papers of John Blacking*, pp. 1–28. Chicago: University of Chicago Press.

Ceribašić, Naila. (2007). "Musical Faces of Croatian Multiculturality." *Yearbook for Traditional Music* 39: 1–26.

Ceribašić, Naila, and Erica Haskell, eds. (2006). *Shared Musics and Minority Identities*. Zagreb; Roč: Institute of Ethnology and Folklore Research, Cultural-Artistic Society "Istarski željezničar."

Clausen, Bernd, Ursula Hemetek, and Eva Saether, eds. (2009). *Music in Motion: Diversity and Dialogue in Europe*. Bielefeld: Transcript Verlag.

Cooley, Timothy J. (2005). *Making Music in the Polish Tatras: Tourists, Ethnographers and Mountain Musicians*. Bloomington: Indiana University Press.

Erol, Ayhan. (2008). "Reconstructing Cultural Identity in Diaspora: Musical Practices of the Toronto Alevi Community." In *Music from Turkey in the Diaspora* (klanglese 5), edited by Ursula Hemetek and Hande Sağlam, 153–162. Vienna: Institut für Volksmusikforschung und Ethnomusikologie.

Flosdorf, Dietmar, and Nicole Marte (Text). (2006). *Pùnkitititi—Mozart für Kinder, Ein Musikvermittlungsprojekt in Wiener Volksschulen mit abschließendem Festival, January–May 2006. Ein Projekt von Wiener Mozartjahr 2006*. Vienna: Musikverlag Alexander May.

Fock, Eva. (1999). "When the Background Becomes the Foreground. Music, Youth and Identity." *Young* 7(2): 62–77.

Fuchs, Bernhard. (2001). "Türkische Musikerträume in Wien: Volkshaus oder Explosion." In *Musik kennt keine Grenzen: Musikalische Volkskultur im Spannungsfeld von Fremdem und Eigenem*, Tagungsbericht Wien 1998 der Kommission für Lied-, Musik- und Tanzforschung in der Deutschen Gesellschaft für Volkskunde (Musikalische Volkskunde 14), edited by Gisela Probst-Effah, 294–304. Essen: Verlag Die Blaue Eule.

Georges, Robert A., and Michael Owen Jones. (1980). *People Studying People: The Human Element in Fieldwork*. Berkeley: University of California Press.

Hall, Stuart. (1994). *Rassismus und kulturelle Identität*. Ausgewählte Schriften 2. Hamburg: Argument Verlag.

Harrison, Klisala, Elizabeth Mackinlay, and Svanibor Pettan, eds. (2010). *Applied Ethnomusicology:Historical and Contemporary Approaches*, Newcastle upon Tyne: Cambridge Scholars Press.

Heinschink, F. Mozes, and Ursula Hemetek, eds. (1994). *Roma—das unbekannte Volk*. Vienna: Böhlau Verlag.

Hemetek, Ursula, ed. (1996). *Echo der Vielfalt: Traditionelle Musik van Minderheiten— ethnischen Gruppen / Echoes of Diversity: Traditional Music of Ethnic Groups-Minorities* (Schriften zur Volksmusik Bd. 16). Vienna: Bohlau Verlag.

Hemetek, Ursula. (2001a). "Music and Minorities: Some Remarks on Key Issues and Presuppositions of the Study Group." In *Glasba in manjšine: Music and Minorities.*, edited by Svanibor Pettan, Adelaida Reyes, and Maša Komavec, pp. 21–30. Ljubljana: Založba ZRC.

Hemetek, Ursula. (2001b). "Music of Minorities Between Exclusion and Ethnoboom. Intercultural Encounter in Austria." *the world of music* 2–3: 139–152.

Hemetek, Ursula. (2004). "Music and Minorities: A Challenge to Our Discipline. Some Theoretical and Methodological Considerations from the Roma in Austria." In *Manifold Identities: Studies on Music and Minorities*, pp. 42–54. Newcastle upon Tyne: Cambridge Scholars Press.

Hemetek, Ursula. (2006). "Applied Ethnomusicology in the Process of the Political Recognition of a Minority: A Case Study of the Austrian Roma." *Yearbook for Traditional Music* 38: 35–58.

Hemetek, Ursula. (2007). "Approaching Studies on Music of Minorities in European Ethnomusicology." *European Meetings in Ethnomusicology* 12: 37–48.

Hemetek, Ursula. (2009). "The Past and the Present: Ethnomusicology in Vienna: Some Considerations." *Muzyka* Rocznik LIV 1(212): 57–68.

Hemetek, Ursula, ed. (2012). *Music and Minorities in Ethnomusicology: Discourses and Challenges from Three Continents* (klanglese 7). Vienna: Institut für Volksmusikforschung und Ethnomusikologie.

Hemetek, Ursula, and Sofija Bajrektarević. (2000). *Bosnische Musik in Österreich. Klänge einer bedrohten Harmonie*. (klanglese 1). Vienna: Institut für Volksmusikforschung an der Universität für Musik und darstellende Kunst Wien.

Hemetek, Ursula, Gerda Lechleitner, Inna Naroditskaya, and Anna Czekanowska, eds. (2004). *Manifold Identities: Studies of Music and Minorities*. Newcastle upon Tyne: Cambridge Scholars Press.

Hemetek, Ursula, Essica Marks, and Adelaida Reyes (eds.) (2014). Music and Minorities from Around the World. Research, Documentation and Interdisiplinary Study. Newcastle upon Tyne: Cambridge Scholars Press.

Hood, Mantle. (1971). *The Ethnomusicologist*. New York: McGraw-Hill.

Johnson, Henry. (2007). " 'Happy Diwali!' Performance, Multicultural Soundscapes and Intervention in Aotearoa/New Zealand." In *Musical Performance in the Diaspora*. Special Issue of *Ethnomusicology Forum* 16(1): 71–94.

Jurková, Zuzana, and Lee Bidgood, eds. (2009). *Voices of the Weak: Music and Minorities*. Prague: Slovo21 and Faculty of Humanities of Charles University.

Kaya, Ayhan. (2001). *"Sicher in Kreuzberg": Constructing Diasporas: Turkish Hip-Hop Youth in Berlin*. Bielefeld: Transaction Publishers.

Kovinjalo, Tanja. (2007). *Sevdalinka und urbaner Raum. Musikalische und textliche Aspekte*. Vienna: Diplomarbeit an der Universität für Musik und darstellende Kunst Wien.

Kuhn, Walter. (1934). *Deutsche Sprachinselforschung. Geschichte, Aufgaben Verfahren*. Plauen: Wolff.

Kuhač, Franjo. (1878–1881). *Južno-slovjenske narodne popievke [South-slavic folk songs]*. 4 volumes. Zagreb: Self Published.

Levin, Ted, and Ankica Petrović. (1993). *Bosnia: Echoes from an Endangered World*. CD with booklet. Smithsonian Folkways SF 40407.

Loughran, Maureen. (2008). "But what if they call the police?" Applied Ethnomusicology and Urban Activism in the United States." *Muzikološki zbornik/Musicological Annual* 44(1): 51–66.

Myers, Helen. (1993). "Introduction." In *Ethnomusicology: Historical and Regional Studies*, edited by Helen Myers. New Grove Handbooks in Music. London: Macmillan.

Nettl, Bruno. (1992). "Recent Directions in Ethnomusicology." In *Ethnomusicology*, edited by Helen Myers, pp. 375–403. New York; London: W.W. Norton.

Nettl, Bruno. (2005). *The Study of Ethnomusicology: Thirty-one Issues and Concepts*. Urbana: University of Chicago Press.

Pesek, Albinca. (2009). "War on the Former Yugoslavian Territory: Integration of Refugee Children into the School System and Musical Activities as an Important Factor of Overcoming War Trauma." In *Music in Motion: Diversity and Dialogue in Europe.*, edited by Bernd Clausen, Ursula Hemetek, and Eva Saether, pp. 359–370. Bielefeld: Transcript Verlag.

Pettan, Svanibor. (1996). "Making the Refugee Experience Different: 'Azra' and the Bosnians in Norway." In *War, Exile, Everyday Life: Cultural Perspectives*, edited by Renata Jambrešić Kirin and Maja Povrzanović, 245–257. Zagreb: Institute of Ethnology and Folklore Research.

Pettan, Svanibor. (2008). "Applied Ethnomusicology and Empowerment Strategies: Views from across the Atlantic." *Muzikološki zbornik/Musicological Annual* 44/(1): 85–99.

Pettan, Svanibor, ed. (2008). *Applied Ethnomusicology, a thematic issue of Muzikološki zbornik/ Musicological Annual* 44(1).

Pettan, Svanibor. (2012). "Music and Minorities: An Ethnomusicological Vignette." In *New Unknown Music: Essays in Honour of Nikša Gligo*, edited by Dalibor Davidović and Nada Bezić, pp. 447–456. Zagreb: DAF.

Pettan, Svanibor, Adelaida Reyes, and Maša Komavec, eds. (2001). *Glasba in manjšine-Music and Minorities*. Ljubljana: Založba ZRC.

Ramnarine, Tina, ed. (2007). *Musical Performance in the Diaspora*, Special Issue of *Ethnomusicology Forum*, 16(1).

Reiterer, Albert F. (1996). *Kärntner Slowenen: Minderheit oder Elite? Neuere Tendenzen der ethnischen Arbeitsteilung*. Klagenfurt: Drava.

Rešidbegović, Belinda. (2002). *Die Sevdalinka—Das bosnische städtische Lied im Repertoire von Ševko Pekmezović*. Vienna: Diplomarbeit an der Universität für Musik und darstellende Kunst Wien.

Reyes-Schramm, Adelaida. (1979). "Ethnic Music, the Urban Area, and Ethnomusicology." *Sociologus* 29: 1–21.

Reyes, Adelaida. (2001). "Music, Migration and Minorities: Reciprocal Relations." In *Glasba in Manjšine—Music and Minorities*, edited by Svanibor Pettan, Adelaida Reyes, and Maša Komavec, pp. 37–46. Ljubljana: Založba ZRC.

Reyes, Adelaida. (2007). "Urban Ethnomusicology Revisited. An Assessment of Its Role in the Development of Its Parent Discipline." In *Cultural Diversity in the Urban Area: Explorations in Urban Ethnomusicology* edited by Ursula Hemetek and Adelaida Reyes (Klanglese 4), pp. 15–26. Vienna: Institut für Volksmusikforschung und Ethnomusikologie.

Rice, Timothy. (2014). "Ethnomusicology in Times of Trouble." *Yearbook for Traditional Music* Vol. 46: 191–209

Russell, Ian. (2006). "Working *with* Tradition: Towards a Partnership Model of Fieldwork." *Folklore 117* (April 2006): 15–32.

Sağlam, Hande. (2007). "Musical Practice of Immigrants from the Former Yugoslavia and Turkey in Vienna II: Musical Identification and Transcultural Process among Turkish Immigrants in Vienna." In *Cultural Diversity in the Urban Area. Explorations in Urban Ethnomusicology* (klanglese 4), edited by Ursula Hemetek and Adelaida Reyes, pp. 63–75. Vienna: Institut für Volksmusikforschung und Ethnomusikologie.

Sağlam, Hande. (2008). "Cosmopolitans and Locals—Music Production of the Turkish Diaspora in Vienna." In *Music from Turkey in the Diaspora* (klanglese 5), edited by Ursula Hemetek and Hande Sağlam, pp. 37–48. Vienna: Institut für Volksmusikforschung und Ethnomusikologie.

Schachiner, Memo G. (2008). *Politik und Systematik. Wiener Musikwissenschaft im Wandel der Zieten. Die Ära Guido Adler (1898–1927)*. Vienna: MC Publishing.

Sheehy, Daniel. (1992). "A Few Notions about Philosophy and Strategy in Applied Ethnomusicology." *Ethnomusicology* 36: 323–336.

Silverman, Carol. (2012). *Romani Routes: Cultural Politics and Balkan Music in Diaspora*. Oxford; New York: Oxford University Press.

Slobin, Mark. (1992). "Ethical Issues." In *Ethnomusicology: An Introduction*, edited by Helen Myers, pp. 329–337. New Grove Handbooks in Music. New York; London: Macmillan.

Slobin, Mark. (1995). "Four Reasons Why We Have No Musical Minorities in the United States." In *Music in the Year 2002: Aspects on Music and Multiculturalism*, edited by Max Peter Baumann, Krister Malm, Mark Slobin, and Kristof Tamas, pp. 31–41. Stockholm: The Royal Swedish Academy of Music.

Solomon, Tom. (2008). "Diverse Diaspora: Multiple Identities in 'Turkish Rap' in Germany." In *Music from Turkey in the Diaspora* (klanglese 5), edited by Ursula Hemetek and Hande Sağlam, pp. 77–88. Vienna: Institut für Volksmusikforschung und Ethnomusikologie.

Statelova, Rosmary, Angela Rodel, Lozanka Peycheva, Ivanka Vlaeva, and Ventsislav Dimov, eds. (2008). *The Human World and Musical Diversity*. Sofija: Institute of Art Studies—Bulgarian Academy of Science.

Statistik Austria. (2011). *Bevölkerungsstand*. Vienna: Stadt Wien.

Stoeltje, Beverley J., L. Fox Christie, and Stephen Olbrys. (1999). "The 'Self' in Fieldwork: A Methodological Concern." *Journal of American Folklore* 112: 158–182.

Stojka, Ceija. (1988). *Wir leben im Verbogenen: Erinnerungen einer Rom-Zigeunerin*. Vienna: Picus.

Stokes, Martin. (1997). "Introduction: Ethnicity, Identity and Music." In *Ethnicity, Identity and Music: The Musical Construction of Place*, edited by Martin Stokes, pp. 1–28. Oxford; New York: Berg.

Tschernokoscheva, Elka. (2008). "Hybridity as a Musical Concept: Theses and Avenues of Research." In *The Human World and Musical Diversity*, edited by Rosmary Statelova, Angela Rodel, Lozanka Peycheva, Ivanka Vlaeva, and Ventsislav Dimov, pp. 13–23. Sofia: Institute of Art Studies.

Temkin, Andrea S. (1988). "Alice Cunningham Fletcher." In *Women Anthropologists: A Biographical Dictionary*, edited by Ute Gacs, Aisha Khan, Jerrie McIntyre, and Ruth Weinberg, pp. 95–101. New York: Greenwood Press.

Titon, Jeff Todd. (1995). "Bi-Musicality as Metaphor." *Journal of American Folklore* 105: 287–297.

References on the Web

www.harristojka.at (2013)
www.ictmusic.org (2013)
www.minderheiten.at (2013)
www.romano-centro.org (2013)
http://profile.myspace.com (2006)

CHAPTER 3

BEING APPLIED IN THE ETHNOMUSICOLOGY OF AUTISM

MICHAEL B. BAKAN

Introduction

APPLIED *ethnomusicology*, writes Jeff Todd Titon, may be defined as "the process of putting ethnomusicological research to practical use" (Titon, 2011).[1] My purposes in this chapter are, first, to describe and critically examine how an ethnomusicology of autism might be conceptualized as a form of applied ethnomusicology so defined, and, second, to position this emergent area of inquiry in relation to relevant epistemological frameworks, including the autistic self-advocacy and neurodiversity movements, disability studies, and the anthropology of autism.

To achieve these purposes, I employ a polyvocal narrative approach, weaving together my own words and ideas with those of children on the autism spectrum with whom I play music, spokespersons from within the autistic self-advocacy movement, and scholars, scientists, and disability rights advocates representing diverse positions and epistemic communities (Harrison, 2012). I ultimately propose an ethnographic model of disability as a potential alternative and complement to the existing social and medical models, arguing that the ethnographic and relativistic tenets of applied ethnomusicology hold the potential to effectively promote neurodiversity and autism acceptance by helping to transform customary tropes of deficit, disorder, despair, and hopelessness into alternate visions of wholeness, ability, diversity, and possibility.

The Artism Ensemble will be my principal ethnomusicological focus. Artism is a neurodiverse music performance collective comprising several children with autism spectrum diagnoses[2] and their co-participating parents, along with a cohort of professional musicians and ethnomusicologists of diverse musicultural background. The ensemble is the cornerstone of the Artism Music Project, an Institutional Review

Board-approved applied ethnomusicology program that has been developed in accordance with all permissions, safety, and ethical requirements and recommendations of the Human Subjects Committee at Florida State University (FSU). I have coordinated and performed with the ensemble since its founding in 2011.

In our collective commitment to fostering a musicultural world that builds foundationally from the agency, imagination, and preferences of the children in the group,[3] Artism endeavors to privilege autistic ability over disability, supportively responding to the creative initiatives and impulses of children with autism, rather than trying to restrain, retrain, or redirect them.[4] Artism additionally serves as a social model in its own right through its concerts and other performance events: a model of inclusive sociality, music making, and cultural co-production that promotes autism acceptance rather than autism awareness; that displays a productive and creative domain of musical praxis built upon the elimination of conventional generational, cultural, musical, and neurophysiological boundaries and barriers; and that in turn challenges traditional assumptions about musical expertise, musical value, and the ostensibly self-evident social hierarchies that exist within group music-making environments.

Artism applies ethnomusicology to practical use in these multiple and interrelated ways. It enables people who have historically been disenabled, builds culture and community in environments where "conventional logic" would seem to deny the very possibility, and publicly performs autistic ability and sociocultural inclusivity as challenges and alternatives to autistic disability and exclusion. Yet it is undeniable that Artism, whatever its merits or aspirations may be, is also a product of the very hegemonic constructs that it resists and challenges. It highlights the staging of autism and the performance of disability. In so doing, it paradoxically resists and is co-opted by an essentially (and essentialist) pathologizing view which posits "autism" in contradistinction to "normal," thus propagating the very constructs of exclusion and hierarchy it aims to overturn, at least in some measure.

Like most manifestations of disability practice and discourse, the Artism Ensemble occupies a complexly contested space in which empowerment and appropriation are dialectically entwined; it invites critical consideration and evaluation. The following discussion endeavors to tease out some of this complexity, while ultimately concluding with the suggestion that Artism and like-oriented applied ethnomusicology projects are worth the effort, despite their inherent limitations and liabilities.

Applied Ethnomusicology, Music Therapy, and Medical Ethnomusicology

It is important to establish at the outset that there are fundamental epistemological and practical differences between engaging musically with autistic individuals in the context of an applied ethnomusicology project like Artism, on the one hand, and treating autism spectrum disorders (ASD) through the use of music therapy–based interventions, on the other. As is explained in the 2012 online article "Music Therapy as a Treatment Modality for Autism Spectrum Disorders," published by the American Music Therapy Association (AMTA) on its website,

> Music Therapy is the clinical and evidence-based use of music interventions to accomplish individualized goals within a therapeutic relationship by a credentialed professional who has completed an approved music therapy program
> .... Music therapy provides a unique variety of music experiences in an intentional and developmentally appropriate manner to effect changes in behavior and facilitate development of skills. ... Music therapy can stimulate individuals [with ASD] to reduce negative and/or self-stimulatory responses and increase participation in more appropriate and socially acceptable ways. ... Because music is processed in both hemispheres of the brain, it can stimulate cognitive functioning and may be used for remediation of some speech/language skills [in persons with ASD].
> (American Music Therapy Association, 2012)

The field of music therapy is highly diverse. The approaches of its researchers and practitioners span a wide gamut, from behaviorism-based studies yielding quantified outcomes to ethnographic and phenomenological methods emphasizing qualitative findings and narrative reports.[5] Yet for all the ways in which they differ, and despite the fact that the cited AMTA article is by no means representative of the discipline in total, I would contend that there is a unifying thread binding together the endeavors of music therapists on the whole: put simply, they are committed to using music for therapeutic purposes, and therapy, by at least one standard definition, is "treatment intended to relieve or heal a disorder."[6]

This treatment-centered orientation is consistent with the AMTA position on ASD accounted for above. From that stance, ASDs are treated by music therapists using "music interventions" that aim to "effect changes in behavior and facilitate development of skills," "reduce negative and/or self-stimulatory responses and increase participation in more appropriate and socially acceptable ways," and "remediate some speech/language skills." This is certainly a valid approach that has yielded benefits for many autistic people, improving quality of life and promoting the development of useful skills. Yet there are many other potentially fruitful approaches as well, and applied ethnomusicology in particular lends itself to a rather different set of epistemological priorities and practical methods.

As an ethnomusicologist who works in the area of autism, my interests are in music making, not music interventions; my epistemological focus is on autism as a cultural way of being, not a disorder (cf. Straus, 2013); my aspiration is to comprehend and engage with people labeled "autistic" on their own terms to the greatest extent possible, rather than to effect changes in their behavior, facilitate the development of specific skills, or remediate their actions in social settings to bring them in line with normative expectations.

In short, my framework is ethnographic rather than therapeutic, musicological rather than pathological. I am not trying to provide treatment or to cure autism through musical methods or any other. Instead, I am trying to better understand and communicate with people identified as autistic by hanging out and making music with them, having conversations and listening well, and getting to know who they are and what matters to them. To the extent that this work is directed toward effecting change of any kind, its main purpose is not to change autistic people in any way, but instead to change the often misguided ways that non-autistic, that is, neurotypical, people and institutions imagine, think about, and respond to autism and people who "have" it.

These priorities distinguish the approach of the present work not only from music therapy, but to a lesser degree from medical ethnomusicology as well. The progenitor of Artism, the Music-Play Project (MPP), which ran from 2005 to 2009 and was the subject of an earlier series of publications (Bakan et al., 2008a, 2008b; Bakan, 2009; Koen et al., 2008), was a medical ethnomusicology endeavor. Emphasizing both qualitative and quantitative measures of "social-emotional growth indicators" and gains in "response-ability," MPP melded ethnographic and therapeutic priorities in a manner that aligned with the health and healing-oriented perspectives of much medical ethnomusicology (and indeed of much music therapy as well). Koen, Barz, and Brummel-Smith, in their introduction to *The Oxford Handbook of Medical Ethnomusicology* (Koen, 2008), define *medical ethnomusicology* as "a new field of integrative research and applied practice that explores holistically the roles of music and sound phenomena and related praxes in any cultural and clinical context of health and healing" (Koen, Barz, and Brummel-Smith, 2008, 3–4).[7] The music-play protocols of MPP provided such a context in the therapeutic dimensions of their intent.

Artism is a different case. It is a project that aligns much more comfortably with the basic tenets of applied ethnomusicology than with those of medical ethnomusicology. Accounting for this difference, at least in part, is a personal history of transformative experiences that traces back to a cathartic musical encounter I had in 2003. From there, the story runs through the life course of the Music-Play Project, then headlong into a moment of crisis in 2010. This, in turn, paves the way for the founding of the Artism Ensemble in 2011, and finally leads to a series of discoveries in the anthropology of autism, disability studies, and the autistic self-advocacy and neurodiversity movements that have subsequently reconfigured how I think about music, autism, and ethnomusicology.

BEGINNINGS

My path to becoming an ethnomusicologist of autism began in the year 2003, when a three-year-old relative of mine, Mark,[8] was diagnosed with a condition called Asperger's syndrome.[9] I had never heard of Asperger's and became quite concerned when I learned that it was an autism spectrum disorder. I had a rather fuzzy image of what autism was at the time, one formed mainly by Dustin Hoffman's performance in the movie *Rain Man* and by occasional encounters with disturbing, sensationalist media images in which autistic children were shown isolated in corners of rooms, rocking back and forth incessantly, banging their heads against walls, erupting into violent tantrums.

Mark certainly did not fit this image. Granted, he didn't come across as your "typical" three-year-old kid either. He was often anxious. He carried his body kind of stiffly, clenching his fists and holding a lot of tension in his shoulders. He tended to avoid eye contact, except with his parents (especially his mother). His English-language vocabulary was large for his age, but he didn't seem very interested in using it to actually communicate most of the time; rather, he spoke mainly in a language of his own invention, Skoofie, which was unfortunately unintelligible to others. When speaking Skoofie, he was very expressive and gestural, but when speaking English he tended to use a flat monotone and to stand or sit still, rarely employing hand gestures or body language. He did not like meeting new people—they scared him, made him anxious—and he would customarily retreat to the comfort of his bedroom whenever visitors came to his home, staying there until they departed. He had meltdowns and tantrums just like other children his age, but was prone to being inconsolable for rather long periods when they occurred.

For all that, he was an adorable, bright, and endearing little guy, a lot of fun to be around except when he was feeling especially out of sorts, and that really wasn't all that often since he was happy much of the time. His bond with his mother was extremely close—theirs was a very warm and loving relationship—and among those whom he knew well he could be affectionate, funny, and expressive.

One night I was at Mark's family's house for a dinner party. He had sequestered himself in his room while the rest of us dined. This was as expected. My new Florida State University ethnomusicology colleague Benjamin Koen was at the gathering as well, and he and I decided to do some drumming together after the meal.

Ben and I were improvising and getting into a nice groove. My eyes were shut, as is my habit when I play. I felt a light tapping on my leg and looked down to see Mark sitting beside me on the floor, looking up. I was surprised, but delighted. He shifted his gaze away from me toward a pair of bongo drums (one of many options in a room full of percussion instruments) that were sitting next to him on the floor. Then he looked back up at me. I surmised that he wanted to jam, too, and that he was asking for permission to do so. I smiled at Mark and nodded encouragingly. He jumped in and started to play, immediately taking the rhythm in an entirely new direction. Ben and I excitedly followed him there. Mark's eyes lit up. Then he took us to another musical place and we went there with him. He lit up some more, and next thing we knew he was singing, too, in a strong, clear, beautiful voice I had never heard before, continuing to drum all the while. It was quite magical.

And then it was over. Eight o'clock arrived, and right on cue Ben's baby daughter melted down and started to cry. Moments later, the baby was bundled up and the Koens were off and away, headed toward home in their minivan. Mark disappeared for a few minutes and I assumed he had returned to the solace of his bedroom for the rest of the night. But then he reappeared in the living room. My wife Megan and I were sitting together on the couch. Mark came over and started talking to us. I don't remember what he said (I wish I did) but what I do remember is that he was like a different kid from the Mark I had known. He looked relaxed, he spoke to us lucidly in English and accentuated his speech with fluid hand gestures and body language, and the tension in his shoulders had melted away. He appeared altogether comfortable, at ease. Something about the social experience of drumming with Ben and me in the free, exploratory, improvisatory environment that we had spontaneously created together seemed to have tapped into something deep.

Precisely what that something was I will never fully know, but at the time and up until the present I remain convinced that it had a lot to do with Mark's sense that Ben and I were really listening to him, listening to what he had to say to us and how he wanted to connect with us through his drumming, his singing, his *playing*.[10] We weren't trying to tell him what to do or how to do it right; we weren't directing the flow of the music or the course of the improvisation, though we were certainly contributing to it. We were paying attention, enjoying, responding, communicating, appreciating, intuitively reaching out to meet Mark where he was and wanted to be, and then traveling elsewhere with him from there. The extent to which we succeeded in these various ventures was not really the point, for I firmly believe that what mattered most for Mark was the simple fact that we were trying. And I firmly believe, too, that with the exception of his mother and a few select others, there had been far too few people in Mark's life who had really done this, who had really tried to co-experience the world through his eyes and ears and thoughts and feelings, rather than assuming they had the right, even the obligation, to try to correct and normalize his "unusual" behavior or, perhaps even worse, to tune him out altogether.

Becoming Applied

That evening of drumming with Mark and Ben had a transformative impact on me. I was inspired by it to move in a new direction as both a musician and an ethnomusicologist, one that would ultimately take me to the new frontier of becoming an applied ethnomusicologist of autism.

A goal of capturing lightning in a bottle was central to that journey. The kind of experience that Mark, Ben, and I had shared was something I wanted to cultivate so that other kids on the spectrum—and other people generally—could enjoy it as well. I didn't see this as a potential cure for autism or as a path toward "normalizing" autistic behavior; these kids were getting enough therapies and interventions already. I just wanted to help make things happen that would enable them to have fun, feel successful, and play and explore the way they wanted to, rather than according to everybody else's rules all the time; and I wanted their parents to be a part of all that, too, both in terms of sharing in the experience actively and getting to see their kids having a good time doing something well, with "doing well" defined not in terms of the criteria of some test or standard of normalcy or functionality, but rather in terms of simply taking some pleasure in the experience of a meaningful activity undertaken in the company of others. These would appear to be rather modest goals, but in the domain of autism, bereft as it has historically been of the most fundamental measures of regard and respect for the integrity and value of autistic personhood, they turned out to be not so modest at all.

From such goals and aspirations was born the Music-Play Project, or MPP, an interdisciplinary venture produced mainly under the banner of medical ethnomusicology, involving a collaborative team led by Benjamin Koen and myself, and including autism research scientists, physicians, and a cognitive psychologist as well (Bakan et al., 2008a, 2008b; Koen et al., 2008, Bakan, 2009). Initially, the project took its name from a different acronym, CHIMP, which stood for the Children's Happiness Integrative Music Project. We were dissuaded from the use of this name, however, when an anonymous reviewer of one of our first grant proposals expressed that it was dangerously suggestive of early experiments in "abnormal psychology" that relied on data culled from studies of monkey and chimpanzee behavior. The name CHIMP was summarily dumped, but not without regret on my part, as I had rather liked the emphasis on happiness and integration that the spelled-out version of the acronym stressed.

So began what I now have come to regard as a process of progressive deterioration for the program, which from that point forward was known as the Music-Play Project. The more deeply I immersed myself in the medical-scientific literature on autism and ASD, with its heavy emphasis on deficits, disorders, and impairments—and on interventions, therapies, and cures—the more fully I was seduced into that literature's paradigmatic assumptions insisting that measurable outcomes of benefits, preferably quantitative ones drawn from the analysis of data collected in randomized clinical trials with controls, would be the only valid measures of the project's success. The more fully I was pressured into accepting the idea that the capacity of MPP to meet its "potential" and make a real "impact" were dependent on our success in securing grants from scientific research funding agencies and having our articles published by peer-reviewed scientific journals, the more I felt the core goals and aspirations that had inspired the project in the first place slipping away from me.

As MPP moved increasingly science-ward, even as I grasped desperately at the evasive notion that this was being done in a synergistic way that did not compromise the project's original intentions (Bakan, 2009), it progressively diverged from what it had been at the start and from what I had always believed it should remain. Try as we did to keep it from doing so, MPP became less about play, less about music, less about the kids and the families, and more about the results, the measures, the documentation of benefits and gains, and the potential impact beyond the immediate environment of the actual people involved.

The Music-Play Project had begun in 2005 and continued, on and off, through several different phases and studies, until 2009. Many wonderful things happened during its course, but the growing disconnect between what had gotten me into it and what it had become eventually became too great. To play in the sandbox of medical-scientific autism research meant to play by the rules of autism science. This translated into identifying and targeting specific areas of social, communicative, and behavioral deficit and impairment associated with ASD and developing testable methods for empirically determining what, if any, benefits our music-play programs were providing in terms of improving the symptoms and lessening the deficits of children participating in our project. In other words, the goal was to effect positive changes toward more "normal" and "functional" ways of acting, reacting, and relating on the part of these kids, which was precisely what I had *not* wanted this work to be about.

This recognition was sobering and disheartening. I snapped. I didn't want to do this anymore. I didn't want to "measure" these kids, "normalize" them, or "cure" them; I didn't want to be doing therapy of any kind. I just wanted to play music with them and give them and their parents a chance to have some fun and blow off some steam, to be creative and social and engaged on their terms instead of somebody else's, to be playful and imaginative without having to worry about measuring up. I craved the comfort and ease that Mark and Ben and I had shared on that pivotal night back in 2003, for the kids and their parents, and also for me. "Sciencing about autism" made no more sense to me than "sciencing about music" ever had, and it constituted a similar affront to my musical and humanistic sensibilities (Merriam, 1964; Bakan, 1999: 15).

So I let it go. By 2009, Ben had moved to China and I had completed a major phase of the Music-Play Project, a randomized clinical trial measuring "social-emotional growth indicators" that was based on the SCERTS model of ASD assessment (Bakan, 2009; Prizant et al., 2006). I presented my findings at the 2010 Society for Ethnomusicology meeting and determined that it was time to close this chapter of my career and move on to something else.

A couple of months later, though, I received a call from Jennifer Hoesing at the Florida Department of State's Division of Cultural Affairs (DCA). She was familiar with the Music-Play Project work and was calling to inquire about whether I might be interested in submitting a proposal for a DCA-administered, National Endowment for the Arts–funded grant in support of the continuation of my music and autism work. Immediately, I envisioned a new path forward. Arts and culture—these were my comfort zones; these were the places I lived as a musician, as an ethnomusicologist. What had been the Music-Play Project, mired down in the priorities of scientific autism research, assessment, and intervention, could potentially become something very different: the Artism Music Project.

Artism would be about playing music and improvising, and about celebrating and modeling neurodiversity. In Artism, kids with autism would be the kinds of people and musicians *they* wanted to be, and they would call the shots. And it would feature a real band, the Artism Ensemble, made up of the kids, their parents, and a talented and diverse group of professional musicians who would together go out and play concerts—concerts where people would get to hear and see all of us having a good time being creative, being ourselves, and being together.

More than any amount of statistical data or academic rhetoric, I reasoned, such a project had the potential to change public perceptions of autistic people for the better, to foster autism acceptance by presenting an alternative and affirming image of lived autistic realities and neurodiversity. Identifying people with labels like "autistic" or "disabled" inevitably creates frames in which particular biases or predispositions toward those individuals are activated. This applies to perceptions and assessments of musical performances as much as to anything else. Yet as the music education researchers Judith Jellison and Patricia Flowers have noted (1991: 323), "when the... actual performance is seen to be unlike that suggested by the label, initial biases have been shown to be overcome."

I was convinced that performances by the Artism Ensemble would do that kind of work, at once celebrating and defying the label of "autistic" in ways that countered all the entrenched mythologies of autistic tragedy and negation. Even more important, I was convinced that this imagined "Artism Ensemble" would offer opportunities and outlets for people with and without autism to experience special moments of comfort, joy, ease, and new understanding, as Mark and Ben and I had on the occasion that had launched the whole thing forward in the first place.

I prepared the proposal and it was successful. The grant was awarded in 2010 and the Artism Ensemble came into existence in January 2011, continuing under the aegis of grant funding through the summer of 2013.[11]

Spinny Chairs

"Come in," I say, inviting my twelve-year-old Artism Ensemble bandmate Mara Chasar into my office on a sweltering hot August afternoon in 2013. Mara enters with eyes downcast and sporting a mild frown. She seems nervous, or at least a bit uncomfortable. For three years now, the main context in which she and I have interacted has been the E-WoMP, or Exploratory World Music Playground, in Tallahassee, Florida. There, together with three or four other children on the autism spectrum, some of the children's parents, and accomplished musicians hailing from locations as far afield as Peru, Bolivia, Trinidad, and China, Mara and I have met regularly to rehearse, play, and make music together. We have also taken the E-WoMP on the road, performing in Artism Ensemble concerts at venues around Tallahassee and in other parts of Florida.

Mara and I have actually known each other and have been playing music together on and off for more than four years by this time. We first became acquainted in 2009 when she and her parents participated in a three-week program of the Music-Play Project. We then reconnected when I invited them to join the Artism Ensemble. They played in the group during its inaugural 2011 season, took a hiatus for a year in 2012, and rejoined in 2013. The 2013 season had concluded with a big concert in Orlando for the Opening General Session of the annual conference of the Society for Disability Studies (SDS), just a few weeks prior to the present meeting in my office.

Now here we are, sitting in the stillness of my fake wood-paneled digs in the College of Music at FSU, surrounded by computer and audio equipment and multiple shelves stuffed with books and folders. It's got to be a bit off-putting for Mara, I think to myself. Maybe this was a bad idea.

But things immediately change for the better the moment Mara feasts her eyes on the nice black office chair sitting adjacent to my desk. She plops herself down and gives it a good kick start.

"Whee!!" she exclaims with glee as she tucks up her knees and whirls about in the chair, over and over and over again. The downcast eyes alight and open wide. The frown becomes a radiant smile and Mara's laughter fills the room.

"I *love* spinny chairs!" she shrieks. "Spinny chair! Everyone loves the spinny chair!!"

She spins and spins, round and round, and she continues spinning as she quickly modulates from her playful tone to a more serious one.

"So what do you want?" she asks me.

I'm a bit thrown off by the question.

"Want?" I say, pondering, searching for just the right way to put it. "Oh, what do I want—well, I just want to talk to you, about autism and Asperger's and stuff like that," I venture, not sure how that's going to go over. Mara continues to spin. "You know," I continue, "you had such wonderful things to say about all that stuff during the question-and-answer session after our Orlando concert with Artism, and since then I've been reading this book written by autistic people—it's called *Loud Hands: Autistic People, Speaking* (Bascom, 2012a)—and what you were saying is really in line with what they're saying. So now I'm trying to write about music, and autism, and Artism and all that, and I think it would be great if you could write with me, because you have such amazing insights and I think having you share those would make the things I'm working on way better than anything I could write by myself."

"So you want me to help you write a book?"

"Well, yeah, a book, some articles, a few different things actually. Is that OK?"

"I think that sounds cool."

"Great. So how about you talk and I'll type out what you say, or else you can just sit here at the computer and type yourself if you prefer. That's fine, too."

"You type," she says. "I like *spinny chairs!*"

"Remember how our concert in Orlando was at that conference, you know, the one for the Disability Studies society?"

"Yeah."

"Well, after the rest of you guys left, I stayed around for the rest of the conference. There was this one session that was run by people who do disability studies but who also have autism themselves, and they thought that our concert was sponsored by this big organization called Autism Speaks. It wasn't, but they thought it was because I had handed out this questionnaire to the audience and one of the questions had to do with 'promoting autism awareness.' Well, it turns out that 'autism awareness' is a phrase that these people, and a lot of other autistic people, too, really hate. They think it's offensive, because what they want is autism *acceptance*, not autism awareness; because a main mission of Autism Speaks is to find a *cure* for autism, to get rid of it, and these people with autism say they don't *want* to be cured, they just want to be who they are and to be accepted for being who they are. So then—"

"Who says autism is a bad thing?" Mara interjects in a tone of righteous indignation. "It sounds like this [Autism Speaks] organization is treating autism like cholera. Autism isn't cholera; it isn't some disease you can just cure. It's just *there*. You don't *need* to be aware of it; you just have to accept that it's there. I mean, you can't accept cholera; it's a disease."

"You told me that a lot of people find this organization offensive," Mara continues, "and honestly, you know, [from what you've said about it,] I do too. Awareness and acceptance are a lot different from each other. Yeah. Awareness means you know it's there, but acceptance means you know it's there and it's not going to go away. Of course, you can't accept something if you don't know it's there, so I guess we have to be aware of it *and* accept it. So if that organization's thing is 'Autism Awareness,' maybe they should change it to 'Autism Awareness *and* Acceptance.' And honestly, curing autism doesn't come in some kind of a pill or medication. And there *is* no cure. There really isn't. It's just there, wound into your personality."

Mara has stopped spinning momentarily. Now she resumes. "Spinning chairs! Spinning chairs make *everyone* happy!" she sings. Then, in a mock serious tone, "I get distracted easily," and after that, throwing back her hair and laughing wildly, "*especially by things like this that are SPINNY CHAIRS!!*"

"You know," I say to Mara, laughing along with her as she continues to spin away, "the scientists and the doctors and therapists and people like that who specialize in autism, and the people in those organizations like Autism Speaks, would say that what you're doing now—spinning and spinning and spinning while we have this conversation—is an example of *stimming*, that it's a 'symptom' of your Asperger's or your autism or whatever."

"Stim-*what*?" Mara asks, seemingly confused. "What *is* that?"

"Stimming," I repeat. "It's a word that they use to describe so-called 'self-stimulating behaviors' that autistic people do when they're, I don't know, feeling stressed or uncomfortable or whatever, or maybe the scientists don't know why they do those things but they know they do them and they say that's one of the things that makes them autistic."

Mara's laughter now escalates to a fever pitch.

"That's just *ridiculous!*" she states incredulously. "I mean, I bet that the president has a spinny chair and sometimes *he* spins around."

"Which president? The president of the United States or the president of Autism Speaks?"

"Both of them," she fires back. "I'm sure they look around and see if their security guards are around, and if they see the coast is clear they just kind of silently spin around in their chair. They probably don't laugh like I do because the president doesn't laugh, or at least lots of people think that, but that's just another stereotype—but still. Spinny chairs. I *like* spinny chairs."

There is a brief pause in the conversation as Mara continues to spin.

"I like to talk a lot," she explains, "but the president likes to talk a lot too. And he gives all those speeches, so why don't they say that the president needs to be 'cured,' because the president talks a lot too. If he's like me in *any* way, he needs to be 'cured,' *doesn't* he?"

I chuckle. Mara stops spinning, leans forward, and points to the spot on my computer monitor where I have just transcribed her last remark.

"Just say that I said that sarcastically," she insists. "I don't want to offend the president."

"I have something else I wanted to say," Mara announces after another brief pause, resuming her spinning at the same time. "You know, I think there should be a type of therapy that involves spinny chairs. There should be a room where there are rows and rows of spinny chairs, and a bunch of people would file in and sit down, and they'd all talk to each other and say, 'I wonder what this new therapy is?' And then the therapist would walk in and tell everyone to be quiet, and then he or she would say, 'Now, spin around in your chairs really fast!' and everyone would at first be really skeptical, but then someone would try it, whirling around and around. They'd say, 'Hey, this is fun!' and everyone else would start to do it, and then the whole room would be spinning around and around, or at least to everyone in the spinny chairs. Or a therapy where everyone gets together and just types or writes stories together. When I'm bored or sad or stressed, I like to sit down, ignore everyone, and just *write* for hours on end.

"You know, when I hear about people saying people with autism aren't 'normal' and get surprised when we do things like use big words or do things they can't, I just think: We *are* normal. We learn things just like 'normal' people do, we talk when we feel like it to who we feel like talking to just like 'normal' people do, we play and dream and laugh and love *just like 'normal' people do*, even if we're too shy to admit it sometimes.

"Some of us have a few problems, but why do 'normal' people have to be the ones to 'fix' them?" Mara asks rhetorically, after which she instructs me to be sure to put scare quotes around each iteration of "normal" and around the word "fix" in the preceding section.

"Why are all the therapists 'normal' and we're not?" she adds. "In fact, the therapists should be people who used to have severe autism or Asperger's, or *whatever*, and then found out how to deal with their problems. Having a Ph.D. in psychology doesn't always make you an expert."

"What about people like me," I ask, "you know, who aren't autistic but work with people who are?"

"Well, you people seem pretty nice," Mara answers matter-of-factly, "and you seem to know what you're talking about, so people like you would be pretty good for that role. But I still like the idea of doctors and stuff who have autism."

Autism and ASD: The Official Story

> Autism spectrum disorder (ASD) is a range of complex neurodevelopmental disorders, characterized by social impairments, communication difficulties, and restricted, repetitive, and stereotyped patterns of behavior. Autistic disorder, sometimes called autism or classical ASD, is the most severe form of ASD, while other conditions along the spectrum include a milder form known as Asperger syndrome, and childhood disintegrative disorder and pervasive developmental disorder not otherwise specified (usually referred to as PDD-NOS).[12] Although ASD varies significantly in character and severity, it occurs in all ethnic and socioeconomic groups and affects every age group. Experts estimate that 1 out of 88 children age 8 will have an ASD. . . . Males are four times more likely to have an ASD than females.
>
> (NINDS, 2013)

So states the "Autism Fact Sheet" published on the website of the US National Institutes of Health's National Institute of Neurological Disorders and Stroke (NINDS). Later in the same document, NINDS declares:

> The hallmark feature of ASD is impaired social interaction. . . . Children with an ASD. . . have difficulty interpreting what others are thinking or feeling because they can't understand social cues, such as tone of voice or facial expressions, and don't watch other people's faces for clues about appropriate behavior. They lack empathy. Many children with an ASD engage in repetitive movements such as rocking and twirling, or in self-abusive behavior such as biting or head-banging. They. . . don't know how to play interactively with other children. Some speak in a sing-song voice about a narrow range of favorite topics, with little regard for the interests of the person to whom they are speaking.
>
> (NINDS, 2013)

Elsewhere, the "Fact Sheet" provides a list of primary indicators leading to an ASD diagnosis, especially in individuals beyond the infancy/toddler years: impaired ability to make friends with peers, impaired ability to initiate or sustain a conversation with others, absence or impairment of imaginative and social play, restricted patterns of interest that are abnormal in intensity or focus, preoccupation with certain objects or subjects, inflexible adherence to specific routines or rituals, and stereotyped, repetitive, or unusual use of language.

As for treatment options, there "is no cure for ASDs," according to NINDS. "Therapies and behavioral interventions are designed to remedy specific symptoms and can bring about substantial improvement. . . . Most health care professionals agree that the earlier the intervention, the better. . . . Therapists use highly structured and intensive skill-oriented training sessions to help children develop social and language skills, such as Applied Behavioral Analysis." (NINDS, 2013).

Deficit-centrism

The official story on autism and ASDs, as represented by the NINDS "Autism Fact Sheet" and other research and informational sources deemed credible and authoritative, is mainly a bleak one. It is the kind of story that affirms anthropologist Olga Solomon's assertion that there is "a remarkable silence, an absence of discourse about hope in biomedicine's views on autism . . . " (Solomon, 2010a: 253),[13] and that motivates comments from autistic activists such as the following one from Temple Grandin:

> I'm certainly not saying we should lose sight of the need to work on deficits. But. . . the focus on deficits is so intense and so automatic that people lose sight of the strengths [of autistic people]. If even the experts can't stop thinking about *what's wrong* instead of *what could be better,* how can anyone expect the families who are dealing with autism on a daily basis to think any differently?
>
> (Grandin and Panek, 2013: 180–181; italics in original)

How indeed? And even Grandin might be accused of not going far enough in her critique of rampant deficit-centrism, for in highlighting the plight of "the families who are dealing with autism," she diverts attention away from autistic people themselves. Consider what the autistic self-advocate Penni Winter has to say on this matter:

> Our Autism is called a "tragedy" or even, by some parent groups, "the enemy" to be fought at all costs, and the [apparent] increase in our numbers is referred to as an "epidemic," as if Autism were some dread disease. We're said to "ruin" our parents' lives and break up marriages, and we get discussed in terms of the "burden" we are on our families, the "difficulty" we cause others. What we might feel or think or want is hardly even asked—because, oh yeah, that's right, we don't *have* feelings or needs. It's the parents and families who are focused on, because they are deemed to be the ones that "matter," not the individuals with Autism.
>
> (Winter, 2012: 119; square brackets in original)

There are exceptions to the pervasive tones of deficit-centrism and bleakness, even in the most mainstream contexts. The NINDS "Autism Fact Sheet" does hold out hope for people with ASDs across the lifespan, indicating that for many, "symptoms improve with age" to the extent that they "are able to work successfully and live independently or within a supportive environment" (NINDS, 2013). The website of Autism Speaks (Autism Speaks, n.d. "a") presents a similar position and adds to it with the pronouncement that "*all* [people with ASDs] deserve the opportunity to work productively, develop meaningful and fulfilling relationships and enjoy life." The same website now includes an "Autism Acceptance" page as well (Autism Speaks, n.d. "b")—presumably a response to the attacks levied against the organization's ubiquitous "Autism Awareness" campaign by autistic self-advocates. And the NINDS "Fact Sheet" has a link to the website of Autism Network International (ANI), a leading autistic self-advocacy organization, on its list of resources for additional information.

Despite such occasional nods to alternate viewpoints and priorities, however, the consistent message from the mainstream remains intact: where autism is concerned, nothing is good unless it gets better, with "good" and "better" equating to an ideal of "normal," "indistinguishable from normal," or at least "closer to normal." Within such an epistemological quagmire, there can be no true achievement of what autistic self-advocates are seeking in their calls for autism acceptance; in their view, this needs to change.

"It starts with the basic, foundational idea that *there is nothing wrong with us. We are fine*," writes Julia Bascom in her foreword to *Loud Hands*.[14] "We are complete, complex, human beings leading rich and meaningful existences and deserving dignity, respect, human rights, and the primary voice in the conversation about us" (Bascom, 2012b: 10).

Building on this premise, Penni Winter explains:

> One of the biggest and most insidious maltreatments [of autistic people] involves the concept and practise of what I call "normalisation," which springs out of the belief that Autism is an inferior or "wrong" state. Thus "becoming normal" is seen by many parents and therapists as the ultimate goal... and the aim of all therapy is to make us "indistinguishable" from our "normal" peers. Autism thus becomes something to be got rid of, no matter what sacrifices must be made. Some would even rather see their child dead than autistic... [What advocates of normalisation fail to see] is the real cost of this normalisation, which can be very high indeed... they are subscribing to a huge fallacy—the one which says that the Autism is somehow separate from, and "burying," the "real" (i.e.: normal) person underneath. Not so. *Autism runs all the way through*. It's a deep neurological difference. It can no more be stripped away or "cured" than our gender or race can be "cured" or taken away. It's that central to our being [cf. Sinclair 2012 [1993]: 16–17].
>
> (Winter, 2012: 115–117)

The autistic author and activist Ari Ne'eman, who served on the US government's National Council on Disability under Obama and was the first president and co-founder of the Autistic Self Advocacy Network, problematizes and nuances the issues raised by Bascom and Winter in the following passages from an essay he wrote on the future of autism advocacy:

> Sadly, the traditional autism community has been driven by a set of priorities different from our own. Led almost exclusively by those not on the autism spectrum, it has made harmful decisions without our input.... It is our belief that the traditional priorities of autism advocacy, which focus on eliminating the autism spectrum rather than pursuing quality of life, communication, and inclusion for all autistic people, need to be reset.... The object of autism advocacy should not be a world without autistic people—it should be a world in which autistic people can enjoy the same rights, opportunities and quality of life as any of our neurotypical peers....

Does this mean that we should not be engaged in trying to ameliorate the many challenges associated with being autistic? Of course not. What it does mean is that, first, we should target our efforts towards the real challenges we face, rather than towards a broader, nebulous concept of "curing" autism that is offensive to many of the people that it aims to benefit. Second, we should in every instance consider the fact that it is often social barriers rather than disability itself that pose the problems we face.

(Ne'eman, 2012: 88–90, 93–94)

The issues are highly complex. Autistic self-advocates such as Bascom, Winter, and Ne'eman share core convictions regarding the guiding priorities of autistic advocacy, but they do not speak in unison, and they hold widely divergent views on a host of matters. Furthermore, the positions they espouse, individually and collectively, are by no means representative of a unified stance where the values and priorities of autistic people at large are concerned. There are many on the spectrum who openly oppose their views, and this does not even account for the large number who do not as yet have any means at all to effectively communicate with other people. The question of who is best qualified to speak and work on behalf of *their* interests—parents or other family members, autistic self-advocates, researchers, clinicians, or therapists—is one of the most vexing and contentious in the entire realm of autism-related discourse and policymaking. And it would be naïve to suggest that the kinds of supports, accommodations, and treatment protocols that have emerged through the dedicated efforts of medical-scientific researchers, clinicians, and therapists have been neither beneficial to nor appreciated by a great many autistic people. Much valuable work has been done, and many lives have been changed positively as a result of it.

In approaching this chapter, then, I am aware that autistic self-advocacy and neurodiversity have their limitations, problems, critics, and internal divisions. But coming from the relativistic epistemological foundation that I do as an ethnomusicologist, I remain convinced that listening to what autistic people have to say—verbally, musically, and otherwise—is the best and most appropriate first step toward an engaged and applied ethnomusicology of autism. A paradigm shift from pathology to neurodiversity is essential to this development.

Toward a Neurodiverse Approach to Applied Ethnomusicology

Mainstream discourses relating to autism and ASD routinely posit a dichotomy of "autistic" to "normal." This is unacceptable from an autistic self-advocacy perspective. The term "normal" must be replaced if the conversation is to move forward productively; *neurotypical* is the suggested replacement word. The autistic scholar and author Nick Walker explains that this is a word which "allows us to talk about members of the dominant neurological group without implicitly reinforcing that group's privileged position (and our own marginalization) by referring to them as 'normal'" (Walker, 2012: 233).

Walker similarly advocates for the term *neurodiversity* for the larger movement of which autistic self-advocacy is a part, and *neurominority* as a designation for autistic culture: "Neurotypicals are the majority; Autistics are a neurominority," he explains to illustrate the latter. As for the former, *neurodiversity* is defined by Walker as "the understanding of neurological variation as a natural form of human diversity, subject to the same societal dynamics as other forms of diversity," such as race, gender, ethnicity, or sexual orientation (Walker, 2012: 233). He argues convincingly of the need for a shift from a *pathology paradigm* of autism (and human neurological variation generally) to a *neurodiversity paradigm*. In the epistemology of the pathology paradigm, there is belief in a "right," "normal," or "healthy" way for human brains and minds to be configured and to function. Substantial divergence from this dominant "normal" standard equates with the blanket assessment that there is "Something Wrong With You" (Walker, 2012: 227). Contrastingly, in the epistemology of the neurodiversity paradigm, variation in the configuration and functioning of human brains and minds is regarded as "a natural, healthy, and valuable form of human diversity," and "all of the diversity dynamics (e.g., dynamics of power, privilege, and marginalization) that manifest in society in relation to other forms of human diversity... also manifest in relation to neurodiversity" (2012: 228).

As Walker attests,

> If you reject the fundamental premises of the pathology paradigm, and accept the premises of the neurodiversity paradigm, then it turns out that you don't have a disorder after all. And it turns out that maybe you function exactly as you ought to function, and that you just live in a society that isn't sufficiently enlightened to effectively integrate people who function like you. And that maybe the troubles in your life have not been the result of any inherent wrongness in you. And that maybe everything you've heard about Autism is open to question, and that your true potential is unknown and is yours to explore.
>
> (Walker, 2012: 237)

THE ARTISM ENSEMBLE: A DIFFERENT WAY TO PLAY

The kind of neurodiverse world that Walker envisions in the above quotation mirrors the kind of musicultural space that the Artism Ensemble aspires to realize. Making music, performing publicly, and doing ethnography are our main tools, relativism and advocacy our epistemological cornerstones. In the E-WoMP, autistic preference and action are not regarded as symptomatic; they are accepted for what they are—viable ways of being human—and they are creatively explored. Challenges and frustrations that arise within the group and between its members—and they do arise—are confronted and dealt with as a matter of course. They are part and parcel of the band's basic social dynamic and are never merely explained away as manifestations of the autism-related problems of particular individuals. The constructs of autism and ASDs—or, as we prefer to call them, ASCs, or autism spectrum conditions—are always out in the open, but in any given situation they are subject to either outright dismissal or vigorous critical assessment on account of their perceived irrelevance, inaccuracy, or inadequacy.

The ensemble itself is a large group of somewhat fluid proportions. On any given occasion, it will include between three and five children diagnosed with ASCs, one or two parents of each child, and anywhere from five to nine staff musicians. The total number of players ranges from about a dozen to upwards of 20.

Artism's Exploratory World Music Playground facility, the E-WoMP, comprises a large array of percussion instruments that both the children and adult players are free to explore, as they wish to and on their own terms, individually or collectively—thus the "playground" identifier in the name. Most of the E-WoMP's instruments were manufactured by project sponsor Remo, and are modeled after traditional drums and other percussion instruments originating in West Africa, Latin America, Native America, and elsewhere. They include djembes, congas, bongos, ocean drums, thunder tubes, cuicas, a Native American-type gathering drum, tom-toms, egg shakers, and steelpans (steel drums).

All instruments selected for the E-WoMP must meet two basic requirements: high yield for low input (i.e., easy to produce pleasing/satisfying sounds without need of specialized training) and safety for use by the children in the program. Flexible rubber swimming pool dive sticks are the main types of mallets, and other mallets and sticks with padded or rubber ends are used as well. The use of rubber-tipped and padded striking implements is important not only for the physical safety of participants, but also for keeping volume levels in check and avoiding harsh timbres. Sensitivities to loud and harsh sounds are common among people with autism, making attention to such sensory issues a priority in any music-centered project.

Artism's staff musicians play both the E-WoMP percussion instruments and their own instruments, including guitar, bass, steelpan, flute, and clarinet. In previous years, other instruments, such as *zheng* and didgeridoo, were also featured. The diverse musical backgrounds of the staff contribute to the profusely intercultural palette of resources from which Artism's music springs. Compositions, arrangements, and directed improvisations by the children reflect this musicultural diversity, as elements of *festejo*, rumba, flamenco, calypso, raga, and gamelan combine with those of jazz, blues, funk, hip-hop, rock, classical, and other genres—as well as with ideas and concepts that are uniquely the children's own and bear no recognizable resemblance to any pre-existing musical genre or tradition per se—to forge the unique sound and approach that define Artism's music.

Applying Ethnography in the Ethnomusicology of Autism

"Medical culture—what has been described and vigorously critiqued within Disability Studies as the *medical model* [of disability]—has certain defining attributes," writes Joseph Straus in his essay "Autism as Culture." "First, medical culture treats disability as pathology, either a deficit or an excess with respect to some normative standard. Second, the pathology resides inside the individual body in a determinate, concrete location. Third, the goals of the enterprise are diagnosis and cure" (Straus, 2013: 462).[15]

Whether describing medical models of disability or pathology paradigms of autism, thinkers like Straus and Walker pinpoint the same basic epistemological premises. Proponents of any such models or paradigms, in their various roles as researchers, physicians, or therapists, as teachers, aides, or even parents, operate from a fundamental position that there is a need to *change* the autistic or otherwise "disabled" person. They are, then, at least in their relations and interactions with their subjects, patients, clients, students, or children, agents of change in search of solutions.

I do not consider myself to be an agent of change in this sense. Neither do I fully see myself as an agent of change in the alternate sense that disability studies scholars such as Tobin Siebers have posited relative to the so-called social model of disability, which "opposes the medical model by defining disability relative to the social and built environment, arguing that disabling environments produce disability in bodies and require interventions at the level of social justice" (Siebers, 2008: 25).

It is principally an ethnographic model, or at least way of thinking, that guides me in working ethnomusicologically on autism. I want to get to know and understand autistic people according to *their* terms and from their perspectives: learning from them, sharing experiences with them, comprehending their conceptions and values of community, personhood, social experience, humor, work and play, pleasure and pain, joy and suffering, and of course music. Toward such ends I concur with Straus's insistence that we must take "the concept of 'neurodiversity' as a point of departure" as we "seek to understand autism as a way of being in the world, a world-view enshrined in a culture... a difference, not a deficit" (2013: 467).

The challenges of working ethnographically on autism and neurodiversity are in some respects unique, but at a fundamental epistemological level they mirror those of ethnographic research generally. Consider, for example, the following comments by Jim Sinclair, which, were it not for the specific references to autism and "your child" (the original context was a presentation for parents of children with ASDs), could readily be mistaken for a passage from an introductory manual on ethnographic fieldwork:

> It takes more work to communicate with someone whose native language isn't the same as yours. And autism goes deeper than language and culture; autistic people are "foreigners" in any society. You're going to have to give up your assumptions about

shared meanings. You're going to have to learn to back up to levels more basic than you've probably thought about before, to translate, and to check to make sure your translations are understood. You're going to have to give up the certainty that comes of being on your own familiar territory, of knowing you're in charge, and let your child teach you a little of her language, guide you a little way into his world.

(Sinclair, 2012 [1993]: 17)

Artism and Applied Ethnomusicology

As an ethnomusicologist, I am interested in the music, thoughts, lives, and musical communities of the autistic children with whom I currently work and play music in much the same way that I was interested in the music, thoughts, lives, and musical communities of Balinese gamelan musicians with whom I worked and played music in Indonesia in the 1980s and 1990s (Bakan, 1999). I did not endeavor to remediate the performance practices of my Balinese fellow musicians, nor cure them of their preference for paired tunings over equal tempered ones. I assumed that these Balinese musicians were competent practitioners of the Balinese musical arts they practiced. I assumed that their distinctive clusters of behaviors, abilities, and attitudes in musical and social practice reflected individual manifestations of a broader Balinese worldview and ontology. I welcomed opportunities to learn from them through musical and social interactions, through performances and conversations that yielded ethnomusicological insights into Balinese ways of being, and of being musical.

I assume similar things and welcome similar experiences and insights in my work with the Artism Ensemble. Entering the E-WoMP, the principal site of Artism musical production, I approach matters much as I did when entering the *bale banjar*, the principal site of Balinese gamelan music production: as a learning musician, a curious and committed ethnographer, and a co-participant in the making of music and cultural community.[16] Here, though, the culture-bearers are not musicians in Bali who play on a gamelan but American children on the autism spectrum who play on an E-WoMP. It is these children who direct Artism's musical proceedings, guiding the course of group improvisations, coming up with musical themes and motives that under their own sure-handed ensemble direction take shape and blossom into full-blown compositions, selecting pre-existing materials—a melody from Liszt's *Hungarian Rhapsody No. 2*, a Bo Diddley beat under an extemporized rendering of Dr. Seuss's *Green Eggs and Ham*, a steelpan-led take on the Beatles' "A Hard Day's Night"—from which to create inspired arrangements that cleverly combine passages of pre-composed and improvised music.

As for the adult members of the ensemble—the professional musicians and "non-musician" parents alike—we are not there to teach or direct the children; rather, we are there to learn from and respond to them. We apply whatever skills and attributes we bring to the E-WoMP, individually and collectively, to nurture the children's creativity, agency, individual and social aspirations (musical and otherwise), and reciprocity.

There are no pre-established repertoires, right or wrong notes, specific musical goals or demands, or defined expectations of any kind beyond ensuring that all participants contribute to maintaining a safe environment emphasizing mutual respect and support for one another.

Typically, rehearsals and concerts move in round-robin fashion from one piece to another, with each child taking charge of the composition/arrangement and ensemble direction duties for one or more of their own pieces per program. This protocol was not created or imposed by me or any of the other adult ensemble members, but was an organic and gradually forming outgrowth of the children's own desires for how Artism's musical process should work, one that was worked out collectively among them in rehearsals (with one child in particular, NICKstr, usually taking a leadership role in the deliberations). The development of this protocol seemed to emerge as a direct response to the children's learning at the outset of the project that the ensemble was not going to function exclusively in a "play lab" environment, as in the Music-Play Project, but would additionally be getting out in public and performing concerts. Once they realized that they were going to have an audience, they almost immediately became committed to the idea of fashioning what one of the children, Coffeebot, referred to as a "high-quality musical product." They also became quite deeply invested in delivering the goods with showmanship and style, that is, showmanship and style defined on *their* terms, which have often been deliciously and provocatively at odds with "conventional" musical tastes and sensibilities.

It was fascinating to witness this strategic and aesthetic shift from a participatory to a presentational mode of performance (Turino, 2008), as well as to both observe and be a participant in the making of the distinctive sound, look, feel, and identity that have come to define Artism's unique musicultural brand over time. The accompanying note includes links to video examples from Artism rehearsals and concerts that provide some sense of the diverse character and range of the group's repertoire.[17]

It is also important to mention that in both broad outlines and specific characteristics, the generative processes of musical production and social engagement that define the Artism Ensemble's approach contrast in key regards with "best practices" positions regarding clinical, therapeutic, and educational approaches to working with people with autism. As Elizabeth Fein explains,

> Individuals on the autism spectrum tend to gravitate toward pre-ordered systems in which the relationship between parts can be predicted based on rules, and struggle to function within open-ended systems requiring flexibility, improvisation, and intuition. They thus gravitate toward and function best under a "stable symbolic and social order," under conditions where social expectations and givens are consistent, explicit, systematic, and shared between interlocutors.
>
> (Fein, 2012: 69–70)

Artism's open-ended approach, reliant as it is on flexibility, improvisation, and intuition, may be seen to push back against such logic to a considerable degree. Moreover, there is no doubt that the children in the group (and also the adults) *do* sometimes struggle with the unpredictability and open-endedness of the process; it is even fair to surmise that their often exacting methods of directing the ensemble, as well as their frequent preference for creating music that can be precisely ordered and structured, reflect desires for increased control and certainty. But over time they have all come to revel in the possibilities for spontaneous invention and co-creation that the E-WoMP affords, too, each in their own way.

On the basis of what I have observed over the past decade, autistic people are no less spontaneous, intuitive, flexible, or improvisatory than other people. They can just appear to be so because they are so often forced to contend with situations and settings in which their particular attributes and preferences for expressing such qualities are demeaned, or are patronized, or are not even recognized by their interlocutors. The evidence coming from the autistic self-advocacy movement, as well as from Artism and similar types of projects (see, for example, Bagatell, 2010; Bascom, 2012a; Fein, 2012), suggests that in situations where autistic people are given opportunities to have their talents enabled rather than disenabled, nurtured rather than quashed, and embraced for what they are rather than being targeted for remediation, they can and will thrive in ways that people without autism would never think possible unless they witnessed it firsthand. A primary purpose of Artism is therefore to provide just such people, that is, neurotypical people, with precisely that opportunity: to witness, enjoy, appreciate, and celebrate autistic ability rather than identify, symptomatize, marginalize, and take pity on autistic disability.

The child stars of the Artism Ensemble, together with their supporting cast of parents and professional musicians, make good and innovative music, make good culture and community, and make change. They do this through their compositions and arrangements, their improvisations, their concerts, and their public presentations of individual and collective selfhood. Change is achieved internally among the group's members through our joint musicultural ventures and all that they reveal. It is achieved externally as we reach out to audiences through concerts in which Artism's players, the children foremost of all, are *applied* to the cause of transforming public perceptions of autism from disability-centered to ability-centered ones, from recognition of a negating sort to recognition of the more affirming and celebratory kind.

A CRITIQUE OF ARTISM FROM MEMBERS OF THE AUTISTIC SELF-ADVOCACY COMMUNITY

Revisions and edits aside, the majority of my foregoing description of the Artism Ensemble and its philosophy was written prior to the group's Society for Disability Studies (SDS) Conference concert in Orlando on June 26, 2013. In the aftermath of that concert and still today, I stand by what I wrote in most every respect. However, an enlightening exchange that I had with several autistic self-advocates a couple of days after the show profoundly impacted my subsequent assessment of not just the concert itself, but also the project overall and possibilities for its improvement and development moving forward. This same exchange also heightened my appreciation for the challenges of doing applied ethnomusicology generally, since determining how and for whom such research is being put "to practical use" is inevitably a complex matter with high stakes attached.

The Artism Ensemble concert at SDS 2013 was the group's most ambitious and complex undertaking to that point. We had previously performed about a dozen concerts, ranging in setting from open-air arts festivals to large concert halls and from state museums to street fairs. We had never traveled beyond our home-base region of Tallahassee/Leon County, however, and had certainly never experienced the kind of visibility that performing at the pre-eminent international conference on disability studies promised to provide.

Any musician knows that taking a band on the road is challenging. There are myriad logistical details to attend to, from transportation and accommodations, to loading equipment in and out of the performance venue, to sound and lighting and other technical matters, to maintaining a collective spirit of camaraderie, patience, and enthusiasm. Take a band on the road in which the featured players are children, and beyond that children with the special sensitivities and proclivities associated with autism, and the venture's complexity and possibilities for difficulty grow exponentially. Add to *that* the complicated audience dynamics of a body such as the Society for Disability Studies, in which most of the members are themselves disabled individuals collectively requiring a wide range of accommodations, and it is easy to imagine a situation in which any of a number—and indeed any number—of things might go wrong.

Yet nothing did, or so it seemed. All six cars in our motley caravan made it through the labyrinth of toll booths, outlet malls, and theme park discount ticket outlets between Tallahassee and Orlando in good time and without a hitch. Our complimentary hotel rooms were nicely acquitted and ready and waiting for us upon arrival. The kids—and the adults, too—were in good spirits and very excited about the show. We had an excellent and efficient dress rehearsal, leaving us ample time for a leisurely dinner before the concert. Everyone on site—the sound and lighting technicians, our SDS host officers and volunteers, the interpreter team assigned to "translate" our concert into sign language (an amazing site to behold)—was as welcoming, competent, and accommodating as we could have hoped for.

The concert itself was a great success. Our program consisted of five main selections, all composed or co-composed by the children in the group: "Steel Drum Madness," by Coffeebot; "Life of Goodness," by E. S.; "The Beat Song," by E. S. with Carlos Silva; and "The Nightmare Before Christmas" (based on the poem and movie of the same name by Tim Burton) and "Purple Eggs and Ham," by Mara (under the stage name "Mara-I-am" on the program). These were followed by a free-improvisation jam session performed as an encore, during which an open invitation was made to the audience to sit in with the band; several audience members came onstage and joined in on various available percussion instruments while others (e.g., in wheelchairs) had instruments brought to them and participated from their seats.

Each of the pieces came off well; all 12 members of the band expressed that this was probably the best concert we had ever done. The audience, about 150 strong, was receptive and enthusiastic. There was a special feeling in the room, perhaps issuing from the fact that this supportive community of scholars and disability rights advocates had an unprecedented depth of comprehension and appreciation for what we were doing. We received a standing ovation, and then there was the aforementioned post-concert Q&A session, which was so enlightening, and in which Mara in particular really shone.

An evaluation questionnaire was distributed to audience members, per our standard protocol under the NEA grant. The responses were overwhelmingly positive. The concert was deemed "Excellent" (1) or "Very Good" (2) by 95% or more of the respondents on every question, and the free comments were almost uniformly enthusiastic. The only criticisms per se were that one respondent felt that "the music this band plays seems to heavily represent the higher end of the [autism] spectrum"[18] and another found that a couple of the comments of one of the band members (i.e., an adult professional musician) seemed "awkward" and this audience member "didn't care for" them. Otherwise, all respondents indicated that they had liked the music very much, had been inspired by the concert, had learned much of value regarding the abilities of autistic children, and so on.

I had no specific feedback of which I was aware, however, from any autistic individuals who had attended the concert, and this, as much as anything, was something I had hoped might emerge. So two days later, during an open Q&A session following a fascinating conference panel titled "Intersectionalities in Autistic Culture(s): A Discussion Instigated by This Posse of Autistics and Friends" (Grace et al., 2013: 42), I took advantage of the opportunity to solicit feedback on our concert.

"Were any of you at the Artism Ensemble concert the other night?" I asked. Several of the panelists, as well as a number of audience members, indicated they had been. "So I was wondering," I continued, "you know, we've never had the opportunity to play for and get feedback from members of the autistic community, and I'd be really interested in hearing your honest assessment of the show."

One of the panelists, the autistic self-advocate Zachary (Zach) Richter, veritably leapt out of his seat to the center of the room.

"Honestly," he said, "well, I'm going to keep this polite, because you don't want to hear the impolite version—"[19]

"That's OK," I interjected. "Don't spare my feelings. I really want your honest opinions."

"Well, I'm going to keep it polite. It's better to keep it polite. You know, I've seen you around the conference, Dr. Bakan"—

"Please, call me Michael."

"No, I'll call you Dr. Bakan—and I wanted to say something to you, but I didn't because I didn't want to be rude. But since you brought up the question, honestly, I found it offensive."

It was a stinging criticism, and of an intensity that quite frankly surprised me, but I managed to maintain my poise.

"How so?" I asked, bracing myself for the response.

Zach proceeded to present an incisive and thorough-going critique. Other panelists and audience members contributed occasional comments, too. These included the panel moderator, Professor Elizabeth J. Grace of National-Louis University, who is autistic, as well as another panelist, Allegra Stout, who is not autistic but is deeply involved in the autistic self-advocacy movement.[20] It was a lively discussion, with expressions of unanimity of opinion on a number of issues, dissension on others. The following is my own summation of the main critical points raised, which I present with advance apologies for inevitable oversimplifications of a richly nuanced and impassioned exchange:

- The concert, with its emphasis on percussion and amplified instruments, demonstrated a lack of sensitivity to the sensory challenges of many autistics.
- My failure to instruct the audience to use "silent applause" (e.g., waving of hands overhead) rather than clapping to express their appreciation was another instance of inattentiveness to autistic sound sensitivities.
- The absence of any autistic adults in the group—or even of consultation with autistic adult musicians in connection with the project—was deemed problematic for several reasons:
  - It deprived the children of the opportunity to have adult collaborators and mentors who, like themselves, were autistic.
  - It implicitly propagated the pervasive mythology that autism is a "children's disease," in turn playing into a common neurotypical tendency to infantilize autism in ways that sabotage autistic self-advocacy initiatives.
  - It inscribed and reinforced a pattern—real, illusory, or otherwise—of the agency of autistic children being constrained by the values and sensibilities of neurotypical adults (myself most especially).
- The absence of explicit political activism and engagement in the manner of presentation diminished whatever potential may have existed for advocacy in support of autistic and broader disability rights causes.

The Scourge of "Autism Awareness"

There was an additional criticism levied by Richter as well, one that did not pertain to the concert performance itself, but rather to an unfortunate item included on the audience questionnaire:

In terms of promoting autism awareness, this concert was:

(1) Excellent (2) Very Good (3) Good (4) Fair (5) Poor

"Why are you asking about autism awareness?" Richter inquired of me, a pained expression on his face. "That's wrong. It should be about autism *acceptance*! Have you received funding from Autism Speaks? That's what I think, and I'm angry because SDS told us this was going to be a safe space for autistics, and then they bring in your group and the whole autism awareness thing, and it's like an Autism Speaks agenda and that makes me—us—mad. I've talked to the conference organizers and told them this shouldn't have happened, and I've blogged about it, too."

This was a nightmare unfolding. I felt defensive, under attack, and yet I could easily see how the chain of events leading up to this moment had resulted in its occurrence, and how from Richter's perspective the charges being raised against me and the whole Artism enterprise were well-founded. A loud silence blanketed the room in anticipation of my response.

"First, Zach, let me assure you, we have received no funding or support from Autism Speaks and have no affiliation whatsoever with that organization," I began. "Second, I feel absolutely terrible. I didn't know how offensive the phrase 'autism awareness' was until now, nor did I know the history behind it that contributed to making it so. You are 100% right, and as soon as I leave this session I'm going to remove that phrase from the questionnaire and free myself of any association with it in everything I write or say from now on. I want to do this thing right. I'm really sorry."

"We can help you with that," Dr. Grace chimed in. "It's easy. If you send me that questionnaire, I can go through and make edits to get rid of that kind of offensive language."

"Thanks. I'd really appreciate that, and I'm sorry for taking up so much of your discussion time on this topic."

"That's OK," she assured me, "but we do need to move on now."

Addressing the Criticisms

The feedback on the Orlando Artism concert that Zach Richter and his fellow autistic self-advocates provided has proven to be invaluable. It has inspired me to think about the Artism Music Project, and more broadly the applied ethnomusicology of autism, in new and challenging ways. Mainly, at this stage, it is making me think long and hard about what in Artism is currently working and what is not. What about the project should be retained, adapted, developed, and nurtured, and what should be tossed, expunged, or at least radically reconfigured?

These are practical questions, not theoretical ones. They address applied ethnomusicology concerns, not intellectual abstractions. And yet, as applied ethnomusicology endeavors consistently teach us, there is no dividing line between the practical and the theoretical, the applied and the intellectual. They always inform and penetrate one another, for every practical decision both reflects the conceptual apparatus involved in its making and affects the conceptual horizons that emerge in its wake.

If we are to endeavor to improve Artism, our best first step is to respond directly, dispassionately, and honestly to the criticisms that have been directed toward it by autistic self-advocates. The following is at least a preliminary effort to do precisely that:

- Criticism: Failure to accommodate the sensory challenges of many autistics, especially their sensitivity to loud sounds.
    - This must be addressed, both within the group itself and in our mode of public performance. Mara has on a few occasions said that the tendency toward loud playing in the group, especially in the compositions of the two boys, Coffeebot and NICKstr, sometimes overwhelms her. There have been occasions when she has become distressed in rehearsals that now, in retrospect, I would attribute to her discomfort at the sheer loudness of the environment. E. S. does not speak verbally about sensitivity to sounds, but she does often cover her ears during rehearsals, which may—or may not—signal that she is experiencing discomfort or displeasure due to loudness.[21] The challenge here is that the two boys in the group *love* to play loud, sometimes really loud, and the philosophy of letting the child lead, especially in their own pieces, creates a dilemma as to whether they should be free to express themselves as they choose or should be reined in (and if the latter, by whom). In the end, however, we will probably do best to heed the advice of Jim Sinclair, who advocates for community norms that protect members with sensitivities from overstimulation (Sinclair, 2012 [2005]: 43). We can all learn to play more softly without ultimate compromise to our expressive potential, and this will need to be a goal for the ensemble in the future, for the sake of certain of its members as well as prospective audience members with heightened sensitivities to sound.
- Criticism: Failure to instruct the audience to use "silent applause" rather than clapping during the performance.
    - This deserves prompt attention. Encouraging future audiences to adopt the practice of applauding silently rather than clapping, which is standard practice at autistic gatherings such as Autreat, will enable us to avoid disturbing autistic or otherwise sound-sensitive audience members. It will additionally provide a great teaching moment on neurodiverse practices and values for our other concert attendees.
- Criticism: Absence of adult autistic musicians in the ensemble.
    - This, too, warrants an active response. If we claim to be a neurodiverse ensemble and to model neurodiversity by way of example, we need to raise the stakes of what is meant by such claims. We have to open ensemble membership not to just autistic adult musicians, but also to autistic "non-musicians" and neurotypical children. The present demographic of the ensemble is too categorical: autistic children, neurotypical adults. It is no wonder that autistic self-advocates would take issue with this arrangement, and it is imperative that this structure be remedied.
- Criticism: It appears that the children are not really the composers of the pieces credited to them.

- This is a complex issue. I can attest to the fact that the children have a great deal of autonomy in conceptualizing, exploring, making manifest, and shaping their own musical ideas on their own terms within the Artism context. That said, this is an improvisation-driven ensemble, and the collective improvisation process inevitably involves significant "co-creation" on the part of other members of the group. The staff musicians, being the experienced and professional players they are, have the capacity to strongly influence the music's direction as it emerges in the course of improvisation, whether intentionally or not. Moreover, since they are often the main (though not only) players of melodic and harmonic instruments, their impact on the shape and development of the children's compositions can be great. My overall impression has been that the children tend to appreciate and value these musical contributions of their adult collaborators; indeed, they have often stated this to be the case. Moreover, they are generally not averse to speaking (or otherwise communicating) their displeasure when they do *not* approve of where their music is being taken by the staff musicians. I believe that on this level we are actually doing quite well (though we can always do better) and that the issue here may be more one of impression than reality.[22]
- Criticism: Absence of political activism in the concert diminished its advocacy potential.
  - While I appreciate and respect this charge, I do not necessarily agree with it. It is my belief that the strongest "political" statement the Artism Ensemble can make on behalf of autistic advocacy, agency, and self-determination is the one that keeps the music in the foreground first, last, and foremost. Play is important, joy is important, shared endeavor is important, and music is important. If autistic and non-autistic people can share in the pleasurable co-creation of culture and music together through a project like Artism, and if other people get to share in that experience as well, whether as listeners or co-participants, then everyone benefits, consciousness is raised, mutual acceptance is cultivated, and good work is done. Sometimes, an absence of explicit political activism is to the advantage rather than the detriment of effective advocacy. Artism performances would seem to hold that potential, though different performance contexts will surely influence whether or not that is the case in the future.

Mara Speaks (Again)

Back to Mara, who is once again spinning in her favorite chair. ". . . and of course the Autism Ensemble [sic] is not a cure," she tells me. "I don't treat it like a cure, because it isn't, and if you call it a cure I will disagree with you. It's simply the kind of way you can calm down and, you know, help with the bad parts of autism without restricting the good parts."

I ask her what she means by that.

"Well, what I mean is, a lot of famous people were autistic or Asperger's or something," she explains. "[My] Mom tells us that people like Einstein and Marie Curie and a bunch of other famous people had it. Mom tells me that a lot of people who have autism and Asperger's can be more creative and insightful than other people, insightful in a way, you know, where they've experienced a lot of the emotions that they're either writing about in stories, or plays, or poems; because a lot of people who have autism can swing between different emotions really quickly. I'm like that. Someone will just say one word and I become like a stereotyped *emo*. (Once again, if you haven't heard it before, an *emo* is one of those really sad, dark people. I just go around telling people 'Life is pointless' when I'm like that.) Of course, the bad parts in my situation are that when I get angry, I get ANGRY!! I mean, like, yelling, slamming-door angry. Of course, I never get physical angry. I don't punch or hit or bite, though I have bitten someone, but that was in third grade. What I meant by helping with the bad parts but not restricting the good parts is that Artism kind of helps with my anger issues without restricting my creativity, and that's all I got to say."

"Well, OK," I say, pausing and trying to figure out a way to get Mara to expand briefly on that last topic. "I know we've been at this for a while, but can you just tell me a little bit more about how that works?"

"It's the fact that I'm allowed to bang on drums for a while—and any instrument I want (as long as I don't break it or it's not meant to be banged)—without anybody telling me I'm supposed to do it *this* way, or I'm supposed to do it *that* way, or I'm supposed to put *this* there or *that* THERE, or I'm doing it wrong."

"Is that the most important one," I ask, "the one about not being told you're doing it wrong?"

"Yeah."

"Why is that so important, not to be told you're doing it wrong?"

"Because I'm told that every day. I want a break from it!" She laughs. "*Spinny chairs!* . . . It's just nice being there with other people without them telling me what to do, or just jabbering about all the things they can do that I can't. . . ."

"If Artism continues next year and you stay in the group," I now ask Mara, shifting gears so as to test out some of Zach Richter's proposals for the group's future development, "what would you think about having an adult musician with autism join the band?"

"That would be good actually; it sounds pretty cool. I'd like that." Mara pauses and redirects her attention. "I like spinny chairs, paper clips, wolves, and a bunch of other things."

"What do you think it would add?"

"It would add to themselves and to us. It would be cool seeing an adult with autism in the group instead of just kids with autism. And the autistic adult would be happy to see so many autistic kids being happy too."

"Are you an autistic kid or a kid with autism?"

"It doesn't matter. It's like asking a zebra, 'Are you black with white stripes or white with black stripes?'"

"Would it be good to have kids who weren't autistic in the group as well?"

"What do you mean?" Mara asks, looking perplexed, as though the question doesn't even make sense. "Well, why not?!" she finally exclaims. "Does it matter? I mean, just because it's called the Artism Ensemble doesn't mean we only have to have autistic kids in there."

"Did it ever bother you that that was the way it was?"

"No, not really. We're all just kids in the end. I mean, that's the whole point. We're all just kids in the end. Who friggin' cares whether we're autistic or not? Why does it matter?"

Concluding Thoughts

Mara is wise beyond her years. Her ideas and insights cut to the core of many current autism and neurodiversity issues and debates.

"Who says autism is a bad thing?" she asks rhetorically. The answer is that a great many people do, indeed the vast majority. Yet Mara, along with autistic self-advocates such as Bascom, Walker, Sinclair, Ne'eman, Winter, Richter, and Grace, begs to differ: autism is not a bad thing, it's just a thing—a difference, not a deficit; a culture, not a disorder.

There "is no cure [for autism]. There really isn't. It's just there, wound into your personality," Mara tells us unequivocally, again echoing the convictions of most autistic self-advocates. No wonder these people decry the extraordinary amount of time, effort, expertise, and expenditure being poured into autism research and interventions aimed at their ostensible normalization, remediation, and cure, into what they equate with efforts at their erasure from a society that does not value or want them, as they are and for whom they are.

"Who friggin' cares whether we're autistic or not? Why does it matter?" Mara challenges us to wonder. Why indeed, for if the neurotypical majority could learn to better listen and respond to the autistic neurominority, to attend to what autistic people say *they* need and want, rather than assuming to know what's best for them, true neurodiversity would become a real possibility. Then whether you're autistic or not wouldn't have to matter so much, or it would matter in different, more productive ways. Working together, we can collectively forge a path away from stigma, exclusion, and disenfranchisement, and toward acceptance, inclusion, empowerment, and agency for all.

"It's just nice being. . . with other people without them telling me what to do, or just jabbering about all the things they can do that I can't." Poignant words again from Mara, and words that are hardly exclusive to autistic people; the relevance of such sentiments is arguably universal. Does it not behoove all of us to create, nurture, and sustain environments in which being together with others in this way can be expected, counted on, and assumed, whether you happen to be black or white, Muslim or Christian, autistic or neurotypical? Awareness is not enough; acceptance is the necessary but not sufficient condition for getting us to where we need to be.

Music provides a powerful vehicle for asserting and reifying the qualities of human dignity, inclusion, acceptance, and neurodiversity that Mara, along with an ever growing chorus of autistic self-advocates, champions of disability rights, and activist scholars across multiple disciplines, are promoting. Ethnomusicology, with its moorings in ethnography and musical co-participation, offers a productive theoretical foundation from which to move forward. Applied ethnomusicology, with its emphasis on putting ethnomusicological research to practical use, sets the merging of productive musical practice, ethnographic epistemology, and social activism in motion. An emergent ethnomusicology of autism is thus an arena of great potential, whether in its possibilities for exploring new horizons of musical sociality and agency, expanding the horizons of ethnographic possibility, or serving the interests of autistic self-advocacy, disability rights, and neurodiversity.

The path is not an easy one. Missteps and pitfalls are inevitable: the prospect of garnering resentment from the very people on whose behalf we presume ourselves to be working is real and palpable; the kinds of understandings we develop, programs we enact, and messages we send may well play into the hands of makers of agendas and images we aim to combat. Indeed, abundant opportunities exist to make things worse rather than better, regardless of our intentions. We may stumble, as I did at the Society for Disability Studies conference. We may propagate the very essentialisms we abhor, for example, in the aftermath of an Artism concert in 2012, when I overheard a departing audience member saying something to the effect of, "Oh, wasn't that special; it's so nice that those autistic kids get to do something fun with music since they surely couldn't play in a *real* band or orchestra."

"No one would claim perfection" in such work, Jeff Todd Titon presciently warned in 1992, since "action is risky, and sometimes one makes mistakes; but consider the alternative, non-action" (Titon, 1992: 320). Indeed, the stakes of taking action are high, but the consequences of not taking action are higher still. The risks are always there, but they are more often than not worth taking, so long as we approach our endeavors judiciously, intelligently, in a well-informed manner, and with compassion and vision. Most important, we must learn to listen and to listen well, even to those who may find it hard to communicate with us in ways that we can readily understand. That is a challenge that should not be beyond us. We are, after all, musicians, and ethnomusicologists; it's what we do.

Notes

1. For alternate definitions and substantive discussions of related issues in applied ethnomusicology, see also Titon (1992), Sheehy (1992), Alviso (2003), Harrison, Mackinlay, and Pettan, eds. (2010), and Harrison (2012).

2. All of the participating children and families in Artism were formerly participants in the ensemble's progenitor, the Music-Play Project, or MPP, as well. They were originally recruited for MPP through the client registry of the Center for Autism and Related Disabilities (CARD) at Florida State University and became involved with Artism when I put out an open call to MPP alumni in 2009 regarding this new, related project.
3. The intersectionality of autistic and child identities in the Artism Ensemble is not addressed explicitly in this chapter for reasons of space and scope. Exploring such intersectionality is of great potential significance, however. Ethnomusicologically oriented, ethnography-informed approaches to the study of children's musical cultures, as exemplified, for example, in publications by Campbell (2010), Marsh (2008), and Gaunt (2006), offer valuable models and possibilities relative to future projects and studies on the musical lives of autistic children.
4. There is continuing debate on the relative pros and cons of using person-first language in discourses on autism. As Elizabeth Fein notes, "In many disability contexts and communities, using 'person-first language' (i.e. *Steve is a person with autism*) is considered to be more respectful than using language that characterizes that person according to their condition (i.e. *Steve is autistic* or *Steve is an autistic*). However, in the autism world, this formulation of the relationship between person and condition is not so straightforward. Many in the autistic self-advocacy community have voiced a strong preference against person-first language, arguing that autism is not, in fact, separate from themselves in the way such language implies. . . . [I]n the absence of a single good answer to the thorny question of respectful language," Fein states, "I have chosen to use both of these formulations and alternate between them as seems appropriate for the context. Whenever possible, I follow the preferences of the person to or about whom I am speaking" (Fein, 2012: ix). I adopt a similar approach here.
5. For a range of approaches in music therapy, see Nordoff and Robbins (1977), Bruscia (1987), Clarkson (1998), Edgerton (1994), Ruud (1998), Aigen (2002), Stige (2002), Kern (2004), Pavlicevic and Ansdell (2004), Whipple (2004), Walworth (2007), Gold (2011), Reschke-Hernández (2011), and Simpson and Keen (2011).
6. This definition of "therapy" is from Oxford Dictionaries online: http://www.oxforddictionaries.com/us/definition/english/therapy (accessed May 28, 2014).
7. On medical ethnomusicology, see also Barz (2006), Koen (2009), Allison (2010), Van Buren (2010), and Barz and Cohen (2011). Of related significance are Roseman (1991) and Friedson (1996, 2009).
8. "Mark" is a pseudonym, as are the identifying names used in this chapter for all child participants in the Artism Music Project with the exception of Mara Chasar. Both Mara and her parents specifically requested that she be identified by her real name in this and other publications related to this research.
9. In the *Diagnostic and Statistical Manual of Mental Disorders*, 5th edition (i.e., DSM-5) (American Psychiatric Association, 2013), the various separate "disorders" of the autism spectrum, including Asperger's syndrome (Asperger disorder), have essentially been collapsed into a single diagnostic category of Autism Spectrum Disorder (ASD).
10. As for Mark himself, he recently told me that me he has no recollection of the events of that evening and explained that "[i]t's actually not that big of a deal to me, because I'm not that into music now anyhow" (personal communication, August 2, 2013).
11. The original 2011 grant and two renewals of it (2012, 2013) were federally funded by the National Endowment for the Arts and administered by the Florida Department of

State's Division of Cultural Affairs. Additional sponsorship of Artism has come from the Florida Council on the Arts and Culture, Remo Inc., the Council on Culture and Arts for Tallahassee/Leon County (COCA), Temple Israel (Tallahassee), the Society for Disability Studies, the Tallahassee Youth Orchestras, and the Florida State University's College of Music, College of Medicine, Center for Autism and Related Disabilities, and Autism Institute.

12. See note 9 above regarding how what were formerly recognized as multiple "disorders" of the autism spectrum have been collapsed into the single diagnostic category of ASD in DSM-5.
13. The anthropological study of autism is a growing field in which significant contributions are being made to epistemological and methodological transformations of autism research and discourse. See also Ochs et al. (2004), Grinker (2007, 2010), Solomon (2010b), Prince (2010), Sirota (2010), Sterponi and Fasulo (2010), Bagatell (2010), Solomon and Bagatell (2010), Brezis (2012), and Fein (2012).
14. *Loud Hands: Autistic People, Speaking* (2012) is an important recent addition to the growing corpus of published works addressing issues of autism and living with ASD that have been authored or co-authored by autistic people. See also Williams (1992), Lawson (2000), Shore (2003) (of additional interest on account of the author's professional status as a musician and music educator), Miller (2003), Prince-Hughes (2004), Biklen (2005), Ariel and Naseef (2006), Tammet (2007), Robison (2007), and Mukhopadhyay (2011 [2008]), among others. Numerous documentary films, blogs, websites, and other media also contribute to the increasingly prominent presence of autistic voices in ASD discourses.
15. Straus's work intersects disability studies, music theory, and musicology. He is central to a cohort of scholars currently working in these areas. Representative works in the emergent literature on music and disability that engage autism-related subjects include Straus's book *Extraordinary Measures: Disability in Music* (2011) and his co-edited volume (with Neil Lerner) *Sounding Off: Theorizing Disability in Music* (Lerner and Straus, 2006). That volume includes autism-related chapters by Headlam (2006), Jensen-Moulton (2006), and Maloney (2006). Of related interest, see Lubet (2011) and Marrero (2012). Of more general relevance to the epistemological orientations and practical ramifications of different models of disability in disability studies (e.g., medical, social), see Davis (2013a, 2013b, 2013c), Shakespeare (2013), Siebers (2013), Garland-Thomson (1997, 2013), Rioux (1994), Titchkosky (2007), Carlson (2009), Ralston and Ho (2010), and Silvers (2010); on autism specifically, see Nadesan (2005), Murray (2008), and Osteen (2008).
16. There is, of course, an inherent flaw in this comparative analogy. Balinese musicians were doing what they do long before I arrived in Bali as an ethnomusicologist in the 1980s, whereas the children in the Artism Ensemble did not know each other, let alone become co-creators of their own musicultural world, until after the program and the E-WoMP were created. I, in collaboration with other non-autistic adults, came up with the idea of the project, made the E-WoMP, and implemented Artism. Therefore, I may rightly be accused of having essentially created the ethnographic field site that I now visit and research. While recognizing that there is some irony in this situation, ethnographically speaking, I hold to the conviction that a large measure of "ownership" of the E-WoMP space, and of Artism's musical and social processes and priorities overall, has been claimed and maintained by the children in the group.

17. "Joobai I," by E. S., may be accessed at http://www.youtube.com/watch?v=2ZVHiDQJLL0; "Steel Percussion," by NICKstr, at http://www.youtube.com/watch?v=SjkrjHf_cSI. Both performances were recorded during a concert at the Florida State University Museum of Fine Arts in the spring of 2013. A rehearsal video of "Purple Eggs and Ham," by Mara, may be accessed at http://www.youtube.com/watch?v=CltqzvA96-E. Note that this video commences with an incomplete take. The full performance starts 40 seconds in, immediately after the point at which one of the children (Coffeebot) is heard saying "Take two."
18. This is a valid observation. Three of the four children who performed in the concert had diagnoses of Asperger's syndrome or high-functioning autism (HFA), and this was a major factor in the group's approach and profile on multiple levels. It is perhaps worth noting, however, that in the Music-Play Project, which enrolled more than 30 children in its programs from 2005 to 2009, the span of different ability and diagnostic profiles along the continuum of the autism spectrum was much larger than it has been in Artism. Several of the participating children in MPP were essentially nonspeaking individuals, for example.
19. This is not an exact transcript of the conversation. My reconstruction effort here is based on notes I took during the panel, journaling I did in its immediate aftermath, and memory-based recollections. I apologize and take full responsibility for any inaccuracies or misrepresentations.
20. I am grateful to Allegra Stout for consulting with me on the present work and for recommending the book *Loud Hands*, which has profoundly affected my perspectives on autism.
21. Since E. S. also frequently covers her ears in other settings, including quiet ones, it is difficult to determine whether this is a sound sensitivity–related matter in her case. This has been an ongoing topic of discussion with her parents and has been explored by the ethnomusicologist Elyse Marrero in her Master's thesis, which focuses on E. S. and her music (Marrero, 2012).
22. I hasten to add, however, that my Artism staff colleague Michelle Jones takes a more critical stance on this matter than I do. She contends that there is a tendency for the staff musicians to "dominate" the course of musical development at times. She also notes that the current arrangement, wherein melodic and harmonic instruments are principally the province of the staff musicians while the children (and parents) mainly play percussion, creates an "imbalance of power" that favors the adult players with professional musical experience.

REFERENCES

Aigen, Kenneth. (2002). *Playin' in the Band: A Qualitative Study of Popular Music Styles as Clinical Improvisation*. New York: Nordoff-Robbins Center for Music Therapy (Steinhardt School of Education, NYU).

Allison, Theresa A. (2010). "Transcending the Limitations of Institutionalized Aging Through Music: Ethnomusicology in the Nursing Home." Ph.D. dissertation, University of Illinois (Urbana-Champaign).

Alviso, J. Ricardo. (2003). "Applied Ethnomusicology and the Impulse to Make a Difference." *Folklore Forum* 34(1/2): 89–96.

American Music Therapy Association (AMTA). (2012). "Music Therapy as a Treatment Modality for Autism Spectrum Disorders," AMTA website: http://www.musictherapy.org/assets/1/7/MT_Autism_2012.pdf (accessed August 19, 2013).

American Psychiatric Association. (2000). *Diagnostic and Statistical Manual of Mental Disorders* (4th ed., Text Revision; DSM-IV-TR). Washington, DC: American Psychiatric Association.

American Psychiatric Association. (2013). *Diagnostic and Statistical Manual of Mental Disorders* (5th ed.; DSM-5). Arlington, VA: American Psychiatric Publishing.

Ariel, Cindy N., and Robert A. Naseef, eds. (2006). *Voices from the Spectrum: Parents, Grandparents, Siblings, People with Autism, and Professionals Share Their Wisdom*. London and Philadelphia: Jessica Kingsley Publishers.

Autism Speaks (website). (n.d. "a"). "What Is Autism: How Is Autism Treated?" http://www.autismspeaks.org/what-autism/treatment (accessed August 26, 2013).

Autism Speaks (website). (n.d. "b"). "What Is Autism: Autism Acceptance" http://www.autismspeaks.org/what-autism/autism-acceptance (accessed August 26, 2013).

Bagatell, Nancy. (2010). "From Cure to Community: Transforming Notions of Autism." *Ethos* 38(1): 33–55.

Bakan, Michael B. (1999). *Music of Death and New Creation: Experiences in the World of Balinese Gamelan Beleganjur*. Chicago: University of Chicago Press.

Bakan, Michael B. (2009). "Measuring Happiness in the 21st Century: Ethnomusicology, Evidence-Based Research, and the New Science of Autism." *Ethnomusicology* 53(3): 510–518.

Bakan, Michael B., Benjamin Koen, Fred Kobylarz, Lindee Morgan, Rachel Goff, Sally Kahn, and Megan Bakan. (2008a). "Following Frank: Response-Ability and the Co-Creation of Culture in a Medical Ethnomusicology Program for Children on the Autism Spectrum." *Ethnomusicology* 52(2): 163–202.

Bakan, Michael B., Benjamin D. Koen, Megan Bakan, Fred Kobylarz, Lindee Morgan, Rachel Goff, and Sally Kahn. (2008b). "Saying Something Else: Improvisation and Facilitative Music-Play in a Medical Ethnomusicology Program for Children on the Autism Spectrum." *College Music Symposium* 48: 1–30.

Barz, Gregory. (2006). *Singing for Life: HIV/AIDS and Music in Uganda*. New York: Routledge.

Barz, Gregory, and Judah M. Cohen, eds. (2011). *The Culture of AIDS in Africa: Hope and Healing Through Music and the Arts*. New York: Oxford University Press.

Bascom, Julia, ed. (2012a). *Loud Hands: Autistic People, Speaking*. Washington, DC: The Autistic Press/The Autistic Self Advocacy Network.

Bascom, Julia. (2012b). "Foreword." In *Loud Hands: Autistic People, Speaking*, edited by J. Bascom, pp. 6–11. Washington, DC: The Autistic Press/The Autistic Self Advocacy Network.

Biklen, Douglas. (2005). *Autism and the Myth of the Person Alone*. New York: New York University Press.

Brezis, Rachel. (2012). "Autism as a Case for Neuroanthropology: Delineating the Role of Theory of Mind in Religious Experience." In *The Encultured Brain: An Introduction to Neuroanthropology*, edited by D. H. Lende and G. Downey, pp. 291–314. Boston: MIT Press.

Bruscia, Kenneth E. (1987). *Improvisational Models of Music Therapy*. Springfield, IL: Charles C. Thomas.

Campbell, Patricia Shehan. (2010). *Songs in Their Heads: Music and Its Meaning in Children's Lives*. New York: Oxford University Press.

Carlson, Licia. (2009). *The Faces of Intellectual Disability: Philosophical Reflections*. Bloomington: Indiana University Press.

Clarkson, Ginger. (1998). *I Dreamed I Was Normal: A Music Therapist's Journey into the Realms of Autism*. St. Louis, MO: MMB Music.

Davis, Lennard J. (2013a). *The Disability Studies Reader* (4th ed.). New York: Routledge.

Davis, Lennard J. (2013b). "Introduction: Disability, Normality, and Power." In *The Disability Studies Reader* (4th ed.), edited by L. J. Davis, pp. 1–14. New York: Routledge.

Davis, Lennard J. (2013c). "The End of Disability Politics: On Disability as an Unstable Category." In *The Disability Studies Reader* (4th ed.), edited by L. J. Davis, pp. 263–277. New York: Routledge.

Edgerton, Cindy Lu. (1994). "The Effect of Improvisational Music Therapy on Communicative Behaviors of Autistic Children." *Journal of Music Therapy* 31(1): 31–62.

Fein, Elizabeth. (2012). *The Machine Within: An Ethnography of Asperger's Syndrome, Biomedicine, and the Paradoxes of Identity and Technology in the Late Modern United States*. Ph.D. dissertation (Comparative Human Development), University of Chicago.

Friedson, Steven M. (1996). *Dancing Prophets: Musical Experience in Tumbuka Healing*. Chicago: University of Chicago Press.

Friedson, Steven M. (2009). *Remains of Ritual: Northern Gods in a Southern Land*. Chicago: University of Chicago Press.

Garland-Thomson, Rosemarie. (1997). *Extraordinary Bodies: Figuring Physical Disability in American Culture and Literature*. New York: Columbia University Press.

Garland-Thomson, Rosemarie. (2013). "Integrating Disability, Transforming Feminist Theory." In *The Disability Studies Reader* (4th ed.), edited by L. J. Davis, pp. 333–353. New York: Routledge.

Gaunt, Kyra D. (2006). *The Games Black Girls Play: Learning the Ropes from Double-Dutch to Hip-Hop*. New York: New York University Press.

Gold, Christian. (2011). "Special Section: Music Therapy for People with Autistic Spectrum Disorder." *Nordic Journal of Music Therapy* 20(2): 105–107.

Grace, Elizabeth J., Aiyana Bailin, Zach Richter, Allegra Stout, and Alyssa Z. (2013). "Intersectionalities in Autistic Culture(s): A Discussion Instigated by This Posse of Autistics and Friends." Program Abstract, Society for Disability Studies 26th Annual Conference (p. 42).

Grandin, Temple, and Richard Panek. (2013). *The Autistic Brain: Thinking across the Spectrum*. New York: Houghton Mifflin Harcourt.

Grinker, Roy Richard. (2007). *Unstrange Minds: Remapping the World of Autism*. New York: Basic Books.

Grinker, Roy Richard. (2010). "Commentary: On Being Autistic, and Social." *Ethos* 38(1): 172–178.

Harrison, Klisala. (2012). "Epistemologies of Applied Ethnomusicology." *Ethnomusicology* 56(3): 505–529.

Harrison, Klisala, Elizabeth Mackinlay, and Svanibor Pettan, eds. (2010). *Applied Ethnomusicology: Historical and Contemporary Approaches*. Newcastle upon Tyne, UK: Cambridge Scholars Publishing.

Headlam, Dave. (2006). "Learning to Hear Autistically." In *Sounding Off: Theorizing Disability in Music*, edited by N. Lerner and J. N. Straus, pp. 109–120. New York: Routledge.

Jellison, Judith A., and Patricia J. Flowers. (1991). "Talking about Music: Interviews with Disabled and Nondisabled Children." *Journal of Research in Music Education* 39(4): 322–333.

Jensen-Moulton, Stephanie. (2006). "Finding Autism in the Compositions of a 19th-Century Prodigy: Reconsidering 'Blind Tom' Wiggins." In *Sounding Off: Theorizing Disability in Music*, edited by N. Lerner and J. N. Straus, pp. 199–215. New York: Routledge.

Kern, Petra. (2004). "Making Friends in Music: Including Children with Autism in an Interactive Play Setting." *Music Therapy Today* 5(4): 1–43.

Koen, Benjamin D. (2009). *Beyond the Roof of the World: Music, Prayer, and Healing in the Pamir Mountains.* New York: Oxford University Press.

Koen, Benjamin D., Michael B. Bakan, Fred Kobylarz, Lindee Morgan, Rachel Goff, Sally Kahn, and Megan Bakan. (2008). "Personhood Consciousness: A Child-Ability-Centered Approach to Socio-Musical Healing and Autism Spectrum 'Disorders.'" In *The Oxford Handbook of Medical Ethnomusicology: Music, Medicine, and Culture*, edited by B. D. Koen, pp. 461–481. New York: Oxford University Press.

Koen, Benjamin D., Gregory Barz, and Kenneth Brummel-Smith. (2008). "Introduction: Confluence of Consciousness in Music, Medicine, and Culture." In *The Oxford Handbook of Medical Ethnomusicology: Music, Medicine, and Culture*, edited by B. D. Koen, pp. 3–17. New York: Oxford University Press.

Lawson, Wendy. (2000). *Life Behind Glass: A Personal Account of Autism Spectrum Disorder.* London and Philadelphia: Jessica Kingsley Publishers.

Lerner, Neil, and Joseph N. Straus, eds. (2006). *Sounding Off: Theorizing Disability in Music.* New York: Routledge.

Lubet, Alex. (2011). *Music, Disability, and Society.* Philadelphia: Temple University Press.

Maloney, S. Timothy. (2006). "Glenn Gould, Autistic Savant." In *Sounding Off: Theorizing Disability in Music*, edited by N. Lerner and J. N. Straus, pp. 121–135. New York: Routledge.

Marrero, Elyse. (2012). *Performing Neurodiversity: Musical Accommodation by and for an Adolescent with Autism.* Master's thesis (Ethnomusicology), Florida State University.

Marsh, Kathryn. (2008). *The Musical Playground: Global Tradition and Change in Children's Songs and Games.* New York: Oxford University Press.

Merriam, Alan P. (1964). *The Anthropology of Music.* Evanston, IL: Northwestern University Press.

Miller, Jean Kerns. (2003). *Women from Another Planet? Our Lives in the Universe of Autism.* Bloomington, IN: First Books.

Mukhopadhyay, Tito Rajarshi. (2011 [2008]). *How Can I Talk if My Lips Don't Move? Inside My Autistic Mind.* New York: Arcade Publishing.

Murray, Stuart. (2008). *Representing Autism: Culture, Narrative, Fascination.* Liverpool: Liverpool University Press.

Nadesan, Majia Holmer. (2005). *Constructing Autism: Unraveling the "Truth" and Understanding the Social.* New York: Routledge.

Ne'eman, Ari. (2012). "The Future (and the Past) of Autism Advocacy, or Why the ASA's Magazine, *The Advocate*, Wouldn't Publish This Piece." In *Loud Hands: Autistic People, Speaking*, edited by J. Bascom, pp. 88–97. Washington, DC: The Autistic Press/The Autistic Self Advocacy Network.

NINDS. (2013). "Autism Fact Sheet." National Institute of Neurological Disorders and Stroke (website). http://www.ninds.nih.gov/disorders/autism/detail_autism.htm (accessed August 26, 2013).

Nordoff, Paul, and Clive Robbins. (1977). *Creative Music Therapy: Individualized Treatment for the Handicapped Child.* New York: John Day.

Ochs, Elinor, Tamar Kremer-Sadlik, Karen Gainer Sirota, and Olga Solomon. (2004). "Autism and the Social World: An Anthropological Perspective." *Discourse Studies* 6(2): 147–183.

Osteen, Mark. (2008). *Autism and Representation.* New York: Routledge.

Pavlicevic, Mercedes, and Gary Ansdell, eds. (2004). *Community Music Therapy*. London: Jessica Kingsley Publishers.
Prince, Dawn Eddings. (2010). "An Exceptional Path: An Ethnographic Narrative Reflecting on Autistic Parenthood from Evolutionary, Cultural, and Spiritual Perspectives." *Ethos* 38(1): 56–68.
Prince-Hughes, Dawn. (2004). *Songs of the Gorilla Nation: My Journey Through Autism*. New York: Harmony.
Prizant, Barry M., Amy M. Wetherby, Emily Rubin, Amy C. Laurent, and Patrick Rydell. (2006). *The SCERTS Model: A Comprehensive Educational Approach for Children with Autism Spectrum Disorders*. Baltimore, MD: Paul H. Brookes.
Ralston, D. Christopher, and Justin Ho, eds. (2010). "Introduction: Philosophical Reflections on Disability." In *Philosophical Reflections on Disability*, edited by D. C. Ralston and J. Ho, pp. 1–18. Dordrecht, Heidelberg, London, and New York: Springer.
Reschke-Hernández, Alaine E. (2011). "History of Music Therapy Treatment Interventions for Children with Autism." *Journal of Music Therapy* 48(2): 169–207.
Rioux, Marcia H. (1994). "Introduction." In *Disability Is Not Measles: New Research Paradigms in Disability*, edited by M. H. Rioux and M. Bach, pp. 1–7. North York, ON: L'Institiut Roeher Institute.
Robison, John Elder. (2007). *Look Me in the Eye: My Life with Asperger's*. New York: Crown Publishers.
Roseman, Marina. (1991). *Healing Sounds from the Malaysian Rainforest: Temiar Music and Medicine*. Berkeley and Los Angeles: University of California Press.
Ruud, Even. (1998). *Music Therapy: Improvisation, Communication, and Culture*. Gilsum, NH: Barcelona Publishers.
Shakespeare, Tom. (2013). "The Social Model of Disability." In *The Disability Studies Reader* (4th ed.), edited by L. J. Davis, pp. 214–221. New York: Routledge.
Sheehy, Daniel E. (1992). "A Few Notions about Philosophy and Strategy in Applied Ethnomusicology." *Ethnomusicology* 36(3): 323–336.
Shore, Stephen. (2003). *Beyond the Wall: Personal Experiences with Autism and Asperger Syndrome* (2nd ed.). Shawnee Mission, KS: Autism Asperger Publishing.
Siebers, Tobin. (2008). *Disability Theory*. Ann Arbor: University of Michigan Press.
Siebers, Tobin. (2013). "Disability and the Theory of Complex Embodiment—For Identity Politics in a New Register." In *The Disability Studies Reader* (4th ed.), edited by L. J. Davis, pp. 278–297. New York: Routledge.
Silvers, Anita. (2010). "An Essay on Modeling: The Social Model of Disability." In *Philosophical Reflections on Disability*, edited by D. C. Ralston and J. Ho, pp. 19–36. Dordrecht, Heidelberg, London, and New York: Springer.
Simpson, Kate, and Deb Keen. (2011). "Music Interventions for Children with Autism: Narrative Review of the Literature." *Journal of Autism and Developmental Disorders* 41: 1507–1514.
Sinclair, Jim. (2012 [1993]). "Don't Mourn for Us." In *Loud Hands: Autistic People, Speaking*, edited by J. Bascom, pp. 15–21. Washington, DC: The Autistic Press/The Autistic Self Advocacy Network.
Sinclair, Jim. (2012 [2005]). "Autism Network International." In *Loud Hands: Autistic People, Speaking*, edited by J. Bascom, pp. 22–70. Washington, DC: The Autistic Press/The Autistic Self Advocacy Network.
Sirota, Karen Gainer. (2010). "Narratives of Distinction: Personal Life Narrative as a Technology of the Self in the Everyday Lives and Relational Worlds of Children with Autism." *Ethos* 38(1): 93–115.

Solomon, Olga. (2010a). "Sense and the Senses: Anthropology and the Study of Autism." *Annual Review of Anthropology* 39: 241–259.

Solomon, Olga. (2010b). "What a Dog Can Do: Children with Autism and Therapy Dogs in Social Interaction." *Ethos* 38(1): 143–166.

Solomon, Olga, and Nancy Bagatell. (2010). "Introduction—Autism: Rethinking the Possibilities." *Ethos* 38(1): 1–7.

Sterponi, Laura, and Allesandra Fasulo. (2010). "'How to Go On': Intersubjectivity and Progressivity in the Communication of a Child with Autism." *Ethos* 38(1): 116–142.

Stige, Brynjulf. (2002). *Culture-Centered Music Therapy.* Gilsum, NH: Barcelona Publishers.

Straus, Joseph N. (2013). "Autism as Culture." In *The Disability Studies Reader* (4th ed.), edited by L. J. Davis, pp. 460–484. New York: Routledge.

Straus, Joseph N. (2011). *Extraordinary Measures: Disability in Music.* New York: Oxford University Press.

Tammet, Daniel. (2007). *Born on a Blue Day: A Memoir (Inside the Extraordinary Mind of an Autistic Savant).* New York: Free Press.

Titchkosky, Tanya. (2007). *Reading and Writing Disability Differently: The Textured Life of Embodiment.* Toronto: University of Toronto Press.

Titon, Jeff Todd. (1992). "Music, the Public Interest, and the Practice of Ethnomusicology." *Ethnomusicology* 36(3): 315–322.

Titon, Jeff Todd. (2011). "The Curry Lecture: Applied Ethnomusicology." Sustainable Music: A research blog on the subject of sustainability and music. http://sustainablemusic.blogspot.com/2011/04/curry-lecture-applied-ethnomusicology.html (accessed April 25, 2011).

Turino, Thomas. (2008). *Music as Social Life: The Politics of Participation.* Chicago: University of Chicago Press.

Van Buren, Kathleen. (2010). "Applied Ethnomusicology and HIV and AIDS." *Ethnomusicology* 54(2): 202–223.

Walker, Nick. (2012). "Throw Away the Master's Tools: Liberating Ourselves from the Pathology Paradigm." In *Loud Hands: Autistic People, Speaking,* edited by J. Bascom, pp. 225–237. Washington, DC: The Autistic Press/The Autistic Self Advocacy Network.

Walworth, Darcy DeLoach. (2007). "The Use of Music Therapy within the SCERTS Model for Children with Autism Spectrum Disorder." *Journal of Music Therapy* 44(1): 2–22.

Whipple, Jennifer. (2004). "Music in Intervention for Children and Adolescents with Autism: A Meta-Analysis." *Journal of Music Therapy* 41(2): 90–106.

Williams, Donna. (1992). *Nobody, Nowhere: The Extraordinary Autobiography of an Autistic.* New York: Harper Collins.

Winter, Penni. (2012). "Loud Hands and Loud Voices." In *Loud Hands: Autistic People, Speaking,* edited by J. Bascom, pp. 115–128. Washington, DC: The Autistic Press/The Autistic Self Advocacy Network.

CHAPTER 4

MOTIVATIONS AND METHODS FOR ENCOURAGING ARTISTS IN LONGER TRADITIONS

BRIAN SCHRAG

> ... I would so far hardly agree that the widely feared greying-out of musical diversity is actually taking place.... It's hard to overstate the harm done to most of the world's peoples by colonialism, capitalism, and globalization, but difficult to make a case for a pejorative evaluation of the musical results. The musical experience of the average individual is much broader today than in the past. The hybrids and mixes resulting from intercultural contact could be interpreted as enrichment as easily as pollution, and old traditions as a class have not simply disappeared.
>
> Bruno Nettl (2005: 434)

NETTL here deftly attempts to remove one of the most galvanizing burrs under the saddles of ethnomusicology's founders: the specter of global musical homogenization. Alexander Ellis validated non-European musical scales (1885), von Hornbostel and others created archives of recordings of non-European musics at the turn of the twentieth century (Koch et al., 2004), and Frances Densmore documented the musics of North American ethnolinguistic communities (1927). Jacob Gruber described these activities as salvaging as many bits of local communities left in colonialism's wake as possible (1970), and Alan Lomax visualized humanity's likely musical future as grey (1968). Ethnomusicology's pre- and early history resonated with an urgency to act in the face of inevitable loss.

Anthropologists, ethnomusicologists, and others have since eschewed this simplistic conceptual framework: colonialism and neocolonialism inexorably lead to the impoverishment of the centuries-old expressive culture of minoritized communities. Rather, we increasingly recognize the hugely complex interactions constantly occurring between Earth's seven billion individuals, their communities, sub-communities, and supra-communities; governmental, commercial, environmental, communicational infrastructures; and other factors we have yet to imagine.

We celebrate the sparks, the glitter that results from colliding cultures (Lipsitz, 1999). We acknowledge the complex histories and natural loss behind the illusions of cultural stability (Wade, 2012). In addition, we realize that communities are not passive receptors of every sign and system they encounter: "Central Africans in suits, Indonesian soap operas, and South Asian brands are no longer inauthentic copies by people who have lost their culture after being swamped by things that only North Americans and Europeans *should* possess. Rather there is the equality of genuine relativism that makes none of us a model of real consumption and all of us creative variants of social processes based around the possession and use of commodities" (Miller, 1995: 144).

Whence, then, come the burgeoning number of art forms populating UNESCO's List of Intangible Cultural Heritage in Need of Urgent Safeguarding (unesco.org/culture/ich)? Why have the Queensland Conservatorium Research Centre and partners invested five years and considerable financial resources in the Sustainable Futures for Music Cultures project, dedicated to the encouragement of endangered "small musics" (www.imc-cim.org/programme/development-and-music)? And why do many of the people I—and, perhaps, you—know in minority ethnolinguistic communities lament the loss of their traditional laments?

I readily acknowledge the labyrinthian nature of human creativity that our explorations unveil. I contend, however, that the maze is neither infinitely complex nor without metanarrative guidance. Individuals at the beginning of the twenty-first century do in fact experience more kinds of artistry than they did a century earlier. However, these "hybrids and mixes resulting from intercultural contact" constitute a rapidly growing percentage of human experience, masking processes of artistic and social change that result in experiential, social, and intellectual impoverishment. Tony Seeger attributes the loss of small traditions to an uneven playing field, one in which majority groups, missionaries, copyright legislation, and other systemic factors "disappear" them (Schippers, 2009).

We need not think in terms of contamination or enrichment. Rather, certain kinds of artistic traditions suffer from identifiable social and environmental changes: motivated by government promotion, lure of financial gain, war, or environmental catastrophes, children and families move from ethnolinguistically centered communities to cities composed of individuals connected by myriad identities. Such migration often results in loss of materials, skills, knowledge, and anchoring domains of use, thereby thwarting our progress toward a world marked by profoundly diverse artistic forms, each thriving and changing. Ethnomusicologists and others fascinated by surprising artistry in its social contexts are uniquely suited to influence this situation for the better.

In this chapter, I first lay out conceptual groundwork that enables arts-in-culture scholars to enter most productively into local, national, and international efforts to increase local artistic thriving. This entails avoiding esoterica and anchoring our research and communication in widely accessible categories related to experienced events. Second, I explore how framing artistic activity in terms of its degree of liminality moves us toward a deeper understanding of a global arts ecology. Third, I assess the health of artistic forms of communication in minority ethnolinguistic communities. Fourth and finally, I describe practical tools we can use as communities work toward more lively artistic futures.

Foundational Concepts

In this section, I describe the need for shared, widely accessible vocabulary in describing artistic traditions, and then outline a small set of such concepts. This foundation flows from prototype theory and from event-based approaches common to ethnomusicologists and anthropologists.

Return to Coherence

Ethnomusicologists are not usually trained to count things. Linguists count languages, biologists count species, sociologists count opinions, international nongovernmental organizations (INGOs) count displaced people, but ethnomusicologists don't have a comparable basic unit of analysis. Except for rhythmic or harmonic divisions *within* musical pieces, we embrace the caprices of communal choice and form, resisting the urge to define an artist or performance as "*this* and not *that*." After an exceptional education in ethnomusicology, I had to teach myself how to create, administer, and analyze the questionnaires supporting my Ph.D. research in Cameroon (Schrag, 2005). Though not uniformly or categorically (see Titon, 1997), we have eschewed Merriam's early positivist goal of "sciencing about music" (1964: 25).

The benefits of our view of research as purposeful dialogue with other humans, rather than observations of data containers, are enormous: We ground our ethics in human relationships by acknowledging individual and corporate agency, the transformative potential of artists and their arts, and the multivalence of people's identities. We avoid imposing the kinds of stereotypes that Jean Kidula—Kenyan Ph.D. in ethnomusicology—encountered when her students at the University of Georgia learned that she was an accomplished classical piano player: "You play keyboard? Oh my God! You are an African." Kidula responds that it's "sad that people try to push you into this box because an African should do this. Or because you're Italian you should only study that Italian stuff. [A]s a musician, you already know that. So what happens is, you get into other music because it makes... you start incorporating it into your own being" (Schrag, 2000).

When we want to contribute to broader conversations of human rights or influence government or community policy, however, we are left without the persuasive data of proportional loss that counting can reveal. Nettl doesn't *know* that "the musical experience of the average individual is much broader today than in the past." It seems like it *must* be true, given our own experiences and the demonstrably pervasive reach of electronic communication. But we don't really know what's going on.

In order to increase our engagement with people who identify with ethnolinguistic minorities, I propose that we refocus our attention on artistic practices and ideas that have coalesced into identifiable entities. There *are* individuals who experience commonality with other individuals around the idea and practices of an ethnolinguistic construction. The International Organization for Standardization has designated SIL International's *Ethnologue* (www.ethnologue.com) as the authority in identifying human languages (ISO 639-3 standard); it lists over 7,100 living languages, each of which serves as an identity marker for a group. People who speak the Mono language and live (or have lived) in one of several areas in northwestern Democratic Republic of Congo, for example, think of themselves as *amono*—Mono people. Ngiemboon speakers in West Cameroon assume enormous amounts of common knowledge, experience, and values with each other. None of these people groups is internally totally homogeneous, completely discrete, or represents its members' sole identity. But myriad communities connected by ethnolinguistic identity exist, and their interactions commonly include artistic forms of communication as well. Even more to the point, communities based on ease and predictability of communication usually betoken a long history of common language use, and thus draw on multigenerational traditions.

To avoid the dangers of essentializing that ethnolinguistic and artistic labels sometimes generate, I ground my analytical categories in prototype theory. First proposed by Eleanor Rosch in the 1970s (see Rosch, 1977), prototype theory provided a framework for the development of Cognitive Linguistics, which pictures cognition as an amalgamation of features of varying importance. This system of graded categorization evaluates how well a given term coheres with a concept under review. In North America, English speakers identify *robin* more frequently and quickly as a kind of bird than they do *ostrich*; a robin is a better example of a bird—a prototype—than an ostrich because robins have more of the popularly conceived important characteristics of birds (Taylor, 2008: 39–42). Researchers have explained how humans from a variety of communities in the world impute order and meaning to their musical sounds based on cognitive marking and neural processes (see Peretz and Zatorre, 2003). Cognitive anthropologists apply experimental psychology and other methods to explain patterns of shared knowledge (see Kronenfeld et al., 2011).

I approach every definition in this chapter as a tool to reveal local concepts that refer to prototypical elements of the arts and art making. They are centered, malleable, and porous starting points, rather than strictly and minutely delimited Aristotelian categories (see Lakoff, 1999, 1987). This means, for example, that I don't try to define a particular community as consisting only and all of the people who share a closed set of features. Rather, prototype construction leads researchers to identify members of a community by a changing set of features, some of which are more important than others; the language(s) someone speaks and her parents' birthplace, for example, may carry more weight than her manner of dress. This means also that my approach favors the discovery of commonalities, shared concepts within a community. Many ethnolinguistic communities are experiencing stress; emphasizing the stable, older elements of their artistry is more likely to lead toward continuity.

Analytical Categories

I have chosen categories and their definitions that flow directly from common ethnomusicological thought and practice, with organic extensions, and the capacity to be viewed through prototype theory: communities, events, artistic genres, genre enactments, and genre enactors. A *community* is any group of people that shares a story, identity, ongoing patterns of interaction, and that is constantly in flux. Examples include groups that share a strong ethnolinguistic identity, clubs of all kinds, families, dance associations, exercise groups, religious centers, and others. *Artistry* is a special kind of communication, marked by greater emphasis on manipulating form than the communication used in everyday interactions. Poetic speech may rely on patterns of sound and thought, such as rhyme, assonance, and metaphor, that a simple exchange of information will not. Circling a drum while repeating a sequence of foot movements relies on form more heavily than simply walking from one place to another. Adopting the facial expressions of a mythical character draws on form to communicate more than allowing a person's face to remain at rest. Artistry may mark events as separate from everyday activities, may touch cognitive, experiential, and emotional ways of knowing, and may contract or expand the information contained in a message. In addition, artistry often reveals its uniqueness as a bounded sphere of interaction. Artistic events have beginnings and endings (no matter how fluid), between which people interact in unusually patterned ways. Ruth Stone describes artistic events as "set off and made distinct from the natural world of everyday life by the participants" (1979: 37).

Artistic events occur in space and time and include artistry; such events are normally associated with one or more communities. An event is something that occurs in a particular place and time, is related to larger sociocultural patterns of a community, and is divisible into shorter time segments. Communities have types of events that include social expectations and patterns. Examples of events include festivals, birthday parties, rites of passage, watching and listening to a music video on an electronic device, studying a museum painting, a mother instructing her daughter with a proverb, and others. An artistic event contains at least one enactment of a genre.

An *artistic genre*—which I often shorten to *genre* in this chapter—is a community's category of artistic communication characterized by a unique set of formal characteristics, performance practices, and social meanings. My rough method of assessing whether an artistic practice constitutes a genre is that it must be at least two generations old, and community members must be able to create within the system. An important internal characteristic is the level of variation supported by a genre. Examples of genre include *olonkho* (Siberia), Broadway musical (New York City), *kanoon* (Cameroon), *huayno* (Peru), *haiku* (Japan), Delta Blues (Southern United States), and *qawwali* (South Asia).

An *enactment* is an instantiation of an artistic genre during an event, or artistry that people produce through a genre's patterns and practices (see Kisliuk, 1998: 12). *Enactors* communicate through an artistic genre. These people are human beings with multiple roles, competencies, knowledge sets, skills, histories, and identities.

Thinking this way has implications for evaluating the health of any kind of artistry. First, events may contain enactments of more than one genre. A commemoration of the death and life of a Bamiléké (Cameroon) king may last a month—one event with many sub-events. During this time, performers from other kingdoms visit to pay their respects, usually including performances of one or more genres, each with unique combinations of music, dance, drama, and visual elements. Second, events are normally longer than enactments of a genre. At a wedding, for example, you may perform a solo from a love song genre. Enactment of the love song genre is just one part of a larger event that includes rituals and other elements. Third, enactments of genres may be found in more than one kind of event. Certain kinds of acrobatic feats, for example, may appear both in circuses and gymnastic competitions. Fourth, many events entail strong expectations of what kinds of genres they can include. For example, an Orthodox icon might jolt worshippers in a Baptist sanctuary. There may be an inflexible association between a certain type of event and a certain genre, or participants in an event may have the freedom to switch out elements from different genres. Finally, genres and events are always changing. Old ones die, new ones are born, creative people innovate. Genres like *soukous* in 1960s Congo have multiple origins, wrapped in unique combinations of features; such fusions are common.

INTEGRAL AND LIMINAL GENRE ENACTMENTS

In April 2012, I attended a performance entitled "From the Arctic to the Middle East (Broken Narratives by an American Flamenco Dancer)" presented by the Clinard Dance Theatre in Chicago. My niece, Marisela Tapia, performed in this work, which was collaboratively created by Wendy Clinard and her students. Wendy is an accomplished performer and teacher of flamenco, and Marisela had built solid foundations through several years of involvement in the tradition. I expected to experience a performance that felt like the few other flamenco events I had seen and heard, but was surprised by my inability to frame it. *TimeOut Chicago* critic Zachary Whittenburg (Clinard, 2012) described "From the Arctic to the Middle East" as a "... joining of classical Spanish, Andalusian folkloric and current American techniques..." that "... spoke to broader cross-cultural themes."

After the performance, Marisela, her father Andrés, and I discussed the audience response to this modern/flamenco/classical Spanish fusion: palpably positive, marked by focused attention and spirited applause. I wondered, however, whether an audience that knows flamenco well would respond differently to a performance that had more of the characteristics typical of a fuller, older flamenco tradition. As I learned more about flamenco's history, sub-genres, and performance practices, I found examples of performances that entail many more people participating in more energetic and historically forged ways: shouts of *ole* and *eso es* at strategic moments, or the expectation of entering into the heightened state of *duende* (Webster, 2004).

Definitions

These experiences led me to hypothesize two broad enactment categories, based on the number and importance of their characteristics flowing from a genre. I call enactments with deep, wide-ranging relationships to a genre *integral*, and others, *liminal*. Integral enactments are profoundly familiar to performers and exhibit a congeries of components characteristic of their normal social and artistic infrastructure, sufficient to cohere as an iteration of a genre. Another way of describing integral performances may be as those most coincident with the participants' community's structuring structures (Bourdieu, 1977).

Liminal enactments, in contrast, do not comprise features sufficient to fully express a genre. Experiencers recognize certain elements, but lack an emergent frame to guide their expectations and engagement. Arnold van Gennep and Victor Turner developed the concept of liminality to explain rituals' capacity to usher someone from one identity to another (1960 and 1967, respectively). Though I here draw on liminality's more popular sense of being-in-transition, anthropologists' technical use provides some insights. For example, the period of resymbolization between two identities in a ritual allows social fluidity and experimentation not condoned on either side of the transformation. Liminal enactments of artistic genres also often entail unusual levels of risk-taking.

SUSSING OUT LIMINALITY AND INTEGRALITY

To explore liminality's usefulness as an analytical tool, we need to compare several pairs of integral/liminal enactments of a single genre. Two primary approaches exist. First, we could describe two genre enactments from different points in its history: one from a period of historical health of the genre, and one from a period of weakness. A less longitudinal solution entails description of two genre enactments from the same time period: one whose performance allows or encourages more integrality, and one whose context results in liminality. In this section, I place our discussion of artistic genres in the context of their historical geneses. Then I present an extended example of two closely related enactments of a single genre, the two differing primarily on their degrees of liminality. Finally, I isolate features that illustrate contrasts between liminal and integral enactments, drawing on other examples in the process.

Rock Enactments

I attended the Rock of Our Salvation Evangelical Free Church in Chicago's Austin neighborhood regularly from 1987 to 1990, with frequent subsequent visits. This predominantly African-American church became my family's spiritual home, and I became an informal apprentice of the choir director and keyboard player, Paul Grant and Charles Butler, respectively. At that time, my musical training and experience had mostly been in eurogenic traditions, so I needed to learn a number of black gospel church performance characteristics. These skills and knowledge included melodic and verbal improvisational techniques, modifications of vocal timbre, patterns of congregation/choir/soloist interaction, repertoire, common verbal couplets, and shared worship expectations and experiences, among others. When Paul Grant chose Andraé Crouch's "The Blood" as my first solo with the choir in the late 1980s, I integrated most of these characteristics through Paul's oral instruction and my imitation of others. The congregation responded with vocal and bodily animation, especially when I added melodic ornaments: "You've got the Spirit now!" The event dynamic, however, remained primarily one of separation between the performers and the audience.

 I discovered a deeper step into the genre during a visit to Chicago in 2011, when friends at the Rock asked me to sing "The Blood" again with the choir. Because by that time I had become more confident in my performance abilities and in the solidity of my relationships with the congregation, when I came to the end of the final chorus, I decided to improvise more freely, repeating phrases in counterpoint with the instrumentalists in ways that lengthened the song. The instrumentalists, director, choir, congregation, and I entered into a heightened communication mode. We focused intently on each other's visual, kinesic, verbal, melodic, and harmonic cues to shape the rest of the enactment. Members of the congregation began to stand, raise their hands, pray to God, cry, and shout affirmations. Their responses encouraged me to continue into a heightened musical and spiritual awareness and engagement. This reciprocal, resonating feedback did not occur in my previous, more liminal performances of the same song in the same genre.

THE EBB AND FLOW OF COMMUNICATION

When humans from one community interact with those from another, we search for or create ways to communicate. The longer and more regular this interaction becomes, the more energy at least one of the communities will invest in accommodating its visual signs, symbolic vocal systems, and social structures to the others'. The results of communication collisions vary widely, dependent on the agency of individuals, structural similarity of the two systems, economic and social capital at stake, and political or ecological forces, to name a few. Contests between ethnolinguistic communities and global economic and social forces, however, follow a common pattern: If the two groups differ substantially in power or status, then the weaker usually accedes more to the stronger's communication patterns. If they both inhabit similar locations in a power hierarchy, their adaptations to each other are likely to be more equal. The period of time, people engaged, and the locations associated with this contact constitute liminal communicational space.

Linguists and sociolinguists have examined many phenomena resulting from such liminal communicational spaces. Their categories most germane to our discussion are languages, pidgins, creoles, and diglossia (McWhorter, 2001: 131–176). In short, *languages* are grammatically and phonologically ordered systems that serve the needs of full communication; about 7,100 languages exist globally (www.ethnologue.com, accessed February 2, 2015). *Pidgins* are simplified communication systems that people use "... for the utilitarian purpose of interacting with [speakers of other languages] for reasons tied to basic sustenance through the exchange of goods and services" (McWhorter, 2001: 132). Examples of pidgins include Russenorsk—used to enable timber trade between Russians and Norwegians in the 1800s—and the system Native American Indians used to barter with European colonists. Language communities use pidgins for needs distanced from their core identities.

Sometimes, however, pidgins become *creoles*: systems of communication that develop a complexity, internal coherence, and intergenerational transmission distinct from all of the languages that spawned it. Papua New Guineans speak Tok Pisin, a creole historically connected to Portuguese, English, and Melanesian languages. Tok Pisin has developed complex grammatical and lexical characteristics, and people in urban areas are learning it as a first language.

Finally, *diglossia* refers to a situation in which a community speaks at least two languages, and each is "compartmentalized so that there is little or no competition between languages within the same function" (Lewis, 2009). In northwestern Democratic Republic of the Congo, speakers of the Mono language routinely use the regional language, Lingala, for trade. This is likely to remain a stable situation as long as most children leave the government educational system before finishing high school (Lubliner, 2002).

The Kera language spoken by about 35,000 people in southern Chad and Cameroon provides an example of a language that is becoming less complex because of interaction with people in another ethnolinguistic community. In rural areas, Kera speakers use three tones in differentiating between nouns. When Kera speakers—especially women—move to urban areas and begin to converse in French, however, they tend to reduce their use of tone when speaking Kera (Pearce, 2013).

Similar simplification results when communities' artistic forms of communication interact. At least until the 1970s, Siberian Sakha people enacted their *dièrètii* sung genre in ways that included its uncommon characteristic of "unfolding mode" (Alekseyev, 1976: 57; Harris, 2017: 28). Alekseyev describes performance of an unfolding mode as one in which "the distance between the neighboring tones of the tune can vary to extremely wide margins, from a whole tone interval to... even a tritone in its 'unfolding.' The latter is usually connected to an increase in emotional energy, often visible within the parameters of one song. In general, the width of the intonational step is generally related to the character of the personage being sung and the tessitura of the tune" (Alekseyev, 1996: 49; http://eduard.alekseyev.org/work20.html). In the last few decades, enactments of *dièrètii* frequently omit this feature, as Sakha scales transition from malleable intervals to more stable, diatonic forms heard in the modern Russian soundscape (Alekseyev, 1986: 213).

My research among Ngiemboon communities of West Cameroon revealed mechanisms of transmission that result in growing, evolving traditions of integral enactments. The robust performances I encountered were marked by a particular dynamic interchange: its artists create tradition through the masterful exercise of the most malleable of their infrastructures, thereby strengthening the most stable (Schrag, 2013).

The dance association DAKASTUM (Danse Kanoon du Secteur Ntumplefet) provides an instructive example of transmission and interaction that leads to integral enactments. This group of about 40 men and a few women live in Cameroon's capital of Yaounde, meet every two weeks in the home of one of their members, and rehearse exemplars of the *kanoon* Ngiemboon artistic genre. They sing and dance while circling a group of percussionists. DAKASTUM's primary motivation in meeting regularly is to perform at *nkem legwés*—death celebrations—that take place in the first few months of the year, about six hours' distance in their home region, Batcham. Songs' refrains (stable infrastructure) provide the song caller time and predictability to compose the next call (a malleable infrastructure), while the caller's addressing important people provides emotion, social context, and interest to keep singing the crucial refrain; the rigid metronomic patterns of instruments like the shakers allow the player of the big drum structure in which to improvise, which increases interest in and energy emanating from the ensemble; the unflinching existence of the paved road between Yaoundé and Batcham enables DAKASTUM and hundreds of other dance associations to frequently climb aboard a bus (malleable infrastructure) to facilitate interaction and learning between urban and rural performers, while tolls from the bus and thousands of other vehicles provide the Cameroonian government enough money to maintain the road.

DAKASTUM members point to performances at *nkem legwés* as the most integral. These performances include competent players for each of six percussion instruments, at least one masterful song caller, at least 15 to 20 dancers, a chain of about a dozen songs, a high degree of energy and volume (accompanied by steadily rising pitch throughout the performance), time for the caller to improvise lyrics related to the location of the *nkem legwé*, and scores of Ngiemboon people watching. DAKASTUM modifies its enactments for other contexts—for example, recordings for popular distribution in Cameroon or singing an anti-AIDS song in a hospital—including shortening their songs, removing the song-chaining feature, and reducing percussive, vocal, and dance improvisation as much as possible (Schrag, 2005: 163–165). These enactments are outside the center of the *kanoon* genre, moving toward liminality.

When interaction between diverse communities occurs, the prospect of imaginative pleasure, or the attainment of political, monetary, or social goals, may draw artists to act in generic contexts foreign to them; by doing so, they enter liminal space. Artists in this space generate artistry through various combinations of generic patterns and conventions. They may remain embedded primarily in a genre they know well, incorporating interesting features from a new genre into enactments of the known. In this case, they flavor or spice their artistic output with foreign elements that symbolically shift experiencers'—including their own—interpretive frames. The creators of the album *Deep Forest*, for example, "fused digital samples of music from Ghana, the Solomon Islands, and African pygmies with 'techno-house' dance rhythms" (Mills, 1996: 59). The album has sold millions of copies. Feld suggests that the creators of *Deep Forest* are able to "borrow" from non-Western groups because they have romanticized them into representing humanity's primal origins; they are *us* thousands of years ago, so it's really *our* music, too (1996: 25). *Deep Forest* extracted bits of timbre, song phrases, and other artistic elements from foreign genres and inserted them into their artistic base, techno-house.

Most fusions have relatively weak potential for sustaining continuing creativity. This happens when new enactments do not develop into generic patterns that allow other people to enter easily. In fusion, you have to give up something. The result can become a new tradition (e.g., High life), but the initial contributors each offered a bit, a flavor of their deeper, broader artistic tradition. If they leave the old tradition for the emerging, they lose that depth and integration. For example, a tabla master playing jazz or pop reduces conceptual foundations (e.g., ragas), repertoire, social integrations and meanings, forms, and other elements to fit new structures and performance contexts.

Factors affecting the results of interaction between two or more sociartistic genres include the relative social status of each tradition, the preponderance and ease of access to each (for example, through radio, internet, oral means, etc.), and the number of practitioners. The stronger will usually influence the weaker more substantially, resulting in more moves toward liminality by the weaker. From a broad view, minority communities with ethnolinguistic identities exhibit more genres in fundamental transition, fewer enactors of their older genres, lower social status of their older genres, and fewer traditional social domains for the enactment of older ethnoartistic traditions. The global picture, then, is one of minority artistic traditions simplifying, assimilating into majority social domains (e.g., entertainment, tourism, global church), and enjoying fewer practitioners, each with diminished skills.

If people attempt to learn another artistic tradition, having no interest in maintaining their own, then their artistic symbolic structures will still influence the resulting performances: borrowing from linguistic terminology, they will perform with an accent. The accent could result from symbolic structures relating to their societies (e.g., ethnolinguistic communities), performance practices, and performance systems (vocal timbre, fabrics worn, languages used, instruments, patterned movements, etc.). If enough people are interested in creating at the point of socioartistic contact, then new artistic genres may be born.

French philosopher Paul Ricoeur describes tradition as "... not the inert transmission of some already dead deposit of material but the living transmission of an innovation always capable of being reactivated by a return to the most creative moments of poetic activity... [A] tradition is constituted by the interplay of innovation and sedimentation" (1984: 68). The transmission of traditions depends on people emitting sounds, visual patterns, objects, and smells from their bodies into the air, with other people then learning and embedding those symbols into their consciousness and bodies. Innumerable factors may influence the progression of a community's artistry.

How Integral and Liminal Enactments Differ

Embedded in communal systems of value, identity, and transmission, integral instantiations of an older genre exhibit a strong cluster of features characteristic of the genre. In contrast, a liminal enactment connects more ephemerally to both genre patterns and community. I offer the following statements as informed hypotheses comparing the effects of each, ready to be tested.

Integral enactments exhibit more complexity than do liminal. People's communication systems generally become more complex with frequent interaction in the system over a long time, and simpler with less internal interaction; this parallels differences between languages and pidgins. The more time people spend with each other creating within a genre, the more communicational nuance, subtlety, and virtuosity are possible.

Integral enactments result in more ecstatic experiences than do liminal. The communicational complexity typical of integral performances serves as a resource for enactors of genres that comprise ecstatic states. Heightened emotional states are part of numerous artistic traditions, including Hausa Bori ceremonies (Nigeria), Zar in Ethiopia, Candomblé in Brazil, Santería in Cuba, Tarantismo in Italy, Bira in Zimbabwe, glossolalia in Pentecostalism (Becker, 2004: 97–99), Catholic mystical traditions, New Age meditation, and many others. Ecstatic states are often foregrounded by specialized terminology, such as groove (Afrogenic popular musics), in the pocket (jazz), *tarab* (Arabic performance), and *duende* (Flamenco).

In "Creativity and Ambience: An Ecstatic Feedback Model from Arab Music," Jihad Racy provides a rich example of the complex knowledge, experience, and interactions necessary for ecstasy to emerge from performance of certain Arabic genres (1991). He argues that the creative process requires not only the skill and artistry of the classically trained composer/performer, but also a communicative audience that shares an understanding of the basic musical materials (e.g., *maqamat*) with the performers. Intelligent, emotional feedback from the listeners affects how the performers spontaneously compose. This emotional exchange helps create in the performer the ecstatic state of *saltana*. I here quote Racy at length (11–12):

Traditional performers, I have interviewed, stress that the *tarab* process first requires that the singer or the instrumentalist belong to the *tarab* culture. Like his audience members, he must be "native" to the *tarab* musical idiom so that he can "feel" the music, or as Fakhri explains, he must understand and sense it properly. He must, for example, play the neutral (microtonal) Arab interval correctly and "feel" their musical effect. Similarly he must understand and respond to the *quaflat* (singular *qafla*), or the emotionally charged cadential formulas at the end of each melodic phrase, particularly in modal improvisations.

In addition, such a performer must be endowed with *ruh*, "soul," or *ihsas* "feeling," namely the emotional power and talent to musically affect, or engage the listener ecstatically. Without this innate quality, a performer may still be accepted for his technical performance skills or his ability to display musical innovations, but is also criticized and even dismissed as someone who plays but does not communicate emotions, or as Sabah Fakhri puts it: "He can play his instrument, but cannot make it speak." Musically, *hsas* implies correct intonation, rhythmic accuracy, and good judgment regarding modal progressions and tonal emphases. "Feeling" also refers to an intuitive ability to affect, for example, finding the desirable delicate musical balance between renditions that are too static and too repetitive to be emotionally engaging, and those that are too excessive and digressive to generate and maintain a true sense of musical ecstasy.

Racy describes performance that is intense, reciprocally communicative, resonant, visceral, and dependent on deep experience and long traditions; integrality is clearly required to produce ecstasy in such Arab classical genres. I've seen Racy perform in contexts where only a few of these characteristics existed, and participants didn't express the same emotional states. Liminality dilutes groove.

Integral enactments result in more deeply contented enactors than do liminal. Beginning in the 1940s, psychologist Abraham Maslow developed the concept of self-actualization, as the pinnacle of his hierarchy of needs: the state of a person who realizes his or her potential, fulfills him- or herself, and does "the best they are capable of doing" (Maslow, 1954: 150). In liminal enactments, artists limit the sounds, sights, and movements they produce because they cannot lean into the patterns and signs of an established genre. Following Maslow, artists without contexts in which they can fully express their art live poorer lives. Researchers have applied the concept of self-actualization cross-culturally to a degree (see Ivtzan, 2008), but more study is needed to know how much it explains globally. I expect that skillful artists thrive in their artistic potential most during integral enactments.

Liminal enactments can lead to the development of new genres. If people invest enough energy into the enactment and institutionalization of liminal forms over time, new genres emerge. Essentially every transnational, transethnic, translinguistic form of artistry reflects this process: Congolese popular music draws historically on West African, Cuban, European, and Central African musicking, propelled to wide influence in part by recording studios in the Congo basin in the 1930s and 1940s (Mukuna, 1992); Punjabi popular music mixes European features with those of their ethnolinguistically tethered arts (Schreffler, 2012); and virtually all North American popular music flows from artistic interactions between enslaved Africans and others (Southern, 1997). This is the artistic water through which nearly everyone connected to the global economy swims.

Liminal enactments can provide spaces for forging social harmony. Communities united by ethnic, political, commercial, or other ties often vie for dominance at the interstices of contact with others. But liminal space is in some ways neutral ground—betwixt and between—and artists with divergent histories and competencies may also find connections therein. To overcome natural frictions, then, efforts to encourage co-operation require intentional rigidity and patient relationship-building. Participants in the Songs for Peace Project (www.songsforpeaceproject.org) drew on this feature of liminality to work toward reconciliation between Muslims and Christians. They gathered ethnomusicologists, composers, cinematographers, missiologists, and various scholars at colloquia in Beirut, Lebanon, and Yogyakarta, Indonesia. They interacted through presentations, discussion, and shared performance (King and Tan, 2013).

Such liminality contributes malleable, invigorating energy into human dialogue. It provides space, for example, to connect people from divergent communities to encourage peace.

Liminal enactments can tickle people's imaginations. Liminal enactments like Wendy Clinard's collaborative flamenco fusion, "From the Arctic to the Middle East," inject energy into genre breaking and novelty. Clinard's intense motivation to explore boundaries and fuse disparate traditions invigorated her for years, resulting in marked newness. Such enactments can also introduce non-aficionados to interesting and valuable artistry, as Wendy's did for me.

Assessing the Health of Humanity's Artistic Traditions in the 2010s

Nettl is likely correct in stating that "[t]he musical experience of the average individual is much broader today than in the past." Their integral experiences, however, may be few. In this section, I first propose a straightforward gauge of an individual artistic genre's health. I then provide a broad historical framework for explaining the general state of minority arts, and present a graded scale for assessing the health of artistic traditions through historical lenses.

For our present purposes, I am most interested in one particular kind of historical artistic genre change, namely the kind experienced by many ethnolinguistic communities in the last 100 years or so. These changes are built on colonial, missionary, commercial infrastructure, and social momentum influences of the late 1800s and early 1900s. Subsequently, the rate of change accelerated due to urbanization and the astounding expansion of communication technologies from the late 1900s until the present.

Measuring the Health of an Ethnolinguistic Community's Artistic Genres

Following Ricoeur's view of tradition as a living process of innovation and sedimentation, the ideal growth pattern of artistic genres is one of grounded creativity through balanced malleable-stable dynamism. Practitioners maintain a sustainable equilibrium between newness and familiarity, allowing the new to invigorate the familiar and the familiar to support the new. A long malleable/stable passing on of a tradition produces complexity, depth, and integration with its community(ies), while allowing for adaptation and novelty. The result is the production of thriving, resilient, flourishing arts.

Quick and Dirty Genre Health Sketch

My time living in the Mono village of Bili in the Democratic Republic of the Congo in the early 1990s and subsequent interactions allow me to suggest a rough model to measure how well a tradition is following this pattern. Three types of data are necessary for such an analysis: the number of times the genre has been enacted in two or more periods separated by a significant passage of time; an assessment of each instantiation's degree of integrality; and indications of the growth of the genre's features in new enactment contexts. From this data, we can approximate the most recent measure of health of the genre and its trajectory for the future.

Table 4.1 roughly illustrates the change in health of the *gbaguru* genre, as enacted by the Mono community in Bili. *Gbaguru* is a long tradition characterized in the main by these traits: sung; performed primarily by men; played on a 7–10 stringed harp, the *kùndi*; lyrics in the Mono language; melody does not move in opposition to linguistic tonal direction; lyrics commonly refer to Mono proverbs; composers' purposes normally include giving advice to someone; and broader social purposes include enforcing social norms.

Longer *gbaguru* enactment contexts include the following: individual enjoyment at home, while walking through a forest, *yangba* and *gbaya* circle dances, and the *gbaza* male initiation rite. All of these have become less frequent since the 1940s, caused primarily by government institution of schools and the expansion of Communauté Evangélique du Christ en l'Ubangi (CECU) churches using foreign arts. The last *gbaza* was performed near Bili around 1974.

Newer *gbaguru* enactment contexts include recording an oral "letter" for someone far away, lyrically and dramatically communicating news, and leading worship in CECU churches. CECU churches began introducing *gbaguru* songs into their services periodically in the early 1990s, and in more regular and extensive ways since 2007. I was purposefully involved in pastors' discussions of embracing *gbaguru* music into the lives of their communities and in contributing to a song-writing workshop in 2007. The 2007 workshop resulted in a dramatic growth in the number of people performing

Table 4.1. Number and Integrality of Gbaguru Enactments, Mono Community

	Number of	Enactments	Integrality	of Enactments
	Longer Traditions	*Newer Traditions*	*Longer Traditions*	*Newer Traditions*
1940s	high	none	high	N/A
1980s	low	very low	medium	very low
1990s	low	low	medium	very low
2011	low	medium	low	medium

and composing *gbaguru* for mostly Christian purposes. Note that I haven't counted the enactments, and so must rely on comparative vocabulary in Table 4.1 to illustrate my points.

Graded Genre Health Analysis

Linguists have tried to understand the rapid rate of language death in the world today by analyzing the nature of each language's use and transmission (see, e.g., Lewis and Simons, 2010). Ethnomusicologists have begun to adapt the concomitant models to artistic forms of communication. Box 4.1 identifies eight possible states of an artistic genre's vitality.[1] Assessing a genre's vitality on a graded scale helps guide the nature of our interactions with a community.

GLOBAL COMMUNITY ARTISTIC HEALTH ASSESSMENT

No one has evaluated the health of the world's artistry as a whole through rigorous quantitative or qualitative lenses; we have as yet neither the conceptual framework nor the methods to make this assessment. Building on this chapter's discussions, I here suggest several possible characteristics of a vigorous global ethnoartistic ecology that may serve as steps toward our capacity to evaluate our status in a useful manner. Building on its origins as a branch of biology concerned with the relationships between living things and their physical context, I use the term *ecology* here to emphasize the interdependence between all embodied, social, communicational, and physical factors affecting the world's artistry. Healthy artistic and biological systems share several characteristics: They benefit from the adaptational value of diversity; they follow finite cycles of growth, decay, and renewal; they exhibit immeasurably complex internal and external connections; and they respond well to humble stewardship at the community

Box 4.1 Graded Health Assessment of Artistic Communication Genres

1. **International**: An artistic genre reaches this level when an international "community of practice" forms around it.
2. **National or regional**: The genre's reputation grows beyond the home community. Community members may receive financial or other support from the regional or national level.
3. **Vigorous**: This is the pivotal level for artistic vitality. At this level, oral transmission and largely traditional contexts of education are intact and functioning. People have sufficient opportunities for performance, and young people are learning by observation, participation, and appropriate educational contexts. A genre can exist comfortably at this level without needing to move higher.
4. **Threatened**: The first level that hints at downward movement, toward endangerment. A genre is still enacted, but changes are becoming noticeable: diminishing performance contexts, increased time given to more recent introductions, more rural-urban movement.
5. **Locked**: The genre is known by more people than just the grandparent generation, but its performance is restricted to tourist shows or other contexts that are not integrated into the everyday life of the community. The performance repertoire is fixed, with no new additions. Participation and creative energy decline noticeably.
6. **Shifting**: The grandparent generation is proficient in this genre, but fewer contexts exist for passing it on to younger people. Possibly the younger people do not express interest (or are perceived that way by their parents and grandparents). The genre is not dead or endangered at this level, and can be revitalized, but signs point to downward movement and likely endangerment.
7. **Dormant**: Functional contexts for performance are gone, but recordings and other ethnographic description exist. A community could reacquaint itself with the genre, but its rebirth would likely take on a different character than the original.
8. **Extinct**: No one in the community is capable of creating or performing in this genre. Probably no performance has occurred in the lifetime of anyone currently living. No documentation exists. This is rarer, as most genres grow into other styles, or stylistic elements are perpetuated in related styles.

level (Titon, 2009). In the vocabulary of dynamism that emerged from my study of Ngiemboon communities, a healthy global artistic system is one in which many older traditions exhibit internally sustainable creativity—a vibrant malleable/stable engine within a growing community. In such a system, the percentage of liminal artistic performances in the world in any given year should not surpass that of integral, and such performances should contribute to a vibrant malleable/stable engine that feeds energy back into local creative ecosystems.

A thriving global ecosystem makes non-destructive use of electronic communication media, which seems more likely than some early predictions would have it

(Green and Ruhleder, 1995). A 2009 study found that ". . . while the [Internet] revolution increased the volume of all communications, it is possible that it has intensified our local communications to a greater extent than it intensified our global communications, simply because we maintain a greater number of local contacts. If this is correct, physical proximity may have become an even *more* important factor in social dynamics compared to the pre-[Internet] era" (Goldenberg and Levy, 2009). Crowdsourcing and other community data gathering approaches also promise the ability to contribute to "local" projects from anywhere (Greengard, 2011). Audio or video internet discussions, then, may energize local traditions by increasing their visibility, and artists in majority traditions acknowledge and affirm local creativity. In addition, many new traditions become vibrant and deeply embedded in communities, but not at the expense of older, existing traditions. Finally, the global artistic panorama contains thriving communities expressing as much fundamentally diverse artistry as possible, resulting in individual and communal well-being and self-actualization.

Examples of Loss in Longer Artistic Traditions

In 2005, six city-raised participants attended a song-writing workshop I led in Yaounde, Cameroon. Most of their parents or grandparents had moved to Yaounde from geographically centered ethnolinguistic communities elsewhere in Cameroon. I asked how many knew one of the traditional song styles of their parents well enough to sing or compose in it. The number: zero. When I lived in the Mono village of Bili (northwestern Democratic Republic of the Congo) in the early 1990s, only two older men played the *mbaza* (xylophone), a few people knew how to play and sing with the *kùndi* (harp), and horn ensembles had all but disappeared. This contrasted markedly with how older people described the community life of one or two generations earlier, when these traditions flourished. In neighboring Central African Republic, the Mpyemo instruments that Gerhad Kubik and Maurice Djenda noted in 1966 (Kubik, 1998: 311) no longer existed by the late 1990s (Brad Festen, personal communication; Djenda, 1992/1993). *Olonkho* epic poem performances in Siberia (Harris, 2017: 3), *alamblak* slit drum speech (Coulter, 2007), and Kaluli *sa-ya:lab* funerary weeping (Feld, 2001: 54–55) in Papua New Guinea all represent artistic genres that have mostly or completely faded from communities since the 1950s. UNESCO contributes bureaucratic and international weight to exposing these phenomena by yearly adding artistic traditions to its Lists of Intangible Cultural Heritage (ICH) in Need of Urgent Safeguarding (www.unesco.org/culture/ich).

Perhaps, as Nettl suggests, the losses we notice represent the natural course of societal evolution—one form dies, another takes its place, and the beat goes on. We may experience melancholy at its passing, but there's usually something new and interesting and solid around the corner. I believe, however, that the global picture of change in human artistry is qualitatively different and more deeply corrosive now than in the last century. I base this conclusion on viewing art forms as ecologically situated systems of communication that respond to global social dynamics in ways similar to languages and physical ecosystems.

As far as I know, nobody has tried to make an exhaustive list of such forms of artistic communication, their histories, and health. Linguists and ecologists, however, have counted languages and species of flora and fauna. Respected (and contested) scholars predict that if losses continue at current levels, 50% of plant and animal species and perhaps 90% of the world's more than 7,000 languages will disappear by the end of the twenty-first century (Krauss, 1992; Wilson, 2002). Linguist Michael Krauss challenges his colleagues: "Obviously we must do some serious rethinking of our priorities, lest linguistics go down in history as the only science that presided obliviously over the disappearance of 90% of the very field to which it is dedicated" (1992: 10). I am not aware of parallel counts of artistic genres, but the examples of loss I have given suggest that such communication may follow similar trends (see Aubert, 2007: 55–56).

Testimonials

My Cameroonian friend Roch Ntankeh is in one of the first generations whose parents moved from rural areas to Yaounde, learning only French and popular music styles. In his late twenties, he began to feel a void that came from his ignorance of the language and arts of his parents' region, Bangangté. With this motivation he has researched that community's arts for an academic degree, and has begun regularly taking his children to Bangangté for lessons in their language and arts.

> The first thing that motivated me to study the music of my own people is the fact that I had important musical skills and social curiosity that permitted me to more quickly understand than someone outside my culture. After that, I realized how little I knew of my own culture. This motivated me to find out more because I learn much through individual study. The feeling that animates me is joy, curiosity, lots of questions; but beyond all of that, the inner peace caused by the fact that I've re-found myself, my own history and my identity. I thus feel affirmed and encouraged. And that motivates me to encourage others to do the same because it's only when you discover what's hidden inside yourself that you can grasp what's hidden in others.
>
> (written communication, May 2013, my translation from French)

Ethnomusicologist Robin Harris conducted research with Sakha communities in northern Siberia, focusing on the epic storytelling genre, *olonkho*. Master *olonkhosut* Pyotr Reshetnikov shared as follows (Harris, 2009; see also Harris, 2017: 161–162):

> The audience for olonkho is less now because they have forgotten how to listen to olonkho, as an oral creation, as an attractive, really, creation of humanity. There used to be lots of olonkhosuts, great olonkhosuts, because there was a community of listeners. In the past, olonkhosuts were elevated, and if the olonkhosut was good,

even great, one whose name was spread around the republic, people would make an effort to come, even from far away to hear.

Both of these artists feel hope, Roch because of his resources and fortitude to take such energetic measures, and Pyotr Reshetnikov because of the revitalization that began after Soviet decline in the 1990s. I have other friends who don't have the resources and fortitude to take such energetic measures, and they feel that their relevance to the world is fading.

I believe that the most crippling injuries triggered by increasing liminality are human existence with less deep pleasure, fewer thriving communities, and unfulfilled friends. The lost satisfaction includes not merely the pleasure related to heightened emotional states, but also the delight in being surprised or the opportunity to encounter myriad artistic milieux that spark curiosity, exploration, creation, and response.

Toward a Thriving Global Artistic Life

A healthy artistic genre has recurring enactments, effective patterns of transmission, and innovation in the context of predictability. At a global level, healthy artistry includes the continual reinvention and interaction of painfully diverse genres. Scholars in culture, communication, and the arts can significantly increase the likelihood of reaching such an enduring, vibrant dynamism.

Global Interest in Longer Artistic Traditions

I first presented a paper at an ethnomusicology conference in the early 1990s. After discussing my efforts to encourage creativity in northwest Democratic Republic of the Congo, an ethnomusicology student offered this advice: "Don't worry about all that activist stuff. Just record the harp music so we can enjoy it—it's beautiful." Speechless at the time, I have since reflected on the effects of various ideological and philosophical strands twisting through ethnomusicology and related fields. The two strands most germane to this discussion are the tension between activism and scholarship, and the role of ethnolinguistic minorities in ethnomusicological research. Regarding the latter, members of the Society for Ethnomusicology (SEM) have, since the organization's founding in the 1950s, noticeably shifted their interest away from ethnolinguistic minority musics toward other subjects (fig. 4.1). This general trend is revealed by the subjects of articles in SEM's flagship journal, *Ethnomusicology*. Editors dedicated most of the issues in the 1950s to formational content for the new discipline of "ethno-musicology": developing bibliographies, building lists of interested people, disseminating information about courses related to the field, making announcements,

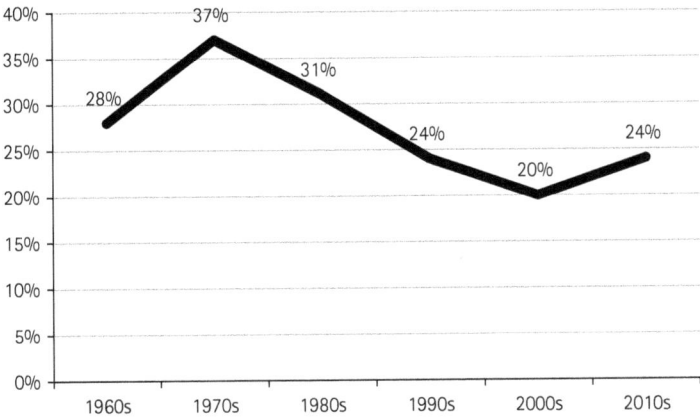

FIGURE 4.1 *Ethnomusicology* articles treating ethnolinguistic minority musics.

and gathering information about audio recordings of national and minority musics. Essentially all of the discussions and information either directly address or assume an interest in music of Others, mostly ethnolinguistic minorities. The first article on the subject of a minority musical tradition appears in the eighth issue, "An Apache Fiddle," by David McAllester (1956).

Following the foundational moment of the 1950s and early 1960s, the percentage of *Ethnomusicology* articles dedicated to ethnolinguistic minorities peaked in the 1970s at 37%, and bottomed out in the 2000s. Figure 4.1 contains the results of a rough, conservative survey of the proportion of articles dedicated to such minorities in *Ethnomusicology*.[2]

Ethnomusicological inquiry and reflection, of course, occur beyond SEM's North American hub. The British Forum for Ethnomusicology (BFE), the *Société française d'ethnomusicologie*, the International Council for Traditional Music (ICTM), and other scholarly organizations provide platforms for international dialogue and publication not included in this survey. In addition, students and scholars in universities all over the world reflect on and write about musics and their communities. And as I suggested in the introduction to this chapter, streams counter to the North American example also flow through the global music scene. UNESCO's Commission on Intangible Cultural Heritage, the Queensland Conservatorium Research Centre's Sustainable Futures, the recent formation of the Minority Musics Section in ICTM, SEM's Indigenous Music Special Interest Group, and Applied Ethnomusicology groups in both ICTM and SEM all point to scholars' and social activists' renewed interest in minority arts. Reasons for this renaissance may include postcolonial shame, acknowledgment of the parochial nature of eurogenic values in many artistic disciplines, and fear of weaknesses in the health of human ecosystems brought on by homogeneity. It may be a sense of nostalgia for moments of surprise at encountering something completely different or discovering never-before-documented genius.

Scholars and activists from minority communities are also recognizing the loss of their traditions and finding stronger voices through organization and internet communication. Even Christian churches are recognizing the loss of the communicative power and inherent value of their older arts. The Congolese participants in a song-writing workshop I helped lead in 2006 wrote a manifesto including these words (my translation from French):

> We have noticed with regret the remarkable absence of traditional music in our churches. This was caused by the arrival of the first missionaries, and traditional music has been erased, leaving in its place modern music, which has given youth the feeling of being despised, wronged. . . . Thus, we participants of this workshop recommend that the Congolese Association for the Translation of the Bible and Literacy of Sukisa-Boyinga ask our churches to help us incorporate traditional music with inspired biblical texts in our respective churches.

A Therapeutic Approach to Communities and Their Arts-Making

Taking action to sustain older artistic traditions will require a methodology with elements that arts advocates can implement and that stakeholders can measure. Creating Local Arts Together (CLAT), outlined in *Make Arts for Life: A Guide* (Schrag and Van Buren, 2018), is one such process.

CLAT consists of seven localizable steps that community members can use to encourage vibrancy in their longer traditions (see Figure 4.2).

1. *Meet a Community and Its Arts*. Explore artistic and social resources that exist in the community. Performing Step 1 allows you to begin relationships, involve and understand the people, and discover the hidden treasures of the community.
2. *Specify Goals*. Discover the goals that the community wants to work toward. Performing Step 2 ensures that you are helping the community work toward aims that they have agreed upon together.
3. *Select Effects, Content, Genre, and Events*. Choose an artistic genre that can help the community meet its goals, and activities that can result in purposeful creativity in this genre. Performing Step 3 reveals the mechanisms that relate certain kinds of artistic activity to its effects, so that the activities you perform have a high chance of succeeding.
4. *Analyze an Event Containing the Chosen Genre*. Describe the event and its genre(s) as a whole, and its artistic forms, as well as in relationship to their broader cultural context. Performing Step 4 results in detailed knowledge of the art forms, information that is crucial to sparking creativity, improving what is produced, and integrating it into the community.

FIGURE 4.2 The Create Local Arts Together (CLAT) methodology.

5. *Spark Creativity*. Implement activities the community has chosen to spark creativity within the chosen genre. Performing Step 5 actually produces new artistic works for events.
6. *Improve New Works*. Evaluate results of the sparking activities and make them better. Performing Step 6 ensures that the new artistry exhibits the aesthetic qualities, produces the impacts, and communicates the intended messages at a level of quality appropriate to its purposes.
7. *Integrate and Celebrate for Continuity*. Plan and implement ways that this new kind of creativity can continue into the future. Identify more contexts where the new and old arts can be displayed and performed. Performing Step 7 makes it more likely that a community will keep making its arts in ways that produce good effects long into the future.

CLAT integrates ethnographic and artistic form research and analysis into an Appreciative Inquiry approach to community development (see Ashford and Patkar, 2001; Tiempo, 2012). Our goal with such methodologies is to see more and more genres moving from Threatened, Locked, and Shifting to Vigorous states (see Box 4.1). In sociolinguistic terms, we want to fortify artistic genres with long histories so that they will remain thriving components of living languages, sometimes developing stable diglossic relationships with regional or international arts.

Action Points for Scholars

Ethnomusicologists' ethical, relational, methodological, and arts-in-culture organicism uniquely qualifies us to help humanity reach the richest artistic future possible, which celebrates artists and artistry in long traditions. I offer a list of steps we can take toward this goal.

- Create a stream of ethnomusicology and related disciplines dedicated to identifying, assessing, and promoting the health of older artistic genres of communication. With communities, we can use a simple tool like a Community Arts Survey (see Appendix) to identify and briefly describe such genres. We can then assess the vitality of the artistic genres on a scale like that in Box 4.1. Finally, we can offer strategizing and catalyzing events that draw on approaches like Creating Local Arts Together (Figure 4.2).
- Integrate the identification, assessment, and promotion of older traditions into our degree programs, courses, publications, community projects, and conferences.
- Devote the majority of our social, financial, and intellectual capital to getting to know and encourage artists representing older, at-risk traditions. Ethnomusicologists and scholars from related disciplines can contribute best when we (1) prefer analytical concepts firmly grounded in experienced events rather than esoterica; (2) employ methods that members of most communities in the world can adapt and implement without extensive education and training; and (3) choose to be guided by our historical ethic of privileging minoritized communities in our engagement.
- Encourage more students to study and promote older minoritized art forms.
- Develop and contribute to living archives of longer artistic traditions. These should be curated, internet-based, appropriately accessible, and designed to spark discussion and creativity (Seeger and Chaudhuri, 2004).
- Increase our engagement with international and national initiatives to support longer artistic traditions, such as UNESCO's ICH. Though often a frustrating mix of common goals and institutional roadblocks (see Grant, 2014), such efforts need our expertise. See Smith and Akagawa (2009) and Barthel-Bouchier (2013) for more on ICH.
- Remove silos separating applied ethnomusicology, indigenous musics, minority musics, medical ethnomusicology, ambitious studies like Sustainable Futures, activist organizations like Cultural Survival (www.culturalsurvival.org), and related

communities. These and other disciplines (see, e.g., Aubert, 2007: 47–51) share many goals and offer unique approaches. Collaborating on demonstrably effective projects will result in a much wider impact on the world's artistry (cf. Nettl, 2010:107).
- Embrace the phenomenological theoretical stream in ethnomusicology most recently championed by Harris Berger (2009, 2014), but extend it to interactions and goals outside academia. Though phenomenology takes the experience of events as primordial—as I do in this chapter—we need to theorize within a cycle that includes external praxis. In fact, an event-anchored, organic, humanized, embodied view of artistry welcomes insights from all of ethnomusicology's conceptual streams: music, dance, and poetic analysis; semiotic approaches to emotion; thick ethnographic description; participation in artistic practice; revealing power differentials in communities' artistry; and others.
- Enlist huge numbers of people around the world in harnessing internet-mediated creativity in the interests of—and following the leadership of—minority artists. Clay Shirky suggests that humans have built up "well over a trillion hours of free time each year" and can access "public media that enable ordinary citizens, previously locked out, to pool that free time in pursuit of activities they like or care about" (2012: 27). We can help spark major investment from this enormous pot of cognitive surplus into celebrating and promoting older traditions. This could include fostering websites, social media sites, audio and video sites, cell phone enactment distribution, and other electronic channels.
- Get used to counting things.

Conclusion

Ethnomusicology stands unique in the world in its rigorous organic treatment of art forms and the communities who experience them. We may sometimes swim unappreciated in the eddies and backwaters of academia, public policy, and community development, but not because our potential contributions are negligible. Rather, I believe our offerings are *too* radical, and thus often incomprehensible to others.

To illustrate, in 2007 I became the International Ethnomusicology Coordinator for SIL International, a faith-based language development international nongovernmental organization (INGO). At the time, SIL's ethnomusicology department operated as an appendage, only vaguely related to our founding discipline, linguistics. I, Tom Avery, and others began to graciously and inexorably force change: We became the

Ethnomusicology and Arts Group; I earned a spot on our International Academic Coordination team, with linguists, anthropologists, literacy specialists, and other already legitimized disciplines; we laboriously followed the bureaucratic trail of forms to create official job descriptions for Arts Specialists; we developed curricula to train people in this multidisciplinary field, culminating in a World Arts M.A. at the Center for Excellence in World Arts and a similar program at Payap University in Chiang Mai, Thailand; UNESCO accredited SIL to provide advisory services to its Intergovernmental Committee on Intangible Cultural Heritage; and we crafted superb promotional materials to attract people to join us.

Throughout this period, we presented ourselves as inhabiting the core of SIL's identity: helping minoritized communities access their local communication systems to work toward a better future. We ethnomusicology and arts people were skilled in interacting with artistic forms of communication (i.e., genres comprising elements of music, drama, dance, verbal arts, and visual arts); everyone else was concerned with prosaic utterances susceptible to linguistic analysis. But we all cared about communication. In some significant contexts, ethnoarts personnel now work hand in hand with linguists and others. However, we continue to work toward integration with many of our colleagues' conceptual and practical framework.

The forces arrayed against local art forms are formidable: urbanization weakens ties between language speakers and their home cultures; globalized communication media relegate local art forms to one choice among millions (Kidula, 2008: 54); media industries relentlessly press their favored art forms into new markets (Kaemmer, 2008: 403); expansive religious traditions use foreign genres, creating unwelcoming environments for artists from their local communities; and engulfing educational, legal, and religious systems destroy long-established traditions of transmission. We may be entering a period of perpetual liminality.

I believe that ethnomusicologists can help minority communities navigate these tides. We can become known, highly regarded in academic and policy-making circles, and be present when influential people make decisions affecting minoritized artistic traditions. We can exert considerable winsome influence in local, regional, and international arenas when we combine a vision of artistically thriving humanity, commitment to artists on the margins of global communities, personal stories of friends in these margins, and rigorous scholarship contributing to a growing body of data. We can move from academic and activist liminality to an exhilarating integrality.

Restating the linguists' lament, we must do some serious rethinking of our priorities, lest ethnomusicologists stand feckless while global forces liminalize the representatives of long artistic traditions whose depth, beauty, function, and power we are uniquely able to appreciate. Bess Lomax Hawes's admonition that ethnomusicologists should lean toward activism with ethnolinguistic minority communities remains telling: We "should be supporting the music alive; rather than just teaching it as though it were gone . . . " (1993), or treating its enactors as though they don't exist.

APPENDIX

Perform a Basic Community Arts Survey

This activity relies on a focus group to develop a preliminary list of artistic communicative events, and can be performed by anybody with some competencies in basic ethnographic questioning. It should take a day or less to perform, and result in a list of the types of artistic communication that are both integral and ancillary to a community. The rough list becomes an essential resource for deciding what kinds of ethnographic and formal analysis that a community wants to perform. These decisions will be based on particular goals associated with literacy, education, community development, justice, well-being, and the like.

1. Gather Community Representatives

Gather a few people from the community of different ages, genders, and socioeconomic backgrounds.

2. Make a Quick List of Event Types When People Communicate Artistically with Each Other

Ask questions such as these:

> When do people sing? Dance? Tell stories? Act? Wear special clothing?

Jot down the name, brief description, and other information that arises, such as kinds of people involved (men, women, youth, children, specialists, a particular socioeconomic group, etc.); when it's usually done (particular days, seasons, months, times of day, etc.); reason(s) for the event (if easily discernable at this early point in the research) and/or connotations.

3. Extend the List by Researching Likely Social Contexts for Artistic Communication Acts

Anthropologists know that cultures often mark important events and transitions with artistically rendered communication. Use the following outline to help identify rituals and special events that exist in a community. Then explore what kinds of communication might be associated with rituals, life-cycle events, historical events, activities, nature, or ceremonies.

Life-Cycle Events

- Birth (birth announcement, lullaby)
- Childhood (funny or nonsense games, teasing, taunting)

- Puberty (girl's songs, boy's songs, initiation)
- Courting (love, courting, proposal of marriage)
- Marriage (wedding, men's events, women's events)
- Death (funeral, burial, mourning)

Historical Events

- Commemorative (disasters, honors, first outsiders, changes in leadership or government, first road, first vehicles, wars, etc.)
- Legend (creation, mythology)
- Local news

Activities

- Work (cutting timber, hunting, fishing, road making, etc.)
- Fighting (preparation for battle, battle, victory, defeat, etc.)
- Dancing (male, female, multiple sexes, social, ceremonial, solo, etc.)
- Recreation

Ceremonies

- Religious (planting, harvesting, fertility, power, prophecy, worship, etc.)
- Social (greeting, farewell, wedding, funeral, completion of a special community project, etc.)

Nature

- Animals (pets and wild animals, including birds, fish, and reptiles)
- Places and things (mountains, rivers, forests, trees, plants, the heavens—including clouds, sun, moon, stars, and sky)
- Time cycles (daily, weekly, monthly, annual)

4. Extend the List by Presenting a Barrage of Eurogenic or Other Outside Communication Genres

Present a list like the following and ask, "Do you have anything like this?"

Exclamation, greeting, calling, imperative, announcement, spiel, exchange, argument, discussion, debate, hortatory, persuasive, report, commentary, narrative, eulogy, prayers, proverbs, riddles, humor, artistic/poetic, meditation, song, proverb, word games, unintelligible speech, story, myth, fable, folktale, chant, parable, and so on.

5. Gather a Little More Information about Each Genre

If time and occasion allow, you can ask a few more questions about each genre:

- A brief description or local name
- Kinds of people involved (men, women, youth, children, specialists, a particular socioeconomic group, etc.)
- When it's usually done (particular days, seasons, months, times of day, etc.)
- Reason(s) for the event and/or connotations
- Whether the event includes special

    - verbal features (e.g., vocal modifications, poetic elements, archaic vocabulary)
    - movement features (e.g., dance, gestures)
    - dramatic features (e.g., one person taking on the character of another, connoting a different reality)
    - musical features (e.g., melody, rhythm)
    - visual features (e.g., designs, colors, shapes).

Notes

1. Slightly revised text from Coulter (2011). See also Harris (2017); Grant (2014); Saurman (2013).
2. Thanks to Center for Excellence in World Arts graduate students Lydia Duggins and Julie Johnson for performing this research.

References

Alekseyev, Eduard Ye. (1976). *Problemy formirovaniia lada: na material yakutskoi narodnoi pesni* [Yakut folk song and the genesis of tonal organization]. Moscow: Muzyka.

Alekseyev, Eduard Ye. (1986) *Rannefol'klornoe intonirovanie* [The Inception of Sung Scales]. Moscow: Sovetskii kompozitor.

Alekseyev, Eduard Ye. (1996). "O muzykalnom voploshchenii olonkho" [On the musical incarnation of olonkho]. In *Monuments of the Folklore of the Peoples of Siberia and Far East*, Vol. 10, *Yakut Heroic Epic 'The Mighty Er Sogotokh*, pp. 42–72. Novosibirsk: Nauka.

Ashford, Graham, and Saleela Patkar. (2001). *The Positive Path: Using Appreciative Inquiry in Rural Indian Communities*. Winnipeg: International Institute for Sustainable Development.

Aubert, Laurent. (2007). *The Music of the Other: New Challenges for Ethnomusicology in a Global Age*, translated by Carla Ribeiro. Burlington, VT: Ashgate Publishing.

Barthel-Bouchier, Diane. (2013). *Cultural Heritage and the Challenge of Sustainability*. Walnut Creek, CA: Left Coast Press.

Becker, Judith. (2004). *Deep Listeners: Music, Emotion, and Trancing*. Bloomington: Indiana University Press.

Berger, Harris. (2009). *Stance: Ideas about Emotion, Style, and Meaning for the Study of Expressive Culture*. Music/Cultures Series. Middletown, CT: Wesleyan University Press.

Berger, Harris. (2014). "New Directions for Ethnomusicological Research into the Politics of Music and Culture: Issues, Project, and Programs." *Ethnomusicology* 58(2): 315–320.

Bourdieu, Pierre. (1977). *Outline of a Theory of Practice*. Cambridge: Cambridge University Press.

Clinard, Wendy. (2012). Program notes for "From the Arctic to the Middle East (Broken Narratives by an American Flamenco Dancer." Chicago: Clinard Dance Company.

Coulter, Neil. (2007). *Music Shift: Evaluating the Vitality and Viability of Music Styles among the Alamblak of Papua New Guinea*. Ph.D. dissertation, Kent, OH: Kent State University.

Coulter, Neil. (2011). "Assessing Music Shift: Adapting EGIDS for a Papua New Guinea Community." *Language Documentation and Description* 10: 61–81.

Densmore, Frances. (1927). "The Study of Indian Music in the Nineteenth Century." *American Anthropologist* 29: 77–86.

Djenda, Maurice. (1992/1993). "De la disparition des éléments culturels chez les Mpyemõ: Observations participantes." *Bulletin of the International Committee on Urgent Anthropological and Ethnological Research* 34/35: 149–160.

Ellis, Alexander. (1885). "On the Scales of Various Nations." *Journal of the Society of Arts* 33: 485–527.

Feld, Steven. (1996). "Pygmy POP: A Genealogy of Schizophonic Mimesis." *Yearbook for Traditional Music* 28: 1–35.

Feld, Steven. (2001). Liner Notes. *Bosavi: Rainforest Music from Papua New Guinea* [CD]. Smithsonian Folkways Recordings and the Institute of Papua New Guinea Studies.

Gennep, Arnold Van. (1960). *The Rites of Passage*. Chicago: University of Chicago.

Goldenberg, Jacob, and Moishe Levy. (2009). "Distance is Not Dead: Social Interaction and Geographical Distance in the Internet Era." *arXiv*: 0906.3202.

Grant, Catherine Fiona. (2014). *Music Endangerment: How Language Maintenance Can Help*. New York: Oxford University Press.

Green, Carolyn, and Karen Ruhleder. (1995). "Globalization, Borderless Worlds, and the Tower of Babel." *Journal of Organizational Change Management* 8: 55–68.

Greengard, Samuel. (2011). "Following the Crowd." *Communications of the ACM* [Association of Computing Machinery] 54(2): 20–22.

Gruber, Jacob. (1970). "Ethnographic Salvage and the Shaping of Anthropology." *American Anthropologist, New Series* 72(6): 1289–1299.

Harris, Robin P. (2009). Interview with Pyotr Reshetnikov in Cherkëkh, Yakutia, June 16, 2009.

Harris, Robin P. (2017). *Storytelling in Siberia: The Olonkho Epic in a Changing World*. Urbana-Champaign: University of Illinois Press.

Ivtzan, Itai. (2008). "Self-actualisation: For Individualist Cultures Only?" *International Journal on Humanist Ideology* 1(2): 111–138.

Kaemmer, John E. (2008). "Southern Africa: An Introduction." In *The Garland Handbook of African Music*, edited by Ruth M. Stone, pp. 382–405. New York: Routledge.

Kidula, Jean Ngoya. (2008). "Music Culture: African Life." In *Music in the Life of the African Church*, edited by Roberta R. King, Jean Ngoya Kidula, Thomas Oduro, and James R. Krabill, pp. 37–56. Waco, TX: Baylor University Press.

King, Roberta, and Sooi Ling Tan. (2013). *(un)Common Sounds: Songs of Peace and Reconciliation among Muslims and Christians*. DVD. Directed by Craig Detweiler. Documentary film.

Kisliuk, Michele. (1998). *Seize the Dance!* New York: Oxford University Press.
Koch, Lars-Christian, Albrecht Wiedmann, Susanne Ziegler. (2004). "The Berlin Phonogramm-Archiv: A Treasury of Sound Recordings." *Acoustical Science and Technology* 25(4): 227–231.
Krauss, Michael. (1992). "The World's Languages in Crisis." *Language* 68(1): 4–10.
Kronenfeld, David B., Givanni Bennardo, Victor C. de Munck, and Michael D. Fischer, eds. (2011). *A Companion to Cognitive Anthropology.* Oxford; Malden, MA: Wiley-Blackwell.
Kubik, Gerhard. (1998). "Intra-African Streams of Influence." In *Africa: The Garland Encyclopedia of World Music*, edited by Ruth Stone, pp. 293–326. New York; London: Garland Publishing, Inc.
Lakoff, George. (1987). *Women, Fire, and Dangerous Things: What Categories Reveal about the Mind.* Chicago: University of Chicago Press.
Lakoff, George. (1999). "Cognitive Models and Prototype Theory." In *Concepts: Core Readings*, edited by Eric Margolis and Stephen Laurence. Cambridge, MA: Massachusetts Institute of Technology 391–422.
Lewis, Paul M. (2009). "The Sustainable Use Model and The Expanded Graded Intergenerational Disruption Scale (EGIDS)." Paper presented at the International Language Assessment Conference (ILAC), Penang, Malaysia.
Lewis, Paul M., and Gary F. Simons. (2010). "Assessing Endangerment: Expanding Fishman's GIDS." *Revue Roumaine de linguistique* 55(2): 103–120.
Lipsitz, George. (1999). "The Changing Scene: Anxiety and Ethnomusicology." Unpublished paper presented at the Thirty-third Annual Meeting of the Society for Ethnomusicology, Southern California Chapter, University of California-Riverside, February 27.
Lomax, Alan. (1968). *Folk Song Style and Culture.* Washington, DC: American Association for the Advancement of Science.
Lubliner, Jacob. (2002). "Reflections on Diglossia." www.ce.berkeley.edu/~coby/essays/index.html (accessed July 30, 2013).
Maslow, Abraham. (1954). *Motivation and Personality.* New York: Harper.
McAllester, David. (1956). "An Apache Fiddle." *Ethnomusicology* 1(8): 1–5.
McWhorter, John. (2001). *The Power of Babel: A Natural History of Language.* New York: Henry Holt and Company.
Merriam, Alan. (1964). *The Anthropology of Music.* Evanston, IL: Northwestern University Press.
Miller, Daniel. (1995). "Consumption and Commodities." *Annual Review of Anthropology* 24: 141–161.
Mills, Sherylle. (1996). "Indigenous Music and the Law: An Analysis of National and International Legislation." *Yearbook for Traditional Music* 28: 57–86.
Mukuna, Kazadi wa. (1992). "The Genesis of Urban Music in Zaire." *African Music* 7(2): 72–84.
Nettl, Bruno. (2005). *The Study of Ethnomusicology: Thirty-one Issues and Concepts.* Champaign: University of Illinois Press.
Nettl, Bruno. (2010). *Nettl's Elephant.* Urbana: University of Illinois Press.
Pearce, Mary. (2013). "Variation with Gender in the Tonal Speech Varieties of Kera (Chadic)." In *Gender and Language in Sub-Saharan Africa: Tradition, Struggle, and Change*, edited by Lilian Lem Atanga, Sibonile Edith Ellece, Lia Litosseliti, and Jane Sunderland, pp. 79–93. Amsterdam: John Benjamins Publishing.
Peretz, Isabelle, and Robert J. Zatorre, eds. (2003). *The Cognitive Neuroscience of Music.* New York: Oxford University Press.

Racy, Ali Jihad. (1991). "Creativity and Ambience: An Ecstatic Feedback Model from Arab Music." *the world of music* 33(3): 7–28.

Rosch, Eleanor. (1977). "Classification of Real-World Objects: Origins and Representations in Cognition." In *Thinking: Readings in Cognitive Science*, edited by Philip Johnson-Laird and Peter Wason, pp. 212–222. Cambridge: Cambridge University Press.

Saurman, Todd. (2013). *Singing for Survival in the Highlands of Cambodia: Tampuan Revitalization of Music as Mediation and Cultural Reflexivity*. Ph.D. dissertation, Chiang Mai University.

Schippers, Huib. (2009). "Ecologies of Creative Diversity." *Griffith REVIEW* 23. https://griffithreview.com/articles/ecologies-of-creative-diversity/

Schrag, Brian. (1994). "Toward a Model for the Evaluation of the Cultural Strength of Various Musics." *Notes on Anthropology and Intercultural Community Work* 16: 3–14.

Schrag, Brian. (2000). "Grooving at the Nexus: The Intersection of African Music and Euro-American Ethnomusicology at UCLA." UCLA Ethnomusicology Department. Los Angeles: University of California, Los Angeles.

Schrag, Brian. (2005). *How Bamiléké Music-Makers Create Culture in Cameroon*. Ph.D. dissertation, University of California, Los Angeles.

Schrag, Brian. (2013). *Creating Local Arts Together: A Manual to Help Communities Reach their Kingdom Goals*. General editor, James R. Krabill. Pasadena: William Carey Library.

Schrag, Brian, and Kathleen Van Buren. (2018). *Make Arts for Life: A Guide*. New York: Oxford University Press.

Schreffler, Gibb. (2012). "Migration Shaping Media: Punjabi Popular Music in a Global Historical Perspective." *Popular Music and Society* 35(3): 333–358.

Seeger, Anthony, and Shubha Chaudhuri, eds. (2004). *Archives for the Future: Global Perspectives on Audiovisual Archives in the 21st Century*. Calcutta: Seagull Books.

Shirky, Clay. (2011). *Cognitive Surplus: How Technology Makes Consumers into Collaborators*. New York: Penguin Books.

Smith, Laurajane, and Akagawa Natsuko, eds. (2009). *Intangible Heritage*. London: Routledge.

Southern, Eileen. (1997). *The Music of Black Americans: A History* (3rd ed.). New York: W.W. Norton.

Stone, Ruth. (1979). *Communication and Interaction Processes in Music Events among the Kpelle of Liberia*. Ph.D. dissertation, Indiana University.

Tiempo, Joshue Zuriel G. (2012). *Using AI Community Development Planning and Transformation Framework: From Roots to Wings*. Ph.D. dissertation, Southeast Asia Interdisciplinary Development Institute.

Taylor, John. (2008). "Prototypes in Cognitive Linguistics." In *Handbook of Cognitive Linguistics and Second Language Acquisition*, edited by Peter Robinson and Nick C. Ellis, pp. 39–65. New York: Routledge.

Titon, Jeff Todd. (1997). "Ethnomusicology and Values: A Reply to Henry Kingsbury." *Ethnomusicology* 41(2): 254–257.

Titon, Jeff Todd. (2009). "Music and Sustainability: An Ecological Viewpoint." *the world of music* 51(1): 119–138.

Turner, Victor. (1967). "Betwixt and Between: The Liminal Period in *Rites de Passage*." In *The Forest of Symbols: The Aspects of Ndembu Ritual*, pp. 93–111 Ithaca, NY: Cornell University Press.

Wade, Bonnie C. (2012). *Thinking Musically: Experiencing Music, Expressing Culture* (3rd ed.). New York: Oxford University Press.

Webster, Jason. (2004). *Duende: A Journey into the Heart of Flamenco*. New York: Broadway Books.

Wilson, Edward O. (2002). *The Future of Life*. New York: Alfred A. Knopf.

CHAPTER 5

ACTIVIST ETHNOMUSICOLOGY AND MARGINALIZED MUSIC OF SOUTH ASIA

ZOE C. SHERINIAN

Hearing and seeing marginal music through participant activism brings ethnomusicologists face to face with our choice of subjects, with self-reflexivity, and with musical value played out in local power politics. It also presents us with new methods such as ethnographic film, dialogical participation, and broader distribution and impact for our scholarship and its meaning. In this chapter I explore how South Asian activist ethnomusicology can contribute methodology and theory to the wider discipline. Focusing on dialogical processes from two case studies of Dalit (formerly "untouchable" or "outcaste")[1] folk music from my fieldwork and filmmaking in the Indian state of Tamil Nadu, I examine ways to approach local contexts where there are intense hierarchies of musical value and where oppressed communities use music to assert identity and cultural politics of revaluation through methods of participant activism that contribute to what I call Dalit Action Theory.

To conduct activist ethnomusicology in the context of South Asia generates theoretical perspectives of musical value within economies of musical style. It forces the ethnomusicologist to engage with the cultural politics (or meaningful action) of marginalized music and musicians in the South Asian geographic area of study in which, until the late twentieth century, scholarship had primarily focused on formal analysis of the elite classical styles of Karnatak and Hindustani music as sound objects.[2] That is, the meaning of the music was interpreted within and not beyond the building blocks of musical performance. It exemplified the fetishization of the object of art and the genius individual artist whom ethnomusicology has typically worked against, especially within the academy. As in the visual arts, where it was thought that there must be an art object that can be preserved, in Western art music it is the composer and the score that are fixated upon as the primary objects of analytical importance and the determinants of meaning. This was the focus and methodological model adopted by early ethnomusicologists of South Asian music. In pre-1980s ethnomusicological field methods, knowledge was understood to lie in the object of the transcription or notation of the collected and recorded music. Such representation of sound then facilitated comparison across lived experience to understand origin and evolution (Titon, 2008: 25).

Since the mid-1980s, using phenomenological and hermeneutic approaches, the point of entry into the "life-world" (ibid.) of the music for ethnomusicologists has more often been the people, their context and the processes that evolve from sound making, the shared experience of performance, and the relationships that evolve through that fieldwork process, as well as music's social cultural process of production, transmission, and reception. The moments of self-reflexivity that reveal transformation enter ethnomusicological ethnographies through close description of shared music making that may be poetic and polemic. Instead of a singular authoritative interpretive approach, we constitute meaning through "sympathetic listening" across multiple personal field relationships and perspectives (ibid.: 27, 29). Our goal is knowledge of people through agreement and lived experience, the analysis of which proceeds through interpretation of shared musical processes (ibid.: 27). These methods are common today in South Asian ethnomusicology. However, repercussions of the pre-1980s inclination toward the formal analysis of classical South Asian music included the reinforcement of long-standing local hierarchies of musical and social identity value that were further codified in the mid- to late twentieth century by postcolonial caste politics and academic choices.[3]

I assert that an alternative engagement with the meaning and value of marginalized South Asian music through the drumming and folk songs of untouchables, or Dalits, inherently changes the way we practice ethnomusicology in South Asia and impacts broader theories of applied ethnomusicology. Preminda Jacob (2009), art historian of Tamil visual culture, argues that methodology is determined by the content of study; it takes on the imprint of the theorist's disciplinary focus. She draws from the work of Georges Didi-Huberman (2003), who poetically described methodology and its impact on the fieldworker as tools in perpetual transformation:

> From the tool kit to the hand that uses them, the tools themselves are being formed, that is to say, they appear less as entities than as plastic forms in perpetual transformation. Let us think rather of malleable tools, tools of wax that take on a different form, signification, and use value in each hand and on each material to be worked.
> (Didi-Huberman, 2003: 38)

Thus, as we move from fetishizing the art/sound object of classical South Asian music produced by and for the elite, using a methodology of formal analysis, to a focus on the use of folk music by the lower castes and Dalits, to assert politics of identity what does this require of our fieldwork and ethnographic methodology? How does it affect the fieldworker, the subject, and the relationship between them? Do each of them also become malleable tools (re/trans)formed in the research process? Finally, what does the resulting theory that evolves from the data/experience look or sound like?

Most important, a focus on folk cultural contexts, expressions, and processes, as well as the lower castes who use and produce this culture (a shift in musical, contextual, and human subjects from earlier studies), forces us to recognize and deconstruct local hegemonies of musical style and our discipline's contributions to the construction and perpetuation of them. This necessitates a self-reflexive, area-focused (South Asia) consciousness of our choices and stance.

I propose that studying the people and meaning behind marginalized music necessitates a participant-*activist* methodology, not only in fieldwork, but in teaching content and academic/community programming. In this chapter I use and theorize *activist* and *advocate ethnomusicology*, as opposed to *applied* or *public sector*, which I feel reflects a job description or title more than a method. I am concerned with the actions of advocacy and engagement in order to emphasize "energy directed toward sociopolitical concerns" (Dirksen, 2012: n.p.), "the uses of ethnomusicology towards solving concrete problems" (Harrison, 2012: 514), or the understanding of advocate ethnomusicology as "any use of ethnomusicological knowledge by the ethnomusicologist to increase the power of self-determination for a particular cultural group" (Pettan, quoted in Harrison, 2012: 509). However, I ground such political action or engagement in the feminist perspective that the personal is the political. Further, I wish to bridge what Rebecca Dirksen calls the "[w]ell-fed false dichotomy between 'pure research' and 'applied work,'" or the perceived juncture between the university and "real life" (2012: n.p.). Barbara Kirshenblatt-Gimblett argues that this split is a "mistaken dichotomy" based on a resistance to reflexively analyze the core, applied character of the discipline of folklore (1988: 141). The activism I examine here includes recognition of the role that ethnomusicologists play within the academy as "advocates" legitimizing the study of *all* music (not just Western art music) simply through our presence in the classroom and committee room every day, transmitting and representing our discipline.

Finally, the use of media such as participatory ethnographic film as a form of knowledge transmission (and production), and as an educational and consciousness-raising tool, not only opens the possibility to reach a wider audience for ethnomusicology, it also requires that the ethnographer and her resulting "texts" become a forum or conduit for her subject's agency and message, while not erasing or denying the scholar's own critical voice. Film provides an accessible medium and greater sensory experience for the audience to which the subjects communicate. It provides a fuller observation of the experiences of the marginalized, and a means to a more transparent lens into the relationship of the subjects with the ethnographer. Further, participant-action ethnographic film, in which cameras are put into the hands of the ethnographic and/or oppressed subjects, can provide a collaborative ethnographic production that is much less mediated by the scholar and potentially highly dialogical.

The shift in methods that result from a shift in subject (classical to folk music, elite to oppressed people) allows us to begin to see, hear, and experience South Asian music differently—from multiple perspectives, no longer as aesthetic objects that reflect the constructs of elite musicians, their values and culture. But instead, we can experience the perspective and creative processes of the oppressed majority and their music that asserts a vision, song, and beat of resistance and liberation. As scholars, we are invited to open ourselves to dance with the thinking, conscious, embodied, agentive Dalit singing her tune, refusing to be silent, but demanding to be heard and seen in a cultural politics of clashing musical styles.

TRANSFORMATIVE MUSICAL MEANING/ ACTION GROUNDED IN THE POLITICAL ASSERTION OF CULTURAL VALUE BY DALITS

Dalit is a self-chosen term of oppositional politics that is used by people throughout India (and in some other parts of South Asia or its diasporas) formerly referred to by the terms *untouchable, outcaste, harajin*, or the contemporary term, *scheduled caste*.[4] The term Dalit comes from Marathi, meaning ground, suppressed, or broken. As a single umbrella term, it undermines *sub-jati* (caste) differentiation and unifies people across identities of oppression including class, gender, race, and religion.[5] The term *Dalit* was first applied in Western India to lower castes and outcastes in the nineteenth century by Jyotirao Phule, the Maharashtran activist and social reformer who worked for the rights of Shudras (lower castes), outcastes, and women (Mendelsohn and Vicziany, 1998: 4). The modern Dalit movement was started in the 1920s by Dr. B. R. Ambedkar (1891–1956), whose work included challenging Mahatma Gandhi's campaign to prevent untouchables from having a separate electorate—that is, their own representation in India's new democracy.[6] The term was made popular again by the Dalit Panthers and in the Dalit literary movement of 1970s in the state of Maharashtra. Dalits also fall under the rubric of the "subaltern," in that as a subject, the subaltern studies group of South Asian historians have studied them in a limited—some would argue, failed—sense (Bhagavan and Feldhaus, 2008). Dalits make up over 16% of the population of India (that is, 260 million). Untouchability was outlawed by Article 17 of the Indian Constitution in 1950. However, prejudice, discrimination, and violence continue as part of the daily experience of Dalits in India and its diasporas. Indeed, historian Dilip Menon calls caste violence "the central fault line of contemporary Indian society" (Menon, 2006: 1).

Dalit Action Theory is politicized agency of the oppressed, asserted through cultural expression, necessitating an activist methodology focused on collaboration, dialogue, and reciprocity. Its action is one of social justice for underrepresented and undervalued culture: an expression of the ideal of worthy intervention and a "guiding sense of social purpose" that has been at the heart of ethnomusicology, particularly applied ethnomusicology, since its inception (Sheehy, 1992: 323; Titon, 1992: 316–317).[7] In ethnomusicology, Dalit Action Theory evolves from political experience, engagement, and exchange; that is, dialogue between culture bearers, researchers, and other activists with whom they are engaged. I have developed this concept from anthropologist Sherry Ortner's idea of subaltern practice theory (1996). While "practice" is a useful concept from performance studies, my emphasis on "action" broadens the concept of practice and performance to recognize a politicized agency of the oppressed, asserted through the arts and the ethnographer's dialogical engagement with them. I am searching for a space between gender theorist Judith Butler's distinction of performance and performativity that would articulate through expressive culture a blended, heightened, conscious "habit" of identity politics (Blacking, 1995: 218; Butler, 1990). Sheehy calls this "conscious practice": the purpose and end game of applied ethnomusicology's strategic action that goes beyond collecting knowledge for knowledge's sake (1992: 323). A phenomenological approach, using examples below from dialogical fieldwork among outcastes of Tamil Nadu, will show how Dalits use music to assert value, power, and empowerment in society, and the means by which knowledge about that process is formulated and transmitted as the foundational lens for methods and theories of advocacy and activist ethnomusicology.

The Classical Ten Percent

In South Asian culture, one continues to find a hierarchy of musical value in which the classical court music and concert music—Hindustani and Karnatak, which are patronized by only about ten percent of the population—are considered of greater worth than other practices, including folk, popular (Bollywood or productions of the regional film industries), and some devotional music. This hierarchical value difference is justified in the following ways. The "classical" practices are theorized in vernacular and Sanskritic texts and thus are considered rooted in "ancient Hindu" culture, which predates the "foreign" cultural influences of Islam and Christianity. However, this essentially erases their influence, or the contribution of anything but upper caste Brahminical Hindu culture, to these "classical" forms of music.[8] Furthermore, the powerful institutions of society (education, media, politics) and the elite (upper caste and class) people who control public discourse consider the classical practices more complex, virtuosic, meaningful, and literally cleaner (or purer) than these other genres, even those practices essential to village Hinduism.

What is as important to this study, however, is that this discourse of ancientness, purity, and essential greater value has been reinforced and codified, whether consciously or unconsciously, by Western ethnomusicologists. The results have been an uncritical impact on our knowledge about and support of the music of elite South Asians and, to a large degree, an erasure of our knowledge and support of the non-elite. In particular, we have ignored the music and culture of Dalits. However, I would also apply this erasure to lower-caste and class hereditary musicians, who also struggle to have the value of their music recognized (Terada, 2000). These musicians who play folk instruments in the village ritual economy, as well as those who play in Brahmin temples, are still believed to repollute themselves through performing drums like the Tamil frame drum called *parai*[9] or aerophones such as the double reed *nagaswaram*. That is because such instrumental performance involves the polluting substances of animal skin or saliva. By maintaining hereditary occupational roles as performers within polluting contexts such as funerals, where the sounding of the instrument is ritually necessary and outcaste participation is demanded within village systems of *kadamai* or slave-like hereditary duty, their status remains low (Sherinian, 2009, 2011).

Folk music scholar Jesudasan Rajasekaran described the dynamics of degradation and low status experienced by folk musicians whom he observed in the 1970s when he first began to study Tamil folk music:

> The status of folk music and also musicians was very, very low. They are not even considered as people that they [the middle classes and castes] can move [with], they can go about and talk to or have any interaction with. Because, they are only used for occasions where they are required. That's all. If it's a karagam dancer, Mariamman festival comes, "ok we pick them up." That is all. The rest of the time these people, they are just on the fringe. They are not very much part of the society, not like the Karnatak musicians, or any other light musicians, or temple musician. That's another hierarchy that is in this thing. Just like in this community, the caste hierarchy is so strong, even [in] the music they have a hierarchy.
>
> (J. Rajasekaran interview, February 15, 2009)

Rajasekaran's analysis highlights a hegemony in Tamil culture that not only parallels, but (re)constructs and transmits a tangible coherence of structures of musical value as hierarchies of the social values of caste and class in South India (Feld, 1984: 406). An even more visceral expression of the coding of the musical value hierarchy in South India came from a Brahman Karnatak *mrdangam* (drum) artist who said that simply hearing folk music made him feel sick to his stomach (personal communication, Aaron Paige). Thus, the untouchability and *unseeability* of low-caste musicians are extended to the sound of their instruments as *unhearable*.[10]

Unfortunately, this value hierarchy has also been reinforced, perpetuated, and codified in the West by the research and teaching choices of ethnomusicologists, including the standard material in world music textbooks (the majority of which focuses on analysis of classical Indian music). Ethnomusicologists have further supported this social hierarchy in the following three ways: (1) by not contextualizing the meaning of specific styles of music within South Asian culture, particularly in economies of caste and class; (2) by erasing the presence of folk and popular voices (who make up a numerical majority in the society) through the music we choose to research, teach, and program in our concert series; (3) by codifying style categories instead of recognizing the flow of cultural influence and exchange through their porous boundaries.

Orientalism and Neo-Orientalism in Ethnomusicology

There is a complex interactive fieldwork dynamic, with specific histories in both the Euro-American academy and the South Asian context, that needs to be deconstructed and scrutinized in order to understand how the more recent choice of subjects from the less valued communities potentially shifts our methodology. This deconstruction is necessary in order to address advocacy from the perspective of marginalized South Asian music and its cultural politics, and therefore to bring the music of lower caste, outcaste, poor, tribal, and rural people to the center of academic inquiry.

The Japanese historian and Pulitzer Prize–winning author John Dower described the idea of value-free scholarship, or "research produced by a completely impartial and dispassionate researcher" (McLean, 2006), in which the field of Asian studies was immersed in the 1960s and 1970s, as the drowning of the academy in highly political and ideological modernization theory that indeed was not value free (Dower, 2004). This apolitical, anti-activist methodology, rooted in the surveillance culture of the McCarthy era of the 1950s, created great fear and purged scholars from Asian studies. David Price shows that social activist-anthropologists working for racial justice experienced a similar politics of sanitization and scrutiny by the FBI starting in the 1940s and 1950s (Price, 2004). In her discussion of the history of applied ethnomusicology and mid-twentieth-century interest in folk culture following the New Deal cultural documentation projects of the 1930s and the burgeoning folk revival movement, Rebecca Dirksen says that "McCarthyism and Cold War politics administered a heavy blow as the FBI investigated folk artists and supporters for alleged communist sympathies." These included the "rigorous investigation" of Allen Lomax and Benjamin Botkin by the FBI (Dirksen, 2012: n.p.; Sheehy, 1992: 325).

The scrutiny and the ideology of value-free scholarship affected the choice by many ethnomusicologists to study classical music and culture in India over less valued forms of music in the mid-twentieth century. It also may have been the least threatening choice for American ethnomusicologists during the heightened tensions of the Cold War, with Pakistan politically aligned with the United States, and India with the Soviet Union. Furthermore, within the music academy, where most ethnomusicologists studied and taught, local struggles over musical value influenced the choice to work with elite Asian court music that could compete with the "sophistication" of Western classical music. This was not only a research choice; it extended to performance teaching, textbook content, and concert presentation. Mantle Hood's concept of bimusicality (that one could be fluent in more than one musical system) and his development of this musicological method, derived from performance skills and music theory/analysis within ethnomusicology, further fueled the study of elite/court-based Javanese, Japanese, and South Asian music (Nettl, 2005: 50). Deborah Wong calls this "research through performance practice" (2008: 81). Drawing on work by Marc Perlman (2004), Wong suggests that the problem with Hood's work was his authorial position and the lack of ethnographic, dialogical, or collaborative presence in his writing, so core to contemporary applied, activist ethnomusicology and, some theorists argue, all ethnomusicology (Harrison, 2012: 507–508):

> His scholarship on gamelan music theory was profoundly shaped by his time and his own training. He spent years interacting with Javanese musicians and learning from them directly, but they are essentially not present in his analytical work; His scholarship on music theory is empirical, produced by a unitary interpretive subject (Hood) and is barely ethnographic.
>
> (Wong, 2008: 81)

In turn, the theoretical and musically complex nature of these practices molded ethnomusicological approaches and methods of interaction with "classical" Asian music. Indeed, Nettl argues that more Western audiences were inclined to embrace Asian elite (while foreign) practices as "music" and further that they might even like, let alone appreciate, them for their complexity (Nettl, 2005: 50). The easy embrace of Asian classical music through introducing gamelan ensembles in the Western academy, bringing "A-grade" artists and academics from Bali and India to teach in Ph.D. programs, and their mentorship of Western students as "disciples" further supported the acceptance of ethnomusicology within music departments that were still committed to the Eurocentrism manifest in the "value-free" ideology of virtuosity and perfection of the Western musical canon.[11] The study of elite court and temple cultures of Asia, with their comparably complex written theoretical and notation systems, more easily validated and facilitated the study of non-Western music in general during the early years of the discipline (1950s). However, this Eurocentric hegemony was not new. It had its roots in Western music and academic studies tainted by the colonialism and racism of the nineteenth century, as well as the orientalism of the eighteenth century.

The focus on elite court cultures of Asia by ethnomusicologists is an example of the continuation of Indology and eighteenth-century orientalism, which historian Thomas Trautmann (1997) calls "Indomania." Trautmann focuses on Sir William Jones, known primarily for his assertion that Sanskrit was a civilized European proto-language, in some respects surpassing Latin and Greek in the development of its grammatical system (1997: 39). In 1784 Jones also wrote Indic ethnomusicology's foundational "Brahmin-musical-centric" (my words) texts with his treatises on Indian classical music, entitled *On the Musical Modes of the Hindus*. Trautmann's form of eighteenth-century orientalism can also be seen in the encouragement of Indian Christian converts by the German Lutheran missionaries in South India to use the elite Karnatak genre of *kīrttaṇai* as the basis for an indigenous hymnody as early as 1714.[12] It was not until the height of imperial colonialism in the mid-nineteenth century that the Eurocentric brand of orientalism Trautmann calls "Indophobia" was more prevalent in British India. In South India its musical traces were perpetuated primarily by British missionaries, including the promotion among converts of four-part harmonic

Western hymnody in English over the earlier modal and odd-meter based indigenous genre of Christian *kīrttaṉai* encouraged by the German Lutherans (Sherinian, 2007, 2014).

Indomania for the elite practices continued among music scholars and their local informants, usually Brahmins in the nineteenth century. For example, Augustus Willard wrote one of the earliest English treatises on Hindustani music in 1834. This was followed in 1914 by A. H. Fox Strangways's early prototype of comparative musicology, *The Music of Hindustan*, and the work of two twentieth-century Protestant missionaries: Emmons White, who published *Appreciating India's Music* in 1957, and H. A. Popley, who drew on the earlier work of Fox Strangways and Captain Day to write *The Music of India* in 1921. White also worked closely with contemporary Brahmin Karnatak theorist P. Sambamoorthy and, in the 1970s, Karnatak ethnomusicologist John Higgins. These missionary and civil servant scholars wrote detailed analyses of the classical raga systems, as well as detailed transcriptions in Western notation from first-hand experience through personal study with a local, typically Brahmin, teacher. While these works contain subtle traces of ethnocentrism, rationalistic comparison, generalization, paternalism, and the impetus to scientifically codify structural procedures and performance practice, they generally were written with a great respect and appreciation for the Karnatak and Hindustani systems. The goal (particularly of Fox Strangways and Popley)—to scientifically and practically "know" the classical systems, particularly of melody—however, strongly contributed to the later methodological focus on music's structure and theory within South Asian ethnomusicology. Further, this focus was devoid of any real sociopolitical analysis of the culturally powerful Brahmin, or upper caste, elite hereditary music communities that produced or patronized these forms of music and the theories about them. This lack, in turn, extended the production of uncritical colonial knowledge past the midtwentieth century, landing us in the middle of contemporary Hindu fundamentalist cultural politics.[13]

In his analysis of the contemporary Hindu fundamentalist movement in *The Saffron Wave*, historian Thomas Hanson shows how "the Brahminical high scriptural tradition that... produced the bulk of Sanskrit texts [was] regarded as the classical center of the Aryan-Vedic high civilization" (1999: 65). He argues that the concept of a single classical Hinduism organized around a central high culture and extending across the subcontinent as a "great tradition" was a production of colonial knowledge. Furthermore, this codification and elevation of Brahminical practices into a Hindu tradition took place with "the active assistance and help of Brahminical western-educated strata, especially in Madras and Bengal where the colonial administration began" (ibid.: 66). The concept of the unity of Hindu culture puts the classical practices at the center, with devalued folk music at the margins, paralleling the geography of most villages, where outcastes, considered spiritually dangerous and impure, are confined to ghettos on the wastelands at the boundaries of the village (Mines, 2010: 226, 232).

Partha Chatterjee describes the Hindu fundamentalist Bharatiya Janata Party (BJP) as more concerned about defending and promoting a unified Indian culture than the religion of Hinduism. He defines the BJP's construct of Indian culture as an authentic ideal, fundamentally unified, ancient, and continuous. Furthermore, he says, the attempts to describe this unified ideal by nationalists "have been largely textual, searching ancient works of religion, philosophy and law written for the most part in Sanskrit. The older the texts, the stronger the claim to belong to the origins of Indian culture and hence to its continuous authenticity" (2003: 1). To counter these claims of cultural unity, and to show the great diversity of practices in India, many of which counter orthodox Hindu practices, Chatterjee cites a recent vast study by the Anthropological Survey of India. He finds that in 4,635 distinct communities, 80% of the population eat fish or meat, racial hybridity is the norm, one-half of all men and one-quarter of all women drink, most are allowed to smoke, and the strong regard for lineage and ancestry "is a trait that belongs only to the upper castes" (ibid.).[14]

Chatterjee furthermore says that while the cultural nationalists may recognize diversity within India, they argue that there is a fundamental cultural unity that cannot be found in the day-to-day practices of the people because those practices have been corrupted by many influences (often constructed as foreign, Muslim, or Christian). They hope to promote this political ideology in order to uphold the national cultural ideal and maintain power in the hands of the upper caste Hindus (ibid.).

In order to understand the dynamics and politics of advocacy in South Asian ethnomusicology, we must confront the local sociopolitical identity of musical style, as well as the contribution of colonial dynamics and scholarship to the construction or reification of these hierarchies. A self-reflexive approach will help us understand our inherent role as advocates or perhaps contemporary Indomaniacs, which ethnomusicologists have played for non-Western music and musicians within the music academy since the founding of the discipline in the 1950s—and in South Asia for over 200 years. Then we must decide the degree to which we were, and continue to be, conscious of the elite or marginalized subjects of our advocacy.

Methods that focus on formal analysis of musical systems (such as raga and tala) help us maintain distance from the "disorientation" of the embodied, often sensually extreme fieldwork experience. It keeps the academic project in a comfort zone away from the "domains of the body, the spiritual, the 'mystical,' 'the exotic,' and the 'primitive'" (Hahn, 2006: 92). Our methods of fieldwork as disciples of classical music gurus have led to extreme levels of embodied (particularly technical) knowledge from which South Asian ethnomusicologists have been able to make great contributions to the understanding of the systematic theory and performance practice of these forms of music, for example, the work of Slawek (1987) and Miner (1993) on the history of sitar, Nelson (1991) on the *mrdangam* drum, and T. Viswanathan (1974) on Karnatak raga improvisation. However, the literature has lacked that self-reflexive mirror that would necessitate greater representation and understanding of the sociopolitical context and processes from which the music evolves and gains its meaning. To generate a new method of South Asian activist ethnomusicology through better understanding the music/dance that have been overlooked in South Asia, I turn to Dalit Action Theory.

Dalit Action Theory on the Ground

Transformative musical action is woven into encounters with politics of cultural value. Key to this action and its meaning is dialogical field engagement, disorientation, and reorientation through reflection. Dislocation when in the field and relocation in the academic world (or vice versa) are also often factors whether one is literally far away from the field site or not (Babiracki, 2008: 168). However, in his study of heavy metal music, Harry Berger describes a critical dialogical process through engaged interpretation with metal performers after a period of ethnomusicological data gathering (interviews and participant observation) (Berger, 2008: 74). This is methodology for theoretical interpretation that crosses the perceived dichotomy between academy and field site, engaging the subjects of research in the production of knowledge through, in Berger's case, dialoguing with the metal heads about Marxist critiques of their music and the politics of music, which in turn resulted in a range of collaborative interpretive insights that supported the agentive voice of the subjects (see case study below and Sherinian, 2005).

In this way, Dalit Action Theory in ethnomusicology *evolves out of data* and *experience* derived from political engagement, participant-action, and exchange of music and ideas between members of the music culture and ethnomusicologists, as well as other activists with whom the people are engaged. Knowledge production is dialogically shared. The goal of the experience and cultural understanding *is* transformative musical meaning/action, grounded in the assertion through performance of a politics of cultural value, resistance, and identity. Key to this action in the field experience is transformation through cultural and musical disorientation (Hahn, 2006; Wong, 2008), which we can perhaps call a subaltern praxis of reversal, reorientation through reflection and interpretation (Freire, 1984 [1970]), and, as Berger has shown, critical dialogical engagement (Berger, 2008).

Using two case studies of Dalit folk music from the South Indian state of Tamil Nadu, I will show how music makers/producers use music to assert value, resistance, and empowerment in society. My focus is to demonstrate how theories of advocacy and activist ethnomusicology evolve from data and experience attained through using an activist ethnomusicological methodology focused on collaboration, dialogue, reciprocity, and mutual transformation in relationship, shared music making/composition/performance knowledge building, and theologizing.

Case Studies from the Dalit Movement: The Subaltern Sing (and Drum!)

Both of the following case studies engage with Tamil Dalits and the cultural politics of Dalit liberation through music. I began writing this chapter with the intention of using the phrase "subaltern action theory," drawing on *subaltern* as a universal, academic designation that can encompass the experience and politics of people such as Dalits throughout South Asia and its diasporas.[15] Antonio Gramsci first applied "subaltern" to those groups excluded from politics, who thus lacked a voice of political representation or participation in the production of history or culture, as the elite understood this process. This included those of "low rank," the proletariat, workers, peasants, and those suffering under the hegemony of ruling elite classes such as Mussolini's Fascist Party (El Habib Louai, 2012: 5).[16] I am further influenced by feminist anthropologist Sherry Ortner's (1996) feminist practice theory focused on gender and power. She theorizes the role that female/subaltern agency can play and how this agency is both constructed and enacted (Ortner, 1996: 16).

The subaltern studies group in South Asian history, especially as exemplified by Gayatri Spivak's essay, "Can the Subaltern Speak?" (1988), uses Marxist and feminist analysis to understand workers and women, drawing on Gramsci's notion of the proletariat and those of low rank in their use of the term *subaltern*. From her analysis of early twentieth-century Indian women's lack of access to the public sphere, Spivak asks the question, "Can the subaltern speak?" She was specifically concerned with the experience of women subjugated by *sati* (or widow immolation), which was primarily middle class and elite women, being solely represented in the writing of British colonials and elite Indians. She also describes subaltern self-representation in scholarship and media as "anonymous and mute."

Those marginalized in today's South Asia similarly have little access to voicing their concerns or representing their identities in mainstream media and to globally networked, or cosmopolitan audiences. So, how can the subaltern speak for themselves, especially without reinscribing their subordinate position in society? I assert and, as I once discussed with Dr. Spivak, attempt to understand the self-representation of many marginal people in India by suggesting that "Can the subaltern speak?" is the wrong question. For those oppressed by caste, class, and often gender, the means of protest communication in South Asia is rarely public speech. It is more often song and performance; that is, the subaltern sing and drum their subjectivity (Sundar, 2007: 160–162).[17] As a method for ethnomusicology (and political science), one must *listen* for the resistive expression of Dalits not as speech, but as music. My primary critique of Spivak's use, and in turn my evolution from the phrase "subaltern practice theory" to "Dalit Action Theory," is the lack of recognition that Dalits or any oppressed peoples inherently have agency. This is the case in South Asia because many upper-caste historians who theorize the "subaltern" have not studied (done fieldwork with), understood, or recognized the contemporary *medium* from which Dalits communicate. Dalit Action Theory in the medium of folk music instead redirects and *answers* the question, "Can the subaltern speak?"

By reorienting and answering this question with a focus on the Dalit action of musical performance and protest, I shift from the limits of a category of identity such as subaltern (which implies a population below some other identity)[18] or even the term *oppressed*, to behavior, or the action of Dalit culture. Because of the daily forms of danger and humiliation that Dalits must resist to survive, they may not speak (in the public sphere or from a political platform) at all. I assert that the Dalit mode of action is to sing and drum their resistance and liberation, using accessible tools of identity such as those evolved from village folk culture that inherently empower them in their own cultural resources (language, nonverbal musical style, instruments, etc.).[19] Further, as I show in the following case studies, Dalits re-sound their empowerment through Dalit musico-theology, through reclaiming the polluted status of their *parai* frame drum, and through interrogating their internalized castism.

Thus, by choosing the term Dalit Action Theory, I allow my theory to evolve from my data and the terminology of local activists across South Asia. The following ethnographic case studies explore and define how Dalits act and what actions can be contained within this term and then applied theoretically more universally. I found that Dalits often act in a unified way across differences (caste, class, and gender); they are more often intersectional. While it is commonly asserted that the liberation of women is at the center of caste liberation (Devasahayam, 1997), Dalit culture encourages acting in an expansive, inclusive, and improvisatory way, as is reflected in the ability to change the lyrics, tunes, rhythms, and other elements, of folk songs (as a medium of action), in order to meet the particular sociopolitical needs of the moment (Appavoo, in Sherinian, 2014). Dalits often act in a loving welcoming way toward those who might hold power over them, while maintaining their integrity of self-understanding and definition (see case of Amulraj below). This exemplifies Sherry Ortner's model of "serious games": "culturally organized social episodes in which players retain some degree of agency... actors play with skill, intention, wit, knowledge, intelligence" (Prieto, 1998: 12).

I draw my concept of action from Sherry Ortner, who emphasizes in her book *Making Gender* the role of practice in social change. Ortner reacts against practice theory as reproduction in the mode of Bourdieu and Giddens (Ortner, 1996: 17), while she continues to argue against the separation of reproduction and transformation. She also avoids the loop of structures constructing subjects, or vice versa. Ortner instead argues for subaltern practice theory that "look(s) for the slippages in reproduction, the erosion of longstanding patterns, the moments of disorder and outright resistance" (ibid.). In her case study of the Hawaiian women's cultural coup that overthrew local gender arrangements, she emphasizes "the disjunctions in, rather than the coherence of the structure,... the creativity of the women within the limits of their traditional politics,... (and) the transformations rather than the continuities that ensued" (1996: 18). Thus, her emphasis lies on "incompleteness, instability, and change" in systems and people (ibid.).

I am interested in the sort of agency from the oppressed that emerges not only from a dynamic cultural context, but also with cultural material such as music, to create change. This is radical action, that goes to the root, often internally, to address core issues of power and hierarchy that affect oppressed communities: the power of the communal arts to radically transform the self in relation to society or one's context. This is negotiation between the constructed ideological forces and the place where real people work out the messiness on the ground to create change. This practice framework has a conscious intent of radical action through the arts for change. Human action not only constructs the arts and individual identity in relation to them, but also transforms them, potentially liberating the actor. The actor inherently shows his or her skill through the arts, manipulating folk song lyrics, tune, rhythm, instruments, and meanings to create an internal, community-based dialogue intended to create action for change.

This action is radical in its disorientation, in the way that it pushes the external limits of habitus (Ortner, 1996: 11). Dalits reverse power structures (Appavoo, in Sherinian, 2014). In village religious practice, Dalits radically transform, from the inside, the internalized roots of the shame of untouchability. The *parai* drum evokes trance states that enable Dalits to make themselves anew. Dalit Action Theory, then, is centered in the power of the arts, the music-dance-narrative, to (re)produce society and history through the intentional action of agents, specifically oppressed agents. Dalits understand the larger forces working against them and are actively—not simply—surviving, and resisting, through daily musical action.

The church in India constructs Christian identity and theology as well as the practice of music. But, through indigenizing Christian music in styles such as folk music that allow for slippages in reproduction and active resistance to dominant ideology, practitioners are able to change lyrics and other musical aspects and, therefore, theology (Sherinian, 2014). Using folk music, Dalit Christians are able to change Christian theology and their associated social identities "from below." With such a musical system, song texts have no authors, hymnbook committees have no control, and there is a built-in "lack of totalization of 'structure' itself.... Hegemonies are always 'partial'... there are always sites [or sounds]... of alternative practice and perspective available, and these may become bases of resistance and transformation" (Ortner, 1996: 18). Folk music in Indian culture is one such site of alternative practice, particularly with the influence of culture broker theologians like Rev. J. T. Appavoo (1940–2005), who was a significant node in a network of change that encouraged this alternative practice of folk music as theology.[20]

Actors as agents with desires and intentions are embedded within games, dramas, stories, and, I would also assert, musical systems and structures with sound and movement. Furthermore, such perspectives inherently recognize, in agency, alternatives—the possibility of doing things differently. As Ortner says, "there are [always] other ways of doing the game of life, even if those alternatives are not immediately available or not subjectively desirable. What is important is that they exist, and thus always prevent closure" (Ortner, 1996: 19). They are understood as possible. They give hope and encourage persistence of action by the oppressed. This is consciousness.

Christianizing "Dalit"

In the early 1980s, Christians throughout India, but particularly in the South, began to embrace the term *Dalit* as a form of identity and to apply it to the creation of a liberation theology that addressed caste as well as class and gender inequalities. This "Dalit Theology" had its roots in the Social Gospel movement of the mid- to late nineteenth century,[21] the Ambedkar movement, Marxist and labor movements, and the anti-Brahmin Dravidian movement in South India (Devasahayam, 1997; Webster, 1992). It also led to the development of a body of literature on Dalit theology.

The academic roots of the Dalit theology movement began at the United Theological College, Bangalore, in April 1981, with a lecture entitled "Towards a Sudra Theology" by A. P. Nirmal. Kottapalli Wilson used the term *Dalit* in 1982 in his book *The Twice Alienated Culture of Dalit Christians*. In 1984, the Church of South India Dalit Bishop M. Azariah (the first Dalit Bishop in the CSI Madras Diocese, who served in 1990–1999) was the first Protestant Church leader to use the phrase "Dalit Theology" in international discourse, with the intent of bringing global concern to the plights of Dalits.[22] One of the most striking problems for Christian Dalits is that the Indian government does not afford them the same degree of compensation (quotas in government jobs and educational seats) as nominally Hindu Dalits.[23] In 1994, Bishop Azariah led a march to Delhi to fight for compensatory rights—affirmative action and quotas in education and government jobs—for Christian Dalits equal to those offered to "Hindu" Dalits. Dalit Christians have also been actively involved in the international struggle for Dalit human rights and recognition of caste discrimination. More recently, many Dalit Christians, including the young women *parai* drummers of the Sakthi Kalai Kuzhu (The Sakthi Folk Cultural Centre), participated in political demonstrations as performer/activists at the 2001 United Nations Conference on Racism in Durban, South Africa, and the 2004 World Social Forum in Mumbai.

CASE ONE: TAMIL FOLK MUSIC AS DALIT THEOLOGY

It was this milieu of activism and musico-theology into which I stepped in 1993 to begin my doctoral fieldwork on the indigenization of Tamil Christian music—only to become disoriented and transformed. In this section I describe how the introduction of folk music by theologians and a folk music process of re-creation of Christian music and theology by Dalit villagers since the 1980s are examples of Ortner's subaltern practice theory, specifically through the reformation of sociomusical identity (Ortner, 1996: 17).

Tomie Hahn articulates how an ethnomusicologist can experience disorientation in fieldwork in the process of discovering the transformative moments that lead to cultural understanding or reorientation (Hahn, 2006: 89). I conducted my dissertation fieldwork at the Tamil Nadu Theological Seminary (TTS) in Madurai, India, in 1993–1994. My original intent had been to study the use of Indian classical Karnatak music by Christians. However, in my first engagement with Rev. Theophilus Appavoo (1940–2005) and his Dalit Christian folk music, I experienced embodied disorientation that critically challenged my understanding of what was significant theologically, musically, and politically in the seminary community.

In Appavoo's first morning chapel service that I observed in the early months of my fieldwork, I was taken aback by the way he arranged the community in the chapel space, mixing women and men in a circle instead of segregated on two sides. Furthermore, he called forth women students to dialogue with him during his sermon, and he used lively participatory folk songs where typically light (film-music style) or classical Christian music was the norm. This experience not only moved me intellectually and musically, but politically (Blacking, 1995: 213–214).[24] The direct and metaphorical ideology of the lyrics and the folk musical style fully engaged my progressive (feminist, socialist, and queer) political values and moved me to commit my project to a greater understanding of the expression and transmission of Appavoo's Dalit Liberation theology through music. I chose to embrace the folk style of this Christian music, the participatory experience of the gender-integrated space, the experience of collaborative music making, and the politics of liberation that these performance practice values articulated. It was not only an academic decision, but also an embodied political one, in the feminist sense of the personal being the political. John Blacking's analysis of the Christian music of the South African Venda people, which applied a folk model of musical performance integrating worship, music, politics, and social life, is a useful comparison:

> The significance of musical freedom in the context of religious worship becomes apparent, and the difficulty of explaining nonverbal action with concepts derived from other modeling system dissolves in the face of a system that relates feeling and bodily experiences to material realities without any sense of contradiction.
>
> (Blacking, 1995: 221)

This initial observational experience in the TTS chapel brought me into Appavoo's sphere and familial community as a student and critical partner in dialogue about music production, style, and transmission in the seminary.

Above I describe Harry Berger's use of critical dialogue in fieldwork and interpretation with particular attention to the "ethics of voice in fieldwork... and the role of power in expressive culture" (Berger, 2008: 74–75). One of my most embodied transformative field experiences at TTS involved a dialogue about vocal style and a folk process of shared production of theology from below through the adaptation or change of lyrics. The result of this embodied experience and interpretive process was a multifaceted understanding of caste and gender politics through recognition of the agency (voice) and stances of all involved in the negotiation of meaning (Berger, 2009). Specifically, the analysis of musical style showed both nonverbal and verbal elements of song expressing the agentive voices of the doubly oppressed: Dalit women.

While learning to perform and lead the classical South Indian Karnatak style, sung liturgy at TTS, I acutely experienced the hegemony of male vocal range. That is, the performance practice of this congregational style liturgy at the seminary required women to sing very high because the keynote, or *sruti*, was determined by a male vocal range, usually a *sruti* of C or D, in a setting in which men and women sing in octave unison. Male instrumental leaders habitually chose the most accessible *sruti* for them (males) to both sing and play on a harmonium keyboard. Thus in order to sing in octaves, the women had to push their range up from the Karnatak music norm of F1 to begin at c2 (middle C) and stretch to g3 (or higher, an octave and a half above. For the majority of the women (including me), the musical result was a strained, thin, often squeaking female timbre, very typical of Indian film music since the late 1940s. My initial analysis and embodied response in my own discomfort of singing that high was that these women were constrained by what I termed a male vocal hegemony. I shared this musical and gendered analysis with Rev. Appavoo, helping him understand my embodied musical experience (Sherinian, 2005).[25] The following was his response:

> I think real research should create some action. So if I do some research that should create something, some change in what we call the subjects of research. As you have been doing. You are doing that, because you always remind us about the women,. . . you know the women's perspective. . . . So this should be research of a person who is committed to humanity in general. All my articles and everything are connected with that kind of thing. It's not just research for the sake of getting a degree.
>
> (interview, Madurai, July 1994)

However, while Appavoo supported my analysis and potential influence on, or "interventions" in, the realm of performance in the seminary (Titon, 1992: 316), through dialogue with the young women singers, I determined that many of them *preferred* and *strove* to sing high with a nasal timbre, as a vocalized film music aesthetic that constructed a modern, sophisticated Indian femininity. Appavoo ultimately recognized this perspective, but concluded that this vocal expression was not "liberating," as an oral symbol of modernity and sophistication, which simultaneously reinforced a domesticated, virginal, and constrained femininity for adult women (Sundar, 2007: 147–148, 169).[26]

Further engagement with Appavoo's own compositional processes, on the other hand, not only created change in his community, or the "subjects" of my research, but in the ethnographer (myself). This manifested through Appavoo's style of dialogical engagement with students and with me. It included praxis, reflection, and change of his compositions, a collaborative process to make them more accessible and theologically relevant and thus as liberating as possible. For example, when teaching his own songs, Appavoo remained open and listened for feedback about lyrics and musical sound from students at the seminary. While I was doing fieldwork with Appavoo's choir, the women spontaneously replaced the lyric that addressed God as *Appa* (father) with *Amma* (mother) in a rehearsal of his song "Manasamātta" (Change of Heart). He thoughtfully broadened the way he addressed God to make it more inclusive of a theological construction as mother as well as father, by switching the term every other refrain (see Sherinian, 2014: Chapter 4, for full analysis of this song and a sound example). This is indicative of Appavoo's embrace of a folk music process. In South Asian classical music, on the other hand, the student is passive, never asking questions of the guru, but simply practicing and patiently waiting for the guru to decide if the student is ready to receive more. It is a role that demands an inherently "uncritical nature" (Groesbeck, 2001: 1; Nettl, 2005: 156–157).

Appavoo did not immediately recognize his own gendered limitations until the women's side of the choir boldly sang back to him their perspective that "God is Mother!" He did not understand my gendered experience of singing the Karnatak liturgy until I shared that the vocal range chosen for me by the male harmonium player, who used it to primarily accompany men, strained my performance/range. In turn, I did not understand the class perspective of the urban Dalit women until another Indian woman friend lent the perspective that while I felt limited by this high vocal range, perhaps the young Dalit women who sang this repertoire in their upper range experienced its thin timbre as an urban sophisticated voice, like that of film stars, and provided them modern, urban, middle-class status through musical emulation. When Appavoo recognized that my strained experience as a women vocalist did not fit his own folk and feminist ideology of accessibility for his music, he consciously scrutinized the starting pitches (or vocal range level) for his compositions, adjusting them to better accommodate women in performance. Others in the seminary who did not share these feminist values, on the other hand, ignored us. Until ethnomusicologists begin to practice an activist methodology and fieldwork space that allows dialogue between multiple perspectives or stances, that challenges the constructionist authority of a white academic, of a male theology professor, of a rising middle-class Dalit female student, and that acknowledges that we ethnomusicologists inherently intervene, we can only achieve a limited understanding of culture.

The re-creative flexibility and transmission process (production, reception, and reproduction) of folk music in the Tamil Dalit Christian context provided the lived experience of people as the experience of creating empowering theology.[27] This included the dialogical and interpretive process of participatory-action that evolved from the lived experience and practice of conducting fieldwork through embodying and negotiating not only politicized lyrics, but nonverbal, culturally coded elements like musical timbre and range (Blacking, 1995: 199–200).

Rev. Appavoo, in turn, put the responsibility back on us, his students, to transmit his theological and political message through engagement with village and town congregations and to nurture these songs in a feedback process that could potentially lead to further theological recreation, particularly by the village Dalit people for whom the music was intended. After inviting me into his family circle and calling me his daughter, he named me *Parattai Kural* (Parattai's voice),[28] bringing to consciousness an identity of being more than a scholar, but also an activist with whom he was willing to trust and share his music. Through this trust and familial closeness, he placed a responsibility on me to spread his message of the praxis of Dalit musico-theology at a more global level.

All of these dialogical field engagements and experiences dislodged, redefined, and reoriented the traditional guru-disciple relationship that I, like so many of my colleagues in South Asian ethnomusicology, had come to expect, particularly within a

Karnatak or Hindustani elite musical context. It was the shift to a folk music milieu and a liberation theology production, transmission, and reception process that facilitated this reorientation.[29]

Jeff Titon describes the particular process of self-reflexivity and transformation for ethnomusicologists as located in the shared experience of playing music together in cross-cultural relationships (Sherinian, 2005, 1; Titon, 2008 [1997]). My engagement in hearing, studying, and performing Tamil Christian folk music, and my participation in the daily rituals of shared eating and in a dialogue of shared values with the community members who gathered around the musico-theology and person of Rev. Theophilus Appavoo created the place from which I locate my participation and self-transformation in my study and activism.

Case Two: Drumming Dalit Documentary Film

In his book *Global Soundscapes* (2008), Mark Slobin essentially asks, "What does music do for film?" I want to extend this question to ask, "What can film do for music as advocacy?" The documentary film, *This Is a Music: Reclaiming an Untouchable Drum*, which I shot in India in 2008–2009 and released in 2011, is an example of ethnomusicological advocacy that is inherently polemic. The title *This Is a Music* came from one of my nine *parai* frame drumming teachers, Amulraj, as he asserted the value of his drum, usually considered polluting, as *music* (*ida oru isai*, or "this is a music," in Tamil).

> TYAGU (FIELD ASSISTANT/TRANSLATOR): To what extent do you accept those who think of you in such a degrading way? To what extent do you accept their views?
> AMULRAJ: We won't get angry if they speak that way. Those who have learned the profession won't get angry. We won't get angry (shakes his head). We will call them and say, "Come here man, *this is a music*! You can't understand this (shakes hand and gestures a throw). It doesn't get through your thick head! That is why you are speaking like this. Go ask people like yourself, but who have traveled, 'what are our abilities?' Don't simply go around talking like scum." We will call them and tell them these things. But we won't get angry with them. (Smiles and shakes his head "no").
> (interview, Amulraj, Munaivendri, Tamil Nadu September 7, 2008)

In the Indian musical economy, where the hierarchy of musical value parallels the caste hierarchy, "polluted" outcaste musicians playing polluting folk music struggle for respect against assertions of degradedness and lack of musicality (personal communication, Rajasekaran, 2009). Thus, Amulraj's assertion that his *parai* instrument, commonly thought of by middle-caste villagers and upper-caste musicians as degraded, "is a music" is a passionate, radical critique of the cultural ramifications of caste hierarchy. By providing Amulraj and his troupe an opportunity through film to voice their agency against this cultural devaluation and to share their ongoing experience of castism in the Indian village in their struggle to become professionalized musicians (laborers), my academic work as a scholar filmmaker embraces this polemic stance. However, my position to support Amulraj's assertions are grounded in traditional ethnomusicological methods— that is, well documented, "hard," systematic musical analysis of the music's structure and performance practice using my informant's own terms (analytical perspectives and metaphors that perhaps do not get through the thick heads of Amul's middle- and upper-caste oppressors). These were gained from spending four months of participatory fieldwork learning to play the *parai* with the members of Kurinji Malar: embodying its rhythms, its structure, its dance, and its meanings.[30]

As significant as formal analysis, however, my film focuses on the negotiation of the *parai*'s ritual value in funerals and village Hinduism, where its sound and sounding is the means to call the deity, analogous to the use of Sanskrit *slokas* in Brahminical Hinduism (personal communication, John Jayaharan, 2009), and the means to take the soul to heaven (*surgam*) (personal communication, Rajasekaran, 2009). Further, we observed how in the contemporary urban folk festival context, *parai* performance has become a source of Non-Brahmin, Tamil cultural identity and entertainment. Finally, within the Dalit civil rights movement in Tamil Nadu, the *parai* drummer has become a cultural icon for empowerment and the drum "a weapon for liberation."

Making this documentary film was experiential and progressive within the discipline of ethnomusicology, as its process and results were highly dialogic, self-reflexive, multivocal, and transformative. Having nine teachers instead of one, as Tomie Hahn has argued, "disoriented" my fieldwork expectations in Munaivendri village (2006: 89). It changed the nature of the guru-student relationship I had grown to expect in the South Asian context. This multivocality of teaching techniques lent itself further to a dialogical engagement throughout the fieldwork and filming process. My teachers challenged my discourse and interpretations, the critical process of which I document in the film narrative. I allowed myself to be vulnerable (to turn the camera on both my subjects and myself, the ethnographer), to show the dialogical process of coming to understand the following: (1) the drummer's worldview (and how it was different from perspectives of middle-class Dalit activists, which I had adopted); (2) how they experienced caste discrimination as musicians; (3) how they experienced the term *parai* (as "a bitter taste on their tongue," or a word that was hard to swallow, as it reminded them of their degraded caste name, *Paraiyar*); and (4) how they would ultimately negotiate a balance between building their self-esteem that resulted from their more positive reception at the Chennai Sangamam urban folk festival with the limitations of their necessary economic engagements with upper-caste patrons in their home village context.[31]

SASHI (CINEMATOGRAPHER): What do you think about *parai*?
ZOE (ETHNOGRAPHER/DIRECTOR): The instrument.
TYAGU (FIELD ASSISTANT): You see, the object. The instrument... what do you think about that instrument. What is its meaning to you?

AMULRAJ (DRUMMER/TEACHER): You mean drumset?
TYAGU: *Parai*?
AMULRAJ: (strongly assertive tone) you mean about drumset! That is honorable (*kouravamana*) work (*velai*). There is no need for us to ask for alms (*pitchai*) from anybody. It is beautiful work. It is super work. It is not that this is being done as hereditary (*parambaram*) habit (*parakam*). Of course it was done as a hereditary habit [duty], but we are not following them (in that way). Music Illaiyaraja [famous Dalit film music producer] is beating, right? Can we simply go and talk about him that way? But, when it comes to learning the profession, no one will acquire it that easily. This profession will come quickly only to the one who created it. [He likely means Paraiyars who are thought to have this ability "in their blood"]. When it comes to beating a single beat... if you ask who can learn it quickly, it comes only to us.
TYAGU: Do others think about drumset as low (*kizha*)? If they think of it as low how do you accept that?
AMULRAJ: Those few others who do not know about this profession, and those who do not know anything of the world, and those who have not gone anywhere [literally outside] and have no knowledge about other places, think of this profession as polluted (*asingama*). Those who have moved away from this place to town and have roamed there would not think of it as polluted. Those who have lived only here, having never been away [traveled], would think "these guys... what they do is definitely polluted. What they do is a bad/mistaken work [*tappana tolil*]." Those who have traveled in four directions would think, "this guy... Beautiful profession! Keen interest!" And, those who know that whatever function it is, only drumset leads the way [literally stand at the front] will not think of it as degraded. Even then, if somebody thinks, "What, drumset! This guy is still (mindlessly) beating *kottu* and roaming around." We would respond "what man, have you (*ni*—informal you) ever traveled around the world?" In this way we have also questioned them and answered with details.... Similarly, anyone who has traveled all the four directions would not think that way. They have said, "It is his profession, sir we cannot beat like him! You see this guy beating, see whether you can beat like that, sir." I have heard this being said with my own ears. (Interview, Amulraj, Munaivendri September 7, 2008)

In her attempt to negotiate agency within practice theory, Sherry Ortner begins by "retaining an active intentional subject without falling into some form of free agency and voluntarism" (1996: 19). She argues for a method that embraces "the unit of practice" as the serious game or structures of agency, not the "agent" (ibid.: 13, 19). This allows us to keep the hopeful and persistent action of agents as well as structures in mind. To remember to hear how agents are "skilled and intense strategizers who constantly stretch the game even as they enact it, and the simultaneous fact that players are defined and constructed (though never wholly contained) by the game" (ibid.: 20).

Amulraj's identity may still be constructed as *Paraiayar*, or untouchable *jati*, by his upper-caste village neighbors, but his movement as a musician outside the ideological, geographical, and discursive limitations of the village allows him to negotiate this, to redefine himself in relation to other forces that show the greater humanity of his music and person. He intentionally talked back to us, the ethnographers who used the reclaimed, ancient term *parai* of the Dalit activists and folk festival organizers, to name his drum/ensemble. He instead assertively favored an English term "drumset" that had more neutral, but valued status in his mind as middle class. He justified this with his claim to an indigenous cosmopolitanism, to a worldliness and understanding of the ruptures in the caste system possible outside his village and region, and the value and agency of his music to help create these.

How was this field encounter mutually transformative? Through my relationship with Kurinji Malar as their student, their advocate, and their friend, these nine drummers became brothers to me. While I was already invested in regional Dalit politics, I came to understand their local village processes, their economic and social context, their sociopolitical reality—which is not mine, which I can step out of without having to take any real responsibility or without it having an impact on my daily life. However, I was further transformed into an activist filmmaker through a relationship of affinity with their situation. I, in turn, created the opportunity for Kurinji Malar to attend the Chennai Sangamam festival through drawing on my contacts with Catholic organizers and other academic activists to get the group invited to the festival, based partly on the fact that I was making a documentary about them.[32] But, the drummers then took this opportunity and ran with it. The networking they pursued with other musicians and organizers at the festival (which I had nothing to do with), along with their professionalism and enthusiasm in performance, led to multiple opportunities that took them twice to national and international events in Delhi, as well as to several other regional festivals. Ethnomusicologists in academia have always networked to create these sorts of opportunities for our teachers/informants, though one might argue that I was acting more like a public sector or applied ethnomusicologist who works in community festival organizing. Ethnomusicologists need to reconsider that, whether creating opportunities for our informants while in the field or producing world music concert series for a school of music, this is musical activism: that ethnomusicologists are all activists and advocates, and the process of becoming so can be transformative of our work, our scholarship, and ourselves as people.

The ethnomusicological method of musical immersion in contexts that bring us face to face with performers, typically as our teachers or collaborators, who produce musical sound, concepts about it, and its cultural meaning, is participant activism. We are not only immersed in contexts, but in relationships of shared music making and dialogues of knowledge production. When we bring these processes into our written or audiovisual ethnographies and are conscious or honest about our roles as actors in the field, we are practicing self-reflexivity.

I have shown that if one works in a context in which the value of the music and musicians are intensely hierarchical and one is focused on those at the margins/bottom, we cannot do our subjects justice unless we engage with the local (and potentially global) politics of value. Thus, in order to participate in critical dialogue with subaltern or Dalit collaborators (to change the way we practice South Asian ethnomusicology), we need more conscious tools and theories that engage us as actors in the field, not passive musical mimetics who primarily produce or translate structural analysis of musical systems. The South Asian musical context in which the value and meaning of caste, class, and gender are still fought over and negotiated everyday, through mediums like folk music and performance, offers Dalit Action Theory for ethnomusicology and cultural studies. This is knowledge production as transformative aesthetic action through embodied disorientation, dialogical processes of praxis, reflection, and critical interpretation, woven in and out of encounters with the politics of cultural value, where oppressed groups use the arts to assert identity and (re)valued agency.

While doing fieldwork, many ethnomusicologists come face to face with the reality of political power dynamics with which our informants struggle. However, for those of us who work in the Western music academy, whether the "world" music we study is elite, popular, or Dalit, and whether or not we consider ourselves "activist/advocate ethnomusicologists," we are still forced to engage with the politics of musical value in these institutions. Applying the perspectives of Dalit Action Theory in our academic departmental contexts may also be a means to the growth and survival of our discipline.

Notes

1. *Dalit* is a term of oppositional politics that can be described as anti-caste. It is an umbrella term that is inclusive of those formerly called outcaste, untouchable, or harajin. It is also a term meaning "oppressed," used by some activists to include lower castes, the poor, and women.
2. Art historian of Tamil media culture Preminda Jacob (2009: 4) argues that the ephemeral and collaborative nature of the production in the Tamil film industry and political banners and cutouts, "almost wholly precluded them from serious consideration by art historians. . . The discipline of art history conventionally requires an object that can be collected and preserved and, in the case of contemporary works, clearly attributed in its authorship to a particular individual" (Jacob, 2009: 4).
3. This includes the reassertion of upper-caste and Brahmin identities through solidification and narrowed control of Karnatak music by urban Brahmins, particularly in Madras/Chennai. This happened through the shift in production control away from the regional courts and kingly patrons to the *sabbhas* or music clubs of the urban areas after the 1860s, but also through institutions like the Madras Music Academy and All India Radio (see Lakshmi Subramanian, 2011).
4. The term *harajin*, (meaning "children of God") was applied to untouchables by Mahatma Gandhi. While many common, politicized outcastes still use the term *harajin*, Dalit activists have extensively critiqued it as patronizing. Some of this is based on the general critique of Gandhi by Dr. Ambedkar, the acknowledged twentieth-century leader of the untouchable movement. Ambedkar critiqued Gandhi for upholding the *varna* system in his ideology and for using strategies such as threatening a fast-unto-death if Ambedkar did not relinquish his goal of achieving a separate electorate or representation for Dalits in India's parliamentary system, which was already available for other minorities. This is extensively documented in the Pune (or Poona) Pact of September of 1932. (See youtube.com/watch?v=ZJs-BJoSzbo for Dr. Ambedkar's 1955 BBC Interview).

5. In common use, however, *Dalit* has often problematically been conflated or used in practice as a simple replacement for outcaste *jati* terms such as *Paraiyar* or *Chakkliyar*. Yet, its meaning in such application still carries a sense of political consciousness of oppression and a rejection of the term *untouchable* or specific caste/jati names thought of as derogatory.
6. In 1924, Dr. Ambedkar founded the organization Bahiskrit Hitakarini Sabha (Outcastes Welfare Association), with the intention of working for the liberation of the outcastes, or untouchables. His goals included the eradication of illiteracy, economic development, and nonviolent action against caste-based discrimination, such as denial of temple entry. (Goldy George, *Salam Bhimrao! Dr. Bhimrao Ramji Ambedkar and the Dalit Movement in India: A Reflection*). http://histhink.wordpress.com/2010/07/19/salam-bhimrao-dr-bhimrao-ramji-ambedkar-the-dalit-movement-in-india-a-reflection/ (accessed October 6, 2013).
7. Daniel Sheehy (1992: 324) describes this worthy purpose of ethnomusicology as seeing "opportunities for a better life for others through the use of musical knowledge, and then immediately to begin devising cultural strategies to achieve those ends."
8. The discourse of a golden age of Hinduism disregards the presence of Christianity in Kerala from possibly the first (if not, certainly the fourth) century and the important patronage and cultural influence of Islam, Sufism, and Muslim hereditary performers in Hindustani music (Qureshi, 1991).
9. The etymology of the term *parai* is "to speak or announce," reflecting the occupation of *parai* drummers as those who announce village ritual and social occasions by playing the semiotically coded patterns of their drum. The term parai is found in Tamil Sangam literature written between the 2nd century b.c.e. and 2nd century c.e.
10. In my previous work I have shown that this value hierarchy extends beyond Hinduism to the music and theological resources of other religious communities in South India, including the Christians (Sherinian, 2007, 2014).
11. The best-known Ph.D. programs in ethnomusicology that were early integrators of Asian ensembles and teachers in their curriculum and faculty include UCLA, Wesleyan, University of Michigan, and University of Washington.
12. In the Martin-Luther University Halle-Wittenberg in Halle, Germany, I located a small collection of *kīrttaṉai* dated 1714 that included *ragas, talas*, and three part *kriti* form, put together in a pamphlet for schoolchildren of the Tranquebar mission in Tamil Nadu. It was against this upper-caste repertoire and the values that it carried that Theophilus Appavoo would create his Dalit liberation theology in folk music in the 1980s.
13. The exceptions to this were Regula Qureshi's (1991 and earlier) work on the erasure of the oral contribution of poor, illiterate Muslim hereditary practitioners of Hindustani music and the Marxist work on the music industry by Peter Manuel (1993). The work since the 1990s of Matthew Allen (1997, 1998), Yoshitaka Terada (2000), Amanda Weidman (2006), Richard Wolf (2009), Douglas Knight (2010), Lakshmi Subramanian (2011), Devesh Soneji (2012), and Anna Schultz (2013) has finally begun to fill in the critical perspective and the sociopolitics needed to understand the production of classical music by upper- and middle-caste Indians.
14. This counters the stereotype perpetuated by orthodox Hindus that Indian society is Hindu, the majority of people are vegetarians who further follow the orthodox strictures that one should neither drink nor smoke, and that there is very little intercaste or love marriage.

15. I do not mean to associate Dalit with something that is somehow "sub" or below anything else. It is not a disempowered position but an empowered, counter expression of opposition to the caste system or to hegemonic systems of power.
16. Louai, El Habib, "Retracing the Concept of the Subaltern from Gramsci to Spivak: Historical Developments and New Applications," *African Journal of History and Culture* 4(1): 4–8, January 2012, http://www.academicjournals.org/AJHCDOI: 10.5897/AJHC11.020ISSN 2141-6672 (accessed October 1, 2013).
17. Pavitra Sundar, citing Raheja (2003), similarly asserts in her discussion of film singer Lata Mangeshkar that "[i]n many parts of India, singing is a crucial mode of female participation in the public sphere" (2007: 162), and that indeed music is "the means by which women enter the nation" (ibid.: 161). Sundar qualifies this, saying that women's presence in the public sphere, at least in the film *Lagaan*, is "non-threatening as they are allowed to participate only in song. The narrative makes no room for female aggression" (ibid.).
18. I am grateful to the Dalit filmmaker-activist Thenmozhi Soundararajan for helping me see the point that Dalits are not "sub" or below anything.
19. In his important article on music, politics, and Christianity (1981), John Blacking showed the significance of nonverbal, folk modeling systems to influence social action, especially in oppressive contexts like South Africa's apartheid system, where the speech of the majority black population was severely repressed and restricted (reprinted in Blacking, 1995: 199, edited by Byron).
20. Rev. Dr. J. T. Appavoo was my teacher. My publication *Tamil Folk Music as Dalit Liberation Theology* (Bloomington: Indiana University Press, 2014) is an ethnomusicological biography of his life and theology as music.
21. The Dalit theology movement is a local movement with over one hundred years of roots in India. It was not directly influenced by the South American movement, though its thinkers read liberation theology works by Paulo Freire and Gustavo Gutierrez.
22. Other important publications include *Towards a Dalit Theology* by M. E. Prabhakar (1988), *Emerging Dalit Theology* by Xavier Irundayaraj (1990), *Reader in Dalit Theology* by Arvind Nirmal (1991), *Indigenous People: Dalits* by James Massey (1994), and *Christianity and Dalits* by Sathianathan Clarke (1998), and the recent anthology that includes chapters by Dalit faculty from TTS and the Chennai Diocese, *Frontiers of Dalit Theology*, edited by V. Devasahayam (1997). *Frontiers of Dalit Theology* includes two articles by Theophilus Appavoo, "Dalit Way of Theological Expression," and "Communication for Dalit Liberation."
23. Many lower-caste and Dalit activists, such as the author Kancha Ilaiah, who wrote *Why I Am Not a Hindu: A Sudra Critique of Hindutva Philosophy, Culture, and Political Economy* (1994), reject being called Hindu and having been appropriated into the Hindu fold. They argue that their religious practice, deities, and origins are completely different from Brahmanical Hinduism. Most unpoliticized lower-caste people, on the other hand, simply accept the term *Hindu* as applied to them by the social and political system.
24. See John Blacking's (1995) work on music and politics within the South African (Venda) churches, specifically his discussion of the form of liberation theology called Black Theology and his stress on the importance of musical style, that is, how people of different denominations sang to mark political associations and consciousness in a process of adaptation or inculturation of European Christianity (specifically hymnody) to African culture (1995: 218).

25. For a full analysis of this incident in my ethnographic experience, see my article "Representing Dalit Feminist Politics Through Dialogical Musical Ethnography" in *Women and Music* 9 (2005): 1–12.
26. Pavitra Sundar argues that three generations of Indians knew the "virginally pure" shrill falsetto timbre of the iconic film music figure of Lata Mangeshkar as the "quintessential and ideal voice" of a modern, middle-class, national, Indian femininity (2007: 145, 147–148). Drawing on Barthes's (1977) theory of the "grain of the voice" or "corporeality of voice," Sundar focuses on a method of using "vocality in theories of the body. . . demonstrating how vocal music works to embody and disembody the nation" (ibid.: 146). She describes this as "materiality of music" and the "audible body" (ibid.: 164) grounded in its sociohistorical context (ibid.: 163). She concludes that Mangeshkar's "desexualized vocal style helped contain the dangerous visual and aural presence of female bodies in public" (ibid.: 149). While it is not a particularly transgressive presence, but a domesticated agency limited to "sexually modest, upper-caste, and middle-class Hindu women" as they contribute to patriarchal nationalist goals (ibid.: 164, 168–169).
27. Harris Berger asserts that "the object of study is not music sound or music structure, it is pieces, performance, sounds, or structures in the lived experience of social persons" (Berger, 2008: 70). Furthermore, he argues that ethnomusicology's proper object is not the reification of texts, but "practices of production and reception" (ibid.: 65).
28. Rev. Appavoo's Tamil folk pen name was *Parattai Annan*, or "big brother with messy hair." He used this anonymous identification in the publication of his songs to encourage people to change the lyrics or music as they saw fit to their sociopolitical context.
29. Advocacy was inherently present in my commitment to share Appavoo's Dalit liberation songs and liturgy with the world. Our mutual enthusiasm to get this message to a global academic and theological audience brought him to my academic milieu in the United States on lecture tour. Tragically, on this tour in 2005, he became sick, and after seven weeks of hospitalization with congestive heart failure, died—a completely transformative experience for me.
30. This is an oral system of drumming based in mnemonics with a clear theoretical organization. There is a relationship between the kinesthetics of the dance patterns, the drum mnemonics, and folk tune genres. Most contemporary performances have a systematic drumming and dance organization of a circle-line-circle over the course of 20 minutes. I learned and recorded on videotape 35 different named beats (*adis*) from these men, all but one of whom have less then a fourth grade education. Further, I interviewed them about their teaching methods, and videotaped and analyzed hours of our lessons.
31. See the film trailer for *This Is a Music: Reclaiming an Untouchable Drum* for more contextualized detail. http://www.youtube.com/watch?v=WPXJAYPHGzI.
32. Besides a general ethical stance of practicing my responsibility to "give back" to this group of very poor and illiterate musicians who had become my teachers, I understood this as an "intervention" and a potentially significant boost in their career trajectory and professionalization (Titon, 1992: 316–317). However, I fully embraced Sheehy's notion that securing Kurinji Malar an invitation to participate in the Chennai Sangamam folk festival would and ultimately did provide them increased financial opportunities, and enhanced self-esteem through contact outside the caste-infected economy of their local area—a strategic practice with a worthy purpose (Sheehy, 1992: 324).

References

Allen, Matthew H. (1997). "Rewriting the Script for South Indian Dance," *TDR: The Drama Review* 41(3): 63–100.

Allen, Matthew H. (1998). "Tales Tunes Tell Tales Tunes Tell: Deepening the Dialogue Between 'Classical' and 'Non-Classical' in the Music of India." *Yearbook for Traditional Music* 30: 22–52.

Appavoo, Theophilus. (1997a). "Dalit Way of Theological Expression." In *Frontiers of Dalit Theology*, edited by V. Devasahayam, pp. 283–289. Madras: Gurukul.

Appavoo, Theophilus. (1997b). "Communication for Dalit Liberation." In *Frontiers of Dalit Theology*, edited by V. Devasahayam, pp. 363–372. Madras: Gurukul.

Babiracki, Carol M. (2008). "What's the Difference? Reflections on Gender and Research in Village India." In *Shadows in the Field*, edited by Gregory Barz and Timothy J. Cooley, pp. 167–182. New York: Oxford University Press.

Bhagavan, Manu, and Anne Feldhaus, eds. (2008). *Claiming Power from Below: Dalits and the Subaltern Question in India*. New Delhi: Oxford University Press.

Berger, Harris, M. (2008). "Phenomenology and the Ethnography of Popular Music." In *Shadows in the Field*, edited by Gregory Barz and Timothy J. Cooley, pp. 62–75. New York: Oxford University Press.

Berger, Harris M. (2009). *Stance: Ideas about Emotion, Style, and Meaning for the Study of Expressive Culture*. Middletown: Wesleyan University Press.

Blacking, John. (1995). *Music, Culture, and Experience: Selected Papers of John. Blacking*, edited by Reginald Byron. Chicago: University of Chicago Press.

Butler, Judith. (1990). *Gender Trouble*. New York: Routledge.

Chatterjee, Indrani. (2013). *Forgotten Friends: Monks, Marriages, and Memories of Northeast India*. New York: Oxford University Press.

Chatterjee, Partha. (2003). "A Subtle Poison: Officially Supported Cultural Nationalism Will Make India Intolerant." *The Telegraph*. January 30. Calcutta, India.

Clarke, Sathianathan. (1998). *Dalits and Christianity: Subaltern Religion and Liberation Theology in India*. Delhi: Oxford University Press.

Devasahayam, V. (1997). "Introduction." In *Frontiers of Dalit Theology*, edited by V. Devasahayam, pp. xi–xv. Chennai: ISPCK/Gurukul.

Dirksen, Rebecca. (2012). "Reconsidering Theory and Practice in Ethnomusicology: Applying, Advocating, and Engaging Beyond Academia." *Ethnomusicology Review* 17. http://ethnomusicologyreview.ucla.edu/journal/volume/17/piece/602 (accessed July 7, 2014).

Dower, John. (2004). "Keynote Talk." The 54th annual Midwest Conference on Asian Affairs in Minneapolis, MN.

Didi-Huberman, Georges. (2003). "Before the Image, before Time: The Sovereignty of Anachronism." In *Compelling Visuality: The Work of Art in and out of History*, edited by Claire Farago and Robert Zwijnenberg, pp. 31–44. Minneapolis: University of Minnesota Press.

Feld, Steven. (1984). "Sound Structure as Social Structure." *Ethnomusicology* 28(3): 383–409.

Freire, Paulo. (1984) [1970]. *Pedagogy of the Oppressed*. New York: Continuum.

Fox Strangways, A. H. (1914). *The Music of Hindustan*. Oxford: Clarendon Press.

Groesback, Rolf. (2001). "Social Categories and Ethnomusicological Field Experience in Kerala." Unpublished paper delivered at the Society for Ethnomusicology conference, Southfield, MI.

Gutierrez, Gustavo. (1973). *A Theology of Liberation: History, Politics, and Salvation*, 15th anniversary ed., translated by Caridad Inda and John Eagleson. Maryknoll: Orbis.
Hahn, Tomie. (2006). "It's the Rush: Sites of the Sensually Extreme." *TDR: The Drama Review* 50(2): 87–96.
Hanson, Thomas Bloom. (1999). *The Saffron Wave: Democracy and Hindu Nationalism in Modern India*. Princeton, NJ: Princeton University Press.
Harrison, Klisala. (2012). "Epistemologies of Applied Ethnomusicology." *Ethnomusicology* 56(3): 505–529.
Ilaiah, Kancha. (1994). *Why I Am Not a Hindu: A Sudra Critique of Hindutva Philosophy, Culture and Political Economy*. Bombay: Samya.
Irundayaraj, Xavier. (1990). *Emerging Dalit Theology*. Madurai: Tamil Nadu Theological Seminary.
Jacob, Preminda. (2009). *Celluloid Deities: The Visual Culture of Cinema and Politics in South India*. Plymouth, UK: Lexington Books.
Jones, Sir William. (1792 [1784]). "On the Musical Modes of the Hindus." *Asiatic Researches* 3 (London): 55–87.
Kirshenblatt-Gimblett, Barbara. (1988). "Mistaken Dichotomies." *The Journal of American Folklore* 101(400): 142–155.
Knight, Douglas. (2010). *Balasaraswati: Her Art and Life*. Middletown, CT: Wesleyan University Press.
Louai, El Habib. (2012). "Retracing the Concept of the Subaltern from Gramsci to Spivak: Historical Developments and New Applications." *African Journal of History and Culture* (AJHC) 4(1): 4–8. http://www.academicjournals.org/AJHCDOI:10.5897/ AJHC11.020ISSN2141-6672 (accessed October 1, 2013).
Manuel, Peter. (1993). *Cassette Culture Popular Music and Technology in North India*. Chicago: University of Chicago Press.
Massey, James. (1994). "Indigenous People: Dalits." *Dalit Issues in Today's Theological Debate*. ISPCK Contextual Theological Education Series 5. Delhi: ISPCK.
Mclean, Craig. "Value Free Research," Dictionary Entry. *The SAGE Dictionary of Social Research Methods*, edited by Vicor Jupp. http://dx.doi.org/10.4135/9780857020116; http:// srmo.sagepub.com/view/the-sage-dictionary-of-social-research-methods/n218.xml (accessed July 22, 2014).
Mendelsohn, Oliver, and Marika Vicziany. (1998). *The Untouchables: Subordination, Poverty, and the State in Modern India*. Cambridge: Cambridge University Press.
Menon, Dilip. (2006) *The Blindness of Insight: Why Communalism Is about Caste and Other Essays*. Pondicherry: Navayana Press.
Miner, Allyn. (1993) *Sitar and Sarod in the Eighteenth and Nineteenth Centuries*. New York; Wilhelmshaven: F. Noetzel.
Mines, Diane. 2010. "The Hindu Gods in a South Indian Village." In *Everyday Life in South Asia*, edited by Mines and Lamb, pp. 226–237. Bloomington: Indiana University Press.
Nelson, David P. (1991). *Mrdangam Mind: the Tani Avartanam in Karnatak Music*. Ph.D. dissertation. Middletown, CT: Wesleyan University.
Nettl, Bruno. (2005 [1983]). *The Study of Ethnomusicology: Thirty-One Issues and Concepts*. Urbana: University of Illinois Press.
Nirmal, Arvind. (1991). *A Reader in Dalit Theology*. Madras: Gurukul.
Ortner, Sherry. (1996). *Making Gender: The Politics and Erotics of Culture*. Boston: Beacon Press.

Perlman, Marc. (2004). *Unplayed Melodies: Javanese Gamelan and the Genesis of Music Theory*. Berkeley: University of California Press.
Popley, H. A. (1966 [1920]). *The Music of India* (3rd ed.). New Delhi: YMCA.
Price, David. (2004). *Threatening Anthropology: McCarthyism and the FBI's Surveillance of Activist Anthropologists*. Durham, NC: Duke University Press.
Prieto, Laura. (1998). Review of Ortner, Sherry B., *Making Gender: The Politics and Erotics of Culture. H-PCAACA*, H-Net Reviews. June 1998.
Prabhakar, M. E. (1988). *Towards a Dalit Theology*. Delhi: ISPCK.
Qureshi, Regula. (1991). "Whose Music? Sources and Contexts in Indic Musicology." In *Comparative Musicology and Anthropology of Music*, edited by Bruno Nettl, pp. 152–168. Chicago: University of Chicago Press.
Raheja, Gloria. (2003). *Songs, Stories, Lives: Gendered Dialogues and Cultural Critique*. New Delhi: Kali for Women.
Schultz, Anna. (2013). *Singing a Hindu Nation: Marathi Devotional Performance and Nationalism*. New York: Oxford University Press.
Sheehy, Daniel. (1992). "A Few Notions about Philosophy and Strategy in Applied Ethnomusicology." In Special Issue: Music and the Public Interest. *Ethnomusicology* 36(3): 323–336.
Sherinian, Zoe. (2005). "Re-presenting Dalit Feminist Politics Through Dialogical Musical Ethnography." *Women and Music* 9: 1–12.
Sherinian, Zoe. (2007). "Musical Style and the Changing Social Identity of Tamil Christians." *Ethnomusicology* 51(2): 238–280.
Sherinian, Zoe. (2009). "Changing Status in India's Marginal Music Communities." *Religious Compass* 3(4): 608–619.
Sherinian, Zoe. (2011). Documentary film: *This Is a Music: Reclaiming an Untouchable Drum*. Oklahoma City: World Premiere deadCENTER film festival.
Sherinian, Zoe. (2014). *Tamil Folk Music as Dalit Liberation Theology*. Bloomington: Indiana University Press.
Slawek, Stephen. (1987). *Sitar Technique in Nibaddh Forms*. Delhi: Motilal Banarsidass.
Slobin, Mark. (2008). *Global Soundtracks: Worlds of Film Music*. Middletown, CT: Wesleyan University Press.
Soneji, Devesh. (2012). *Unfinished Gestures: Devadasis, Memory, and Modernity in South Asia*. Chicago: The University of Chicago Press.
Spivak, Gayatri C. (1988). "Can the Subaltern Speak?" In *Marxism and the Interpretation of Culture*, edited by Cary Nelson and Lawrence Grossberg, pp. 271–313. London: Macmillan.
Subramanian, Lakshmi. (2011). *From the Tanjore Court to the Madras Music Academy: A Social History of Music in South India*. New York: Oxford University Press.
Sundar, Pavitra. (2007) "Meri Awaaz Suno: Women, Vocality, and Nation in Hindi Cinema." *Meridians: Feminism, Race, Transnationalism* 8(1): 144–179.
Terada, Yoshitaka. (2000). "T. N. Rajarattinam Pillai and Caste Rivalry in South Indian Classical Music." *Ethnomusicology* 44(3): 460–490.
Titon, Jeff Todd. (1992). "Music, the Public Interest, and the Practice of Ethnomusicology." *Ethnomusicology* 36(3): 315–322.
Titon, Jeff Todd. (2008 [1997]). "Knowing Fieldwork." In *Shadows in the Field: New Perspectives for Fieldwork in Ethnomusicology*, edited by Gregory Barz and Timothy J. Cooley, pp. 25–41. New York: Oxford University Press.
Trautmann, Thomas. (1997). *Aryans and British India*. Berkeley: University of California Press.

Viswanathan, T. (1974). *Raga Alapana in South Indian Music*. Ph.D. dissertation, Wesleyan University.
Willard, Augustus. (1834). *Treatise on the Music of Hindostan: Comprising a Detail of Ancient Theory and Modern Practice*. Calcutta: Baptist Mission Press.
Webster, J. C. B. (1992). *A History of the Dalit Christians in India*. San Francisco: Mellen Research University Press.
Weidman, Amanda J. (2006). *Singing the Classical, Voicing the Modern: The Postcolonial Politics of Music in South India*. Durham, NC: Duke University Press.
White, Emmons. (1957). *Appreciating India's Music: An Introduction to the Music of India, with Suggestions for Its Use in the Churches of India*. Madras: Christian Literature Society.
Wilson, Kottapalli. (1982). *The Twice Alienated Culture of Dalit Christians*. Hyderabad: Booklinks.
Wolf, Richard. (2009). *Theorizing the Local: Music, Practice, and Experience in South Asia and Beyond*. New York: Oxford University Press.
Wong, Deborah. (2008). "Moving: From Performance to Performative Ethnography." In *Shadows in the Field: New Perspectives for Fieldwork in Ethnomusicology*, edited by Gregory Barz and Timothy J. Cooley, pp. 76–89. New York: Oxford University Press.

Interviews

Amulraj, Munaivendri, Tamil Nadu, September 7, 2008.
Appavoo, J. Theophilus, Madurai, Tamil Nadu, July 1994.
Jayaharan, John, Madurai, Tamil Nadu, February 2009.
Rajasekaran, J., Madurai, Tamil Nadu, February 15, 2009.

PART III
INDIGENOUS PEOPLES

CHAPTER 6

DECOLONIZATION AND APPLIED ETHNOMUSICOLOGY

"Story-ing" the Personal-Political-Possible in Our Work

ELIZABETH MACKINLAY

Introduction: Beginnings

THIS chapter is told as story. It is my personal-is-political story and a narrative that speaks to the philosophical, theoretical, and methodological past and present colonial violence in the her/his stories of our discipline. It gives an account of why I come to be speaking about decolonization and applied ethnomusicology in this moment. I realize before I begin that by speaking a story and engaging in talk about decolonization work, I have already ventured onto dangerous and contested ground. I am a white settler colonial woman, and others like me who occupy a settler position have long laid imperialistic claim to the power to speak the truth about Indigenous others. How is the story I propose to tell any different? I am tempted to justify my storytelling approach by carefully choosing words from the writing of Indigenous scholars Sium and Ritskes, who tell us that in Indigenous epistemologies, stories are theory in action and decolonization demands "personal and relational understanding" and the "richness and creative vitality that storytelling brings" (2012: 11). Yet, here they are referring directly to the authority and authenticity of stories told by Indigenous people in a decolonizing space, and the position of a settler speaking is highly contested in this landscape—indeed, who does the storytelling and from what perspective they enter the story are critical (Sium, Desai, and Ritskes, 2012: 11).

Doing decolonization work as a non-Indigenous narrator is not an easy position to occupy or authenticate—but neither should it be. Engaging in what Pillow terms "uncomfortable reflexivity—a reflexivity that seeks to know while at the same time situates this knowing as tenuous" (2003: 188), I would argue, is an ethical necessity for those who want to interrupt and interrogate colonial ways of being, doing, and knowing, which habitually appropriate the voices we speak of/to (Sium, Desai, and Ritskes, 2012: 11; cf., Kelsky, 2001). The reflexivity is uncomfortable, and inevitably so is the story, and such narratives might, as Fanon suggests, more "properly be called a literature of combat" (1967: 193) for they evoke dangerous truths about disciplinary history and identity that "won't stand still" (Denzin, 2006: 334). I am aware that storytelling of this kind is not usual or perhaps even readily accepted practice in ethnomusicology; however, I smile and share with you Richardson's assertion that anyone who thinks the "creative and analytic are contradictory and incompatible" is a dinosaur waiting to be hit by a meteor (Richardson, in Richardson and St. Pierre, 2005: 962). Greene's voice joins Richardson's in support of the urgency to challenge dominant modes of researching and writing:

> Allowing myself to be carried along by the great conversation initiated by others (and, indeed, maintained by others) I would not have to disrupt. I would not have to begin anything; I would need only to be swept along by what the great ones have said and remain partially submerged by them. But then I think of how much beginnings have to do with freedom, how much disruption has to do with consciousness and the awareness of possibility… we have to keep arousing ourselves to begin again.
>
> (1994: 109)

Indeed, this chapter as story is a provocation to become and remain fully and truly "wide awake" (Greene, 1994: 112) to the issues of colonial power and privilege, which refuse to go away in ethnomusicology. Being "wide awake" to colonialism leads to questioning of a critical kind into the uncomfortable landscape of "race," and the lens of critical race theory sits on the ground as a signpost in front of us as a place to begin such a discussion. A critical race theory perspective insists that "race [read colonialism] still matters" (Ladson-Billings, 2009: 18) and does not allow us the option to walk away from, deny, or silence the understanding that "race is always already present in every social configuring of our lives" (Ladson-Billings, 2009: 19). Critical race theory confronts us with our complicity in processes of colonization and asks us as ethnomusicologists to see the ways in which we knowingly or unknowingly enact, sustain, and benefit from our white power and privilege. Critical race theory in ethnomusicology might usefully be defined then as a set of basic insights, methods, and practices that seek to "identify, analyze, and transform those structural and cultural aspects of [ethnomusicology] that maintain subordinate and dominant racial positions in and out of the [field]" (Solórzano and Yosso, 2002: 25). Just like decolonizing storytelling, critical race theory as method is often expressed as story and includes "counter-stories" told by racially marginalized and oppressed peoples to talk back to "monovocals, master narratives, standard stories, majoritarian stories" (Solórzano and Yosso, 2002: 25) produced by white settler colonial privilege. Just like decolonizing "story-ing," the same question about my authority and authenticity to tell stories about colonialism as a white settler colonial woman applies— am I not simply redeploying the same kind of privileged gagging and disempowerment?

The colonizer and the colonized are inextricably in relation—without one there cannot be the other, and in this sense colonization is a "shared culture" (Smith, 1999: 45), or, as Memmi (2013 [1965]) would have it, both colonizer and colonized are "bound" and "chained" in colonial relationship in "relentless reciprocity" and dependence. Both are implicated in the stories of the other; Smith (1999: 45) further explains that what this means is that both colonized peoples and colonizers share a language and knowledge of decolonization. This story is told then in the language and knowledge I have as a white settler colonial woman and the sense of "response-ability" I have that it is time to come clean, to own up, to use my colonial power and privilege to shake, rattle, and roll ethnomusicology into a more ethical way of attending to our colonial complicity. Our "response-ability" as ethnomusicologists, our capacity to respond to the call to decolonize, takes center stage. In the telling of this story, I want both writer and reader to trouble and be troubled by the relationships it invokes (Gandhi, 1998: 4) between who we are as non-Indigenous researchers-as-colonizers in our discipline, the colonizing relationships we have with Indigenous peoples and knowledges we work with, the kinds of colonial violence we embody and perform as ethnomusicologists, the tangled-up colonial past and present in which we find ourselves, and who we might be in the process of becoming once we start talking loudly about decolonization. As I write, I can already sense the resistance that begins to exude from some of you as readers—the direct and indirect privileges and power we hold as colonizers because of the "erasure and assimilation of Indigenous peoples is a difficult reality to accept" (Tuck and Yang, 2012: 9). But I did not promise that this chapter was going be pleasant "feel good" reading; in fact, if it were, it would not be achieving one of its central aims—to unsettle and disrupt. After all, as Fanon reminds us, "decolonization, which sets out to change the order of the world, is, obviously, a program of complete disorder... it cannot come as a result of magical practices, nor of a natural shock, nor of a friendly understanding" (1963: 36).

There are three characters in this story, playfully named: Ms. White Settler Colonial, Professor Decolonization, and Dr. A(pplied) Ethnomusicology. Their stories are unique but become intertwined as they realize the inevitable entanglement of relationships, representation, and research in which they find themselves. Literature is reviewed in the dialogue they speak; theory is evoked in the actions they take and the colonial settings in which they find themselves. This story does not intend to survey all that has been written and thereby define applied ethnomusicology—others in this Handbook and elsewhere (e.g., Harrison and Pettan, 2010) have already done this task justice. Decolonization is the setting, the main character, and the plot line. Some readers may have already decided that this chapter is not for them—putting objections or discomfort to the alternative writing style aside, the terms "colonial," "colonizer," and "colonized" may seem irrelevant, out of step, and yesterday's news, for aren't we already living in a *post*-colonial world? Listen carefully as you read—to the whispering that asks ethnomusicology to respond to decolonization. How do we as non-Indigenous applied ethnomusicologists read, respond to, and reimagine the multiple ways our white race power and privilege are embedded in our lived experience as non-Indigenous peoples? Do we want and what can we hope to achieve in terms of social justice for Indigenous peoples by adopting a decolonizing framework in applied ethnomusicology? Is decolonization a move we want to make in our discipline, and why might applied ethnomusicology offer the best hope yet?

Ms. White Settler Colonial Becomes an Ethnomusicologist

Ms. White Settler Colonial sat down on her most comfortable couch, shoes off, cup of coffee in hand, ready and primed for some reminiscing. Her photo albums lay on the floor next to her, a large pile of black-covered books with plastic pockets keeping her memories safe. She sits still and the albums remain unopened, lost in the historical moment of remembering how she became an ethnomusicologist. In her first-year introduction to ethnomusicology class at university, Ms. White Settler Colonial had watched an Aboriginal song man and song woman from the remote Pitjantjatjara community at Indulkana in the Western Desert of Australia perform, sitting cross-legged on the floor of a tiered lecture room and singing several song verses from a Dreaming song called *Inma nyi nyi* (A. Ellis, 1982; C. Ellis, 1985). While she can see their faces clearly in her memory, Ms. White Settler Colonial cannot remember their names. They were "objects" that she gazed at, their songs were transcribed and analyzed later in tutorials, their voices and identities distanced, disembodied, and therefore ultimately "captured" in her own imperial understanding. With a university music degree in hand, Ms. White Settler Colonial eagerly set forth on an Honours research project in ethnomusicology to return to that moment when she was first introduced to Indigenous Australian Dreaming songs. With no thought about her right to know, she enrolled in Pitjantjatjara tribal [sic] singing classes at the Centre for Aboriginal Studies in Music (CASM; Tunstill, 1989) and found herself the only White Settler Colonial woman in the room. During the first week of classes, the other students variously glared and whispered at her, "Don't you know, you're not Aboriginal—you're white! And you think you have a right to be hear/here!" Ms. White Settler Colonial put her head down, got on with her role as participant/observer/researcher, and sat alone with her as yet unrecognized colonial complicity. One Aboriginal woman, Robin, was watching her closely and waiting to find out—what kind of white settler colonial woman was she? Two, three, and four weeks passed until one day Robin caught her eye and casually asked, "Where you from sis?" The question opened up the possibility of a different kind of encounter, one that began with a gesture of generosity and hospitality from the "colonized" to the "colonizer" and continued with cups of tea in the local café, gigs at art galleries, conversations in lounge rooms late at night, and a burgeoning friendship across that which might divide them—here a friend, there a researcher, but what of the in-between? This question remained unanswered. At the end of the year Ms. White Settler Colonial handed in her Honours thesis and felt duly entitled to call herself an ethnomusicologist.

Ms. White Settler Colonial picked up one of the albums and flicked quickly to the memory she was searching for. She saw herself, a year later, sitting in the "field" in the remote town of Burrulula in the southwest Gulf of Carpentaria in the Northern Territory of Australia as a doctoral student with the tools of her trade—a notebook, a camera, a tape recorder, and stark white skin she had not yet noticed. She is surrounded by people, performers, and a community of Aboriginal people making songs and ceremony in the photo; but Ms. White Settler Colonial sits with her head down once more, trying to "capture" in black ink on white pages that which she calls "music" but which Yanyuwa, Garrwa, Mara, and Gudanji people call something else completely (see Bradley and Mackinlay, 2000, for a discussion of Yanyuwa terms for music). Aside from a short visit to Burrulula in the mid-1960s by Alice Moyle (1988), Ms. White Settler Colonial was the first music researcher to focus attention on Aboriginal performance at Burrulula. She believed proudly and completely in her mission to fill this gap in the musicological record; after all, Ms. White Settler Colonial carried with her a research legacy that must be sustained. No sooner had she thought this, than the whispering returned, "And you think that gives you the right to be hear/here? Who gives you the power and the privilege to be hear/here White girl?" Ms. White Settler Colonial felt the sting of settler naiveté, innocence, and arrogance reach forward from her memory to sharply slap her face and angrily pushed the albums from her lap onto the floor.

Ms. White Settler Colonial sighed—her life and work as an ethnomusicologist has "always-already" been complicated, confused, and conflicted. When she sat down at CASM to learn tribal [sic] singing, she found herself next to the Yanyuwa man who became her husband. She went to Burrulula as his wife and was introduced to the Yanyuwa, Garrwa, Mara, and Gudanji community by her mother-in-law and husband's grandmother as family (see Muir, 2004). "Meet my grandson's wife," her husband's grandmother had said with a smile, as she took Ms. White Settler Colonial by the hand and heart to meet her Yanyuwa family. Soon after arriving at Burrulula she was called *Nungarrima*, the right way "skin" or female kinship name in relation to her husband. No one called her by her first name after that, and she reciprocated; she and they were variously now *baba* (sister), *marruwarra* (cousin), *manjikarra* (sister-in-law), *kujaka* (mother), *kulhakulha* (daughter), *ngabuji* (paternal grandmother), and *kukurdi* (maternal grandmother). Many years later, she would be given a "bush" name linking her to the traditional country of Manankurra and the Tiger Shark Dreaming (see Bradley, 1988), of her husband's grandmother. She became a non-Aboriginal mother to Aboriginal children and *kundiyarra*, a partner in song (Mackinlay, 2000). Despite her sense of belonging to her Yanyuwa family, every so often Ms. White Settler Colonial would turn around and notice her white shadow, and with that recognition came the whispering once more, "Don't forget, you are still *white*, white girl! Can you are you here/hear yet white girl?"

As Ms. White Settler Colonial's personal, professional, political, and performative lives became inextricably entangled, she could no longer see herself clearly in her role as ethnomusicologist, at least not in the way she had been traditionally trained. When she went to Burrulula in 1994, Ms. White Settler Colonial entered a community ravaged by the ongoing effects of colonization, and she idealistically and paternalistically thought her work as an ethnomusicologist would—and could—make a difference. Ms. White Settler Colonial has told this story in other places before (e.g., Mackinlay, 2009, 2010) and she finds it hard, just like every other telling, to find the right words. In this moment of standing still, the "truth" would seem to suggest that nothing has changed. The Burrulula she met 20 years ago is in many ways very much the same Burrulula today, and for her, that is simply not good enough. Her breath catches in her throat as Ms. White Settler Colonial realizes that perhaps it is also that ethnomusicology, at least as she knows it, is no longer good enough. From the corner of her eye she spies her white shadow lurking in the corner and nodding in agreement. She wants her academic work to somehow translate into "something better" for the women, men, and children whom she calls family. Better homes, a fair education, an end to racism, and the reinstatement of Indigenous Australians as a sovereign people—all of these things she feels are more important than black dots on a white page and any fancy analytical account she might be able to give of them. Ms. White Settler Colonial knows that the PhD she completed and the journal papers she subsequently wrote about the social and musical lives of Aboriginal women and men at Burrulula did not change anything for her family, despite how well she wrote them and the prestige of the publications in which they appeared. She realized that while people might be hearing the words she spoke at conferences and reading those that appeared in her writing (e.g., Mackinlay, 2005), they were not listening—not with their hearts. Ms. White Settler Colonial knew that there was more, and indeed that she had to do more, to engage the thinking hearts of her colleagues, students, and friends. In this moment of "wide-awakeness," she found herself at odds with the disciplinary flow of ethnomusicology, and once again she heard the whispering, "Well hello there white girl, perhaps you are beginning to be hear/here!" Now that Ms. White Settler Colonial has begun to hear the whispering, she finds that she cannot ignore it. It plays around in her head constantly. She does not know what else to do except return to her fallback position of researcher to try to find its source.

Whispering in Ethnomusicology about Decolonization

While there are many ethnomusicological discussions that discuss the colonial contexts and the colonial repositories of our work (Emoff, 2002; Seeger, 1986; Waterman, 1990), "decolonization" is a term that remains largely unfamiliar to ethnomusicological vocabulary. In step with anthropological debates in the 1970s sparked by the work of Geertz (1973) and feminist thinkers such as Rosaldo and Lamphere (1974) about the nature of fieldwork, the power and authority of researchers, and texts as representation acts, Gourlay (1978) provactively challenged the concept of the ethnomusicologist as both "omniscient and non-existent" in the writings of colleagues such as Merriam (1967) and Nettl (1964). Gourlay (1978: 3) was critical of the insistence, on the one hand, that ethnomusicologists become fully immersed in fieldwork if they are to truly learn, understand, and interpret the music of another culture, and yet on the other hand, completely silence the performers and their own subjectivities in the texts which result from participatory observation research. He questioned the relevancy and ethics of neutrality and objectivity in ethnomusicological work and called for the "missing ethnomusicologist" to become visible in recognition of the messy reality of the subject-object relationship (1978: 4) inherent in social science research. Indeed, Gourlay (1982) called for a "humanizing ethnomusicology" that would simultaneously resist ethnocentric and dominant Western ways of knowing, doing, and being in relation to music, and seek to bring the worldviews of Self and Other "into an interpenetrating dialectical relationship through which the investigator is himself investigated" (1982: 416). Alongside Gourlay's provocation, feminist thinkers in the discipline (e.g., Herndon and Ziegler, 1990; Koskoff, 1987) had also begun to question ideologies of dominance, and specific attention was given by them to exploring the status of women in music cultures globally, the nature of gender relationships and gender structures on musical roles, and the positioning of the gendered fieldworker in ethnomusicological settings.

However, it would be another 15 years before the first in-depth and sustained critique of the *colonial* past and present of the discipline arrived on the scene with publication of the edited text *Shadows in the Field*, edited by Gregory Barz and Timothy Cooley. The first edition of *Shadows* (1997) attempts to bring into open space discussion of the "crisis of representation" that categorizes postmodern social science, and Barz and Cooley clearly acknowledge the linking of "ethnographic fieldwork, as well as representation, to colonial, imperial, and other repressive power structures" (1997: 4). The need to recognize that being in the field and being with/out Others, being out of the field and being with/out Others, being in the business of representation with/out Others in and with/out of the field is ultimately an exercise of power takes center stage in this text. I use the hyphenated phrase with/out to signify and question the capacity of ethnomusicologists to ever *really* leave the field. If the field *really* is an intersubjective and intercorporeal shared moment of performativity and experience, then the field never *really* leaves us—we are never with/out the field and the shadows we cast are with/out the field at the same time because, on the one hand, they never *really* leave us, and on the other, they remain elusive and incapable of erasure.

In relation to the thinking about decolonization, then, our shadows are shaped by colonialism, and recent work by Vass (2013) would suggest that they are indeed white. White bodies mark the colonial history and disciplinary performance of ethnomusicology, and pale imperial shadows take center stage in talk about decolonization. The second edition of *Shadows* reached audiences in 2008, and what is at once surprising and distressing about this revised text is the silence of talk about decolonization. Yazzie laments, "while the world decolonization process is almost complete, it has not yet begun for Indigenous peoples" (2000: 39) and if *Shadows* is representative of current disciplinary thinking about decolonization, it remains a sharply closed door on an open moment of possibility. "Decolonializing" [sic] processes are referred to by Meizel (in Cooley, Meizel, and Syed, 2008: 96) as relevant only to studies where issues of power and cultural Otherness appear "outstanding," and although she does not explicitly state so, here we can read her words as referring to ethnomusicological studies that engage directly with Indigenous and colonized peoples. In this context, Meizel suggests, the onus is on the researcher to "understand his or her responsibilities in the way others experience their musical worlds" (Meizel in Cooley, Meizel, and Syed, 2008: 96). Certainly, decolonization is one of the most pressing issues for those of us working with Indigenous peoples today, and one that we must take personal response-ability to engage with epistemologically, methodologically, and ontologically, but what of the response-ability of the discipline? If everyone is in agreement that the colonial history pervades past and present practice, do we not have a disciplinary response-ability to decolonize, or at the very least, to begin to dance toward it? Why is it that decolonizing talk in ethnomusicology remains a whispering that many are too afraid to heed? Why do we assume that it's up to Indigenous people alone to decolonize? What kind of discipline is ethnomusicology with/out decolonizing talk, and further, is talk alone enough to decolonize?

Dr. A(pplied) Ethnomusicology Meets Professor Decolonization

Ms. White Settler Colonial found herself a job working in a university teaching ethnomusicology within the context of Indigenous Australian Studies. She decided that she would add the word "applied" to her title and began calling herself Dr. A(pplied) Ethnomusicology—Dr. A. for short. She felt this new term better reflected her personal-is-political agenda. One morning, she was halfway through a lecture on applied and advocacy work in ethnomusicology, when Dr. A. was interrupted by a loud knock at the door.

"Just hold on a moment," she said, and excused herself to see who was there. "Oh my goodness it's you! Prof. D.! I didn't think you were coming! Look everyone; it's my good friend Professor Decolonization! You know, the one I promised to talk to you about before?"

Several students nodded their head in agreement. They thought they recognized her from the discussion earlier but were not quite prepared for the reality.

"What are you doing in town, Prof. D.? I didn't realize you were even in Australia!" Dr. A. was surprised to see her colleague and friend.

"Well, you know how it is, Dr. A., I'm never quite sure if I'm going to be welcome at this kind of gig, but I could see that this was a conversation you needed to have with someone like me by your side—the colonizer and the colonized are bound together, you know, we are *both* implicated in colonization *and* decolonization. Don't forget Phillips and Whatman (2007: 6) who contend, 'because we are all products of a shared colonial history, we are *all* subjects of the enquiry.' The only problem is that you, Dr. A.—a.k.a. Ms. White Settler Colonial—have dominated that conversation for far too long!" Prof. D. winked at the class and settled herself into a spare chair. "So, how far have you got with your class discussions on applied ethnomusicology and decolonization? Has anyone walked out yet? Raised a hand in objection? Wrinkled up their noses or—and I wonder about this response—smiled with empathy?"

Dr. A. grimaced. "Actually, no—well, not yet anyway. We were just about . . . "

Prof. D. interrupted, "Oh, you must have only just started then. . . I know where you're at sister. You haven't told them yet have you?"

Dr. A. hesitated.

"Oh no, don't tell me! You're not nervous, are you, Dr. A.? After all this time?" Prof. D. let out a loud sigh. "Remember, Dr. A. 'everything is in danger of colonizing—everything is suspicious' (Cary, 2004: 77), and that includes your unwillingness to begin the discussion—so go on, off you go. I can hold your hand if you need me to."

Dr. A. swallowed deeply and reached for a sip of cool water to moisten her lips and throat. She realized that the silence between her voice and Prof. D.'s was becoming thick and heavy, you could cut the tension with a knife; the class was expecting her to speak. She began with a safe response.

"Let's start with what we mean when we use terms like 'applied.' In anthropological discourse, the term 'applied' refers to research practices that use theory and method to solve practical human problems. 'Applied' is about 'the dynamics of partnership' between the scholar and the social subjects involved in ethnomusicological research (Hofman, 2010: 22). Many applied ethnomusicological projects run on a collaborative field research and epistemological approach whereby the researched actively participates in the research process alongside the researcher (Hofman, 2010: 23)—as co-researchers, co-authors, and co-constructors of knowledge. Border crossing and shape shifting happens a lot in our work, and many traditional divisions are broken down in such an interactive and dialogic way of working. Sheehy tells us that applied ethnomusicology emphasizes the tendency to see 'opportunities for a better life through. . . musical knowledge' (1992: 324) by asking 'to what end?' (1992: 323)." Dr. A. looked at Prof. D., hoping that maybe this was enough to set the context. Prof. D. didn't need to say a word; she simply reversed the gaze. Dr. A. took a deep breath and continued.

"Sheehy's work put the consequences of our work high on the agenda and challenged us to think about ethnomusicological work as 'strategy guided by a sense of social purpose' (1992: 335). Certainly, there is often a social justice agenda rippling beneath the surface or displayed boldly on a billboard at the front of much applied work in ethnomusicology today, and words like 'benefit,' 'reciprocity,' and 'relationships' figure prominently in these discussions. Ethnomusicologists continue to grapple with the ethical response-abilities they hold toward the communities from whom they collect and gather musical knowledge, a dilemma that becomes even more complex as they shift in and out of academic fields of play. In many ways, applied ethnomusicology represents an attempt to bring this tension to the front and center of our practice so that it can no longer be ignored, but rather demands an active response." Dr. A. finished speaking and looked expectantly at Prof. D.

Prof. D. shook her head in frustration. "To what? What are applied ethnomusicologists responding to? Oh come on Dr. A., you can do better than that! Now's the time to practice what you preach—where's your heart in all of this? Why don't you *really tell them* about decolonization? All of this is just appeasing white settler colonial guilt and pandering to a claim to innocence of the same kind."

Dr. A. knew that Prof. D. wanted more from her, but decolonization was a relatively new word for her, too. Despite all of the whispering she had heard over the past 10 years, she still did not feel she had the right words to explain it, or that she even had a right *to* explain it.

"For me," she began, "the one characteristic I keep returning to is the potential of an applied approach to view our work as musical, personal, *and* political all at once. If we start thinking and talking openly about relationships and response-abilities, then through this lens we are enabled to address the uneasiness that many of us feel when we position ourselves and our discipline in the context of colonization, white power, and white privilege. Indeed, the 'idea of privilege is at the heart of the colonial relationship' (Memmi, 2013 [1965]). It's a matter of urgency, how we as non-Indigenous researchers address the complex relationship between our histories, our disciplines, and ourselves as colonizing culture. Our white settler colonial identity brings us enormous power and privilege in relation to Indigenous peoples, and yet in many research contexts it remains hidden under carefully guarded discourses of 'for their own good,' 'soothe the dying pillow,' 'researcher as expert,' 'document and preserve at all costs,' and, 'saviours of a disappearing race, music, and culture.'"

Prof. D. raised her eyebrows, "Those are pretty harsh words."

"For sure," Dr. A. agreed, but continued with her critique. "But they need to be. Interrogation of the ways in which we continue to embody and enact colonialism is not comfortable business, nor it is an apology for being a colonizer. What it does mean is taking on board, believing, and living words like decolonization."

"That's my baby!" Prof. D. exclaimed. "But it makes me really sad to think that nobody really knows me yet, even when I walk down the corridor to the tea room, many people quietly close their office doors to keep me out. What do they think I'm going to do? Rip their pristine white research chairs from right under their backsides? Do you know what? One day I just might—and that's what everyone is scared of." Prof. D. paused and then continued carefully, "I know that you've been trying to introduce me for some time in your own work Dr. A. (Mackinlay, 2005, 2010, 2012). But maybe it's time for me to start telling the story."

Dr. A. knew that placing emphasis on unveiling inequalities, deconstructing power relations, and reflection and action as pathways to change are important in any dance toward to decolonization. As a non-Indigenous person working with Indigenous communities in applied ethnomusicological contexts, words like "reconciliation," "hope," "action," and "social justice" were everywhere in her writing because they gave her assurance that performance of her white power and privilege as Ms. White Settler Colonial had good intentions. They provided her with "immunity," as Youngblood Henderson (2000: 32) contends, from recognizing and responding to herself as part of the problem. She consistently saw herself as the ethnomusicologist "doing decolonizing good"—one who proudly wore her anti-racist, social justice, and reconciliation politics on her invisible White sleeve and wasn't afraid to call neo-colonial and racist *praxis* in ethnomusicological research for what it was, where and when she saw it. She realized now that while she had might have heard the whispering, she had not really ever listened, and it was time to start.

"Settle in Dr. A., we might be here for a while." Prof. D. shifted in her chair to find a more comfortable position and began. "Some of us—and by 'us' I mean the 'colonized'— have been talking about decolonization for a long time. Decolonization is a concept which takes on different meanings across different contexts—it simultaneously evokes a historical narrative of the end of empire, a particular version of postcolonial political theory, a way of knowing that resists the Eurocentrism of the West, a moral imperative for righting the wrongs of colonial domination, and an ethical stance in relation to self-determination, social justice, and human rights for Indigenous peoples enslaved and disempowered by imperialism. Indigenous scholars frame decolonization in both congruent and contested ways."

"And that's part of it, isn't it?" Dr. A. added, "Discourses such as Orientalism (Said, 1978) and Aboriginalism (Hodge, 1990; McConaghy, 2000) want to construct and imagine an essentialized homogenous colonized group in historical and contemporary terms, but Indigenous peoples' experiences of colonization vary across time and space, and responses to colonization are equally as diverse."

Prof. D. nodded, "Fanon's thinking asserts exactly that. He writes that decolonization is not a formal administrative term but rather a 'restructuring of subjects into agents of history'" (in Kohn and McBride, 2011: 69). Smith (1999) similarly argues that decolonization necessarily empowers Indigenous people to re-claim, re-name, re-write and re-right and in this way the colonized emerge from the fog of the colonial imaginary as liberated people. Wilson and Yellow Bird expand on this and suggest 'decolonization is the intelligent, calculated and active resistance to the forces of colonialism that perpetuate the subjugation and/or exploitation of our minds, bodies and lands' (2005: 2). Others such as hooks have turned their attention more intensively to the prospect of decolonizing minds as a powerful move to 'militantly confront and change the devastating psychological consequences of internalized racism' (1994: 205). Fanon, too, felt strongly about this, writing pro- and evocatively that 'imperialism leaves behind germs of rot which we must clinically detect and remove from our land but our minds as well' (1965: 36)."

"Let's come back to the issue of land in a moment," Dr. A. suggested. "I've read Battiste's work (2000), and she similarly emphasises the need to decolonize Indigenous minds from 'cognitive imperialism, our cognitive prisons' (2000: xvii) and suggests that this can be accomplished by 'harmonizing Indigenous knowledge with Eurocentric knowledge'" (2000: xvi). In a way this reminds me of what a lot of applied ethnomusicology tries to do—make a space where musical and cultural knowledges of the researched and the researcher can performatively come together to empower the former. Applied ethnomusicology when viewed from this perspective might shift us closer toward a critical practice and assist us in deconstructing the unequal power relationships between the researcher and the researched by giving oppressed peoples control over how they are depicted."

"In some senses, yes," Prof. D. continued. "Smith describes decolonization as a process, rather than a product, linked to political action such as social justice and self-determination grounded politically in contexts, histories, struggles, and ideals (1999: 4). We owe a lot to critical scholars and our feminist sisters for giving us the theoretical grounding to expose the lingo of research as vehicles of sustained oppression and tools of colonization (Mutua and Swadener, 2004: 14). For naming colonization for what it is—not discourse and practice that exist in the past, but a machine that continues to dominate our worlds as Indigenous and non-Indigenous people today."

Dr. A. agreed. "I guess you're right, the shift from a colonized to decolonized state doesn't occur in a tidy and linear progression from imperialism through to colonization, and then hey presto, we've got decolonization. It seems to me that thinking about colonialism and decolonization as dialogical is key to us being more responsive and responsible (Le Sueur, 2003: 2). It's a constant dovetailing, circling in and around, backward and forward, and once passed through, any of these stages can be revisited or reversed. That makes it a pretty complicated agenda to take on as a researcher and I am still not sure where, how, and why non-Indigenous people—colonizers like me—should, could or can enter the conversation."

"Yes, and we would insist that colonization is indeed alive and well. There is no *post*-colonialism here (cf., Smith, 1999, 2000); the colonizers have *not* left yet" (Smith, 1999: 24). Prof. D. spoke animatedly, "But we need to start somewhere, Dr. A., we need to *begin*. The first step is to produce counter-narratives to those texts and contexts which sustain the dominance and power of the West over Indigenous peoples. Easy enough, you might say, but to be 'completely' decolonizing, research must go one step further to strive to change lives, stop people from dying, and respond to reality" (Mutua and Swadener, 2004: 10; Smith, 1999: 3).

"You know what? You're right." Dr. A.'s face flushed with shame. "The lived experience of Indigenous peoples is the 'unfinished business of decolonization' (Smith, 1999: 7)—and in the enthusiastic rush to dive into deconstruction of imperialism, we as non-Indigenous researchers maybe too easily forget or dismiss the realities of life for Indigenous peoples because we refuse to make them part of our own. It's too easy for us to step back into settler colonial innocence, sitting pretty under the umbrella of social justice."

Prof. D. reached over and placed her hand gently on Dr. A.'s shoulder. "Dr. A., decolonization is not a metaphor, nor is it a 'metonym for social justice' (Tuck and Yang, 2012: 21). In the opening article of the new journal *Decolonization: Indigeneity, Education and Society*, Tuck and Yang provide us with this stark reminder: decolonization is not converting Indigenous politics to a Western doctrine of liberation; it is not a philanthropic process of 'helping' the at-risk and alleviating suffering; it is not a generic term for struggle against oppressive conditions and outcomes. The broad umbrella of social justice may have room underneath for all of these efforts, but this is not decolonization."

Dr. A. dropped her head into her hands. All of a sudden, her earlier talk about decolonization as linked to social justice in ethnomusicology and applied ethnomusicology felt awkward—exactly as Tuck and Yang intended. Their words were harsh, and there were more to come; Prof. D. had not finished.

"Tuck and Yang are critical of the way in which decolonizing discourse is too easily adopted 'without mention of Indigenous peoples, our/their struggles for the recognition of our/their sovereignty, or the contributions of Indigenous intellectuals and activists to theories and frameworks of decolonization' (Tuck and Yang, 2012: 3). In this guise, it becomes nothing more than a metaphor, and Tuck and Yang stress that this 'kills the very possibility of decolonization; it recenters whiteness, it resettles theory, it extends innocence to the settler, it entertains a settler future. Decolonize (a verb) and decolonization (a noun) cannot easily be grafted onto pre-existing discourses/frameworks, even if they are critical, even if they are anti-racist, even if they are justice frameworks'" (Tuck and Yang, 2012: 3).

Dr. A. rubbed her eyes. "I don't know, Prof. D, there are too many questions swirling around, muddying the waters and making everything messy. How do we read and respond to the multiple ways our colonial settler power and privilege is embedded in our lived experience as non-Indigenous peoples, in our relationships with and responsibilities to Indigenous peoples? How do we begin to link our awareness and acceptance of this reality with 'an agenda which does not accept the dichotomies implicit in the terms colonizer/colonized... but rather explores the relations of power through dialogue, creating spaces for transformation, for new [ethnomusicological] and methodological strategies' (Fox, 2004: 91)? What is our applied ethnomusicological work if it is not linked to social justice? What can and should it be?"

Dr. A. realized, as soon as she asked these questions, that she had already slipped back into a colonizing decolonizing search for 'settler futurity' and 'settler normalcy' (Tuck and Yang, 2012: 35), desperate to find the comfort of 'settler innocence' once more through use of words such as dialogue (read: reconcile, negotiate, settle). Prof. D. sat quietly for a moment staring at Dr. A., almost as though she could read her mind. This next part of the conversation was not going to be easy.

"Unsettling, isn't it, Dr. A.? Land is central to colonization—discovery, conquest, exploitation, distribution, appropriation—all of these are violent acts which form part of the white possessive logic that Moreton-Robinson (2004) speaks of, which disavows Indigenous sovereignty. We can see that land and place are central in ethnomusicological work, too—think about the word 'field' and our insistence on 'fieldwork.' What kinds of white possessive logic do we invoke when we use those terms? Smith (1999: 7) asserts that the 'linguistic and cultural homeland of the colonizers is somewhere else, their cultural loyalty is to some other place'; is this not true, too, for many ethnomusicologists, applied or otherwise? Is not the claiming of a 'field' through 'fieldwork' the same kind of colonial move but in a different guise? In the 'field' are we not laying colonial claim to epistemologies and discursive traditions of knowledge which are *not* ours?"

Dr. A. felt tied up in knots. She knew that what Prof. D. was telling her made sense; it's no longer whispering she hears but shouting, screaming, and yelling. Her husband's and children's voices, those of her family at Burrulula, her Indigenous friends and colleagues are all part of this loud and noisy chorale. Now that her White Settler Colonial laundry hangs plainly on the line for all to see, what is she to do? What are her response-abilities? How can she respond in a way that enacts an ethic of response-ability in relation to the demands of decolonization?

RESPONSE-ABILITY AND BEING-IN-RELATION AS DECOLONIZING WORK

How might we then begin to decolonize applied ethnomusicology? How can decolonizing theory inform actual applied ethnomusicological work? These questions sit uneasily in this story, each and every one of us wanting and needing a neatly packaged way forward through our discomforts and uncertainties. Decolonizing theory asks us to rethink, reimagine, and reconstruct our research identities, relationships, and agendas as existing within a colonial framework, which wants and needs to know, fix, and capture the Other. This is our response-ability—a word written in this way throughout this chapter quite deliberately to remind us that we have an ethical obligation to act on such wide awakeness to the ways in which we continue to "be-in-relation" to colonialism. "Being-in-relation" is a concept that provokes us into personal and political kinds of thinking about the ethical and moral obligations we have to enact a nonviolent research relationship toward the Other, a relationship which deconstructs and breaks down the colonial project. This is dangerous work because it means placing ourselves in a vulnerable position where our reason for being as applied ethnomusicologists is under threat. "Being-in-relation" is a different kind of thinking in applied ethnomusicology—it refuses, as Audre Lorde (2003) would have it, to use the master's tools to dismantle the master's house. The absence of "being-in-relation" to colonialism and our White Settler Colonial subjectivities weakens our capacity to work toward less violent and more socially just practices and projects in applied ethnomusicology. "Being-in-relation" means placing colonial relationship at the center of our practice at every epistemological, ontological, and methodological turn. Sitting there in the middle—whispering and reminding us—colonial relationship calls other ethical modes of being into the research space. Response-ability, respect, re/search, rights/rites, and attentiveness to re/presentation begin to make their way into the motivations, means, and modes of working with Others as applied ethnomusicologists, and become crucial for putting in place a decolonial and ethical way of knowing, being, and doing. Without such attentiveness, colonial ways of working remain unchallenged, undisturbed and unaccountable. "Response-ability" and "being-in-relation" cannot be easily scripted or written into a fieldwork manual or a step-by-step guide on how to decolonize applied ethnomusicology—they are intimately about our individual personal, political, philosophical, and performance relationships that each of us has with colonialism and the people with whom we work. But they can become the beginning of the research conversation.

Conclusion: Applied Ethnomusicology Talks about Decolonization

A story like this has no ending, it is, as Greene would have it, a "narrative in the making" (1995: 1). Dr. A., Ms. White Settler Colonial, and Prof. D. continue to talk, and this chapter represents the way that my "thinking heart" is attempting to "cultivate multiple ways of seeing and multiple dialogues in a world where nothing stays the same" (Greene, 1995: 16; cf. Mackinlay, 2010). Indeed, it is not for me to complete this narrative for readers; it is a story that needs to become uniquely their own. My dialogic and dialectic role as storyteller has simply and most complexly been to introduce a new character into the plot line of applied ethnomusicology, that of decolonization, and the intention has always been to ensure that the ways that Indigenous scholars are thinking, talking, and writing around this concept speak loudly and clearly. Is applied ethnomusicology ready to listen to the voices of decolonization? Are we ready to ask the uncomfortable questions about the ways that we perform and reproduce White Settler Colonial power and privilege from the beginning to the end and back again in our research projects and products, our classrooms, and our engagements with communities? Are we ready and do we have the response-ability? If we are ready to acknowledge and become "wide awake" to our personal-political-disciplinary identities as White Settler Colonial and hold that decolonizing our discipline is one of the most urgent ethical and moral questions of our time, the search must be ongoing, for we are not there yet. We are already performing some of the theoretical and methodological moves we need to make—many of us enthusiastically embrace dialogic and collaborative research processes; we lay bare a willingness to engage with and enact a set of politics that link applied work with advocacy work; we openly enter into a reflexive engagement with the intersubjective and performative nature of what we do; and, we demonstrate a preparedness to ask what kind of research, for whom and by whom, under what circumstances, to what ends—and then to ask them all over again.

In this sense then, to paraphrase bell hooks (1994), applied ethnomusicology, with all of its limitations, remains a location of possibility to begin to decolonize. If applied ethnomusicology can embrace that "research exists at the interstices between political ideology (the idea that shape any given praxis), space/place (the spaces that give life to such projects) and community (the people that carry out such work)" (Zavala, 2013: 65), we begin to decolonize. If we are vigilant in our attendance to and act upon a "wide-awakeness" to the white settler colonial possessive logic of our practice; we begin to decolonize. If we ask whether our projects are ultimately about white settler colonial futurity or Indigenous futurity, we begin to decolonize. If our applied ethnomusicological work places an accountability of "place" (Zavala, 2013: 60) (and by extension, land, sovereignty, and self-determination) at the center of what we do, we begin to decolonize. If we position applied ethnomusicology as within/against colonizing structures, knowing that we forever are between and on the way, we begin to decolonize. If we refuse to engage in the kind of "politics of distraction" (Corntassel, 2012: 91) and reimagine words such as rights as response-ability, resources and research as relationships, and reconciliation as resurgence (Corntassel, 2012: 91), we begin to decolonize. Being white settler colonial in this space means we have to make a radical break from business as usual and perform an ethical turning inside out to imagine a different kind of applied ethnomusicology encounter, "an encounter that both opposes ongoing colonization and that seeks to heal the social, cultural, and spiritual ravages of colonial history" (Gaztambide-Fernández, 2012: 42) and the colonial present in which we find ourselves entangled. Decolonization is everyone's business; it "implicates and unsettles everyone" (Tuck and Yang, 2012: 60). The narrative remains unfinished, and it cannot be built upon metaphor. It is now up to each and every one of us to commit to producing a different kind of decolonizing story.

References

Battiste, Marie (2000). "Introduction: Unfolding the Lessons of Colonization." In *Reclaiming Indigenous Voice and Vision*, edited by Marie Battiste, pp. xvi–xxx. Vancouver, BC: University of British Columbia Press.

Bradley, John J. (1988). *Yanyuwa Country: The Yanyuwa People of Borroloola Tell the History of Their Land*. Richmond, VIC: Greenhouse Publications.

Bradley, John J., and Elizabeth Mackinlay (2000). "Songs from a Plastic Water Rat: An Introduction to the Musical Traditions of the Yanyuwa Community of the Southwest Gulf of Carpentaria." *Ngulaig* 17: 1–45.

Cooley, Timothy J., Katherine Meizel, and Nasir Syed (2008). "Virtual Fieldwork: Three Case Studies." In *Shadows in the Field: New Perspectives for Fieldwork in Ethnomusicology* (2nd ed.), edited by Gregory Barz and Timothy J. Cooley, pp. 90–107. Oxford: Oxford University Press.

Corntassel, Jeff (2012). "Re-envisioning Resurgence: Indigenous Pathways to Decolonization and Sustainable Self-Determination." *Decolonization: Indigeneity, Education & Society* 1(1): 86–101.

Denzin, Norman K. (2006). "Pedagogy, Performance and Autoethnography." *Text and Performance Quarterly* 26(4): 333–338.

Ellis, A. M. (1982). *Inma Nyi: Nyi: The Song of the Zebra Finches*. Adelaide, SA: Centre for Aboriginal Studies in Music, The University of Adelaide.

Emoff, Ron (2002). "Phantom Nostalgia and Recollecting (from) the Colonial Past in Tamatave, Madagascar." *Ethnomusicology* 46(2): 265–283.

Fanon, Frantz (1963). *The Wretched of the Earth*. New York: Grove Press.

Fanon, Frantz (1965). *A Dying Colonialism*. New York: Grove Press.

Fox, Christine (2004). "Tensions in the Decolonisation Process: Disrupting Preconceptions of Postcolonial Education in the Lao People's Democratic Republic." In *Disrupting Preconceptions: Postcolonialism and Education*, edited by Anne Hickling-Hudson, Julie Matthews, and Annette Woods, pp. 99–106. Flaxton, QLD: Post Pressed.

Gandhi, Leela (1998). *Postcolonial Theory: A Critical Introduction*. Sydney, NSW: Allen & Unwin.

Gaztambide-Fernández, Rubén A. (2012). "Decolonization and the Pedagogy of Solidarity." *Decolonization: Indigeneity, Education & Society* 1(1): 41–67.

Geertz, Clifford (1973). *The Interpretation of Culture: Selected Essays.* New York: Basic Books.
Gourlay, Kenneth A. (1978). "Towards a Reassessment of the Ethnomusicologist's Role in Research." *Ethnomusicology* 22(1): 1–35.
Gourlay, Kenneth A. (1982). "Towards a Humanizing Ethnomusicology." *Ethnomusicology* 26(3): 411–420.
Greene, Maxine (1994). "Postmodernism and the Crisis of Representation." *English Education* 26(4): 206–219.
Greene, Maxine (1995). *Releasing the Imagination: Essays on Education, the Arts and Social Change.* San Francisco, CA: Jossey-Bass Publishers.
Herndon, Marcia, and Susanne Ziegler, eds. (1990). *Music, Gender and Culture.* Wilhelmshaven: Florian Noetzel Verlag.
Hodge, Robert (1990). "Aboriginal Truth and White Media: Eric Michaels Meets the Spirit of Aboriginalism." *Continuum: Journal of Media & Cultural Studies* 3(2): 201–225.
Hofman, Ana (2010). "Maintaining the Distance, Othering the Subaltern: Rethinking Ethnomusicologists' Engagement in Advocacy and Social Justice." In *Applied Ethnomusicology: Historical and Contemporary Approaches*, edited by Klisala Harrison, Elizabeth Mackinlay, and Svanibor Pettan, pp. 22–35. Newcastle upon Tyne: Cambridge Scholars Publishing.
hooks, b. (1994). *Teaching to Transgress: Education as the Practice of Freedom.* New York: Routledge.
Kelsky, Karen (2001). "Who Sleeps With Whom, or How (Not) to Want the West in Japan." *Qualitative Inquiry* 7(4): 418–435.
Kohn, Margaret and Keally McBride (2011). *Political Theories of Decolonization: Postcolonialism and the Problem of Foundations.* Oxford: Oxford University Press.
Koskoff, Ellen ed. (1987). *Women and Music in Cross-cultural Perspective.* Westport, CT: Greenwood Press.
Ladson-Billings, Gloria (2009). "Just What Is Critical Race Theory and What's it Doing in a Nice Field Like Education?" In *Foundations of Critical Race Theory in Education*, edited by Edward Taylor, David Gillborn, and Gloria Ladson-Billings, pp. 17–36. New York: Routledge.
Le Sueur, James D. (2003). "An Introduction: Reading Decolonization." In *The Decolonization Reader*, edited by James D. Le Sueur, pp. 1–6. London: Routledge.
Lorde, Audre (2003). "The Master's Tools Will Never Dismantle the Master's House." In *Feminist Postcolonial Theory: A Reader*, edited by Reina Lewis and Sara Mills, pp. 25–28. New York: Routledge.
Mackinlay, Elizabeth (2000). "Maintaining Grandmothers' Law: Female Song Partners in Yanyuwa Culture." *Musicology Australia* 23: 76–98.
Mackinlay, Elizabeth (2005). "Moving and Dancing Towards Decolonisation in Education: An Example From an Indigenous Australian Performance Classroom." *The Australian Journal of Indigenous Education* 34: 113–122.
Mackinlay, Elizabeth (2009). "In Memory of Music Research: An Autoethnographic, Ethnomusicological and Emotional Response to Grief, Death and Loss in the Aboriginal Community at Borroloola, Northern Territory." In *Music Autoethnographies: Making Autoethnography Sing/Making Music Personal*, edited by Brydie-Leigh Bartleet and Carolyn Ellis, pp. 225–244. Bowen Hills, QLD: Australian Academic Press.
Mackinlay, Elizabeth (2010). "Big Women from Burrulula: An Approach to Advocacy and Applied Ethnomusicology with the Yanyuwa Aboriginal Community in the Northern Territory, Australia." In *Applied Ethnomusicology: Historical Approaches and New*

Perspectives, edited by Klisala Harrison, Elizabeth Mackinlay, and Svanibor Pettan, pp. 96–115. Newcastle upon Tyne: Cambridge Scholars Publishing.

Mackinlay, Elizabeth (2012). "Pearl: A Reflective Story About Decolonising Pedagogy in Indigenous Australian Studies." *The Australian Journal of Indigenous Education* 41: 67–74.

McConaghy, Cathryn (2000). *Rethinking Indigenous Education: Culturalism, Colonialism, and the Politics of Knowing*. St Lucia, QLD: Post Pressed.

Memmi, Albert (2013 [1965]). *The Colonizer and the Colonized*, trans. H. Greenfield. Hoboken, NJ: Taylor & Francis.

Merriam, Alan P. (1967). *Ethnomusicology of the Flathead Indians*. New York: Wenner-Gren Foundation for Anthropological Research, Aldine.

Moreton-Robinson, Aileen (2004). "The Possessive Logic of Patriarchal White Sovereignty: The High Court and the Yorta Yorta Decision." *Borderlands e-journal* 3(2).

Moyle, Alice M. ed. (1988). *Songs from the Northern Territory*. Canberra, ACT: Australian Institute of Aboriginal Studies.

Muir, Hilda Jarman (2004). *Very Big Journey: My life as I Remember It*. Canberra, ACT: Aboriginal Studies Press.

Mutua, Kagendo and Beth Blue Swadener (2004). "Introduction." In *Decolonizing Research In Cross-Cultural Contexts: Critical Personal Narratives*, edited by Kagendo Mutua and Beth Blue Swadener, pp. 1–26. Albany: State University of New York Press.

Nettl, Bruno (1964). *Theory and Method in Ethnomusicology*. New York: Free Press of Glencoe.

Phillips, J., and S. Whatman (2007). "Decolonising Preservice Teacher Education: Reform at Many Cultural Interfaces." In *Proceedings The World of Educational Quality: 2007 AERA Annual Meeting*, 194–209. Chicago: AERA.

Pillow, Wanda S. (2003). "Confession, Catharsis, or Cure? Rethinking the Uses of Reflexivity as Methodological Power in Qualitative Research." *Qualitative Studies in Education* 16(2): 175–196.

Richardson, Laurel, and Elizabeth Adams St. Pierre (2005). "Writing: A Method of Inquiry." In *The Sage Handbook of Qualitative Research* (3rd ed.), edited by Norman K. Denzin and Yvonna S. Lincoln, pp. 959–978. Thousand Oaks, CA: Sage.

Rosaldo, Michelle Zimbalist, and Louise Lamphere, eds. (1974). *Woman, Culture and Society*. Stanford, CA: Stanford University Press.

Said, Edward W. (1978). *Orientalism* (1st ed.). London: Routledge.

Seeger, Anthony (1986). "The Role of Sound Archives in Ethnomusicology Today." *Ethnomusicology* 30(2): 261–276.

Sium, Aman, Chandni Desai, and Eric Ritskes (2012). "Towards the 'Tangible Unknown': Decolonization and the Indigenous Future." *Decolonisation: Indigeneity, Education and Society* 1(1): i–xiii.

Smith, Graham Hingangaroa (2000). "Protecting and Respecting Indigenous Knowledge." In *Reclaiming Indigenous Voice and Vision*, edited by Marie Battiste, pp. 209–224. Vancouver, BC: University of British Columbia.

Smith, Linda Tuhiwai (1999). *Decolonizing Methodologies: Research and Indigenous Peoples*. London: Zed Books.

Solórzano, Daniel G., and Tara J. Yosso (2002). "Critical Race Methodology: Counter-Storytelling as an Analytical Framework for Education Research." *Qualitative Inquiry* 8(1): 23–44.

Tuck, Eve, and K. W Yang (2012). "Decolonization Is Not a Metaphor." *Decolonization: Indigeneity, Education and Society* 1(1): 1–40.

Tunstill, Guy (1989). "An Overview of the Centre for Aboriginal Studies in Music, 1988." *Australian Aboriginal Studies* 1: 29.

Vass, Gregory (2013). *White Shadows in the Classroom: Race-making Pedagogies in an Australian School.* Unpublished PhD thesis, Brisbane, University of Queensland.

Waterman, Christopher A. (1990). "'Our Tradition is a Very Modern Tradition': Popular Music and the Construction of Pan-Yoruba Identity." *Ethnomusicology* 34(3): 367–379.

Yazzie, Robert (2000). "Indigenous Peoples and Postcolonial Colonialism." In *Reclaiming Indigenous Voice and Vision*, edited by Marie Battiste, pp. 39–53. Vancouver, BC: University of British Columbia Press.

Youngblood-Henderson, James (Sákéj) (2000). "The Context of the State of Nature." In *Reclaiming Indigenous Voice and Vision*, edited by Marie Battiste, pp. 12–38. Vancouver, BC: University of British Columbia Press.

Zavala, Miguel (2013). "What Do We Mean by Decolonizing Research Strategies? Lessons from Decolonizing, Indigenous Research Projects in New Zealand and Latin America." *Decolonization: Indigeneity, Education & Society* 2(1): 55–71.

CHAPTER 7

ANDES TO AMAZON ON THE RIVER Q'EROS

Indigenous Voice in Grassroots Tourism, Safeguarding, and Ownership Projects of the Q'eros and Wachiperi Peoples

HOLLY WISSLER

Introduction: Reciprocity

THE support for and ability of indigenous people to express their own voice regarding the use of their music in tourism, representation, safeguarding, and material production projects are often impeded by the restrictions and agendas of local government and nongovernment organizations, as well as tour companies. The efficacy of projects based around any of these activities is often directly proportionate to how much that voice is listened to, ideally in balance and equal partnership with the counterpart they are working with. The question of *how* to gauge efficacy in music projects and representation has been a debate in applied ethnomusicology in the past few decades (Alviso, 2003; Bradley, 1989; Davis, 1992; Grant, 2012; Hutchinson, 2003; Lomax Hawes, 1992; Long, 2003; Sheehy, 1992). In this chapter I discuss the representation of music in indigenous tourism, preservation, safeguarding, and CD production through the lens of two case studies. I use these themes to focus on hands-on indigenous action regarding self-representation and how the choices of action are related to satisfactory reciprocal relationship (or lack thereof) between the indigenous people with the applied ethnomusicologist, foreign tourists and students, and Peru's Ministry of Culture.

The first study is the internationally known highland Quechua Q'eros people in the Cusco Region of southern Peru and their choices regarding indigenous tourism and effective sharing of their music in touristic ventures; and the second is the near-extinct Amazonian Wachiperi[1] people, also in the Cusco Region, and their choice to make their own CD production of their now inactive songs, intentionally negating a CD production proposition from the Cusco division of the Ministry of Culture. When it comes to presenting music in the public sphere, both the Q'eros and Wachiperi assert their own guidelines in active resistance, even if on a very small scale. Indeed, my intention for sharing these two case studies is to advocate for the value and efficacy of micro-scale grassroots applied music projects, executed in small groups and even one-on-one, versus large-scale operations, events, and stagings that involve organizational participation. Applied ethnomusicology can be effectual on the smallest of scales, and in my experience that is where it has been the most fruitful.

The measurement of success of projects with both the Q'eros and the Wachiperi is gauged by the effectiveness of *reciprocity*, an age-old theme in anthropological and ethnomusicological studies, which was first systematically studied in the groundbreaking work of Marcel Mauss in his comparisons of Polynesian, Melanesian, and Native American exchange systems. Reciprocity also premises the social, economic, and spiritual systems in the Andes and the Amazon, as shown in the lives of the Q'eros and the Wachiperi. Mauss's classic book, *The Gift* (1954, first edition in English) examines reciprocity in large-scale contexts with detailed description of the North American potlatch, the *kula* ring exchanges based on Malinowski's work with the Tobriand peoples, and in the meetings, assemblies, markets, festivals, and seafaring expeditions of various Polynesian and Melanesian groups. Similarly, the Inca Empire (1436–1532) functioned on a large-scale system of reciprocity known as *mit'a*, whereby a tribute tax was paid to the Inca king and nobility in the form of labor and production (food, weaving, ceramics, metallurgy, mining, and the building of temples, palaces, roads, and irrigation canals, to name a few). In return, all areas of production, that is, all peoples who were incorporated into the Inca system, received periodic distribution of food and clothing from the massive state storage system of *qollqas* (storehouses). Instead of common markets that were the life centers of many Asian and European empires, the Incas had intricate trade networks among the coastal, Andean, and Amazon regions joined by Qhapaq Ñan (royal stone roads). An enormous variety of goods was produced all along the Andean vertical ecology,[2] made possible due to the multitude of ecosystems found in the extreme range of altitudes situated in tropical latitudes. Through labor tax reciprocated by provision of goods to all, the Incas created a successful social system that propelled the largest pre-Columbian empire in the New World. This system of reciprocity was intrinsically linked to the social and personal relationships among those who made the exchanges, so that reciprocity on the local level extended to the empire level. The first decades of the post-Spanish invasion (1532–1570) experienced a tragic shift to a newly introduced European slave feudal system that caused the breakdown, demoralization, and mass deaths of many Andean, coastal, and Amazonian groups, indicative of the devastation that a non-reciprocal system can incite (see Hemming, 1993: 334–359).

Today, as in the past, relationship is key to Andean livelihood and is what must be nurtured above all else. *Ayni* is the system of reciprocity that ensures good relationship among people with their fellow community members, animals, and the powerful spirits that hold sway over their quality of livelihood (see scholarship that includes discussions of *ayni*: Abercrombie, 1998; Allen, 1997, 2002, 2008; Arnold with Juan de Dios Yapita, 1998; Bastien, 1978; Bolin, 1998; Butler, 2006; Cummins, 2002; Flores Ochoa, 1977, 1988; Gow, 1976; Harris, 2000; Isbell, 1978; Mamani Mamani, 1990; Mannheim, 1986, 1991; Rozas Alvarez, 2002 [1979]; Schaedel, 1988; Silverman, 1994; Stobart, 2006; Tomoeda, 1996; Webster, 1972; Wissler, 2009a; Zuidema, 1964, 1982, 1990). In living and working with the Q'eros since 2003 I have come to see how this operative principle is essential in every relationship, and can cause offense, even harm, if not upheld.

The Quechua word *ayni* refers to mutual aid in nearly every aspect of community life, such as sharing food and labor, gift-giving, and political and ritual offices as part of a community's *cargo* system.[3] This understood web of social obligations ensures that everyone in the community is taken care of in social, political, and fundamental ways. While exchanges are not often direct, *ayni* is an implied and tacit obligation that ensures that "what goes around, comes around." On the smallest scale, home visits should be accompanied with a simple gift, such as potatoes or *coca*,[4] and neighbors help one another in farming, herding, and home building. On the community level, a festival *carguyoq* (sponsor) solicits food, drink, and *coca* from fellow community members so that his *cargo* (festival responsibility) goes well. If *ayni* is not fulfilled, one risks damaging a relationship with a neighbor or the entire community. Anthropologist Catherine Allen, in her moving ethnography *The Hold Life Has*, succinctly describes the vitality of *ayni*: "Reciprocity is like a pump at the heart of Andean life" (Allen, 2002: 73).

This system of interactive reciprocity in the Andes exists not only among humans, but among all vital energies, as Allen states:

> Every category of being, at every level, participates in this cosmic circulation. Humans maintain interactive reciprocity relationships, not only with each other but also with their animals, their houses, their potato fields, the earth, and the sacred places in their landscape.
>
> (Allen, 1997: 76)

All entities—human and non-human—have *animu*, an animated essence, so the maintenance of respectful relationships with all beings is essential for a good, functioning life (Wissler, 2009a: 42–45). In Q'eros, and many traditional Andean communities, the most potent relationship to be upheld is with the supernatural forces, the *Apu* (mountain gods) and *Pacha Mama* (mother earth), as they hold the most power and influence on quality of life. If this crucial relationship is not maintained and renewed through numerous offerings, the spirits can inflict ill, sometimes in dramatic ways: crops fail; lightning strikes a person or an animal; a puma attacks a baby llama or alpaca; or a family member dies prematurely. In this case, "what goes around, comes around" can literally have deadly consequences. Conversely, if the reciprocal relationship is attended to, the powers can bestow good luck, healthy crops, and herd procreation. I have witnessed these beliefs and realities as daily life in the Q'eros community, with Q'eros' songs as one of the many offerings used in order to uphold good relationships with these all-powerful spirits (see Wissler, 2009: 109–207). Similarly, the Amazonian Wachiperi have their own system of reciprocity, as described later in this chapter.

Mauss expounds the idea that gifts received are not inactive, which is why gift-giving can be so powerful and binding (and in some cases, potentially dangerous). An example he details is *hau*, which, according to the Maori, is the soul and power of objects that create ties on a soul-level because of the animation/spirit of the object (Mauss, 1990: 11–12). The Q'eros' animal fertility rituals are pinnacle moments of circulatory *ayni* among all sentient beings, when there is an abundant flow of energies and conspicuous co-consumption in intentional exchange of *ayni* among the supernatural powers, people, animals, and a variety of ritual objects (see Allen, 2002; Stobart, 2006; Wissler, 2009).[5] Sound and song have vital roles in these circulations of offerings (Wissler, 2009: 182–207). Other continuous offerings include libations of alcohol, and intricate offerings with many ingredients, to include food items and coca leaves, that are then burned for the *Apu* to consume via the smoke, while the ashes are consumed by *Pacha Mama*.

Mauss determines reciprocal gift-giving as a total social phenomenon, since it involves legal, economic, moral, religious, social, aesthetic, and spiritual dimensions. Mauss lists the benefits of reciprocity as numerable: It creates mutual ties and satisfaction on the individual, familial, community, inter- and intra-community, and institutional levels; enhances solidarity such as kinship links, alliances, and friendly relations; creates permanent commitments; is obligatory and binding; promotes honor and integrity; and is the basis of moral and material life. Reciprocity, as the intrinsic social underpinning of life for the Q'eros and the Wachiperi, is therefore the naturally preferred mode of interaction in our projects as well.

Background: Andes and Amazon, Q'eros and Wachiperi

The Andean Quechua Q'eros and the Amazonian Harakbut Wachiperi live on extremes of the same River Q'eros, both in the Paucartambo province within the region of Cusco,[6] in southeast Peru (see Figures 7.1 and 7.2). The Q'eros nation consists of five communities, with the largest community of Hatun Q'eros, the site of my work, located on the river's source at 11,000 feet above sea level. This source is fed by glacial headwaters originating at 16,000 feet, flows through the llama, alpaca, and potato zones of Hatun Q'eros, down through their cloud forest territory, plunges through impassable gorges, and eventually arrives in the rain forest foothills at the Wachiperi community located on the river's mouth, at 1,000 feet.[7] Not only are the Q'eros and Wachiperi located on the furthermost ends of the same river, but both groups represent extremes of indigenous cultural prosperity: The Q'eros are a flourishing Quechua group, having tripled their population in the past one hundred years, with their traditional and changing customs expressive of pre-Hispanic culture, such as songs, weavings, and offerings to the mountain spirits.

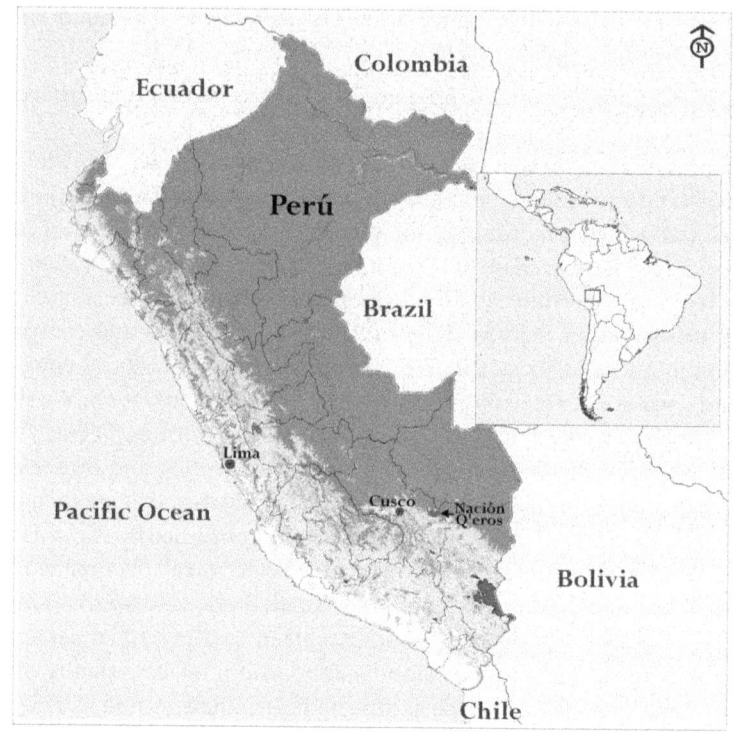

FIGURE 7.1 The location of the Q'eros Nation in Peru. The Wachiperi region is due north of the Q'eros Nation, in the beginning of the green Amazon section.

(Map courtesy of ACCA, Asociación para la Conservación de la Cuenca Amazónica, Cusco, Perú. www.acca.org.pe)

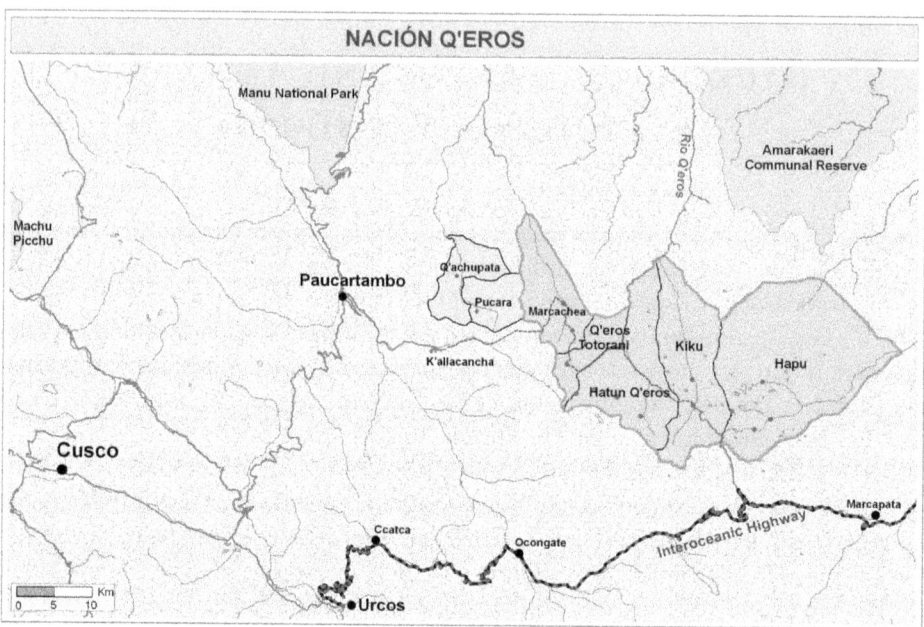

FIGURE 7.2 The location of the Q'eros Nation and the Q'eros River in reference to the Department capital of Cusco and province capital of Paucartambo.

(Map courtesy of ACCA, Asociación para la Conservación de la Cuenca Amazónica, Cusco, Perú. www.acca.org.pe)

This is a result of their ancestral exploitation of three vertical ecological zones located on the eastern watershed of the Andes, spanning from 15,000 to 6,000 feet in a vertical drop of about 25 miles. These zones provide all animal and crop resources for sustainability, so that their ethnic and cultural integrity is intact and the continued integrity of their cultural practices is fostered. The Q'eros are an admirable example of a people who are not tied to the cash economy within their own community, though this is rapidly changing due to urban migration and the arrival of a car road into the community (2014), which connects them to urban amenities and trappings more than ever before in their history.

By contrast, the Wachiperi, of the Harakbut linguistic family, suffered great loss and relocation during forced enslavement and displacement from their original territory caused by the early twentieth-century rubber terror, particularly under the exploits of Peruvian rubber baron Carlos Fitzcarrald, who made the Madre de Dios region, original home of the Wachiperi, a major area for capturing slaves and labor under the pain of death. Later, many Wachiperi were relocated to a mid-century (1946) establishment of a North American Baptist Mission, followed in 1948 by a small pox epidemic that coincided with the opening of the road to Cusco, which severely reduced the population. Today only some one hundred or so Wachiperi remain.[8] The Wachiperi songs, like the people and their language, are on the border of extinction.

Q'eros and Wachiperi music has much in common, as is true for many indigenous cultures: The songs express their environment with topics about the landscape, revered animals and birds; they are used for personal expression of grievances, complaints, and loss; both are used for healing in some form; and the songs fortify identity and social ties (Allen, 2002; Olsen, 1996; Seeger, 2004a; Stobart, 2006; Turino, 1993; Uzendoski, 2005; Wissler, 2009a). The principal difference is that the Q'eros still embody and retain the original context for musical practice (carnival, animal fertility rituals, corn harvest), while the Wachiperi lost their context for musical production during relocation to the Protestant mission and prohibition of the drinking of *masato*, fermented yucca beer. Community singing for the Wachiperi had been traditionally organized in *masateadas* (communal drinking rituals) in large communal homes, and their communal singing ended with the prohibition of this ritual.

In September 2010 I collected, digitized, and repatriated 50 years of audiovisual archives to the Q'eros, and in December of the same year I digitized and returned University of California Berkeley anthropologist Patricia J. Lyon's 1964 and 1965 reel-to-reel recordings of 206 Wachiperi songs to the Wachiperi. This was the first time in the history of both communities that audio-visual archives had been repatriated to them (see Figure 7.3).[9] In the case of the Wachiperi, the repatriation of song archives was my introduction to the community, whereas with the Q'eros I had accumulated years of research and reciprocal relations that opened doors on both communal and individual levels. It is this foundation of years of trust and collaboration with the Q'eros that has allowed for the co-creation of exchanges with tourist and student groups, with music as focal point, which are fulfilling and often very potent for both the Q'eros and the guests. I have married my role of 30 years as tour leader and cultural translator in mountain

FIGURE 7.3 Digitized archives returned to the Queros-Wachiperi community. Estela Dariquebe and Manuel Yonaje, front, are the only two elders alive who recorded with Patricia Lyon in 1964 and 1965.

(Photo by Holly Wissler, December 11, 2010)

areas of Peru with 15 years as music researcher in the same mountains, to successfully incorporate the Q'eros and their music into our mutual livelihood of tourism in a way that benefits both parties on various levels, without changing or creating a new form of the performance aspect of their music.

THE QUECHUA Q'EROS AND THEIR MUSIC IN INDIGENOUS TOURISM

When indigenous music is introduced into tourist realms, it quite often undergoes the construction of a new or altered musical form (Harnish, 2005), a folklorization of the original music (Mendoza, 1998, 2000), or a staging of indigenous culture and identity negotiation for political purposes (Oakdale, 2004). Indigenous music that is commoditized for touristic purposes often becomes "self-conscious 'cultural performances'" (Rios, 2012: 6), a self-conscious presentation of self (Senft, 1999), or, in the ecological analogy of Titon, "like chemical fertilizers, artificial stimuli that feed the plant but starve the soil...." (Titon, 2009: 122). In my work with the Q'eros and the introduction of their music into tourism, they do not reconstruct a performance of identity, or display an objectified image of their cultural heritage, which could be very tempting for them given that they are often associated (on the national and international level) with a romantic Inca past, as a people who still harmoniously live in untouched, ancient tradition (Corr, 2003).

I argue that what supports the maintenance of authentic, unpackaged musical performance, as well as the facilitation of deep sharings of musical and life experiences between two extremes of culture (indigenous, rural Andean with modern, urban US), is the very small, grassroots level in which we work. These exchanges are not so "small" after all, when one considers the inner experience of rich benefit and growth, and, in the case of the Q'eros, personal benefit plus economic compensation. It is in the arenas of tourism and work with students on study abroad programs in Peru where I have experienced direct, immediate, and long-lasting impact in the service of applied ethnomusicology.

Indigenous Tourism and Ideas of Authenticity

In past decades there has been a growing interest in, implementation of, and debates about indigenous tourism, which includes activities where indigenous people are directly involved, and their culture, including musical presentation, serves as the essence of attraction (see Boniface and Robinson, 1998; Butler and Hinch, 2007; Knudsen and Waade, 2010; Ryan and Aicken, 2005; Xie, 2001). Butler and Hinch state in their introduction to their edited volume *Tourism and Indigenous Peoples*, "Indigenous cultures have become a powerful attraction for tourists and as such they have drawn the attention of tourism entrepreneurs, government agencies and academics" (Butler and Hinch, 2007: 2). Many of the case studies in this volume discuss whether indigenous tourism is an opportunity for the indigenous to "gain economic independence and cultural rejuvenation to whether it presents a major threat of hegemonic subjugation and cultural degradation" (ibid.). These are two extremes of the continuum, and the editors do clarify that "[a] parallel range of opinions exist at operational levels of debates about the *size* of indigenous tourism markets, the appropriateness of various marketing practices and the business models that are most suitable for indigenous tourism operations" (ibid., my emphasis). The overall premise of all cases presented is that there is not one guiding set of principles that assures success in indigenous tourism models; rather, each case is unique to time, place, and size. I agree with this conclusion, and have myself experienced models that both work and do not work regarding tourism with the Q'eros.

280　INDIGENOUS PEOPLES

Boniface and Robinson (1998) discuss how tourism can help preserve cultures and resurrect forgotten traditions, while at the same time challenging cultural norms, which can lead to situations of conflict, in which much tension, and even violence, can result. Many issues must be confronted when cultures meet, such as social and economic power relations, and even moral and legal rights. The majority of the case studies in both Butler and Hinch and Boniface and Robinson deal with fairly large-scale tourist operations. I emphasize the word *size* as quoted above because it is on the smallest level where I have felt and seen the most effective results, literally one-on-one, or a ratio of roughly two to one, when I introduce US guests and the Q'eros to one another (Figure 7.4). The group sizes I work with are anywhere from four to thirty total people involved. The effectiveness of these encounters is probably more immediate and impactful when compared to

FIGURE 7.4　Two US tourists with three Q'eros, learning about the Q'eros pinkuyllu flutes.

(Photo by Holly Wissler, July 17, 2014)

many other models that deal with interactions on a larger scale, such as stagings of musical presentations to a sizable audience.

The issue of authenticity in tourism—its definition and implementation—has been a much-debated issue in the study and practice of indigenous tourism. One of the first critics of inauthentic tourist experiences was the American historian and social critic Daniel Boorstin, whose groundbreaking book *The Image* discussed the effect of mass media on American culture that resulted in contrivance and a valuing of the fake over the genuine. He critiqued the tourism industry as a whole, saying it once offered real experiences but came to insulate travelers from the places they were visiting and, instead, provided artificial products and presentations for tourists who expect to see scenes out of the movies (Boorstin, 1961). Boorstin's seminal critique is still influential in authentic tourism debates today.

Fifty years later, Knudsen and Waade discuss "a hunger for reality and the indexical authenticity" and "a striving for the real" in regard to authenticity in indigenous tourism (Knudsen and Waade, 2010: 2). Authenticity is not observers (tourists) observing staged authenticity (the idea of tourist as observer and host culture as observed; Urry, 2002), but "the nature of authenticity is *experiential*" (Johnson and McIntosh, 2005: 36, my emphasis). Along these lines, Knudsen and Waade discuss that the longing for the authentic in tourism is not a "... 'thing' you can possess, nor a 'state of mind,' but something which people *do* and a feeling which is *experienced*" (Knudsen and Waade, 2010: 1). I agree that *experience* and *experiential* are key components in authentic exchange in indigenous tourism, which includes accessing deeper meanings of indigenous music by the students/tourists involved.

Knudsen and Waade use the term "performative authenticity" to marry object-related and subject-related modes of authenticity. Object-related refers to concepts that are "out there": place, the tourists' projections, narrations, and identity constructions about place, and pre-conceived ideas in general, such as the desire for a non-technological, natural environment and experience in their travels. "Indexical authenticity" refers to the inner experience of the tourist who is affected by and has intense feelings for place (object-related) (ibid.). Subject-related refers to the inner, affected, tactile, corporeal, emotional, and inter-relatedness that the tourist actually experiences (ibid.: 12–16). Performative authenticity, therefore, is the combination of preconceptions that conjure up images and sensations with the subjective inner affected experience and existential personal quests that happen in the moment. In simpler terms, the projected combined with the experienced.

Sustainability scientist Ning Wang writes in his article "Rethinking Authenticity in Tourism Experience," "Existential authenticity refers to a potential existential state of Being that is to be achieved by tourist activities. Correspondingly, authentic experiences in tourism are to achieve this activated existential state of Being within the liminal process of tourism" (Wang, 1999: 352). Wang discusses authenticity in terms of intrapersonal (the sensations of authenticity the person feels) and interpersonal (the authentic bonding among peoples). I believe the concepts intra- and interpersonal, sensations and bondings, are key in the success of interactive, exchange tourism and indigenous musical sharings. In our exchanges, the tourists and students have direct and intimate contact with the Q'eros and their musical offerings. The tourists' experience is more than observing, but a taking part in, a participation of—when emotions, thoughts, sensations, and even spirit become involved. I believe we achieve authentic sensations and mutual bonding in our exchanges, which are connected to both pre-conceived ideas of place and identity, combined with actual, corporeal, and emotional experience, which I expand on below.

Interpretations and meanings of "authenticity" have been critically examined in contemporary ethnomusicology, and many ethnomusicologists have discussed authenticity in regard to the incorporation of indigenous music in touristic ventures and festivals (see Stokes, 1994). Jeff Titon quotes the definition of folk cultural traditions from the Smithsonian's Center of Folklife Programs and Cultural Studies *Guidelines for Research*, which is meant to guide fieldworkers' decisions on what is and is not authentic:

> . . . community-based forms of knowledge, skill and expression learned through informal relationships and exhibiting intergenerational continuity. Typical genres include oral tradition, social custom, material culture and its supportive knowledge, and the folk arts. Forms of folk culture are traditional to the extent that they maintain standards or values, which have continuity with, and are informed by, past practice. They are living traditions to the extent that they are practiced, and are socially integrated within community life and speak to its cognitive, normative, affective, and aesthetic concerns (Office of Folklife Programs 1988).
>
> (Titon, 1999: 123–124)

Based on this definition, the Q'eros' music-making I organize for tour groups is solidly rooted in "intergenerational continuity" and a "living tradition." While they are not playing in the ritual context (i.e., drinking the ceremonial *chicha*—corn beer—involved in multiple offerings for the mountain spirits or carnival merry-making), the execution of their music is not modified or staged. The renderings are more subdued than during their inebriated ritual contexts and more akin to the way they sing around their family hearths or while herding their llamas and alpacas out in the Andean heights: a simple playing and singing of their songs in an intimate, private setting, as they did for me during my fieldwork, so that they share the community's affective and aesthetic concerns. To use Thomas Turino's definition, this is participatory music that does not become staged or presentational. Rather, it is a simple rendition of participatory music (Turino, 2008).

In contrast to simple renderings of music in intimate settings, many of my Q'eros friends have expressed feelings of *p'enqay*, or shame, and a sense of being used and manipulated as they are put on stage by the Ministry of Culture, which solicits them to perform their songs and the traditional sounding of announcement on conch shells (*pututu*) for specific ceremonies based around achievements of the Ministry. Both the Q'eros and the Wachiperi are regularly called upon to travel long distances from their communities and perform for special Ministry of Culture events, thereby symbolizing the Ministry's investment in heralding and safeguarding the traditions of both peoples. While the Q'eros' musical performances for the MC are similar to the ones they do for my tour groups—a simple rendition of songs—the *experience* is dramatically different. One is an uncomfortable staged obligation for a political entity, with little understanding or significance of the music imparted, and centered around an event that often has nothing to do with the people performing, versus an intimate, often mutually meaningful experiential exchange between US tourists/students and the Q'eros, which is directly focused on the Q'eros, who they are, and the layers of musical meaning. In my experience, it is the latter musical representation that engenders a sense of "authentic."

Indigenous Tourism and the Q'eros Identity

I first heard of the Q'eros upon moving to Peru in 1982 as the exotic last stronghold of "pure" indigenous Andean people surviving today. It was this romantic reputation that led me 20 years later to choose the Q'eros' ritual music as my dissertation research topic. The fame and attraction of the Q'eros to foreigners evolved from mid-twentieth century onward due to many factors that link them to an ancient, and even Inca, past.[10] One version of the Q'eros' origin myth of Inkarí, the mythical Inca who founded the Inca Empire, tells how the Q'eros were privileged with the power of wisdom, while the Incas received the political power. The first academic expedition into Q'eros headed by Cusco University (Universidad Nacional de San Antonio Abad del Cusco) in 1955 highlighted the connection to an Inca past with sensational editorials in the Lima newspaper, *La Prensa*, such as: "Living museum from the Inca era being studied by Peruvian scientists," and "Q'ero is an admirable testimony of a pre-Incan city in Peru" (journalist Demetrio Tupac Yupanqui, August 21 and 22, 1955, respectively). These editorials brought national attention to the Q'eros. Fifty years later, their legal establishment of the *Nación Q'eros* (Q'eros Nation, consisting of five Q'eros communities, approximately 3,000 population) is indicative of the Q'eros' self-identified identity/ethnicity, and their wish to preserve and promote themselves as a unified group. In 2006, Peru's then National Institute of Culture—today the Ministry of Culture—declared the Q'eros people "Cultural Patrimony," the first case of its kind in Peru in which a people were so named.[11] Because of this renown, streams of foreign and local filmmakers and researchers have been drawn to Q'eros' romanticized identity over the past 50 years.

As mentioned, the Q'eros' continued practice of their community traditions has much to do with their location in three diverse ecological zones on the eastern watershed of the Andes, all in relatively close proximity, which has fostered self-sustainability, and less need for trade and outside movement than more dependent Andean groups. The Q'eros are likely one of the few remaining ethnic groups of the diverse mosaic of cultural groups in existence in southern Peru at the time of the Spanish invasion, versus ethnic Incas (see Mannheim, 1998: 383–384; Rowe, 1948: 185; Webster, 1972: 7–9). In sum, the Q'eros, with their intact cultural and ethnic identity, have many platforms and an eager audience from which to assert this identity, which they articulately connect to an ancient

Inca past, as their origin myth tells them; they are proud of their identity, and articulate and utilize it to their benefit. This makes tourism highly attractive for and to the Q'eros.

Today the Q'eros are particularly sought out by a specific niche of foreigners (US and European) who seek spiritual guidance, and have come to look to the Q'eros as *the* teachers and holders of Andean Native American spiritual tradition. They are known as spiritual leaders, because every head of family—usually the men, and sometimes the women—is a ritual specialist, having inherited the knowledge of how to make precise offerings for the mountain deities (*Apu*) and Mother Earth (*Pacha Mama*), whereas other Andean communities have only one or a few ritual specialists. This corresponds to their version of the origin myth, Inkarí, in which the Q'eros inherited vast spiritual knowledge. Many Q'eros are invited abroad to teach their knowledge, and visitors to Peru hold learning sessions with them in and around the Cusco region, while the hardier will travel to Q'eros.[12] This type of "mystical/esoteric/New Age tourism," as it is called in the tourist trade, comes with a lot of hot critique; many argue that because of the forces of commerce and capitalism, the Q'eros have sold out or exploited their ritual expertize to spiritually empty Westerners who look outside their own home for fulfillment, or, conversely that the Q'eros representatives, such as tour companies, have created an exaggerated mystique around the Q'eros that the Q'eros comply with and cultivate in order to simply earn the much-needed income to support their families. Certainly, the Q'eros are a spiritual people, and the issue of spiritual tourism is complex and multi-faceted.

In spite of the Q'eros' renown and attractiveness to outside visitors, they do not have any community-based tourism (CBT) in place, where the community could potentially manage their own touristic operations to the control and benefit of the community;[13] rather, separate tour companies and individuals employ Q'eros who are looking for work in tourism as they become more connected to/dependent on the cash economy. In the past decade there has been significant Q'eros migration to Cusco, which comes with new economic trappings: building homes, paying for their children's education, and buying food from the market that they used to grow in their community. Tourism is now a main form of income for many in-community and migrant Q'eros, and they are savvy in securing their own work contacts to make offerings for tourists and sell their handmade textiles.

This system of individual enterprise fosters capitalistic competition and often jealousies among community members, yet many Q'eros have stated that they prefer to be their own individual agents in securing tourist activities versus any kind of CBT where equality would be enforced. Francisco Quispe from Q'eros stated bluntly that they do not want to create CBT that would instill and obligate an equal sharing of tourist earnings. "Many don't want to share, because they think that if they do a rotation system then there would be 'less for me.' We prefer to work with people we already know; with contacts we already have and continue to make" (personal communication, July 19, 2013). This contrasts with the Taquile island CBT model, where, in the 1970s, the Taquileños created an innovative, community-controlled tourism system, with home stays and cultural activities, to combat mass tourism to their island that was run by outsiders. The Q'eros region is vast, not a single island, and the Q'eros individually, not collectively, discreetly invite tourists to their homes in the mountains, or meet tour groups in Cusco. This is completely in character with their savvy negotiation of "Inca identity" that they use in political, social, and tourist arenas; it is also in line with their decades of astute control regarding which outsiders can and cannot film, research, and witness rituals in their community.[14] They have taken control of tourism in their region and are not interested in any CBT that may not serve their own individual desires and needs, which is fascinating considering that they still live by traditional communal rules in regard to intracommunity social matters.

Case Study: Q'eros-Tourist Exchanges with Music as Focal Point

Knudsen and Waade discuss authenticity in indigenous tourism as "the desire for insight into the intimate back-stage life of others," and this insight is what we achieve in our small, face-to-face meetings with the Q'eros (Knudsen and Waade, 2010: 10). Even though I am regularly solicited to take groups and individuals into Q'eros because of my research profile, I only travel to Q'eros with select, close friends because in this way I feel we can share quality exchanges inside the intimate space of the Q'eros' homes. In other words, I take friends to meet friends. I have only led one tour group into Q'eros, and I sensed varied agendas and interest in the clients' meeting the Q'eros, so that any meaningful exchange was compromised, and the trip felt unsatisfactory. This experience, coupled with the high-altitude rigors and inclement weather involved in arriving to the community that took a toll on the original intent of cultural exchange, led me to conclude that I will not take tourists into Q'eros again. What works for us (the Q'eros, visitors, and me) are the close meetings between select Q'eros and small tour and student groups in Cusco, specifically using music as focal point and a window into Q'eros' life and perspective.

The Q'eros call me *chakawarmi* (bridge-woman) because of my ability to conjoin my compatriots with the Q'eros in meaningful colloquy. I work with about 10 Q'eros families whom I rotate for the exchanges. The group I have chosen are the ones who committed to my work years ago when I began my initial music research in Q'eros, so we have a long working history together. In this way I continue *ayni*, reciprocal social obligation, in exchange for all the favors and time they gave in helping me understand their music. In some cases, the Q'eros' earnings with groups are through selling their textiles, but mostly we are hired to meet with small tour and student groups, so that the Q'eros make a much-welcomed wage.[15]

The tourist demographic we meet with are generally high-powered, well-educated professionals from the United States who have just two weeks or so vacation a year. Many check into their workplace regularly via Smartphones, often adding stress to their once-in-a-lifetime visit to Peru. Knudsen and Waade (2010) expand on ideas from Gilmore and Pine (2007), stating that "the craving for authenticity is a reaction to a strong technologically mediatised, commercialised and socially constructed reality. One could think of this 'craving' as a 'longing' for the immediate, non-commercialised, brute natural world, characterized by the real authentic" (Knudsen and Waade, 2010: 1). Most of the visitors we meet with come away with a sense of having experienced the "real authentic," even if in one session and on a small scale.

Certainly the meeting location has a powerful, underlying influence: the capital of the Inca Empire, with the final goal of the mystical citadel of Machu Picchu. The clients/students are already under the spell of having finally arrived in the majestic Andes, a place that has been their dream for years. They are in the midst of the "indexical authenticity" and "emotional geography" of the tourist's inner experience, affected by and having intense, often projected, feelings for place (Knudsen and Waade, 2010: 5–16). This emotional investment in place and history is conducive to their openness for and interest in a meeting with the Q'eros.

Upon meeting the Q'eros, the guests first see the physical representation of authentic: The men in pre-Hispanic *unku* tunics under their hand-woven ponchos, with the knee-length *calzuna* pants; the women in brightly-colored finely-woven *lliklla* shawls with typical Q'eros designs and *bayeta* (woven cloth of sheep and alpaca fiber) skirts. All wear the simple *ojota* sandals, and often their feet are mud-caked from recent work in their homes, fields, and travel by foot over a mountain pass to arrive at the road and take the bus to Cusco. Soon after, social features of the authentic begin to be expressed: warm hugs from the Q'eros to the guests, most of whom are unaccustomed to such affection upon first meeting. Barriers begin to break down. The tourists soften, smile, and even laugh at this unexpected warmth and physicality. Next come greetings in their native Quechua, a language they have not heard in person, and most likely have not heard of before their journey to Peru. These are not formal speeches, as are sometimes performed on stage for Ministry of Culture functions just before musical performance, but direct, personal greetings in this ancient language of the Andes.

We sit in chairs in a small circle, versus two lines facing one another ("us" and "them"), or the Q'eros on a stage and the guests as audience, as in Ministry of Culture presentations. Often we hike together, sharing magnificent Inca archaeology and Andean scenery (Figure 7.5). I ensure that the sessions are dialogue; that is, I invite the Q'eros to ask questions of the clients, and vice versa. There are many questions that I could easily answer in regard to the Q'eros' lifestyle, and interpretation and meaning of their music, but I defer to the Q'eros so that they reply first in their own words, and I then add what I have discovered and learned through years of research, in terms that are more easily understandable to Western thinking. Therefore, my translation is both literal from Quechua to English, with the addition of cultural translation.

Next, I facilitate the sharing of a music the guests have neither heard nor imagined before: men simultaneously play *pinkuyllu*—four-holed end-notched vertical bamboo flutes—"out of tune" and dissonant, while the women sing with full force from the gut, intentionally expelling all air at the ends of phrases ▶. Each *pinkuyllu* is tuned to itself, but not to another, so that if there are two or three *pinkuyllu* the sound is inevitably

FIGURE 7.5 A Q'eros couple sharing music with US tourists from inside an Inca niche.

(Photo by Vicki Groninga, October 13, 2013)

bitonal or tritonal. I let the Q'eros choose which *pukllay taki*, or carnival song, they wish to sing, about the sacred and medicinal plants, flowers, and birds in their environment. It is taboo to sing the animal fertility songs out of ritual context, but it is precisely the tritonic *pukllay taki* sung by a woman combined with the tritonic *pinkuyllu* complementary melody that is normally sung out of carnival context throughout daily activities such as herding and weaving. I see it over and over again: the spellbound look of awe on the visitors' faces, taking in this extraordinary experience of indigenous Andeans vigorously singing and playing, and *just for them*.

In our ensuing post-listening dialogue I explain how the basic life tenet of *ayni*—reciprocity—is manifested in Q'eros music. I begin with the significance of the song topic and basic elements of music such as tuning, and the complementarity of the men's playing and the women's singing.[16] I help the guests understand what is usually a new musical aesthetic for them: that starting and stopping together is not a musical criterion;

in fact, in Q'eros it is just the opposite. The space must be continually filled with sound so that the offering of songs, particularly in animal fertility ritual, is plentiful and non-stop.[17] If the group shows keen interest, then I particularly expand on one of the most exciting musical discoveries in my years of singing in ritual with Q'eros women: Their self-identified vocal technique, *aysariykuy*, which is the notable prolongation and expulsion of air at the end of alternate refrains. I share my passion about the idea that the Q'eros' worldview is encompassed in a single vocal technique that is a ritual blowing of the person's *samay*, or animated essence, which is sent out in offering to the *Apu*, mountain deities, in propitiation for the return of *ayni*.[18] This ritual blowing of the song, just like the ritual blowing (*phukuy*) of coca leaves, is, in the Q'eros' words, *chayanankupaq*—"so that the song arrives," and *uyarichinankukama*—"until they [the *Apu*] are made to hear." The people hope to be reciprocated with the health of their crops, herds, and overall livelihood. I elucidate how they taught me that if they don't sing and play with *aysariykuy*, then the *Apu* won't hear the song, thereby not receiving the song offering, which places *ayni* in jeopardy. If the song is not received and *ayni* is not reciprocated, bad occurrences take place—and in extreme cases, death. The people take direct responsibility for unreciprocated *ayni*, stating that perhaps they did not sing properly, give enough offering bundles, libations of alcohol and coca leaves, in order to ensure complete reciprocity.[19]

With university and high school student groups that are part of an in-depth study abroad program, I distribute song text and we sing along with the Q'eros, so they can experience the sensation of *aysariykuy* (see Figures 7.6 and 7.7). Many of these student groups have a Quechua component, so I am able to delve deeper and breakdown the meaning of the term *aysariykuy*. Quechua is a language in which multiple infixes and suffixes are added to basic verb roots to enhance the meaning. The root of *aysariykuy* is *aysay*: "to pull," "to drag," "to haul," or "to throw." Added to *aysay* are three suffixes: the first, *ri* [*ru*],[20] indicates an action with speed and urgency; the second, *yu*, implies an action performed with intensity; and finally, *ku*, which indicates an action executed with much enthusiasm, affection, and in quantity. For ease in pronunciation, *ri-yu-ku* becomes *riyku*, so the final word is *aysariykuy*. Thus, the essence of the full translation is something akin to "The song is pulled or thrown with urgency, intensity, and affectionate enthusiasm" and "with much quantity of breath." More than just simply infusing the song with *samay*, or life essence, that *samay* must be moved and "thrown" in a particular way, with "urgency, intensity, and affectionate enthusiasm." The vocal technique is then packed with intention that the guests learn about through singing and are privileged to share with the Q'eros. Explanations, demonstrations, and participation through music are singular, major connectors for the guests to gain a profound glimpse into the deep meaning of Q'eros life. Sometimes the Q'eros break out in endearing laughter at the tentative attempts at *aysariykuy* in the guests' singing, and the humanness of these moments is fun and unifying.

The final portion of our sharing moves into spontaneous dialogue when I facilitate a conversation, and mutual questions and answers between Quechua and English.

FIGURE 7.6 A young US high school student on a National Geographic student group tour in Peru learns a Q'eros song.

(Photo by Holly Wissler, July 18, 2014)

Occasionally we will share about the Q'eros' singing their loss and grief in improvised song text in the animal fertility songs and rituals. Since those rituals are about life, they are also about death and remembrance of time when *ayni* was not reciprocated (see Wissler, 2009: 182–207). This topic only comes up when our conversation leads into it in some fashion, when all those involved are sharing about difficulties and loss in life. All sessions end with the Q'eros selling textiles that the women present have woven themselves, so that the money goes directly to that woman and her family and not through a broker.[21] Everything about the experience is intimate and direct. I believe this is as close a view and understanding of Q'eros music that one can possibly get within the structured framework of a two-hour session, outside of Q'eros.

FIGURE 7.7 A Q'eros man gives a "high five" to a US student on a National Geographic student group tour who has sung a Q'eros song with him.

(Photo by Holly Wissler, July 18, 2014)

Mutually Beneficial Exchange

Both the Q'eros and visitors have articulated numerous benefits from these sessions. Below is a sampling of quotations from some Q'eros and guests who have participated in these exchanges, which illuminate the resultant gains and expansive learning on both sides. I am referred to as *comadre* in the interviews with the Q'eros.[22]

Francisco Quispe Flores from Q'eros stated, "*Noqa thak kashani*"—'I am in peace' [with this work]. I feel a solidarity and *cariño* (affection) because this work is more personal," and Santos Machacca Apasa noted, "When we share about our lives and customs,

I feel *hatun sonqoyoq* (with a big heart)." Santos's mother, Beatríz Apasa Flores, described the fun and happiness she feels:

> *Nishu kusisqa kashani* (I am very happy). We talk, we laugh, we sing. It is fun to hear them sing our songs. They try to do *aysariykuy*, but it is very funny and we laugh. They are immersing themselves. This makes us happy, gives us satisfaction that others want to know our songs. And they can take the songs in their hearts to their family in the US.
>
> (all, personal communication, July 19, 2013)

Equal sentiments of the emotional affects of intimate sharing have been expressed by the foreign guests. Gayle Goschie, a client from Oregon who trekked with me on the Inca Trail to Machu Picchu in 2010 remembered:

> It was so exceptional to be sitting side by side, exchanging a little of ourselves with Holly's interpreting, hearing the feelings of the Q'eros through song. Such a personal experience that transported me back to ancient, ancient times. I will always remember sitting next to Juana, listening to her sing, and admiring the beauty of her and her loosely woven black skirt with its texture of burlap. The big wide diverse world was a little smaller at that moment.
>
> (personal communication, May 21, 2013)

Paralleling Gayle's sentiment, Bonnie and Krishna Arora from San Diego, California relayed:

> We first met the Q'eros while on a day hiking trip in the Sacred Valley [of the Incas]. They performed a prayer offering and, since it was our 34th wedding anniversary, they blessed our marriage. That day they touched us with the genuine love and kindness they showed, and we felt an instant connection. Meeting the Q'eros definitely impacted and changed our lives in many ways and we share that message and the story often with our friends.
>
> (personal communication, August 20, 2013)

Because of that first impactful meeting, Bonnie and Krishna returned to travel with me twice to Q'eros, donating family foundation funds to help build a much-needed bridge to connect the potato and corn zones, and becoming godparents to a Q'eros boy.

The Q'eros and visitors use many adjectives to describe a shared sense of opening, connection, and well-being that is attained during these exchanges: peace, *cariño*, with open-heart, satisfaction, exceptional, personal, and genuine expressions of love and kindness. "The big wide diverse world a little smaller" described by Gayle Goschie is the solidarity and personalized affection that Francisco Quispe addressed. Beatríz touches on the exchange aspect, that the Q'eros feel pride and satisfaction to share their music with the foreign guests, which they can take away to their country and family.

The exchanges facilitate a reciprocal learning and accessibility to one another's lives, which is directly related to the size and intimacy of our interactions, as Francisco articulates: "It is good to work in small groups and rotate the Q'eros who work. Sometimes I work, then another couple works. It is not good to invite a lot of Q'eros, because our sharing is not as good, not as close, and we don't sell as many weavings." Santos relays, "I learn about their lives too. We are always remembering them afterwards. They leave good memories." Santos continued to describe how large group size is an impediment:

> Last year A "Four Winds" trip[23] had 300 tourists in one group, with about eleven or twelve buses and one to two Q'eros per bus. This for me is commercial. Jealousies are created. The Q'eros do not have a voice; we cannot talk that much. We are representatives, but without a voice. It is the same thing with our performances for the Ministry of Culture. It is the small groups that are more valuable, where we do have a voice.
>
> (personal communication, July 19, 2013)

Equally, the tourists and students commented on the value of intimacy. Sarah Mayer, an undergraduate student in Iowa State University's Peru Program, 2013, and Staci MacCorkle, client on the Inca Trail trek to Machu Picchu in July 2010, report:

> The opportunity to have a genuine two-way discussion with the Q'eros was exceptionally unique. It is often really difficult to understand a culture, religion, or way of life so different from our own, but having the connection through Holly that could bridge the gap in understanding gave me a better appreciation of the Q'eros culture that is alive, vibrant, and meaningful, not stuff of strange folklore or mythology.
>
> (Sarah Mayer, personal communication, July 5, 2013)

> Having the opportunity to speak essentially one-on-one with community members was tremendously special and unique. So often, "village visit" activities arranged for international tourists are staged and motivated by particular issues and/or messages. This was very different. Speaking candidly with the Q'eros about their hopes, fears, and day-to-day concerns was both enlightening and, yet, normal. It was normal in the sense that our hopes, fears, and concerns are not that different; I could have been speaking with any of my American peers about the same topics. It was enlightening for the very same reason—no matter where we are in the world and where we call home, people are people; we have the same basic concerns about our quality of life and the resources available to enjoy a quality life.
>
> (Staci MacCorkle, personal communication, June 2, 2013)

The small size of our groups and direct conversations make it so there is no audience; every person involved has a voice, a place to ask questions and share thoughts. There is no agenda, no particular message, other than mutual learning and respect. Francisco stated that in large groups sharing was not as close, and Santos in particular described the frustration of the Q'eros not having a voice in large stagings by tour operators and the Ministry of Culture. He keenly differentiated between representative and voice: that the Q'eros are often representatives, but without a voice. Small groups allow the Q'eros to have a voice, providing an opportunity to share who they are without jealousies that arise when large groups of Q'eros work together. In the exchange held among the Q'eros in the tour group with Staci MacCorkle, we all realized, after about an hour of discussion, that in fact we were expressing the very same preoccupations about our personal lives: family welfare, money, health, and education. In this moment of discovery, we all fell silent and felt a strong sense of connectedness and solidarity. I would go so far as to say we experienced anthropologist Victor Turner's seminal definition of *liminality* and *communitas*: many felt a sense of awe, being in the moment, a bonding, and even love, that unites people of vastly different backgrounds and social realms (Turner, 1969, 1974).

Due to the small group size, a university student experienced the genuineness of the people who are not the "stuff of strange folklore or myth." The director of the Iowa State University program, Nancy Guthrie, called this "foundational reality," in her description:

> I think that our encounter with you and the Q'eros as individuals was a pivotal moment for some of my students in terms of having a window into this culture and people. Before that time together, they were somewhat ethnocentric in their language about Peru. Meeting the Q'eros and hearing about their music, weavings, animals, and way of life provided a foundational reality. This was not something they were reading about in a book.
> (personal communication, July 2, 2013)

Mutual respect, so necessary in this global and violent age, is garnered through this foundational reality. Different lifestyles and cultures can reveal the sameness in humanity through real exchange, as expressed by Staci MacCorkle, and also by Robin Davis, violinist and pharmacist from Boise, Idaho, after she spent many days with Agustin Machacca Flores in Q'eros in 2007:

> Agustín was a proud man with a self-effacing sense of humor. He was an affectionate husband and devoted father of four. He was determined to preserve the skills and customs of the Q'eros by promoting literacy in his family, and working closely with scholars such as Holly. As my admiration for him grew, I realized we shared a matched intelligence; mine applied in the technical realm of Western medicine, and his in the tenuous and demanding mountain existence of the Q'eros.
> (personal communication, July 11, 2013)

Robin came to find respectful equality in such differently manifested realities. Agustín was also able to articulate this shared equality through the process of debunking preconceptions and stereotypes that often results from direct encounters. The Q'eros are simply natural, just being who they are, and with dignity and professionalism they guide in the truthful sharing about the meaning of their music, as explained by Agustín:

> Before the tourists arrive they see photos of the *campesinos* (Andean people who live in the mountains). They feel *pena* (pity) for how we live, how we used to live. But when they meet us they learn about and appreciate how we can live in communities so far away. And we too are concerned about how they live. There is a camaraderie—a confidence that we build together. It is in this confidence that we come to understand one another. It is not that the Q'eros are more *tristes* (sad, poor) and the tourists less so. In the end we are in the same situation. We want to play our music for other tourists, but nobody understands the music. No one can explain it. *La comadre entendichishan* (makes it to be understood). *Chayachinakama* (until [the understanding] is made to arrive).
>
> When we sing and play for the tourists we feel like it is our profession. We are very proud. Our way of playing for them has *sinchi hatun valiq* (extreme value), because we share our customs and our music *ñawi ñawipura* (eye to eye), not via Internet or recording. Our music is very old, from our ancestors' time, and the *comadre* is the *chakawarmi* (bridge woman). The contact is very human, and we end knowing one another, hugging one another.
>
> We have taught *la comadre* the truth about our music. We included her in everything. And now she shares this truth with others. Everything is good because it is done in the basis of knowledge and truth. All of our hard work together is now bearing fruits. She doesn't invent some romantic story about us, like many do. We are in a school together, we are dispersing our knowledge little by little. *Q'ala rimarakushanchis, q'alamanta* (We converse clearly, transparently).
>
> (personal communication, July 19, 2013)

I believe it is of paramount importance to allow foreign guests to experience the Q'eros as they are, thus shattering any preconceptions, such as poor Andeans or romanticized Incas frozen in time, which can be seeds for breakthroughs about other cultural stereotypes. It is in face-to-face learning about one another when preconceptions can fall away. Part of the educational process of seeing the Q'eros, and other indigenous peoples as they are, is through simple and honest renderings and explanation of their music. Agustin takes rightful ownership in lovingly stating that it was the Q'eros who taught me about their music, so that we can pass it on to others through shared learning "in a school together." He is proud for having taught me, and respectfully acknowledges that I am the one that is necessary for "making it be understood," a direct agent, no middleman—from them to me to the foreign guests. It is this genuine presentation of their music that speaks to the hearts of the foreign guests.

Many experience a shift in perception about Q'eros music, and come to learn about the spiritual significance of their music through direct exchange, as Bonnie Arora states:

> Their music was quite different to us. At first it sounded very simple and repetitive, as it seemed to have a span of only a few notes. Then as we learned more of their deep spiritual connection with nature and we began to recognize the whiff of air as they sung as

a way to share their song, their happiness and sadness with nature, and the spirits that reside in the mountains and earth. The impact was overwhelmingly beautiful.

(personal communication, August 20, 2013)

Two undergraduate students in the ISU Peru program report on their perception of Q'eros music:

Our session was like nothing I had ever experienced before. Before traveling to Peru, I had taken a class about indigenous music in the Andes. However, the interaction we had with the Q'eros taught me things a book never could. I was able to see firsthand how excited they were to share an immense part of their culture. To them, music is their life. Without it, the *Apus* and *Pacha Mama* will not hear their prayers. I was in awe with their great reverence for their gods and how they utilized music to show this reverence.

(Kelsey Trejo, personal communication, July 2, 2013)

There are a few moments in my life that I look back on and feel as though it changed my life or perception of the world. For me, I feel that this encounter with the Q'eros will be one of them. Listening to their music and seeing their true passion for their indigenous language and culture not only opened my eyes to a different way of life, but it made me more curious and proud of my culture.

(Kelly Gifford, personal communication, July 2, 2013)

Even a class session conducted virtually by internet with Q'eros in Cusco and a Brandeis University (Boston) World Music class was able to transmit the deep meaning of the music, as Brandeis student Emily Altkorn describes:

What struck me most about our Skype class was intimate connection between Q'eros music and the daily lives of the Q'eros themselves. The Skype session showed me that the Q'eros aren't just "going through the motions"—the songs really do evoke the strong emotions that they are meant to and are an integral part of Q'eros life. Often when I'm in synagogue I find my mind wandering, as I wonder what I'll be doing later that day or when the service will be over. It was clear, though, that Inocencia did not feel this way about her ritual song. In some ways I think I envy her connections to her rituals and music, since I've never been able to feel a connection to my religion or my music (as they are separate to me) in such a pure, honest way.

(personal communication, April 22, 2014)

And Judy Eissenberg, professor of the Brandeis World Music class and professional violinist, experienced the meaning of Q'eros music, as she heard it in Q'eros, as a natural part of life's narrative.

It took a while before someone decided to sing, and when it happened, it was part of the flow of the evening. Earlier that day, I had seen the birds, the llamas, and flowers that were in the songs. I laughed at the earthy teasing of the women in one of the songs. . . . I was part of the world that these songs described. So the music was not so much an object at that moment, it was part of the evening, part of the narrative of life being lived.

(personal communication, August 21, 2013)

It is direct, interpersonal exchange that makes possible deep learning about the meaning of a vital music that goes beyond book learning. I believe when the exchanges spark analysis about one's own culture, as in the case of students Kelly Gifford and Emily Altkorn, that the sessions then have the possibility to reverberate through a person's continuing growth, encouraging self-reflection of one's own person and culture, which ultimately extends to respect for other cultures as a whole. Q'eros music in these settings is not a performed, staged object, but a lived narrative that goes far beyond the boundaries of a classroom and touches souls.

It is evident that the sharing of Q'eros music and life with foreign visitors has a profound impact for all involved. The Q'eros take pride in sharing their traditions (weavings, music, discussions of lifestyle), which are re-enforced and valued by them in the process of performance and transmission, while guests experience a new sound that promotes insightful, visceral, even life-changing learning about another people. For the guests, through the experience of listening and participatory singing, the music becomes insight into a people who live a vastly different lifestyle, yet this difference becomes accessible through perceiving their music as lived experience and "not stuff of strange folklore . . . " or any sort of staged and removed performance. The Q'eros have the opportunity to break through "poor Andean" and "romantic Inca" stereotypes, and be real people, on an equal sharing-basis. The Q'eros are their own "interpretive authorities" and active agents in how they present and explain their music, with my assistance as translator (Titon, 1999: 9). All of the above testimonies show that the mutual sharing of affect, sentiment, connection, dignity, and respect, as well as perception changes and deep learnings about Q'eros music, are only possible because of the eye-to-eye (*ñawi ñawipura*), firsthand, intimate, and direct conversations.

Chris Ryan, in his discussion of indigenous tourism, states, "Successful indigenous tourism products require awareness and exercise of a guardianship and/or teaching role" (Ryan, 2005: 9). Agustín discussed the learning/teaching element thoroughly: the guests learn about the Q'eros and their music, and the Q'eros continue to value their traditions through the mirror of our sessions. The guests begin to assimilate rich aspects of an Andean people and music they have never heard of before, fully enhancing their journey to Peru that otherwise would likely be just visits to archaeological sites without exposure to the people of the high Andes these sites are historically associated with. The Q'eros and myself monitor guardianship in the intimacy of the sessions: they are in charge of how they perform and what we say about it. There is no one else involved.

The Q'eros acknowledge the much-needed economic gain either through sale of their textiles or receiving a wage for their participation. Many times guests will reflect on differences in economic status in the global arena, and, acknowledging their economic advantage, will sometimes work with me afterward to see how they can satisfactorily donate some of their abundant resources toward a project that will benefit the Q'eros. These donations are unexpected bonuses that are born exclusively from the exchanges and are not a part of the original motivation or any agenda. From some of the resultant donations we were able to build the much-needed footbridge (2007), and have seed money for building a primary school in one of the Q'eros valleys that had no school (2010). Boniface and Robinson (1998) discuss how social and economic power relations must often be confronted, even if unspoken, when cultures meet. These issues are often less conflictive when dealt with at the personal level, when the guests have met and talked directly with the people to whom their donation will benefit, and can keep in touch about the projects via internet with me as liaison. Donating toward a needed community project is sometimes one way the US visitors deal with "white guilt" and economic difference in a way that is both personally satisfying to them and benefits the Q'eros.

Reciprocity in Indigenous Tourism with the Q'eros

Three of the principal attributes of successful exchange in our indigenous tourism activities that include music are *size, experience*, and *reciprocity*, which are interrelated and feed on one another. In regard to size, Ingram (2005), and Johnson and McIntosh (2005) touch on the lack of establishing one-on-one relationships as an impediment that leads to distortion when visiting the host groups Maori in New Zealand and aboriginal Australian. In the seminal Fourth 1986 International Colloquium "Traditional Music and Tourism" held in Kingston, Jamaica, Prime Minister Seaga of Jamaica declared: "[the] problem of presenting folk material in an authentic yet appropriate manner is the major barrier between traditional music and tourism" (Kaeppler and Lewin, 1986: 211). Prime Minister Seaga was referring to the inclusion of music in the large tourism industry in the Caribbean. What we do is nearly the opposite: there is nothing large-scale or national, or even regional, that our exchanges entail. What we achieve is orchestrated in an "appropriate manner," without "distortion," precisely because of the small numbers of people involved with direct dialogue. Distortion and unwieldiness are more likely to happen when presentation and exchange are on a larger scale and the intermediaries are not so intimately involved with the culture-bearers and their music.

Small-scale interaction allows Knudsen and Waade's "performative authenticity" to come to life, when projections about place and emotional state are successfully intertwined with in-the-moment tactile, emotional, corporeal, and interrelated experience (Knudsen and Waade, 2010: 12–16). They add, "Through the notion of performative authenticity we wish to point to the transitional and transformative processes inherent in the action of authentication . . . " (ibid.: 1). The transformative processes are actively co-created in sessions of deep learning exchange between the Q'eros and foreign guests. It is in these intense moments of co-creation that two aspects of performative authenticity emerge: relating empathetically to the other and/or connecting affectively to the world (ibid.: 2). Empathy and connecting affectively arise (such as similar preoccupations, as we experienced in one session) when travelers are not insulated and products are not artificial (Boorstin, 1961). Guests are not part of a distant audience; they are right there, up close and personal, in the midst of all experience, discussion, and musical presentation.

The most powerful exchanges are based in the experiential (i.e., not book learning or observation, but interaction). To reiterate Knudsen and Waade's idea of "Authentic" in tourism is neither a "... 'thing' you can possess, nor a 'state of mind', but something which people *do* and a feeling which is *experienced*" (Knudsen and Waade, 2010: 1, my emphasis). The director of the Iowa State University program echoed this idea when she stated that the "foundational reality" of the Q'eros' actions are "things that must be experienced to be understood," and cannot be read in a book. Through experience, the guests sing and *discover aysariykuy*; they gain an embodied perception of a basic life concept that is a driving force of a people whose life is expressed differently on the outside, yet cultural impasse is markedly lessened as we explore and experience more about one another. The experience of both listening to and active embodied participation of music are rich beginnings of understanding what makes another people tick. Ideally, the experience engenders emotional bonding that is a promotion of empathy and understanding between two very different cultures at a singular point in time, when the experience "transcend[s] the tourist frame to become real" (Titon, 1999: 8).

Tourists and students often express that in their short visit they feel as if they have met the "real" people of Peru. My understanding of this statement is that they are referring to the salt-of-the-earth indigenous Andeans, the original backbone of the pre-invasion populace, versus the urbanized service people (guides, hotel receptionists, drivers, etc.) with whom they spend the majority of their tour, and who are more similar in lifestyle. The success of our exchanges has much to do with equal reciprocity, that is, the ideal situation of *ayni* that has premised Andean relationship since pre-Hispanic times, and is the norm of operation with the Q'eros today.[24] The vast scale of exchange throughout the Andean, coastal, and Amazonian regions of the Inca Empire was premised on the effect that a particular good or service had on local relationship, that is, the empire's success was founded on local, small-scale reciprocity that nourished the web of imperial expansion. Through small-scale reciprocal sharing, we respond and collaborate spontaneously in song and discussion, preconceptions are debunked, and we gain a more real sense of one another, thus affecting relationship that can then expand into a larger web, as expressed in the above testimonies.

What is often brought forth are our genuine selves in awe of what we are experiencing. Both the guests and the Q'eros are served by experiences that are heart-opening and/or that change perceptions, providing quality insight into the other, and a sparking of new awarenesses that can continue into daily life. Guests make donations, treat the next person differently, learn about the life-and-death aspect of a vocal technique; the Q'eros learn about the real lives of foreigners, who otherwise would be just tourists walking on the busy street. In this way, the indigenous music of the Q'eros is co-experienced, not falsified or performed artificially—it is merely, and deeply, shared.

While ratios of Q'eros and guests in groups of 5, 10, or even 30 are small scale, often there is a vastness that opens up in the intimacy of exchange that is not small scale at all. The meeting of a few people and changes of perception that are stirred up often extends to how we interact with others as a result of what has happened to us in the exchange. In other words, in the intimacy of a focus, worlds open up. There is a temporary dissolving of separateness, and what results is gratitude and satisfaction.

I contend that these meetings are more effective human exchanges that result in a deeper, longer-lasting transmission of musical information and knowledge to the visitor than other styles of indigenous tourism where indigenous music is part of a staged program, folklorized or distanced from its original meaning. In the space we co-create together, the Q'eros have their own voice to share their music and lives, and equally, so do the tourists and students since all talking is dialogue and participation. This is an example of an active indigenous voice that we have nurtured together, and a meaningful way we have found to bring Q'eros knowledge and music to foreign visitors to Peru.

Adverse situations can occur when that voice is not nurtured and when reciprocity is not experienced as equal. This was the case with the Wachiperi community, who chose to revive some of their near-extinct songs upon emotional listening to archives of their deceased relatives, and who took issue with Cusco's Ministry of Culture, negating a CD publication proposition and instead took charge of their own production. A nearly opposite case, the Wachiperi voice strongly emerged under these very different, conflictive, and emotional circumstances. The story is as follows.

THE WACHIPERI: SONG REVIVAL AND UNESCO

Half of today's 7,000 spoken languages are on the brink of extinction, and over 600 of these have less than 100 speakers (Davis, 2009: 3–5). Wachiperi is one of these apocalyptically endangered languages. The Peruvian Amazon, like all of South America's Amazonia, has suffered tremendous decimation and active disappearance of land and peoples since the European invasion and the introduction of new diseases and devastation caused by the early twentieth-century rubber exploitation, when *caucheros* enslaved and relocated the people of the Harakbut linguistic group from their homeland region on the lower Madre de Dios River to the river's headwaters, which led to infighting among the Harakbut subgroups (Gray, 1996: 14).

In the twentieth century, forces such as mining, logging, evangelism, and cattle farming continue to contribute to the depletion of Amazonian culture and natural resources. Anthony Seeger states, "It's not as though these [musical cultures] are just disappearing, they're 'being disappeared'; there's an active process in the disappearance of many traditions around the world" (quote from Schippers, 2009 152). This has been the case with the Wachiperi of the Madre de Dios River Basin, located just north of the Q'eros Nation territory.

Today, there are approximately 50–60 Wachiperi who know their indigenous language, a sub-group of the Harakbut linguistic family.[25] This linguistic family includes the seven subgroups of languages and people: Arakmbut, Sapiteri, Kisamberi, Pukirieri, Asaraeri, Toyeri, and Wachiperi, many of which are extinct or drastically reduced in numbers.[26] When a language dies, naturally so do the songs that express the soul of the people—in this case the Wachiperi's expression of their healing knowledge and interdependence on the rivers, plants, animals, and birds in their jungle environment. Similar to other indigenous Amazonians, the Wachiperi used to live primarily from fishing, hunting and gathering, and small agricultural production of products such as corn and coca leaves. Since the early 1970s, gold mining has been a source of income for many Harakbut from gold deposits in the Madre de Dios river basin (see Gray, 1983, 1997a, 1997b). Today, many are now part of the urbanized world and hold typical jobs such as shop owners, work with various Amazonian products, such as lumber and coca, or migrate for work in larger cities of Puerto Maldonado and Cusco.

The Harakbut social and spiritual regulating mechanism, like that of the Q'eros, is based in reciprocity (see Alvarez, 2012; Gray, 1996, 1997a, 1997b; Moore, 1975; Tello, 2013). Among the Harakbut the principle of reciprocity is most visible in the relationship between people and nature. Nature constantly gives to the people (food, medicinal plants and products for subsistence, and today gold). The giving of nature to people can sometimes be activated by shamans who are guided by dream revelations. In return, the people must treat the diverse elements of nature with respect, otherwise they risk susceptibility to spiritual sanctions from natural sources.

Among the Harakbut, the patrilineal clan is the primary source of solidarity and reciprocity, and the classic articulation of reciprocal relationship between the men and nature is the hunt. The hunter dreams of his prey, and then upon waking departs to hunt it. If successful, the hunter must generously share his catch with extended family members, who expect to receive some portion of the meat, thereby reinforcing clan bonds Tello, 2013. In modern times, generosity has extended to the profits made from mining gold, which is used to buy food products (such as canned goods that are a luxury) and beer, which are shared with extensive family and community.

Key aspects of reciprocity in social contexts and relationships between Harakbut people and nature are generosity and respect. Some of the sanctions that ensue due to breeches in reciprocity and respect of people with nature are ostracism, and physical and spiritual damage, and even death from natural forces. Mutual respect between animals and humans is imperative. A Harakbut myth relates of an animal rebellion as a warning to people who do not treat animals with the due respect of a solemn hunt, particularly younger men who hunt with frivolity and sport and are then punished by the animals' spirits. For example, a person's soul can be trapped by the Amazonian growth and taken over by the physical and/or character aspects of an animal as a result of the more severe transgressions of reciprocity and lack of respect (Gray, 1997a). So the lowland Harakbut, like the highland Q'eros, take responsibility for their part in their relationship with and the consequences of their reciprocal relationships with the natural and spiritual powers.

Unlike the highland Q'eros who have inhabited their territory for centuries, the Harakbut Wachiperi are new to their recently established community on the Queros River. The Wachiperi historically did not have permanent settlements; rather, like many Amazonian inhabitants in sync with the rhythms of natural abundance, they lived off the plant, animal, and fishing resources of one river area, and then relocated every half year or so to let the area replenish while they exploited the resources from another. In this cyclic migration they were walkers of interfluvial territory as hunters, gatherers, fisherman, and later, farmers.

The Wachiperi lived in large, communal longhouses distributed among the many rivers of the Madre de Dios river basin, but were relocated in the 1950s and 1960s to tributaries farther upstream on and near a North American Baptist Mission. In the mid-1960s the majority of the Wachiperi consolidated into two native communities, La Comunidad Nativa de Queros (often just called Queros-Wachiperi) and Santa Rosa de Huacaria, which gained official legal community status in 1990 and 1985, respectively.[27] In 2008, the Amazon Conservation Association (ACA), a nongovernmental organization (NGO) based in Washington, D.C., along with their sister NGO in Cusco, *Asociación para la Conservación de la Cuenca Amazónica* (ACCA, Amazon Basin Conservation Association) addressed the historical displacement of the Wachiperi family groups from the Queros-Wachiperi community and brokered an agreement between the people and Peru's National Institute of Natural Resources (INRENA) to create the world's first land concession to be managed by an indigenous group located near their community. The Haramba Queros Wachiperi Conservation Concession protects 17,238 acres of highly diverse rainforest, a public land resource that is entrusted to the Wachiperi for a 40-year renewable concession in exchange for their active investment in conservation and sustainable development projects. The concession secures the Wachiperi water supply, sustains their access to forest products, and ideally helps the community maintain their cultural traditions.

ACA and ACCA were aware of my research with the Q'eros, and in 2010 they invited me to visit Queros-Wachiperi to share my work and see if there could be the possibility of cultural work with them as part of the land concession projects. Excited by the possibility of collaborating with people in Amazonia, in December 2010 I digitized and returned 15 reel-to-reels containing 206 Wachiperi songs that anthropologist Patricia J. Lyon had recorded with this community in 1964 and 1965. Lyon had recorded with the direct family elders of today's Queros-Wachiperi community, though even when she recorded they were no longer performing their songs due to their severe population loss and mission prohibition of *masateadas*, the communal gatherings for drinking, singing, and dancing; rather, the singers sang from memory, so that the songs were already in declension 10 or so years prior to Lyon's work with them.

The Wachiperi experienced profound, emotional reactions upon the unexpected hearing of their deceased relatives singing their indigenous songs—songs that many of the younger generation had not ever heard—which galvanized the community into discussion about the revival and preservation of a selection of these songs before the onset of total loss.[28] I received some basic funding support from ACA and ACCA to travel to the community and conduct workshops focused on song and cultural preservation, which mainly consisted of long days listening to Lyon's recordings, discussions about their meaning, and reminiscing about the past. The only three remaining elders alive from the Queros-Wachiperi community, Manuel Yonaje, Carmen Jerewa, and Estela Dariquebe, recounted how they used to walk long distances from their disperse river homes for community gatherings in one host home, drink *masato*, and express their connection to spirits, plants, and animals through days-long drinking and singing (Figure 7.8). These *masateadas* were times of joyful reconnection with other Wachiperi whom they had not seen for some time, "back when we were many people," Manuel recalled.

Manuel described the gatherings: before the drinking of masato started, one by one the men would sing *embachiha*, solo unaccompanied songs that invoked birds, animals, and natural elements such as the moon and stars, with layers of meaning about migrating birds, which are metaphors for the people meeting and departing in welcome and farewell, and also code about the white people's invasion. Later in the night when the *masato* began to flow, they sang *embachinoha*, which they also refer to as *cantos de borracho*, or improvised drunken songs. This was the permissible time and space to

FIGURE 7.8 Estela Dariquebe, Carmen Jerewa, Manuel Yonaje: The three elders of the Queros-Wachiperi community who remember the traditional songs.

(Photo by Holly Wissler, May 12, 2012)

vent personal aggressions, when both men and women expressed individual grievances through song, some quite directly about and toward other community members, often sparking verbal and physical fights (Lyon, 1967: 73–74).

I recorded a number of *embachiha* with old Manuel. One of the songs we were able to revive with a group of about eight Wachiperi was *Kapiro*, about the great egret that returns annually, and is therefore a song of return and welcome. [▶ and ▶ "Kapiro" recorded in 2010 and 1965 respectively] Our project had forward momentum in the first year after my return of the archives, when we shared many touching moments of listening and singing a few temporarily revived songs, such as "Kapiro." A core of about six community members, all of whom spoke Wachiperi, proved to be the most committed to learning some songs. However, the initial idea of reviving many different topical songs proved to be difficult and slow, partly because of division and friction between the urban Wachiperi who had migrated years ago to the more modern community of Pilcopata on the road, and the families who still lived in the community inside the forest. In our third year together we eventually, and mutually, let go of the idea of long-term song revival, simply because Wachiperi music is not sustainable. Jeff Titon defines sustainability of music as "a music culture's capacity to maintain and develop its music now and in the foreseeable future" (Chapter 5 of volume 1). Wachiperi musical culture lacks the resilience "to recover and maintain its integrity, identity, and continuity when subjected to forces of disturbance and change," which, in this case, are critically reduced numbers of Wachiperi and native speakers and loss of original singing context (ibid.).

We did, however, manage to add to the community archive by recording and thoroughly discussing seven *esüwa*, or Wachiperi healing songs, a genre that Lyon did not record during her time with the community 50 years prior. *Esüwa* are not sung during the *masateadas*; rather, these healing songs are passed down through generations of healers (*wamanokkaeri*) and performed privately in intimate one-on-one (healer/patient) contexts, usually at nighttime when the forest spirits are more active.[29] A *wamanokkaeri* visits the ill person invokes the appropriate plant or animal spirits to assist in the healing, and uses a combination of singing *esüwa* (with no instrumental accompaniment) blowing, spitting, and application of plant salves to begin the healing process. Because of the personal nature of *esüwa*, the Wachiperi feel strongly that this genre is not to be exposed in the public arena; so our recordings were solely intended to add to the community archive, and the elders profoundly enjoyed remembering these songs and sharing them with me.

In March and May of 2011, I recorded seven *esüwa* with Carmen Jerewa and Estela Dariquebe, the only two remaining elders of the Queros-Wachiperi community who had once been practicing healers. Carmen still occasionally performs healings with *esüwa*, yet in general the actual practice is in rapid decline. Estela is now blind and simply too frail and with fluctuating lucidity to practice healing. We recorded the seven *esüwa* songs they could draw from memory, and documented information about each one as part of our mutual learning process in our sessions together. In addition to Carmen and Estela, there are some four or five members of the Santa Rosa de Huacaria community who remember these songs and practice healing with them. In particular I remember hearing about Alejandro Dumas from Huacaria, who lived to be nearly 100 and had the regional reputation of being a master healer. He died in early 2010, just before I started my work with the Wachiperi, and his daughter, Lidia, lamented not having taken the initiative to learn *esüwa* healing practice from him, and now it is too late. It is for these reasons—less than 10 elders who know and practice *esüwa* healing with its transmission in severe decline—that UNESCO nominated the *esüwa* to the List of Intangible Cultural Heritage in Need of Urgent Safeguarding on November 25, 2011.

Esüwa Healing Songs

The *esüwa* I recorded and discussed with Estela Dariquebe and Carmen Jerewa were the following:

1. *Bapokate esüwa*. Recorded with Carmen Jerewa, March 19, 2011. For calming hurricanes and strong winds in order to prevent serious damage.
2. *Ekuchirite esüwa*. Recorded with Carmen Jerewa, March 19, 2011. For healing debilitating headaches and migraines.
3. *Wamiekate esüwa*. Recorded with Carmen Jerewa, March 21, 2011.
   For healing diarrhea. This song describes many different kinds of dogs and their varied colorful markings, symbolic of the way an ill person's diarrhea may look.
4. *Ekpuguyte esüwa*. Recorded with Carmen Jerewa, March 21, 2011.
   For curing pulled ligaments. *Ekpuguy* has the repetitive invocation in a mantra or chant style of many types of particularly strong plants and animals. They relayed to me that "just like the plants are humans, like a human, and we believe in the plants, it is because of this we invoke the strong plants with urgency so that the ligament will be strong."
5. *Mbpehekaieesüwa*. Recorded with Estela Dariquebe, March 21, 2011.
   To call back a person's *animo* or spirit, when he or she is near death. The healer sings, "why do you want to leave when we are doing well here? Don't go, come back, come back." The song tells of the clear trail that one walks on when we are dying, but the healer places plants as obstacles in the path so that the person's spirit will return.
6. *Emepükete esüwa*. Recorded with Carmen Jerewa, March 21, 2011.
   For healing *susto*, a phenomenon experienced in both the Andes and the Amazon when one has experienced a great fright, causing a person's spirit to leave the body, thus making it vulnerable for malignant spirits to enter. The healer sings, "Where have you gone, why did you leave, why did you go so far, come here, come here, your spirit is scared, in every place I am calling your spirit to return."
7. *Etakte esüwa*. Recorded with Carmen Jerewa, May 13, 2011.
   For the prevention or cure of a fishbone getting stuck in your throat. The song names many birds that have the proper phlegm to swallow fish easily, such as the *hakuypina*—snakebird (*Anhinga anhinga*).

In addition, Peru's Ministry of Culture created a list of the following *esüwa* in 2013: *Bihichindign* (snakebite cure); *Totochindign* (to cure when one's spirit is trapped by evil forces); *Wewëchindign* (to cure high fever); *Ekmimichindai* (to cure hemorrhages); *Washisopachindign* (to cure cramps); *Nokirëngte emanokkae* (to free the patient from the negative energy of a deceased person that keeps the patient trapped between life and death); *Ekhen* (to lessen a river's flooding, thereby creating a riverbank so that one can cross unharmed to the other side); *Ugate emanka* (to tame the enemy. The enemy's bad energy is absorbed, converted to good and used so that both sides live peacefully; so that a person's love will be reciprocated; and also a technique to tame birds before the hunt); *Ewäsösuwa* (to remove or alienate a person); *Hindakkoichindign* (to cure cut wounds) (*Cantos Wachiperi* CD liner notes, 2013).

Every *esüwa* is a chant-like repetition that invokes animal, plant, and forest spirits, and describes manifestations of the illness usually through metaphor. Often vocables are added to ends of words, for example a nonsensical suffix is added to plant names in *Ekpuguyte esüwa*, for rhythmic ease of rapid-fire repetition. The Wachiperi openly discussed their beliefs about the *Oteri*, or powerful benevolent forest spirits, who are called upon to help in the healing. These spirits are rarely seen because they reside in particularly dense and untouched areas of the forest, which they articulated as an important reason for forest conservation on their land concession. I asked Carmen to perform a healing on me for *susto*, to help with a particularly anxiety-producing situation I was dealing with at the time (see Figure 7.9). After singing the song, Carmen spit and blew the song on various parts of my body. The idea of "blowing the song" for healing and to connect a person with spiritual powers is similar to *aysariykuy* in Q'eros songs: the expelled breath that sends the song out to the *Apu* for connection in offering.[30]

It is because of my preliminary research of the *esüwa*, and the trust I had garnered with one of the two Wachiperi communities, that I wanted to participate in, and felt I should be a part of, the Cusco Ministry of Culture's team that was responsible to UNESCO for the safeguarding[31] of the Wachiperi *esüwa*.[32] At that point in time, I was the only person actively working on the research of the newly nominated *esüwa*. I presented my work to the Cusco director of the Ministry of Culture, David Ugarte, who officially (via written document) invited me to be a part of the team; however, ensuing differences in work ethic with the Ministry of Culture proved to be obstacles in my working with them.

Issues with the Safeguarding of *Esüwa* and Song Ownership

I have observed many struggles and conflicts of interest between the Wachiperi and the Cusco division of the Ministry of Culture (MC-DDCC, Dirección Desconcentrada de Cultura, Cusco, which I refer to as MC hereafter) since UNESCO's naming of the *esüwa* as Intangible Cultural Heritage (ICH). A principal issue is that the Wachiperi emphatically state that any recordings of the *esüwa* are not to be used or distributed publicly, due to the fact that this is sacred knowledge and transmission is only through the act of healing. The safeguarding measures proposed by the MC on the application to UNESCO

FIGURE 7.9 Carmen Jerewa, the only active healer and esuwa singer in the community of Queros-Wachiperi.

(Photo by Holly Wissler, February 19, 2012)

conflict with this taboo, such as Article 1d of section 3b, entitled "Safeguarding measures proposed": "Promotion and dissemination of the *Eshuva* songs: Production of a CD-ROM with a selection of *Eshuva* songs selected and performed by the Huachipaire"[33] and "Production of a documentary in DVD-ROM format depicting the main features of the *Eshuva*."

When I discussed this issue with Regis Andrade, long-term anthropologist employed by the MC, former member of the MC's ethnodevelopment plan with the highland Q'eros and member of the MC's *esüwa* safeguarding team in 2013, he explained that the intended use of any of the MC's recordings of *esüwa* will be in the Intercultural Bilingual Education (EIB) curricula in both communities. The ideal model in the EIB system is that teaching goes beyond instruction in two languages (for example, Quechua/ Spanish in Q'eros, and Wachiperi/Spanish in Queros-Wachiperi and Santa Rosa de Huacaria), to include the indigenous community's traditional knowledge in the school curricula alongside the national curricula, via committed family members who collaborate regularly with the teachers and students. In this way the MC is proposing a completely new form of transmission of the *esüwa*: that the traditional intergenerational transmission of the genre, which is nearly nonexistent, be replaced by collaborative, inter-institutional and familial cooperation in the public education system. Andrade justifies that this use of the *esüwa* recordings is not public since it will not go beyond the schools of the Wachiperi communities (personal communication, September 17, 2013). However, there is no plan as of yet for the implementation of *esüwa* in the EIB curricula of the communities, and only initial discussions have begun with the communities about this idea. The larger issue here, though, is the lack of knowledge about, in Anthony Seeger's terms, "local ideas of appropriate control over transmission of knowledge" (Seeger, 2012: 28). This is the case with the MC who, according to personal accounts from some Wachiperi, lack communication with the communities as to what would be appropriate regarding the safeguarding measures of the transmission of *esüwa*. Meanwhile, the main safeguarding activity between the MC and the communities has been the collaborative editing of the Harakbut dictionary (first of its kind, publication 2015), which the MC envisions as a tool for language preservation.

I believe both the MC and the Wachiperi are still in a time of adjustment to the UNESCO nomination, including any sort of mutual understanding as to what this exactly means, and with no long-term safeguarding plan yet in place—four years after nomination. Many Wachiperi have articulated their dissatisfaction, expressing that any efforts at safeguarding made thus far are superficial. For example, the MC has built a *Casa de la Memoria*—Memory House—in both Queros-Wachiperi and Huacaria. This is simply a large building (based on the former Wachiperi communal longhouse model) that provides the Wachiperi with a physical space to "perform the *Eshuva* and a place for the local elderly to transmit to the youth other expressions of their intangible cultural heritage" (safeguarding objective 1b). Yet on the day of the official inauguration of the *Casa de la Memoria* in Santa Rosa de Huacaria, August 30, 2013, the President of the community, Marisabel Dumas, specifically asked the Cusco director of the MC, David Ugarte, about a plan and funding for use. Ugarte curtly replied that the MC does not have a budget for any projects, and that this should come from UGEL (*Unidades de Gestión Educativa Local*), the local education office that serves the Wachiperi communities. So at this point the shell of the building exists, with no proposed plans or budget for use, other than a suggestion to use the space to "remember Wachiperi traditions." If there is little intergenerational transmission of *esüwa* in the privacy of family homes, it seems absurd to think that the people will walk over to the large building to do it.

Alberto Manqueriapa, an outspoken Wachiperi leader and healer from Santa Rosa de Huacaria, was offended by the colorful pamphlets the MC printed in early 2012 that announce the declaration of *esüwa* as ICH by UNESCO. He highlighted one incorrect statement that informs that the *esüwa* are sung during the drinking of *masato*, and are therefore associated with inebriation. Alberto, with others, posed for the pamphlet photos in their *cushma*, or newly adopted "traditional" dress made of tree bark, yet he says he feels like a *payaso* (clown) when he does this. Wachiperi traditionally wore no clothes, and it is only in recent times that they have adopted the *cushma* as "traditional" dress. He explained that it seems ironic to don the *cushma* as public Wachiperi identity when it was never their original dress and the reality is that in daily life the Wachiperi use Western dress. Alberto, like my Q'eros friends, expressed acute aggravation at feeling used by the MC when he is called on to represent the Wachiperi at MC celebratory events in Cusco. He angrily added that he feels like the token Wachiperi on stage in his *cushma*, while his wife is at home working hard to get food for their children and the people of his community need education. He stated unequivocally that he has little faith in the safeguarding plan of the MC (personal communication, September 10, 2013). The ex-President of the Queros-Wachiperi community, Walter Quertehuari, expressed that the MC seems like *pura pinta* (pure makeup), and he asked, "To what benefit is it to the community that we work on these songs with them?" (personal communication, February 19, 2012). These statements indicate that some Wachiperi, in particular the community leaders, feel as if the process of donning Wachiperi identity and safeguarding traditions and songs are exercises they do for the MC, versus any sort of collaborative commitment.

Renato Cáceres, former director of the Ethnodevelopment Department of the Direction, Production, and Diffusion of Culture in the MC, who also became active in initial *esüwa* safeguarding efforts before choosing to leave the MC, stated that the MC does not know what true safeguarding is. He acknowledged the complexity of effective safeguarding, adding, "neither do I." He pointed out that the MC holds no training seminars or studies of other successful safeguarding models in the world in order to learn about effective safeguarding measures, neither during the application process nor after nomination. He reiterated that the *esüwa* should not be recorded or used lightly, and so that even the proposed superficial safeguarding plan could not be implemented since so much is based on recording.

Professional archaeologists in the field in Peru express similar inadequacies in regards to the MC's safeguarding and management of the area's spectacular Inca archaeological sites. Global case studies of successful management of a culture's major archaeological inheritances are also not consulted; rather, a common complaint is that the MC works in a very local, willy-nilly way, roping off sections of archaeological sites for no apparent reason, and reconstructing Inca walls in ways that have proved controversial, such as the use of cement instead of local materials.

In the case of the *esüwa*, it seems that what is essentially missing is focus on safeguarding plans about preservation and sustenance of the practice per se, versus the recording and archiving of *esüwa* songs that are one aspect of the holistic healing process. The tradition bearers do not have a sense of empowerment, or even collaboration, with the government entity that applied for this international recognition on their behalf. In my discussions with some of the Wachiperi, they complain that they were not included in the design of the safeguarding action plans from the beginning, which is one of the nomination shortcomings noted by past Secretary General of ICTM (International Council for Traditional Music) Anthony Seeger in his informative article on the evaluation process of ICH nominations to UNESCO (Seeger, 2009: 122). The fact that no funding has yet been sought from UNESCO for safeguarding relieves the MC and the Wachiperi of any sort of obligation to UNESCO (ibid.: 116), so that ineffectual safeguarding, confusions, and even conflicts between the MC and the Wachiperi are simply the current status. MC anthropologist Andrade commented that without the UNESCO nomination, the Wachiperi would simply continue to be neglected by the

Peruvian government, as they have been for decades. He reiterated that at least now, with the nomination, they are gaining much public attention and hopefully effective interinstitutional safeguarding plans in the future (personal communication, September 17, 2013). The question that arises, then, is about the value of such attention if it comes rife with conflict and misunderstandings.

Taking Action into Their Own Hands: Wachiperi CD Production

In late October 2011 the MC offered me a contract, from newly disbursed Ministry funds, to produce a CD of Wachiperi songs with the Wachiperi—a project that suddenly became more poignant after the UNESCO naming a month later. They wanted the CD production to include many of Lyon's archival recordings, as well as my recent ones of *embachiha* (songs of animals, birds, and natural elements), and also some of the newly nominated *esüwa*. At that point in time, the seven *esüwa* that I had recorded with the community were only intended for the community archive. The MC made it clear that these funds would roll over at year-end (i.e., in three months), so I felt institutional pressure to complete the CD production with the Wachiperi as soon as possible. At first I was enticed by the idea of funding for a collaborative CD production with the Wachiperi, something we had talked about during our sessions in the Queros-Wachiperi community but had not yet moved forward on, but I needed to consult with the community first.

I had already planned my annual November sojourn to the United States and the Society for Ethnomusicology (SEM) conference, so only on December 4 was I able to present the idea of an MC-sponsored CD production to the Queros-Wachiperi community. This meant we had a short month to complete a CD production if they decided that was what we wanted to do. I was surprised to discover that they did not yet know of the UNESCO naming that had happened over a week prior, which I had candidly mentioned. In reaction, Walter Quertehuari, the President of the community at the time, complained about the lack of consultation on the part of the MC with the community about the application process in the first place. While they did express interest in having a product they could use to promote their Wachiperi identity, particularly when tourists came to their community (which is minimal due to lack of infrastructure and a solid community-based tourism plan), they were also clear that they did not want to work on the production under the auspices of the MC. Quertehuari was direct in his exasperation at the fact that I had done the footwork regarding the return of archives and holding workshops with the community throughout the year, and that we should not allow the MC to suddenly take credit for a production that borrowed both from the community archives (Patricia Lyon's recordings and my new ones) and our work sessions together, which had been partially funded by other entities: the nongovernmental organizations ACA and ACCA. The community agreed in consensus, so that in this moment I witnessed the Wachiperi taking ownership of their work and archives. Fully understanding and accepting their position, upon return to Cusco I broke the news, to the consternation of the MC, and did not enter into contractual agreement with them. Personally I was relieved, as I was beginning to experience the common operating procedure of the MC's bureaucracy, which is a system of delayed, mid-year disbursement of funds for projects that are expected to be completed in insufficient time before year-end. This enforced urgency, combined with a lack of project longevity and vision due to regular turnover in directive staff that is based on the changing political calendar, make the MC projects based in personal agendas, in Cácere's words, versus long-term, collaborative, and visionary projects.

In reaction, the community suggested that we do our own CD production, a proposal that was undoubtedly born from strong feelings of ownership of Patricia Lyon's archives, which I was moved to see them guard so unambiguously. As Seeger states, "Ideas about rights over music are often closely intertwined with important concepts of person, ideas about the origin and significance of sound, and also about relations of power" (Seeger, 2012: 32). The small community of Queros-Wachiperi was fiercely guarding the significant sound recordings of their direct family members, thereby negating a government power that regularly attempts to implement cultural support in ways that lack communication (no conversation about nomination plans and announcement, plans for safeguarding), and that often seem useless (building of the *Casa de la Memoria* as a space to revive cultural tradition), violable (a contract to record *esüwa* for possible public use), and degrading (demeaning staged performances for MC agenda).

With the idea now sparked, we began conversations of how to do a CD production, with no or limited funding. We saw the opportunity of linking the CD production to the first ever Jungle Ultra Marathon, an international event to be held the Kosñipata district in May 2012, the district location of the Queros-Wachiperi and Santa Rosa de Huacaria communities. This six-day mega race with professional runners from around the world, covered by international press, was to be staged to raise international awareness about the multiple conservation efforts in the region. I proposed that we produce the CD in time to be sold at this event to raise awareness about Wachiperi culture, and the community was enthusiastic about the idea. I used all the remaining funds I had received from ACA for my work with the Wachiperi for this production, which was in line with the meeting in late 2011 when group consensus negated funding from the MC. This, then, became a project by and for the community.

We mutually decided on the round number of 20 songs for the CD, 17 from Patricia Lyon's archives and three that I had recorded in 2010 and 2011 with Manuel Yonaje. All of the 10 singers whom Lyon recorded were to be represented, and song topics were to be varied. The small group of community members involved in song selection cherished the time listening to all 10 singers (Manuel Yonaje and Estela Dariquebe were the only two of the 10 still living), and selecting the songs that represented a variety of Amazonian birds and mammals, such as the mealy parrot, great egret, macaw, howler monkey, jaguar, and spectacled bear. The community decided we should list the singers' Wachiperi names along with the names they adopted for, and are known by, in the urban world. For example, Estela's name in Wachiperi is Yorine, and Manuel's is Meyopa. *Embachinoha*, or *cantos de borracho*, were also selected. It was clear that no *esüwa* were to be included, as the MC had wanted, for the obvious reasons outlined above.

The production was inexpensive and completely homemade. We touched up some of the sound from Lyon's recordings when possible, and I completed the master in my home office and ordered two hundred copies to be burned at a CD/DVD production store in a crowded local mall in Cusco. I selected three photographs of the living elders, Manuel, Carmen, and Estela, and collected photos of two deceased singers from family members, and designed a few cover options in a graphic design shop in Cusco. Inside the cover we included a small synopsis of the original singing context and song genres, which was co-written by two educated Wachiperi (the President of the community, Walter Quertehuari, and a university graduate living in Cusco, Joel Jawanchi, son of one of the original singers) and myself. In this summary they were able to include what they felt accurately represented the community, and I was able to add information about Patricia Lyon, an imperative since most of the songs on the CD were from her archives. In the end we were up against the deadline of the start of the marathon, and I was not fully satisfied with the information (mostly the writing style), but the content was satisfactorily inclusive and representative. Due to this last-minute rush, our final communications and decision-making about the CD summary notes were all by cell phone and internet to the Wachiperi who lived in Pilcopata on the road, since there is no electricity, internet, or phone service in the community itself (see Figures 7.10 and 7.11).

This final flurried and constant communication about the last details of the CD production with the Wachiperi in the Peruvian Amazon is a far cry from the days when Anthony Seeger made a collaborative music CD with the Suyá of Brazil (1976), when a single communication often took weeks or months. I was able to send mp3 files via the internet for final approval, while Seeger would mail a cassette tape that would take weeks to arrive and often be unplayable due to broken cassette players or lack of batteries (Seeger, 2008: 276). What remains the same, though, is that "the process, as much as the product" was important for both parties (ibid.: 275). This collaborative process is addressed by Luke Lassiter opens his groundbreaking book *The Chicago Guide to Collaborative Ethnography* with a section from the El Dorado Task Force Papers of the American Anthropological Association:

> The El Dorado Task force insists that the anthropology of indigenous peoples and related communities must move toward "collaborative" models, in which anthropological research is not merely combined with advocacy, but inherently advocative in that research is, from the outset, aimed at material, symbolic, and political benefits for the research population, as its members have helped to define these.
>
> (Lassiter, 2005: ix)

Today it seems that collaborative, advocative research aimed toward the benefit of and defined by the research population is much more possible as the world becomes "smaller," with quick communication and easier road travel. It was the Wachiperi

FIGURE 7.10 Front cover, Wachiperi CD: *Cantos Wachiperi: Familia lingüística Harakbut, Grupo étnico Wachiperi*.

(Photo of the Queros (Q'eros) River in the background)
(Recently "Harakmbut" has become the more acceptable spelling of the linguistic group)

themselves who took the reins and insisted we not work with the MC (political stance); rather, create a product that would stand for who they are now (independent choice, material and symbolic benefit) and what their history is, with symbolic representation including the wealth of Patricia Lyon's materials, and equal representation of their past community members.

Over the next months we sold the CDs at the typical low, affordable CD price (10 soles for locals, about $4, and 20 soles to tourists if they were willing). We sold directly, via various avenues: to marathon spectators; at a hotel reception in Pilcopata; a popular café in Cusco; and to many friends via word of mouth. Every Wachiperi family received their own copies. The sales were slow, but after a year and a half I returned the proceeds to the

1) Apane: *Jaguar* (Jaguar); interpretado por Mariano Dariquebe (Darikewe).
2) Hadndari: *Oso de anteojos* (Spectacled bear); interpretado por Francisco Jerewa (Dactakewerepa).
3) Toyore: *Coto Mono* (Red Howler Monkey); interpretado por Manuel Yonaje (Meyopa).
4) Mawäi: *Loro Boliviano* (Blue-and-yellow macaw); interpretado por Alejandro Jahuanchi (Darikiking). Derechos Reservados © 2012.
5) Miritkewa: *Loro verde de las alturas* (green parrot); interpretado por Carlos Jerewa (Yorampa).
6) Mireng: *Loro verde pequeño*, (small green parrot); interpretado por Alejandro Jahuanchi (Darikiking). Derechos Reservados © 2012.
7) Towaro: *Loro aurora* (Mealy parrot); interpretado por Mariano Dariquebe (Darikewe).
8) Kapiro: *Garza* (great egret), Canto de Bienvenida; interpretado por Mariano Dariquebe (Darikewe).
9) Canto de Fiesta: Interpretado por Estela Dariquebe (Yorine).
10) Pu'hügn Hörokhe: "*La luna ya no sale*", (The moon has not yet risen); interpretado por Benjamin Marenyo (Sanenwa).
11) Canto de confraternidad con los Toyeri: (Remembering the Toyeri people); interpretado por Francisco Jerewa (Dactakewend'epa).
12) Canto de Fiesta: Interpretado por Maria Dariquebe (Dactachihenembio). Derechos Reservados © 2012.
13) Canto de Fiesta: Interpretado por Mercedes Hybue (Nakohikembe).
14) Canto de Fiesta: Interpretado por Palomino Nanchiwakepa, (Hankosi).
15) Korawa: *Estrella* (Star); interpretado por Carlos Jerewa (Yorampa).
16) Wambedn: *Pájaro de color rojo de la altura*; interpretado por Mariano Dariquebe (Darikewe).
17) Canto de Fiesta: Interpretado por Estela Dariquebe (Yorine).
18) Kapiro: *Garza* (great egret), Canto de Bienvenida; interpretado por Manuel Yonaje (Meyopa).
19) Tombahoya: El rio se los está llevando, ("The River is carrying them away"); interpretado por Manuel Yonaje (Meyopa).
20) Iwande: *Canto de Despedida* (Farewell Song); interpretado por Manuel Yonaje, (Meyopa).

Cantos 1-17 recopilados por la antropólogo Patricia J. Lyon entre 1964 y 1965.
Cantos 18-20 recopilados por la etnomusicóloga Holly Wissler entre 2010 y 2011.

Reserva Haramba Queros Wachiperi

www.queros.net
E-mail: comunidad@queros.net

QUEROS WACHIPERI

COMUNIDAD NATIVA

2012 todos los derechos reservados por la Comunidad Nativa Queros-Wachiperi

FIGURE 7.11 Back cover, Wachiperi CD. CD song contents.

community, and they agreed by consensus that all profits were to go toward the purchase of medicines for the three elders.[34] In this way the production was by the Wachiperi, for the Wachiperi, a record of their past and present, done in their way, with their choices and voice, with resultant proceeds that went to the only three elders who remember this invaluable, nearly extinct, song tradition.

The MC's interest in using selections from Lyon's archives in a CD production initiated questions of ownership and nervousness at possible co-option on the part of the MC. We took this opportunity to investigate at INDECOPI (*Instituto Nacional de Defensa de la Competencia y de la Protección de la Propiedad Intelectual*—the national institute that protects intellectual property), only to discover that the Wachiperi would need to show legal proof of song inheritance in order to register ownership of the community's (anonymous) songs—that is, that the song authors had imparted these songs on legal documents to the current community members. They have the right to interpret the songs in the same way their deceased family members did, but "interpreters do not have rights to ownership," as the INDECOPI employee explained to us. As Seeger points out, copyright laws originated in (white, urban upper-class) Europe, were "intimately linked to the figure of the author," and "little thought was given to creating legislation for unwritten and unpublished traditions," that were performed by illiterate, oral cultures (Seeger, 2005: 78). It seems this colonial practice is still in existence in Peru, and this community's songs and collective knowledge cannot be legally protected. The Wachiperi perception is that the original author of their songs was the *gallinazo*, or turkey vulture, who created the songs when the bird was still human. But again, as Seeger indicates in reference the ownership rights of the Suyá songs of Mato Grosso, Brazil, "How does one define a jaguar as individual author?" (Seeger, 2004: 76).

Seeger also points out that, apart from sound, "Music is also a web of rights and obligations that both establish relationships among people and organizations and are also an expression of those relationships" (Seeger, 2004b: 70). In this case, the expression of relationship by the Wachiperi was to say a direct "no" to the powerful Ministry of Culture, and assertively do a CD production in their way, reclaiming the possession of their traditional intellectual property.

In 2013 the MC did produce a CD entitled *Cantos Wachiperi*. Renato Cáceres was sent to record the three song categories for this CD, *embachiha*, *embachinoha*, and *esüwa*, with elders in Santa Rosa de Huacaria and Queros-Wachiperi communities. This was one of his final assignments with the MC before resigning due to differences in work ethic. He stated that he felt "false, hypocritical, and deceitful" during recording, since he had no pre-established relationship with the singers or the Wachiperi as a whole, and he was beginning to understand that the *esüwa* should not be recorded in this superficial manner (personal communication, July 15, 2013). In this CD production, the MC no longer raised the possibility of implementing songs from Patricia Lyon's archival recordings, and in the end did not add the *esüwa* to the CD due to the insistence of the Wachiperi, and instead housed these *esüwa* recordings in the MC archives for the time being.

A recent conversation with a member of the MC *esüwa* safeguarding committee, who preferred to remain anonymous, shed light on the latest status of safeguarding measures. He stated that the original plan leading up to UNESCO nomination was to record and diffuse as many *esüwa* as the MC could, but since the Wachiperi are not in agreement, it is up to them to decide what the safeguarding plan should be. This simplistic explanation and delegation of responsibility to the Wachiperi has currently put a standstill to any safeguarding efforts (personal communication, February 9, 2015). Teresa Campos, area coordinator for indigenous community rights at the MC, and overseer of the *esüwa* safeguarding team in Cusco, succinctly said that safeguarding efforts are currently *congelado*—frozen (personal communication, February 11, 2015). So it seems that what is in store for the future between the MC and the Wachiperi is a total re-assessment of effective safeguarding measures and implementation—or not. Ideal applied ethnomusicology in this scenario would be collaboration and mutual work ethic from all involved parties (MC, ethnomusicologists, anthropologists, community members), yet, when this is not possible, it is ultimately up to the people themselves to take their own stance, which the Wachiperi have and do.

Conclusion

The important components of efficacy and measures of success in specific music projects with the Q'eros (indigenous tourism) and the Wachiperi (CD production) are the combination of small-scale shared experience, co-collaboration, and equal status of everyone involved. The established base of reciprocity that upheld the ancient Inca empire, and Andean and Amazonian communities historically and currently, is also imperative and operative on the smallest of levels for respectful human interaction and exchange. In our projects, many aspects of a mutually beneficial relationship are present and operative. It makes sense that reciprocity is the preferred interaction in projects when it is the foundation of life among the Q'eros and the Wachiperi.

In the case of the highland Q'eros, their active voice in indigenous tourism has been an organic process that we have been developing and fine-tuning for about ten years now. We have learned, together, about what kinds of interactions work in such a way so that everyone is satisfied. The Q'eros authentically and directly express who they are, so that self-representation is in their hands. They have a sense of serenity—*thak!*—about this representation, knowing their voice is heard. More than heard, it is often deeply received in the vibrant space of co-creation, when the foreign guests see their wholeness, versus an Andean stereotype. We never know what will happen or come up in these spaces, which makes the interaction a symbiotic, spontaneous process, versus a more controlled, practiced, and staged event. This is because each individual involved—tourist and Q'eros—is allowed to express him- or herself freely in complementary dialogue. The quality of reciprocal giving and receiving (ideal *ayni*) is more possible in small groups, where active participation is on an individual level that results in people sharing freely and unmasked, engendering expansion and learning on both fronts. The outcome is often heart-opening and connecting, versus sharing from the ego with a pitying ("poor Andean") or exalting ("wealthy foreigner"/"ancient Inca stuck in time") perspective, which is hierarchical and separating. I would go so far as to say that there are grains of emotional healing involved in such interactions. The profound glimpses we experience into the life of the "other" in unhurried, still moments engender a sense of solidarity that can be soothing—a salve to the soul. In this context the Q'eros' music is shared, heard, and received, so that for a brief moment a foreign guest whose life is completely different can gain a sense of understanding and connection into a world he or she has never experienced, or imagined.

In contrast, many Q'eros and Wachiperi discuss feelings of being used by the Ministry of Culture when they perform their music on stage in celebratory functions of achievements by the MC. One example is the May 20, 2013 celebration in Cusco, which announced UNESCO's nomination of the *Qhapaq Ñan*, Royal Inca Highway, as a World Heritage Site, marking the first time in history a multinational application has been sent to and nominated by UNESCO (Argentina, Bolivia, Colombia, Chile, Ecuador, and Peru). The MC called on many Q'eros and Wachiperi to be representative "original people" from the Inca Imperial Period when the usage of this road system was at its peak, requiring them to sing and dance (dance in the case of the Wachiperi) on a large stage in typical dress. The Q'eros and the Wachiperi with whom I discussed this event expressed that the experience was uncomfortable and felt degrading. In this case it is not equal sharing; there is a clear hierarchy involved when the orders come from above, and the indigenous are the *payasos* (clowns), as a Wachiperi leader said. What is glossed as a celebration of their indigeneity is actually experienced as demeaning. Political power relations win out, and the Q'eros and Wachiperi must find other means to wholly express themselves.

In the case of the Wachiperi, the means they took was an active stand when they felt encroachment of political power in response to the MC's suggestion of a CD production about their music, using the community's archives. They said a clear "no," and took it one step further: they came up with a satisfying solution of their own production that enhanced self-esteem and made it so they could represent Wachiperi identity in their way. We mutually agreed and worked together to realize the production, so that I had an equal relationship with the Wachiperi in our work together. The entire production involved about ten people at the most, which is very grassroots, except when you consider that that is about 10% of the entire Wachiperi population. Profits were only 800 soles (about $320), which covered over a year's supply of medicines for the three community elders. It is precisely at this level that such a precarious group must step forth in self-defense. The mutual service I provided was the return of archives, assistance in song selection and CD liner notes, and the know-how of a homemade CD production. Their benefit was an independent production, and mine was collaboration in it, being witness to their courage and ambition in satisfactory representation, and the necessary and willing surrender on my part to do it their way. At this moment, our work together flowed in effective co-collaboration and was service in the sense of equal and reciprocal empowerment. We enjoyed the flow of spontaneous collaboration versus the hierarchical making of a CD in which one entity (the MC) would have final production choice that likely would have been fraught with enhanced feelings of resistance and resentment on the part of the Wachiperi that were already present.

Significantly, what transpired from our intensive song workshops together, and my discussions with Daniel Sheehy, director of the Smithsonian Center for Folklife and Cultural Heritage, about the possibility of a CD production entitled "Music of the River Q'eros," to include both Q'eros and Wachiperi songs, was an invitation to participate in the 2015 Smithsonian Folklife Festival that focused on Peru. In the festival, five representative Wachiperi had the opportunity to express their culture and traditions in their own terms. Also significant is that they were the only indigenous group to represent all of Peru's Amazonia in the festival.

Though we eventually let go of our original idea of reviving songs, as explained above, the most meaningful times were those of group listening, learning, and discussion in a small group with three generations of Wachiperi, which did not result in a product or presentation, but were simply moments of deeply shared experience at a singular point in time. Just that alone, I contend, is valuable. Many, like Nely Ninantay, Manuel's granddaughter, articulated that our listening and discussions were extremely valuable in raising awareness about Wachiperi heritage. Nely stated that she was not even aware of the existence of these songs and their prevalence and place in the Wachiperi past, and she felt proud to receive this heritage.[35] If one single Wachiperi person, like Nely, receives benefit from our small-scale work, then it has been worth it.

Manuel Yonaje died on January 27, 2014. With him passed a substantial quality of lived Wachiperi knowledge since he was one of three Wachiperi elders, and the *only* elder man, of the Queros-Wachiperi community. During our time together from 2010 through 2013, I was able to see how vibrant and grateful he was when listening to Lyon's song recordings, when singing in his recordings with me and discussing the old days "when we were many people" (see Figure 7.12). I would sit for hours in the hot sun or under the dark sky and listen to him reminisce about the old days of Wachiperi history, music, and life. I remember one magical moment when we were sitting in the grass and

FIGURE 7.12 Manuel Yonaje listens to Patricia J. Lyon's Wachiperi archive recordings.

(Photo by Holly Wissler, February 19, 2012)

I saw a small yellow bird up high on a branch, and asked, "Is there a song for that bird?"—to which he burst into singing that bird's song. I am reminded of a powerful quote by anthropologist, ethnobotanist, and conservationist Wade Davis: "Is the wisdom of an elder any less important simply because he or she communicates to an audience of one?" (Davis, 2009: 5). In Manuel's bringing forth his wisdom, I witnessed individuals' perspective and awareness of their own Wachiperi tradition and heritage change, mainly his granddaughter, Nely, and daughter-in-law Odette.[36] These one-to-one relationships were profoundly and mutually beneficial, touching the depths of reciprocity at a most basic level: One elder died with the satisfaction that his people's music was relived and shared with the younger generation of his family, not to be forgotten. I, as "applied ethnomusicologist"—but mainly friend—was privileged to be a part of this process and can now share Manuel's wisdom and life with his community, and in broader contexts, such as the Cusco community, Peru, academia, and the 2015 Smithsonian Folklife Festival. In my work with both the Q'eros and the Wachiperi, we searched together through experience to discover and shape equal, reciprocal, and deeply beneficial relationships, and it is this mutual service that we experience with one another that sustains our projects and my relationship with these extraordinary people—that is, people as individuals, versus a group in staged presentation.

Notes

1. In many publications they are acknowledged as the Huachipaeri group, but recent collaborative work between the Wachiperi and the Ministry of Culture on the first Harakbut dictionary (2015) that has established the Harakbut alphabet has changed the spelling to Wachiperi. Equally, the spelling of Harakmbut has changed to Harakbut.
2. Ethnohistorian John Murra provided groundbreaking research on the usage, exploitation, and sustainability of Andean, Amazonian, and coastal ecosystems, which he termed "vertical ecology" (see Murra, 1972, 1980).
3. The *cargo* system was introduced by Spain mainly for service in Catholic religious offices, such as sponsoring a patron saint festival and liturgical rituals, as well as administrative offices.
4. *Coca* leaves are used practically, socially, and ritually in Andean life. See Allen (2002) for a full discussion of the use of *coca* in Andean communities.
5. As in Q'eros rituals of extreme reciprocal exchange, Marcel Mauss writes about the excessive co-consumption of the North American Indian potlatch rituals (Mauss, 1954).
6. Peru is divided into 25 large regions (formerly called departments).
7. While historically Andean and Amazonian groups have been linked through essential trade networks that complemented the sustenance and ritual necessities of both regions, I have not found any clear historical or ethnographic evidence that confirms that the Q'eros and Wachiperi have historical connections. I have found suggestions of possible ancestral connection of the Q'eros to Amazonian territory beyond their current cloud forest region, which is subject to further investigation, and beyond the scope of this article.

8. The exact number of Wachiperi population is difficult to ascertain since many Wachiperi today are mixed with Amazonia Matsiguenka and highland Quechua groups, and there has been no government census of the Wachiperi. In 2008 the Wachiperi calculated that 57 remained in their population for a diagnostic report prepared by the Asociación de la Conservación de la Cuena Amazónica (Amazon River Basin Conservation Association, ACCA), a nongovernmental organization based in Cusco that works in various conservation projects with the Wachiperi. In a recent workshop (January 2015) with the Wachiperi to prepare for their participation in the Smithsonian Folklife Festival they estimated about 120 total Wachiperi, therefore numbers are subjective and fluctuate.
9. The repatriation of audiovisual archives to the Q'eros is the topic of a forthcoming chapter, "'Where Dead People Walk': Repatriation of Fifty Years of Audio-Visual Archives to Q'eros, Peru" in *The Oxford Handbook of Musical Repatriation*, Eds. Frank Gunderson and Rob Lancefield. In Press.
10. For a detailed discussion of Q'eros' identity, see Wissler dissertation (2009a: 35–41): "Identity: La Nación Q'eros; Q'eros and/ or Inca?"
11. The naming of a "people," versus a tangible or intangible cultural heritage, has received much criticism locally and nationally.
12. If one "googles" "Q'eros," there are numerous websites that offer spiritual tourism activities with the Q'eros.
13. See Boniface and Robinson (1998) for impact of influences on host communities in the tourism industry, and Berno (2007) for the indigenous voice in designing tourism in a case study the South Pacific.
14. See Cohen (1986) and Wissler (2009b) for candid accounts of the challenges of filming in Q'eros.
15. The exchanges are with a varied demographic, through the following organizations: US-based travel companies *Wilderness Travel* and *National Geographic/Lindblad Expeditions*, and US study abroad programs, such as The Center for World Music, SIT World Learning, Iowa State University, and UC Davis. The high-end Peruvian travel company COLTUR Peru (www.colturperu.com) has recognized the value of these exchanges and employs us on a regular basis to meet with a wide spectrum of clientele (spiritual tourists, economists, university alumni, to name a few). In addition, we do video conferences from Cusco with Brandeis University Spanish and music classes.
16. See Wissler (2009: 84–108) about the Andean concept of *yanantin* (male/female complementary duality) and its manifestation in Q'eros ritual music and the relationship between the women's singing and the men's *pinkuyllu* in a transcription design that shows this relationship.
17. See Wissler (2009a), Stobart (2006), and Allen (2002) for the importance of continuous, nonstop music-making in Andean ritual.
18. This is also called *sami*. See Allen (2002) for an in-depth discussion of *sami*.
19. Steven Feld's classic work, *Sound and Sentiment* (1982), addresses reciprocity in the music of the Kaluli in Papua New Guinea.
20. The suffix *ri* is really *ru*, but in this case the *u* changes to *i* for ease of pronunciation, based on the subsequent suffixes.
21. Ingram (2005: 33) discusses a survey of tourists' interactions with Australian aboriginal culture, where they doubt the authenticity of objects being sold.
22. *Comadre*, or co-mother, is a social tie and obligation obtained during *chukcha rutuy*, a pre-Hispanic ritual when the hair of a young child is cut for the first time, a rite of passage from

infancy into humanhood. I become *madrina*, godmother, to the child, and co-mother with the parents.

23. *The Four Winds Society* specializes in "spiritual expeditions" and regularly works with the Q'eros in Peru.
24. I stress *ideal ayni*, since *ayni* is not always reciprocated, which I contend is one of the main reasons the Q'eros express their grief through improvised singing in animal fertility rituals that are all about offerings intended for ideal reciprocal *ayni*. The sung grief is a remembrance of times when *ayni* was not reciprocated (see Wissler, 2009a, Chapter 8).
25. This number includes silent speakers, that is, people of the younger generation who understand Wachiperi but do not speak it.
26. Arakmbut has the most number of speakers (approximately 200).
27. *La Comunidad Nativa de Queros* (Queros-Wachiperi community) has a fluctuating population of about 20 people all of Wachiperi origin, and Santa Rosa de Huacaria has a population of about 150, composed of Wachiperi, Matsiguenka (Amazon group of Arawak origin), and Quechua from the highlands.
28. View a five-minute YouTube of this archive return and ensuing discussions at http://youtu.be/Y8hfmoZi__Y. There is a brief section of *esüwa* in this video clip, which the Wachiperi approved since it is momentary, versus exposing the entire song and practice.
29. There are also two types of protection songs: *esütateika*, when the healer sings for the protection of an individual against possible harm, danger, disease, and *ewasütuteika*, for the protection of a group, such as family, families, or the entire community. These protection songs, like the *esüwa*, are performed privately.
30. Many scholars who have worked in the Andes and Amazon areas of South America have shown how people are agents in the intentional and causal movement of breath, blowing, and spitting, sometimes through song, for interaction with the spiritual, invisible, and intangible forces around them (Allen, 2002; Guss, 1989; Olsen, 1996; Uzendoski, 2005).
31. See Chapter 5 by Jeff Titon in this volume, "Sustainability, Resilience, and Adaptive Management for Applied Ethnomusicology," for a thorough discussion of safeguarding.
32. It is specifically the Cusco division of the Ministry of Culture, not the central office in the capital city of Lima, that is responsible for the safeguarding of *esüwa* since the Wachiperi reside in the Cusco Region.
33. *Esüwa* (versus *Eshuva*) is the more recent spelling asserted by the Wachiperi, which correspond to the newly established Harakbut alphabet and pronunciation.
34. Similarly, when I completed my DVD documentary *Kusisqa Waqashayku* (2007), about the annual cycle of the Q'eros' musical rituals (when I also employed much collaborative input about representation), I returned my documentary production, along with $4,500 in DVD sales and donations, to the Q'eros community. They chose to use the proceeds for the building of their new town council building, completed in 2010.
35. Nely Ninantay is the first Wachiperi student at Cusco University (Universidad de Cusco San Antonio de Abad) to write about her people in an academic thesis. She completed her degree in tourism in 2014 with her thesis on the topic of eco-tourism in her home community of Queros-Wachiperi.
36. I believe that Odette Ramos Dumas, in her mid-twenties, is a notable culture-bearer of the Wachiperi. She is the granddaughter of the renowned shaman Alejandro Dumas, mentioned earlier in this chapter, and inherited much wisdom from him. She is fluent in Wachiperi, and was passionate about our work together and would sit at length by Manuel's side listening to and learning about the songs.

References

Abercrombie, Thomas A. (1998). *Pathways of Memory and Power*. Madison: University of Wisconsin Press.

Allen, Catherine J. (1997). "When Pebbles Move Mountains." In *Creating Context in Andean Cultures*, edited by Rosaleen Howard-Malverde, pp. 73–84. Oxford: Oxford University Press.

Allen, Catherine J. (2002). *The Hold Life Has*. Washington, DC: Smithsonian Institution Press.

Allen, Catherine J. (2008). *Rethinking Andean Animism*. Unpublished MS. Department of Anthropology, George Washington University.

Alvarez del Castillo, Juan Alex. (2012). La Propiedad Compleja Gobernanza de la Tierra y Conservación en la Amazonía La Reserva Comunal Amarakaeri Madre de Dios, Peru. PhD dissertation, The Graduate Institute, Geneva.

Alviso, J. Ricardo. (2003). "Applied Ethnomusicology and the Impulse to Make a Difference." *Folklore Forum* 34(1–2): 49–59.

Arnold, Denise Y., with Juan de Dios Yapita. (2001). *River of Fleece, River of Song: Singing to the Animals, an Andean Poetics of Creation*. La Paz: ILCA, Seria Etnografías no. 2 and Bonn: University of Bonn: BAS series no. 35.

Asociación para la Conservación de la Cuenca Amazónica. (2008). *Diagnóstico Social de la Comunidad Nativa de Queros*. Cusco, Peru: ACCA.

Bastien, Joseph. (1978). *Mountain of the Condor: Metaphor and Ritual in an Andean Ayllu*. St. Paul: West Publishing.

Berno, Tracy. (2007). "Doing it the 'Pacific Way': Indigenous Education and Training in the South Pacific." In *Tourism and Indigenous Peoples: Issues and Implications*, edited by Richard Butler and Thomas Hinch, pp. 28–39. Oxford: Butterworth-Heinemann.

Bolin, Inge. (1998). *Rituals of Respect: The Secret of Survival in the High Peruvian Andes*. Austin: University of Texas Press.

Boniface, Priscilla, and Micheal Robinson, eds. (1998). *Tourism and Cultural Conflicts*. Centre for Travel and Tourism: University of Northumbria.

Boorstin, Daniel. (1992 [1961]). *The Image: A Guide to Pseudo-Events in America*. Random House: New York.

Bradley, Hank. (1989). *Counterfeiting, Stealing, and Cultural Plundering: A Manual for Applied Ethnomusicologists*. Seattle: Mill Gulch Music.

Butler, Barbara. (2006). *Holy Intoxication to Drunken Dissipation*. Albuquerque: University of New Mexico Press.

Butler, Richard, and Hinch, Thomas. (2007). *Tourism and Indigenous Peoples: Issues and Implications*. Oxford: Butterworth-Heinemann.

Cantos Wachiperi. (2013). One compact disc. Cusco: Dirección Desconcentrada de Cultura Cusco, Ministry of Culture.

Cohen, John. (1986). "Among the Q'eros: Notes from a Filmmaker." *Folklife Annual: A Publication of the American Folklife Center at the Library of Congress*, pp. 22–41. Washington, DC: Library of Congress.

Corr, Rachel. (2003). "Ritual, Knowledge, and the Politics of Identity in Andean Festivities." *Ethnology* 42(1): 39–54.

Cummins, Tom. (2002). *Toasts with the Inca: Andean Abstraction and Colonial Images on Quero Vessels*. Ann Arbor: University of Michigan Press.

Davis, Martha Ellen. (1992). "Careers, 'Alternative Careers,' and the Unity between Theory and Practice in Ethnomusicology." *Ethnomusicology* 36(3): 361–387.

Davis, Wade. (2009). *The Wayfinders: Why Ancient Wisdom Matters in the Modern World*. Toronto, ON: House of Anansi Press.

Feld, Steven. (1982). *Sound and Sentiment*. Philadelphia: University of Pennsylvania Press.

Flores Ochoa, Jorge. (1977). "Aspectos mágicos del pastoreo: Enqa, enqaychu, illa y khuya rumi." In *Pastores de Puna*, pp. 211–237. Lima: Instituto de Estudios Peruanos.

Flores Ochoa, Jorge. (1988). "Mitos y canciones ceremoniales en comunidades de puna." In *Llamichos y paqocheros: Pastores de llamas y alpacas*, pp. 237–251. Cuzco: Centro de Estudios Andinos.

Flores Ochoa, Jorge, and Juan Núñez del Prado, eds. (2005). *Q'ero: El último ayllu Inca* (2nd ed.). Lima: Instituto Nacional de Cultura y Universidad Nacional Mayor de San Marcos.

Gilmore, James H., and Joseph Pine II. (2007). *Authenticity: What Consumers Really Want*. Cambridge, MA: Harvard Business School Publishing.

Gow, David. (1976). *The Gods and Social Change in the High Andes*. Ph.D. dissertation, University of Wisconsin-Madison.

Grant, Catherine. (2012). "Rethinking Safeguarding: Objections and Responses to Protecting and Promoting Endangered Musical Heritage." *Ethnomusicology Forum* 21(1): 31–51.

Gray, Andrew. (1983). *The Amarakaeri: An Ethnographic Account of Harakmbut People from Southeastern Peru*. Oxford: University of Oxford Press.

Gray, Andrew. (1996). *The Arakmbut: Mythology, Spirituality and History*. New York and Oxford: Berghahn Books.

Gray, Andrew. (1997a). *The Last Shaman: Change in an Amazonian Community*. Oxford: Berghahn Books.

Gray, Andrew. (1997b). *Indigenous Rights and Development: Self-Determination in an Amazonian Community*. Oxford: Berghahn Books.

Guss, David. (1989). *To Weave and Sing: Art, Symbol, and Narrative in the South American Rain Forest*. Berkeley: University of California Press.

Harnish, David. (2005). "'Isn't This Nice? It's Just Like Being in Bali': Constructing Balinese Music Culture in Lombok." *Ethnomusicology Forum* 14(1): 3–24.

Harris, Olivia. (2000). *To Make the Earth Bear Fruit: Ethnographic Essays on Fertility, Work and Gender in Highland Bolivia*. London: Institute of Latin American Studies.

Hemming, John. (1993). *The Conquest of the Incas* (3rd ed.). London: Pan Macmillan.

Hutchinson, Sydney. (2003). "Confessions of a Public Sector Ethnomusicologist." *Folklore Forum* 34(1–2): 119–131.

Ingram, Gloria. (2005). "A Phenomenological Investigation of Tourists' Experience of Australian Indigenous Culture." In *Indigenous Tourism: The Commodification and Management of Culture*, edited by Chris Ryan and Michelle Aicken, pp. 21–34. Amsterdam: Elsevier.

Isbell, Billie Jean. (1985 [1978]). *To Defend Ourselves: Ecology and Ritual in an Andean Village*. Prospect Heights, IL: Waveland Press.

Johnson, Henare, and Alison J. McIntosh. (2005). "Understanding the Nature of the Marae Experience: Views from Hosts and Visitors at the Nga Hau E Wha National Marae, Christchurch, New Zealand." In *Indigenous Tourism: The Commodification and Management of Culture*, edited by Chris Ryan and Michelle Aicken, pp. 35–50. Amsterdam: Elsevier.

Kaeppler, Adrienne L., and Olive Lewin. (1986). "Fourth International Colloquium "Traditional Music and Tourism," Held at Kingston, and Newcastle, Jamaica, July 10–14, 1986. *Yearbook for Traditional Music* 18: 211–212.

Knudsen, B. T., and A. M. Waade. (2010). "Performative Authenticity in Tourism and Spatial Experience: Rethinking the Relations Between Travel, Place and Emotion." In *Re-Investing Authenticity: Tourism, Place and Emotions*, edited by B. T. Knudsen and A. M. Waade, pp. 1–19. Bristol: Channel View Publications.

Lassiter, Luke. (2005). *The Chicago Guide to Collaborative Ethnography.* Chicago: University of Chicago Press.

Lomax Hawes, Bess. (1992). "Practice Makes Perfect: Lessons in Active Ethnomusicology." *Ethnomusicology* 36(3): 337–343.

Long, Lucy M. (2003). "Making Public the Personal: The Purposes and Venues of Applied Ethnomusicology." *Folklore Forum* 34(1–2): 97–101.

Lyon, Patricia. (1967). *Singing as Social Interaction among the Wachipaeri of Eastern Peru.* Ph.D. dissertation, University of California, Berkeley.

Mamani Mamani, Manuel. (1990). "Myth and Music in the Livestock Marking Ritual of the Chilean Andes." *Latin Americanist* 25(2): 1–7.

Mannheim, Bruce. (1986). "The Language of Reciprocity in Southern Peruvian Quechua." *Anthropological Linguistics* 28(3): 267–273.

Mannheim, Bruce. (1991). *The Language of the Inka since the European Invasion.* Austin: University of Texas Press.

Mannheim, Bruce. (1998). "A Nation Surrounded." *Native Traditions in the Postconquest World: A Symposium at Dumbarton Oaks*, October 2–4, 1992, pp. 383–420. Washington, DC: Dumbarton Oaks Research Library and Collection.

Mauss, Marcel. (1990 [1950]). *The Gift.* New York: W. W. Norton.

Mendoza, Zoila. (1998). "Defining Folklore: Mestizo and Indigenous Identities on the Move." *Bulletin of Latin American Research* 17(2):165–183.

Mendoza, Zoila. (2000). *Shaping Society Through Dance: Mestizo Ritual Performance in the Peruvian Andes.* Chicago: University of Chicago Press.

Moore, Thomas. (1975). Resumen de la Organización Social y Religión Harakmbut. Unpublished manuscript.

Murra, John. (1972). "El control vertical de un máximo de pisos ecológicos en la economía de las sociedades andinas." In *Visita de la Provincia de León de Huánuco en 1562*, editado por John Murra, pp. 427–476. Huánuco, Perú: Universidad Hermilio Valdizán.

Murra, John. (1980). *The Economic Organization of the Inca State.* Greenwich, CT: JAI Press.

Nomination Form ICH-01 for Inscription (of *esüwa*) in 2011 on the List of Intangible Cultural Heritage in Need of Urgent Safeguarding. Ministerio de Cultura, Dirección Regional de Cultura, Cusco.

Oakdale, Suzanne. (2004). "The Culture-Conscious Brazilian Indian: Representing and Reworking Indianness in Kayabi Political Discourse." *American Ethnologist* 31(1): 60–75.

Olsen, Dale A. (1996). *Music of the Warao of Venezuela: Song People of the Rain Forest.* Gainesville: University Press of Florida.

Rios, Fernando. (2012). "The Andean Conjunto, Bolivian Sikureada and the Folkloric Musical Representation Continuum." *Ethnomusicology Forum.* 21(1): 5–29.

Rowe, John. (1948). "Inca Culture at the Time of the Spanish Conquest." In *The Handbook of South American Indians*, Vol. 2, edited by J. H. Steward, pp. 183–330. New York: Cooper Square Publications.

Rozas Álvarez, Washington. (2002 [1979]). "Los paqo en Q'ero." In *Q'ero: el último ayllu inka* (2nd ed.), edited by Jorge Flores Ochoa and Juan Núñez del Prado, pp. 265–276. Lima, Perú: Instituto Nacional de Cultura y Universidad Nacional Mayor de San Marcos.

Ryan, Chris. (2005). "Introduction: Tourist-Host Nexus—Research Considerations." In *Indigenous Tourism: The Commodification and Management of Culture*, edited by Chris Ryan and Michelle Aicken, pp. 1–14. Amsterdam: Elsevier.

Ryan, Chris, and Birgit Trauer. (2005). "Visitor Experiences of Indigenous Tourism—Introduction." In *Indigenous Tourism: The Commodification and Management of Culture*, edited by Chris Ryan and Michelle Aicken, pp. 15–20. Amsterdam: Elsevier.

Ryan, Chris, and Michelle Aicken, eds. (2005). *Indigenous Tourism: The Commodification and Management of Culture*. Amsterdam: Elsevier.

Seeger, Anthony. (2004a [1987]). *Why Suyá Sing: A Musical Anthropology of an Amazonian People*. Cambridge: Cambridge University Press.

Seeger, Anthony. (2004b). "The Selective Protection of Musical Ideas: The 'Creators' and the Dispossessed." In *Property in Question: Value Transformation in the Global Economy*, edited by Katherine Verdery and Caroline Humphrey, pp. 69–83. Oxford: Berg Publishers.

Seeger, Anthony. (2005). "Who Got Left Out of the Property Grab Again? Oral Traditions, Indigenous Rights, and Valuable Old Knowledge." In *CODE: Collaborative Ownership and the Digital Economy*, edited by Rishabe Aiyer Ghosh, pp. 75–84. Cambridge, MA: MIT Press.

Seeger, Anthony. (2008). "Theories Forged in the Crucible of Action: The Joys, Dangers, and Potentials of Advocacy and Fieldwork." In *Shadows in the Field: New Perspectives for Fieldwork in Ethnomusicology*, edited by Gregory Barz and Timothy J. Cooley, pp. 271–288. New York: Oxford University Press.

Seeger, Anthony. (2009). "Lessons Learned from the ICTM (NGO) Evaluations of Nominations for the UNESCO's Masterpieces of the Oral and Intangible Heritage of Humanity, 2001–5." In *Intangible Heritage*, edited by Laurajane Smith and Natsuko Akagawa, pp. 112–128. London: Routledge.

Seeger, Anthony. (2012). "Who Should Control Which Rights to Music?" In *Current Issues in Music Research: Copyright, Power, and Transnational Music Processes*, edited by Susana Moreno Fernández, Salwa El-Shawan Castelo-Branco, Pedro Roxo, and Iván Iglesias, pp. 27–49. Lisbon: Edições Colibri.

Senft, Gunter. (1999). "The Presentation of Self in Touristic Encounters. A Case Study from the Trobriand Islands." *Anthropos* 94 (1–3): 21–33.

Schippers, Huib. (2009). "Three Journeys, Five Recollections, Seven Voices: Operationalising Sustainability in Music." In *Applied Ethnomusicology, Historical and Contemporary Approaches*, edited by Klisala Harrison, Elizabeth Mackinlay, and Svanibor Pettan, pp. 161–179. Newcastle upon Tyne, UK: Cambridge Scholars Publishing.

Schaedel, Richard P. (1988). "Andean World View: Hierarchy or Reciprocity, Regulation or Control?" *Current Anthropology* 29(5): 768–775.

Sheehy, D. (1992). "A Few Notions about Philosophy and Strategy in Applied Ethnomusicology." *Ethnomusicology* 36(3): 323–336.

Silverman, Gail. (1994). *El Tejido Andino: Un Libro de Sabiduria*. Lima, Perú: Banco Central de Reserva del Perú.

Stobart, Henry. (2006). *Music and the Poetics of Production in the Bolivian Andes*. Burlington, VT: Ashgate.

Stokes, Martin, ed. (1994). *Ethnicity, Identity and Music: The Musical Construction of Place*. Oxford and New York: Berg Publishers.

Tello, Rodolfo. (2013). *Hunting Practices of the Wachiperi: Demystifying Indigenous Environmental Behavior*. North Charleston, SC: CreateSpace Independent Publishing.

Titon, Jeff T. (1999). "'The Real Thing': Tourism, Authenticity and Pilgrimage among the Old Regular Baptists at the 1997 Smithsonian Folklife Festival." *the world of music* 41(3): 115–139.

Titon, Jeff T. (2009). "Music and Sustainability: An Ecological Viewpoint," *the world of music* 51(1): 119–137.

Tomoeda, Hiroyasu. (1996). "The Concept of Vital Energy among Andean Pastoralists." In *Redefining Nature: Ecology, Culture and Domestication*, edited by Ellen Roy and Katsuyoshi Fukui, pp. 187–212. Washington, DC: Berg.

Turino, Thomas. (1993). *Moving Away from Silence: Music of the Peruvian Altiplano and the Experience of Migration.* Chicago: University of Chicago Press.

Turino, Thomas. (2008). *Music in the Andes.* New York: Oxford University Press.

Turner, Victor. (1969). *The Ritual Process.* Chicago: Aldine Publishing Company.

Turner, Victor. (1974). "Passages, Margines and Poverty: Religious Symbols of Communitas." In *Dramas, Fields and Metaphors.* Ithaca, NY: Cornell University Press.

Urry, J. (2002). *The Tourist Gaze: Leisure and Travel in Contemporary Societies.* Thousand Oaks, CA: Sage.

Uzendoski, Michael. (2005). *The Napo Runa of Amazonian Ecuador.* Chicago: University of Illinois Press.

Wang, Ning. (1999). "Rethinking Authenticity in Tourism Experience." *Annals of Tourism Research* 26(2): 349–370.

Webster, Steven. (1972). *The Social Organization of a Native Andean Community.* Ph.D. dissertation, University of Washington.

Wissler, Holly. (2009a). *From Grief and Joy We Sing: Social and Cosmic Regenerative Processes in the Songs of Q'eros, Peru.* PhD dissertation, Florida State University.

Wissler, Holly. (2009b). "Grief-Singing and the Camera: The Challenges and Ethics of Documentary Production in an Indigenous Andean Community." *Ethnomusicology Forum* 18(1): 33–49.

Xie, Philip Feifen. (2001). *Authenticating Cultural Tourism: Folk Villages in Hainan, China.* PhD dissertation, University of Waterloo, Ontario, Canada.

Zuidema, R. T. (1964). *The Ceque System of Cuzco: The Social Organization of the Capital of the Inca.* Leiden: E. J. Brill.

Zuidema, R. T. (1982). "Bureaucracy and Systematic Knowledge in Andean Civilization." In *The Inca and Aztec States, 1400–1800*, edited by G. A. Collier, R. I. Rosaldo, and J. D. Wirth, pp. 419–458. New York: Academic Press.

Zuidema, R. T. (1990). *Inca Civilization in Cuzco.* Austin: University of Austin Press.

Index

Note: Tables and figures are indicated by t and f following the page number

Abayudaya (Jewish) community, 70, 70f, 75–82, 76f, 87–93
Aboriginal Australia, 297
Aboriginalism, 263
ACA (Amazon Conservation Association), 301, 302
ACCA (*Asociación para la Conservación de la Cuenca Amazónica,* Amazon Basin Conservation Association), 301, 302, 319
Action points, 210–211
Active resistance, 273
Active voice, 315
Activism, 7, 24, 27, 29
    CASES methodology, 81–87, 83f
    participant, 241
    Titon on, 74, 178
Activist ethnomusicology, 222
Adler, Guido, 99–100
Advocacy, 6, 10, 21, 25, 27, 55, 59, 67–249. *See also* Intercultural mediation
    and activism, 81–87, 83f
    Autistic Self Advocacy Network, 162
    capacity assessment and project conceptualization, 75–78, 76f
    CASES methodology, 78–91, 83f
    Clifford on, 69
    community partnerships, 78–79
    early history of, 27
    education, 88–90
    energy and commitment in, 91–92
    impact on research, 93–94
    lessons from service learning, 73–74
    partnerships, 80–81
    personal motivation for, 71–73
    Pettan and Harrison on, 80–81
    reciprocal impact of, 94–95
    scholar *vs.* advocate roles, 69
    self-advocates, 162–163, 169–172
    service, 87–88
    setting limits, 92
    with subaltern cultures, 86–87
    success and expectations, 93
    sustainability, 90–91
    in Uganda, 69–96, 70f
Advocate ethnomusicology, 82–83, 222
Aerophones, 225
Africa, 37
Akadongo (lamellaphone), 84
Akiva, Rabbi, 70
Akuseka Takuwa Kongo Group, 84, 94
Alamanzani, Katerega, 94–95
Alamblak slit drum speech, 204
Alevism, 142
Al Jazeera, 86
Allen, Catherine, 274
Allen, Matthew, 243
All India Radio, 242
Altkorn, Emily, 295, 296
Amazon Basin Conservation Association (*Asociación para la Conservación de la Cuenca Amazónica,* ACCA), 301, 302, 319
Amazon Conservation Association (ACA), 301, 302
Amazonia. *See* Quechua Q'eros; Wachiperi
Ambedkar, B. R., 223
Ambedkar, Ramji, 242, 243
American Folklife Center (Library of Congress), 23
American Musicological Society (AMS), 16
Amono (Mono people), 190, 195
Analytical categories, 191–192
Andes. *See* Quechua Q'eros

328 INDEX

Andrade, Regis, 306–309
Ang, Ien, 129
ANI (Autism Network International), 162
Annan, Parattai, 245
Anthropology, 180
Apasa, Santos Machacca, 290–291, 292–293
Appalachian mountains, 5
Appavoo, J. Theophilus, 233, 234–238, 243, 244, 245
Applied (term), 261
Applied: in other disciplines, 35–36
Applied anthropology, early, 19–20
Applied ethnography, 166–167
Applied ethnomusicology, 149–151.
 See also specific topics
 advocacy in, 6, 27, 55
 Artism and, 167–169
 of autism, 148–181
 being, knowing, and doing, 8–9
 Berger on, 33
 conscious practice, 31, 34, 224, 261
 cultural policy interventions, 5–6
 and decolonization, 267–268
 definitions of, 3–4, 31–33, 49–50, 148
 early work, 19–20
 education, 6
 as emergent movement, 1
 in environmental sound activism and ecojustice, 7
 in epistemological orientation, 8
 history of, 19–29
 insularity, 9
 intercultural mediation with, 99–143
 International Council for Traditional Music and, 46–49
 in journalism, 7
 in law and music industry, 7
 in libraries, museums, and sound archives, 7
 Loughran on, 99
 in medicine, 7
 music and minorities and, 99–104
 neurodiverse approach to, 163–164
 vs. non-academic work, 32
 in North America, 5–8
 peace and conflict resolution, 7
 power imbalance, 32–33
 professionalization, 17–19
 public, 8
 vs. public folklore, 7–8

 vs. public-sector ethnomusicology, 7–8
 scope, 3–4
 Sheehy on, 261
 Sheehy's categorization of, 115
 small scale, 273
 in United States, 9–29
Applied Ethnomusicology: Historical and Contemporary Approaches (Harrison, Mackinlay, and Pettan), 27, 31
Arakmbut, 320
Archive of Folk Culture (Library of Congress), 23
Archives, 7
Arora, Bonnie, 291, 294–295
Arora, Krishna, 291
Artism Ensemble, 148–150, 164–165
 applied ethnomusicology, 167–169
 critiques of, 169–172, 172–173
 efforts to address criticisms against, 173–175
 Exploratory World Music Playground (E-WoMP), 156, 164–165, 167, 180
 Mara on, 175–177
 origins, 151, 155–156
 participants, 179, 181
 SDS Conference concert (Orlando, 2013), 169–172
Artism Music Project, 148–149, 155–156, 173
Artistic events, 191
Artistic genres, 191–192. *See also* Artistic traditions
 dormant, 203b
 enactments of, 192–193, 194
 extinct, 203b
 health assessment of
  graded, 202, 203b
  health measurement, 201
  quick and dirty sketch, 201–202
 international, 203b
 locked, 203b
 national, 203b
 regional, 203b
 shifting, 203b
 threatened, 203b
 vigorous, 203b
Artistic traditions
 example losses, 204–205
 foundational concepts, 189–192
 global, 202–206, 206–211
 global interest in, 206–208

health assessment of, 187, 200–202, 202–206
as living processes, 200
longer, 206–208
testimonials on, 205–206
Artists and artistry, 191
  basic community arts survey, 213–215
  motivations and methods for encouraging, 187–215
  therapeutic approach to arts-making, 208–210
Arts Specialists, 212
ASCs (autism spectrum conditions), 165
ASDs (autism spectrum disorders), 150, 160, 179
Asian classical music study, 227
Asociación para la Conservación de la Cuenca Amazónica (ACCA, Amazon Basin Conservation Association), 301, 302, 319
Asperger's syndrome, 151, 179
Assessment. *See* Health assessment
Ausnahmsweise Zigeuner, 115–116, 116f, 119–120
Australia, 36–37
  aboriginal, 297
Austria
  Bosnian refugees in, 104–105, 106t, 109, 120–127, 140
  comparative musicology in, 99–100
  discrimination in, 106–107, 108–109
  "Embedded industries—Immigrant Cultural Entrepreneurs in Vienna," 130, 141
  ethnic minority groups in, 105–106, 106t
  foreign population, 105
  historical background, 104–108, 142
  immigrants in, 104–107, 106t, 109, 127–139, 141, 142
  integration process, 106–107
  minorities in, 104–139
  music, 99–104
  "Music Making of Immigrants in Vienna," 130
  National Inventory of Intangible Cultural Heritage, 119, 142
  nongovernmental organization (NGOs) in, 107–108
  political background, 104–108, 142
  refugees in, 104–106, 106t, 109, 120–127
  Roma in, 108–109, 109–120, 112t, 140
  Turkish immigrants in, 105, 106t, 109, 127–139, 141, 142
  Volksgruppengesetz (Ethnic Groups Act), 105, 113
Authenticity, 17
  indexical, 281
  performative, 281, 297–298
  in tourism, 279–283
Autism, 160, 177–178
  anthropological study of, 180
  applied ethnography in, 166–167
  applied ethnomusicology of, 148–181
  Bascom on, 157, 162
  ethnomusicology of, 148–181
  Grandin on, 161
  Loud Hands: Autistic People, Speaking (Bascom), 157, 162, 180
  Music-Play Project (MPP) for, 151, 154–155
  Ne'eman on, 162–163
  neurodiversity paradigm of, 164
  pathology paradigm of, 164
  polyvocal narrative approach to, 148
  self-advocates for, 162–163, 169–172
  Siebers on, 166
  Sinclair on, 166–167
  spinny chairs and Mara, 156–159, 175–177
  Straus on, 166
  Walker on, 164
Autism awareness, 172–173
"Autism Fact Sheet" (NINDS), 160, 161–162
Autism Network International (ANI), 162
Autism Speaks, 157–158, 161, 173
Autism spectrum conditions (ASCs), 165
Autism spectrum disorders (ASDs), 150, 160, 179
Autistic Self Advocacy Network, 162
Autochthonous ethnic minorities, 105
Avery, Tom, 211–212
Ayni, 273–274, 287–288, 297–299, 315, 320. *See also* Reciprocity
Aysariykuy, 288, 291, 298
Azariah, M., 234
Azra project, 34–35, 120

Bagisu circumcision songs, 82
Bagwere people, 84
Bahiskrit Hitakarini Sabha (Outcastes Welfare Association), 243
Bajrektarević, Sofija, 121, 123–124, 125–126, 127
Balitwegomba Choir, 84

Barz, Gregory, 74, 88, 140, 259
Bascom, Julia, 157, 162, 163, 177, 180
Battiste, M., 263
Bauböck, Rainer, 106
Bausinger, Hermann, 138
Being, knowing, and doing, 8–9
Being-in-relation, 266
Berger, Harris M. (Harry), 33, 211, 230, 235, 245
Berliner, Paul, 25
Bezić, Jerko, 40, 101
BFE (British Forum for Ethnomusicology), 207
Bharatiya Janata Party (BJP), 228–229
Bildik, Mansur, 132–134, 133f, 137
Bili, Democratic Republic of the Congo, 201–202, 202t, 204
Bi-musicality, 17, 22
Bira, 198
BJP (Bharatiya Janata Party), 228–229
Blacking, John, 235, 244
Black Theology, 244
Boas, Franz, 10, 12
Bogdal, Klaus Michael, 109–110
Boniface, Priscilla, 279, 280, 297, 319
Boorstin, Daniel, 281
Bosnia, 40, 101, 105, 109, 121, 122, 124, 125, 127
Bosnia: Echoes from an Endangered World (Petrović and Levin), 121–122
"Bosnian evening," 124–128
Bosnian refugees, 34–35, 104–105, 106t, 109, 120–127, 140
Botkin Benjamin, 226
Brahmins, 242
Brandeis University, 295, 319
British Forum for Ethnomusicology (BFE), 207
Buber, Martin, 70
Burgenland Roma, 116, 117
Burton, Tim, 170
Butler, Charles, 193
Butler, Judith, 224
Butler, Richard, 279

Cáceres, Renato, 308, 314
Campbell, Patricia Shehan, 21
Campos, Teresa, 314
Candomblé, 198
Cantos Wachiperi: Familia lingüística Harakbut, Grupo étnico Wachiperi, 313f, 314
Capacity, assessment of, 75–78, 76f
Cargo system, 318

Caribbean, 297
Casa de la Memoria (Memory House), 307, 310
CASES methodology, 78–91
  advocacy and activism, 81–87, 83f
  community partnerships, 78–79
  education, 88–90
  partnerships, 80–81
  service, 87–88
  sustainability in, 90–91
CASM (Centre for Aboriginal Studies in Music), 256, 257
CBT (community-based tourism), 284–285
CD recordings, 118
  Bosnia: Echoes from an Endangered World, 121–122
  Cantos Wachiperi: Familia lingüística Harakbut, Grupo étnico Wachiperi, 313f, 314
  Deep Forest, 197
  Delicious Peace, 70, 82–90, 93, 94
  Sevdah in Vienna, 127
  Wachiperi production, 309–314, 312f, 316–317, 317f
CECU (Communauté Evangélique du Christ en l'Ubangi) churches, 201–202
Center for Excellence in World Arts, 212
Centre for Aboriginal Studies in Music (CASM), 256, 257
Ceribašić, Naila, 115
Chałubiński, Tytus, 114
Chasar, Mara (Mara-I-am), 156–159, 170–171, 175–177, 179, 181
Chatterjee, Partha, 228–229
Chennai Diocese, Frontiers of Dalit Theology, 244
Chennai Sangamam folk festival, 239, 241, 245
Chicago, Illinois, 5
The Chicago Guide to Collaborative Ethnography (Lassiter), 312
CHIMP (Children's Happiness Integrative Music Project), 154
Christensen, Dieter, 53
Christian folk music, Dalit, 234–238
Christianity, 233, 244
Circumcision songs, 82
Clarke, Sathianathan, 244
Classical music
  Asian, 227
  Indian, 220–221, 243
Classical ten percent, 224–225

CLAT (Creating Local Arts Together), 208–210, 209f
Clifford, James, 69
Climati, Antonio, 30
Clinard, Wendy, 192, 200
Clinard Dance Theatre, 192
Coca, 274, 288, 300, 318
Coffee. *See also* Peace Kawomera Fair Trade Coffee cooperative
  Delicious Peace coffee, 93
Coffeebot, 168, 170
Cognitive linguistics, 190
Cohen, Judah M., 74
Colonial, Ms. White Settler, 255, 256–258, 267. *See also* Decolonization, Professor; Ethnomusicology, Dr. A(pplied)
Colonialism, 86–87, 255, 314. *See also* Decolonization
  cultural impoverishment of minorities from, 187–188
  culture shared between colonizer and colonized, 254–255
  history and attitudes of, 59
Colonized people, 254–255
Colonizers, 254–255
COLTUR Peru, 319
Commission on Intangible Cultural Heritage (UNESCO), 207
Commitment, 91–92
Committee on Applied Ethnomusicology, SEM, 26
Communauté Evangélique du Christ en l'Ubangi (CECU) churches, 201–202
Communication
  ebb and flow of, 194–198
  fusions, 196–197
Communitas, 293
Community, 191, 293
  therapeutic approach to, 208–210
Community arts survey, basic, 213–215
Community-based tourism (CBT), 284–285
Community empowerment, 85
Community partnerships, 78–79
Community service learning (CSL), 78
Comparative musicology, 12–13
  vs. folk music research and ethnomusicology, 38–39, 39t
  origins of, 99–100
Comunidad Nativa Queros-Wachiperi (Queros-Wachiperi), 301, 310

Casa de la Memoria (Memory House), 307, 310
CD production, 309–314, 312f, 316–317, 317f
population, 320
Conceptualization, project, 75–78, 76f
Conflict resolution: music for, 7, 58
Congolese popular music, 199
Conscious practice, 224
Consultant-researcher cooperation models, 140
Cooley, Timothy, 114, 115, 140, 259
Cooperation
  among peoples, 58
  consultant-researcher, 140
Copyright, 313–314
Corey-Moran, Ben, 86
Corntassel, J., 267–268
Creating Local Arts Together (CLAT), 208–210, 209f
Creativity: sparking, 209
"Creativity and Ambience: An Ecstatic Feedback Model from Arab Music" (Racy), 198–199
Creoles, 195
Critical race theory, 254
Croatia, 39–40, 42–43
Crouch, Andraé, 193
CSL (Community service learning), 78
Cultural heritage. *See* Intangible cultural heritage
Cultural impoverishment, 187–188
Cultural institutions. *See specific institutions*
Cultural markers, 113, 119
Cultural nationalism, 229
Cultural patrimony, 283
Cultural performance, 278–279
Cultural policy interventions, 5–6
Cultural politics, 220–221, 223–224
Cultural resources. *See specific resources and types*
Cultural Survival, 210–211
Cultural trauma, 5
Culture
  hip-hop youth culture, 134–137, 134f
  medical, 166
  national, 113
  political assertion of cultural value, 223–224
  Romani, 111–113
  shared between colonizer and colonized, 254–255

Curricula
    applied domain in, 51–52
    Intercultural Bilingual Education (EIB) curricula, 306–307
Cusco University (Universidad Nacional de San Antonio Abad del Cusco), 283, 320
Czechoslovakia: refugees from, 104–105, 106t

DAKASTUM (Danse Kanoon du Secteur Ntumplefet), 196–197
Dalit Action Theory, 58, 223–224, 230, 242
Dalit liberation theology, 234–238, 243
Dalit Panthers, 223
Dalits, 220, 242, 244
    Christian, 233
    Christianizing of, 233–234
    political assertion of cultural value, 223–224
    polluting aspects, 224–225, 231–232
    rejection of Hinduism, 244
    scholar ignorance of, 224
    singing (and drumming), 230–233
    Tamil, 58
    terminology for, 223, 242, 243, 244
    This Is a Music: Reclaiming an Untouchable Drum, 238–242, 245
Dalit theology, 233–234
    liberation theology, 234–238, 243
    Tamil folk music as, 234–238
Dalit theology movement, 244
Danse Kanoon du Secteur Ntumplefet (DAKASTUM), 196–197
Dariquebe, Estela, 278f, 302, 302f, 303–305, 310–311
Davidová, Eva, 117
Davis, Martha Ellen, 26
Davis, Robin, 293
Davis, Wade, 318
Day, Captain, 228
Decolonization, 25, 253–268
    applied ethnomusicology and, 267–268
    Barz and Cooley on, 259
    being-in-relation, 266
    Gourlay on, 258–259
    Meizel on, 259–260
    with non-indigenous narrator, 253–254
    response-ability, 266
    story-ing fundamentals, 253–254
    terminology, 258–259
    uncomfortable reflexivity in, 253–254
    whispering about, 258–260
    wide-awakeness, 258, 267–268
    work beginnings, 253–255
Decolonization, Professor, 255, 260–266, 267
Deep Forest, 197
Deficit-centrism, 161–163
Delicious Peace (CD), 70, 82–90, 93, 94
Delicious Peace (coffee), 93
Densmore, Frances, 187
Dersim, 142
Dersim massacre, 142
Dersim Rebellion, 142
Devasahayam V., 244
Development, sustainable. *See* Sustainability
Development programs. *See specific programs*
Dialogical knowledge production, 140
Diasporas, 128–129
Didi-Huberman, Georges, 221
Dièrétii, 195–196
Difference(s), 128–129
Diglossia, 195
Direct intervention, 120
Direct mediation, 35
Dirksen, Rebecca, 27, 222, 226
Discrimination, 106–107, 108–109
Diversity
    neurodiversity, 163–164, 166
    Roma, 111, 112t
    voices of, 129
Djenda, Maurice, 204
Documentation. *See* Archives; Recordings
Dormant genres, 203b
Dorson, Richard, 17
Dower, John, 226
Dress, 307–308
Drums and drumming, 152–153
    parai (Tamil frame drum), 224–225, 231–233, 238–242, 243
    parai oral system, 245
    subaltern, 230–233
    This Is a Music: Reclaiming an Untouchable Drum, 238–242, 245
Duende, 198
Duggins, Lydia, 215
Dumas, Alejandro, 320
Dumas, Marisabel, 307
Dumas, Odette Ramos, 320
"Dunjaluče," 123–124
Dyen, Doris, 26

Ecojustice, 7
Ecology, 202–203
Ecomusicology, 7
Eco-tourism, 320
Ecstatic states, 198, 199. *See also* Trance states
"Educate our Children," 84
Education, 6–7, 58. *See also* Music education
    CASES methodology, 88–90
    higher education, 78
    Intercultural Bilingual Education (EIB) curricula, 306–307
Eissenberg, Judy, 295–296
Ellis, Alexander, 12, 187
"Embedded industries—Immigrant Cultural Entrepreneurs in Vienna," 130, 141
Emotional states, 198
Empowerment, community, 85
Enactments, 192
    fusions, 196–197
    gbaguru, 201–202, 202t
    integral, 193, 198–200
    liminal, 193, 198–200
    Rock, 194
Enactors, 192
Encouraging artists, 187–215
Endingigdi (one-string tube fiddle), 84
Energy, 91–92
Engagement: university in, 71–72
Environmental sound activism, 7
Epistemological orientation, 8
Eria, Muyamba, 82
Esoteric tourism, 284
Essentialism, strategic, 140
Esütateika protection songs, 320
Esüwa healing songs, 303–309, 320
    safeguarding and ownership of, 305–309, 314, 320
Ethnic cleansing, 109
Ethnic groups, 105–106, 106t.
    See also specific groups
Ethnicity, 140–141
    construction of, 128–129
    definition of, 128
    as different, 128–129
Ethnic music, 108–109
Ethnic roots, 118
Ethnographic film, participatory, 222
Ethnography, applied, 166–167
Ethnolinguistic communities, 201

Ethnologue (SIL International), 190
The Ethnomusicologist, 8
Ethnomusicologists. *See also specific individuals*
    advocacy by, 69–96
    personalities and attitudes, 8–9
    places of employment, 3–4
    as public folklorists, 23–24
    training for, 213
    White Settler Colonial, Ms., 256–258
Ethnomusicology. *See also specific topics*
    applied ethnomusicology
    action points for, 210–211
    activist, 222
    advocate, 82–83, 222
    applied, 149–151
    Berger on, 245
    Dalit Action Theory in, 230
    definitions of, 3, 13–14
    vs. folk music research and comparative musicology, 38–39, 39t
    humanized, 25
    humanizing, 259
    medical, 59, 149–151
    neo-orientalism, 226–229
    orientalism, 226–229
    public, 8
    public-sector, 7–8
    purpose of, 243, 245
    research agendas, 189–190
    Sheehy on, 243
    SIL International's work on, 211–212
    South Asian, 220–221
    urban, 100, 130–134
    whispering about decolonization, 258–260
    work in, 5–6
Ethnomusicology (journal), 8, 14, 15
    articles on minority musics, 207, 207f
    subjects of articles, 206–207
Ethno-Musicology (Kunst), 13
Ethnomusicology: A Very Short Introduction (Rice), 55
Ethnomusicology, Dr. A(pplied), 255, 260–266, 267
Ethnomusicology and Arts Group, SIL International, 211–212
Ethnomusicology Review (journal), 27
Eurocentric hegemony, 226–227
Europa erfindet die Zigeuner (Europe Invents the Gypsies) (Bogdal), 109–110

Europe
    applied ethnomusicologies, 41–43
    ethnomusicologies, 38–41, 39t, 41–43
European Union (EU), 131
Evaluation. *See* Health assessment
Events, artistic, 191
Ewasütuteika protection songs, 320
E-WoMP (Exploratory World Music
    Playground), 156, 164–165, 167, 180
"Exceptional Gypsies," 115–117, 116f
Expectations, 93
Exploratory World Music Playground
    (E-WoMP), 156, 164–165, 167, 180
Extinct genres, 203b

Fair trade coffee. *See also* Peace Kawomera
    Fair Trade Coffee cooperative
    Delicious Peace coffee, 93
Fakhri, Sabah, 199
Fanon, F., 263
Fein, Elizabeth, 168, 179
Feld, Steven, 74, 319
Festen, Brad, 204
Festival of American Folklife (Smithsonian
    Folklife Festival), 5
Fieldwork: partnership model of, 113, 140
Film
    participatory ethnographic, 222
    *This Is a Music: Reclaiming an Untouchable
        Drum*, 238–242, 245
Fitzcarrald, Carlos, 277
Fletcher, Alice Cunningham, 11, 100
Flores, Agustín Machacca, 293–294, 296
Flores, Beatríz Apasa, 291
Flores, Francisco Quispe, 290–291, 292
Flowers, Patricia, 156
Fock, Eva, 103
Folk Arts Division, National Endowment for
    the Arts (NEA), 23–24
Folklore
and activism, 24
    history of ethnomusicology and, 10, 12, 17,
        23, 40–41, 44
    Lomax, Alan, and, 23–24
    public, 7–8, 23–25, 55
    in U.S., 7–8, 23–24
Folklore Forum, 27
Folk music, 220, 221. *See also specific regions
    and types*
    research on, 38–39, 39t

    revival of, 23
    Tamil, 234–238
Forced migrants, 120–121
Former Yugoslavia: immigrants and refugees
    from, 106t, 109
Foundational concepts, 189–192
Foundational reality, 293, 298
Four Winds Society, 320
Fox Strangways, A. H., 228
Frame drums. *See Parai* (Tamil frame drum)
Freire, Paulo, 244
Frontiers of Dalit Theology, 244
Fuchs, Bernhard, 132–133
Fusions, 197

Gandhi, Mahatma, 223, 242
Garfias, Robert, 25
Gbaguru, 201
Gbaguru enactments, 201–202, 201t
Genres. *See* Artistic genres; *specific genres*
Germany: Turkish immigrants in, 131
Gifford, Kelly, 295, 296
The Gift (Mauss), 273
Gitan Coeur (Stojka), 118
Giving back, 11
Global arena, 30–54
    Africa, 37
    applied ethnomusicology in, 31–33
    artistic life, thriving, 206–211
    artistic traditions, 202–206
    Australia, 36–37
    European views, 38–41, 39t, 41–43
    homogenization of music, 187
    individual views, 49–52
    International Council for Traditional
        Music, 43–46
        on applied ethnomusicology, 46–49
        Society for Ethnomusicology and, 53–54
    intervention in, 30–31, 32
    North America, 37–38
    personal stance on, 33–35
    power imbalance in, 32–33
    South America, 37
    Southeast Asia, 37
    thriving artistic life, 206–211
    vignette on, 30–31
    worldwide overview, 36–38
Glossolalia, 198
Goals, 209
Górale (highlanders), 114

Goschie, Gayle, 291
Gourlay, Kenneth, 25, 258–259
Government. *See specific government-sponsored programs*
Grace, Elizabeth J., 171, 173, 177
Graded health assessment, 202, 203b
Grammy Awards, 82
Gramsci, Antonio, 231
Grandin, Temple, 161
Grant, Catherine, 36
Grant, Paul, 193
Grassroots tourism, 272–320
Greene, M., 267
Groove, 198
Gruber, Jacob, 187
Guthrie, Nancy, 293
Gutierrez, Gustavo, 244
Gypsy people, 109–110. *See also* Roma
 "Exceptional Gypsies," 115–117, 116f
 Vienna Gypsy Music School, 120
Gypsy Soul/Garude apsa (Stojka), 118

Hahn, Tomie, 234, 239
Hall, Stuart, 141
Halpert, Herbert, 12
Hanson, Thomas, 228
Harajin, 223, 242
Harakbut linguistic family, 300, 318. *See also* Wachiperi
Haramba Queros Wachiperi Conservation Concession, 301
Harris, Robin, 205–206
Harrison, Klisala, 27, 80–81
Hatun Q'eros, 275. *See also* Q'eros
Hausa Bori, 198
Hawes, Bess Lomax, 212
Haydon, Glen, 12, 13
Healing songs, 303–309, 320
 safeguarding and ownership of, 305–309, 314, 320
Health assessment for artistic traditions, 187, 200–202, 202–206
 graded health assessment, 202, 203b
 health measurement, 201
 quick and dirty health sketch, 201–202
Heightened emotional states, 198
Heine, Heinrich, 125
Heinschink, Mozes, 115–116
Hemetek, Ursula, 38–39, 42
 on minorities, 102
 on Roma, 110
 Sevdah in Vienna (Bajrektarević and Hemetek), 123–124, 125–126, 127
Henderson, Youngblood, 262
Heritage, 24, 41, 44. *See also* Intangible cultural heritage
 and tourism, 6, 10, 58, 115, 197, 272–299
Herzegovina, 101, 105, 121
Herzog, George, 12–13, 14–15, 23
Heschel, Abraham Joshua, 95
Heth, Charlotte, 25
Higgins, John, 228
Higher education, 78
Hinch, Thomas, 279, 280
Hinduism, 228, 239, 243
 Dalit rejection of, 244
Hindustani music, 220–221, 224–225, 243
 early treatises on, 227–228
Hip-hop youth culture, 134–137, 134f
History of cultural conservation, U.S.
 American Folklife Center, 23
 NEA Folk Arts Division, 23–24
 Office of Folklife Studies, 23
History of ethnomusicology, U.S., 9–29
 advocacy, 6, 27, 55
 applied, origins and early work, 17–21
 Boas in, 10, 12
 comparative musicology, 12–13
 critiques, 27–28
 doctoral training, 22
 Dorson in, 17
 Dorson-List-Merriam era in, 17
 Dyen and Davis in, 26
 Ethnomusicology, 14, 15
 European roots of, 12–13
 Fletcher in, 11
 Folk Arts Division of NEA, 23–24
 folklore, 23
 folk music revival, 23
 founding generation's research, 21
 giving back, 11
 Herzog in, 12, 14–15, 23
 Hood in, 21
 humanistic turn, 25
 institutional demand for professors, 22
 institutional growth, 21–22
 International Folk Music Council and, 16–17
 Keil in, 25
 Kunst in, 10, 13
 Lomax in, 5, 11–12, 23

History of ethnomusicology, U.S., (*cont.*)
  Matthews in, 10
  McAllester, Merriam, Rhodes, and Seeger's new direction, 15–16
  McAllester in, 14–15
  Merriam in, 14, 16–19
  music as culture move, 24
  Nettl in, 13–15
  Newsletter, 15
  in 1950, 10, 13
  popular interest, 21–22
  postcolonial applied ethnomusicology, 25
  pre-1950, 10
  professionalization, 18
  Seeger in, Anthony, 12
  Seeger in, Charles, 12
  Sheehy in, 11, 25
  skepticism in, 19
  Smithsonian in, 23–24
  Society for Ethnomusicology, 14, 15
    Committee on Applied Ethnomusicology, 26
    current activity, 27
    Section on Applied Ethnomusicology, 26
    theorization in, 27
HIV/AIDS, 74
Hoesing, Jennifer, 155
Hofman, Ana, 72–73, 86–87
The Hold Life Has (Allen), 274
Homogenization, 187
Hood, Mantle, 8, 14, 21, 226
hooks, bell, 267
Horvath, Gisela, 117
Huacaria. *See* Santa Rosa de Huacaria
Humanism, 25
Humanizing ethnomusicology, 259
Hungarian uprising, 104–105
Hungary: refugees from, 104–105
Hurston, Zora Neale, 12
Hymnody, 244

ICH. *See* Intangible cultural heritage
ICTM. *See* International Council for Traditional Music
Identity
  construction through music in diaspora, 128–129
  for minorities, 103
  national, 113
  Q'eros, 283–285

Identity markers, 190
IFMC (International Folk Music Council), 16–17, 43
Ilaiah, Kancha, 244
Illich, Ivan, 74
Immersion, musical, 241, 291
Immigrants. *See also* Migration and migrant communities; *specific communities*
  in Austria, 105–109, 106t
  discrimination against, 106–107, 108–109
  "Embedded industries—Immigrant Cultural Entrepreneurs in Vienna," 130
  integration of, 106–107, 138
  "Music Making of Immigrants in Vienna," 130
  Turkish, 105, 106t, 109, 127–139, 131f, 141, 142
Impoverishment, cultural, 187–188
Inca Empire, 273, 298, 315–316
Incas, 283–284
INDECOPI (*Instituto Nacional de Defensa de la Competencia y de la Protección de la Propiedad Intelectual*), 312–313
Indexical authenticity, 281
India. *See also* South Asia
  Christianity, 233
  classical music, 220–221, 243
  early treatises on music in, 227–228
  frame dramas (*see Parai* (Tamil frame drum))
  musical values, 225, 238–239
Indigenous Music Special Interest Group, SEM, 207
Indigenous peoples, 251–325
Indigenous tourism, 272–320
  authenticity in, 279–283
  music in, 278–279, 285–299, 287f, 289f–290f
  mutually beneficial exchanges, 290–299
  with Quechua Q'eros, 278–299, 280f, 287f, 289f–290f, 315–318
  reciprocity in, 297–299
Indirect intervention, 120–127
Indirect mediation, 35
Indomania, 227–228
Indophobia, 227
Initiative Minderheiten (Initiative Minorities), 107–108
Inkari, 283
INRENA (National Institute of Natural Resources) (Peru), 301

Institute of Folk Music Research and Ethnomusicology (University of Music and Performing Arts Vienna), 139, 141
Instituto Nacional de Defensa de la Competencia y de la Protección de la Propiedad Intelectual (INDECOPI), 312–313
Instruction, music. *See* Music education
Insularity, 9
Intangible cultural heritage (ICH). 6, 19, 42–43, 57, 108, 119, 142, 188, 204, 207, 212, 279, 304. *See also* Heritage
  Commission on Intangible Cultural Heritage (UNESCO), 207
  List of Intangible Cultural Heritage in Need of Urgent Safeguarding (UNESCO), 188, 204, 305, 307–308
  National Inventory of Intangible Cultural Heritage (Austria), 119, 142
Integral enactments, 193, 198–200
Integrality, 193–194
Integration of immigrants, 106–107, 138
Intellectual property, 312–314
Intercultural Bilingual Education (EIB) curricula, 306–307
Intercultural mediation, 99–143
  Barz and Cooley on, 140
  with Bosnian refugees, 109, 120–127, 140
  consultant-researcher cooperation models, 140
  Pettan on, 139, 142
  Rice on, 140
  with Roma, 108–109, 109–120, 140
  Slobin on, 139–140
  theoretical background, 99–108, 142
  with Turkish immigrants, 109, 127–139, 141
Intergovernmental Committee on Intangible Cultural Heritage, UNESCO, 212
International Academic Coordination team, SIL International, 212
International Council for Traditional Music (ICTM), 43–46, 207
  on applied ethnomusicology, 46–49
  current intention, 45
  Minority Musics Section, 207
  name, 56
  objectives of, 44–45
  origins of, 43–44
  and Society for Ethnomusicology, 52–54
  Study Group on Applied Ethnomusicology, 104, 140, 207
  Study Group on Music and Minorities, 101–104, 139, 140, 142
  World Conference, 104
International Folk Music Council (IFMC), 16–17, 43
International genres, 203b
International Hillel, 78
International Organization for Standardization, 190
Intervention, 30–31, 32
  direct, 120
  indirect, 120–127
Introduction to Musicology (Haydon), 13
Invested in Community: Ethnomusicology and Musical Advocacy, 55
Iowa State University, 295
Irundayaraj, Xavier, 244
Islamophobia, 109, 131, 138

Jacob, Prema, 221, 242
Jamaica, 297
Jawanchi, Joel, 311
Jellison, Judith, 156
Jerewa, Carmen, 302, 302f, 303–305, 306f
Jews
  Abayudaya community, 70, 70f, 75–82, 76f, 87–93
  of Syrian descent, 74
Johnson, Julie, 215
Jones, Michelle, 181
Jones, William, 227
Journalism, 7
Jovanović, Ilija, 115–116
Jovanović, Jelena, 55n11
Jungle Ultra Marathon, 310

Kalderaš-Serbian Roma, 116, 118
Kaluli *sa-ya:lab* funerary weeping, 204
Kaluli people, 74
Kalyi jag, 116
Kanoon, 196–197
"Kapiro," 303
Karnatak music, 220–221, 224–225, 229, 242
  early treatises on, 227–228
Karpeles, Maud, 43–44, 53
Keil, Charles, 25
Keki, J. J., 83–84, 85, 86, 93, 94–95
Kera language, 195
Kidula Jean, 189
Kirshenblatt-Gimblett, Barbara, 222
Knight, Douglas, 243

Knowledge for its own sake, 4, 19
Knudsen, B. T., 281, 285–286, 297, 298
Kongo (lamellaphone), 84
"*Kraj tanana šadrvana*," 125–126
Krauss, Michael, 205
Krzeptowski-Sabała, Jan, 114
Kubik, Gerhad, 204
Kugelmass, Jack, 95
Kuhač, Franjo, 40
Kunst, Jaap, 10, 13, 43
Kurinji Malar, 238–239, 241, 245
Kusisqa Waqashayku, 320
Kvitka, Kliment, 56

Lach, Robert, 40
Languages, 195
Lassiter, Luke, 312
Law, 7
Lederach, Jean Paul, 82, 85
"Let All Religions Come Together," 84, 94
Levin, Theodore, 121–122
Liberation theology, Dalit, 234–238, 243
Libraries, 7
Library of Congress
    American Folklife Center, 23
    Archive of Folk Culture, 23
Liebesforschung, 118
Liminal enactments, 193, 198–200
Liminality, 193–194, 293
Lindblad Expeditions, 319
Lingala, 195
Linguistics, cognitive, 190
List, George, 14
Listening, sympathetic, 221
List of Intangible Cultural Heritage in Need of Urgent Safeguarding (UNESCO), 188, 204, 305, 307–308
Living tradition, 282
Local projects, 203
Locked genres, 203b
Lomax, Alan, 187, 226
    "Appeal for Cultural Equity," 11–12
    encounter with Herzog, 23
    folk music revival, 23–24
    radio broadcasts, 5
Lomax, John, 12
Lorde, Audre, 266
Lost artistic traditions, 204–205
Loud Hands: Autistic People, Speaking (Bascom), 157, 162, 180

Loughran, Maureen, 99
Lovari Roma, 111, 116, 118–119
Lugwere, 84
Luwempele (instrumental accompaniment), 84
Lyon, Patricia J., 277–278, 278f, 301, 309–312

MacCorkle, Staci, 292, 293
Mackinlay, Elizabeth, 27
Madras Music Academy, 242
Malm, Krister, 42
Malm, William, 14
Mangeshkar, Lata, 245
Manqueriapa, Alberto, 307–308
Manuel, Peter, 243
Maori, 275, 297
Mara-I-am (Mara Chasar), 156–159, 170–171, 175–177, 181
Marginalized music
    of South Asia, 220–245
    subaltern singing (and drumming), 230–233
    Tamil folk music, 234–238
    This Is a Music: Reclaiming an Untouchable Drum, 238–242, 245
Marrero Elyse, 181
Marxism, 243
Maslow, Abraham, 199
Massey, James, 244
Matsiguenka, 320
Matthews, Washington, 10
Mauss, Marcel, 273, 275, 318
Mautner, Konrad, 115
Maximoff, Mateo, 116
Mayer, Sarah, 292
Mbiko Aisa Farmers Embaire Group, 94–95
McAllester, David, 14–15, 15–16, 21, 207
The Media (Boorstin), 281
Mediation
    direct *vs.* indirect, 35
    intercultural, 99–143
Medical culture, 166
Medical ethnomusicology, 7, 59, 149–151
Meizel, K., 259–260
Memory House *(Casa de la Memoria),* 307, 310
Merriam, Alan P., 14, 16–19, 53
Migration and migrant communities. *See also specific communities*
    forced migrants, 120–121
    Reyes on, 102–103
Minorities. *See also specific groups*
    in Austria, 104–108, 108–139

autochthonous, 105
cultural impoverishment of, 187–188
definition of, 101
ethnic, 105–106, 106t
Fock on, 103
Hemetek on, 102
ICTM Study Group on Music and
　　Minorities, 101–104, 139
identity, 103
music and, 99–104
Nettl on, 102
neurominority, 164
Reyes on, 102–103
Stokes on, 103–104
Minorities research, 100
　Fletcher on, 100
　Pettan on, 100–101
Minority musics, 207, 207f
Minority Musics Section, ICTM, 207
Mngeshkar, Lata, 244
Mondo films, 55
Mono language, 190, 195
Mono people *(amono)*, 190, 195
　Bili village *gbaguru* enactments,
　　201–202, 202t
The Moral Imagination (Lederach), 85
Moreton-Robinson, A., 265
Morra, Mario, 30
Motivations and methods
　for encouraging artists, 187–215
　personal motivation, 71–73
Moyle, Alice, 257
MPP. *See* Music-Play Project
Mpyemo instruments, 204
Murra, John, 318
Museums, 7
Music. *See also specific types and cultures*
　classical, 220–221, 227, 243
　construction of place, ethnicity, and
　　identity through, 128–129
　cultural domain of, 4
　ethnic, 108–109
　folk, 220, 221
　Hindustani, 220–221, 224–225, 227–228, 243
　Indian, 227–228
　in indigenous tourism, 278–279, 285–299,
　　287f, 289f–290f
　in the city *vs.* of the city, 130
　Karnatak, 220–221, 224–225, 227–229, 242
　marginalized, 220–245

　and minorities, 99–104
　minority musics, 207, 207f
　popular, 199–200
　Q'eros-tourist exchanges, 285–299, 287f,
　　289f–290f, 319
　Quechua Q'eros, 278–279
　rap, 137
　Romani, 111–113, 117
　sustainability of, 303
　Tamil folk music, 234–238
　transformative meaning/action of, 223–224
　Western art, 220–221
Musical immersion, 241, 291
Musical Performance in the Diaspora
　　(Ramnarine), 129
Musical value, 225, 238–239
Music education, 6–7. *See also* Education
　Vienna Gypsy Music School, 120
Musicians. *See specific musicians and
　　communities*
Music industry, 7
"Music Making of Immigrants in Vienna," 130
*Musicologica: A Study of the Nature of Ethno-
　　musicology, Its Problems, Methods, and
　　Representative Personalities*, 43
Musicology, comparative, 10, 12–13, 15–16
　origins of, 99–100
Music-Play Project (MPP), 151, 156, 168, 179
　history of, 154–155
　participants, 179, 181
Music therapy, 149–151
Mutually beneficial exchange, 290–299
Mystical tourism, 284

Nabutta, Saban, 84, 94–95
Nación Q'eros (Q'eros Nation), 275, 283
　location, 275–277, 276f
　songs, 277
Nagaswaram, 225
Narrative, polyvocal, 148
National cultures, 113
National Endowment for the Arts
　　(NEA), 23–24
National genres, 203b
National Geographic, 289f, 290f, 319
National identity, 113
National Institute of Culture, Peru.
　　See Peru, Ministry of Culture
National Institute of Natural Resources
　　(INRENA), 301

National Institute of Neurological Disorders and Stroke (NINDS), 160, 161–162
National Inventory of Intangible Cultural Heritage, Austria, 119, 142
Nationalism, cultural, 229
National Socialism (Nazism), 113
National traditions, 113
Native Americans. *See* Quechua Q'eros
NEA (National Endowment for the Arts), 23–24
Ne'eman, Ari, 162–163, 177
Neocolonialism, 187–188
Neo-orientalism, 226–229
Nettl, Bruno, 54
  early work, 13–16, 19–20
  on health assessment of artistic traditions, 200
  on health of artistic traditions, 187
  ICTM work, 54
  on losses in artistic traditions, 204
  on minorities, 102
Neurodiversity, 164, 166
Neurominority, 164
Neurotypicals, 163–164
New Age tourism, 284
Newsletter, 15
New York, New York, 5
New Zealand, 297
Ngiemboon communities, 196, 203
NGOs (nongovernmental organizations), 80, 107–108
Nikolić-Lakatos, Ruža, 111f, 118–119
Ninantay, Nely, 316–317, 320
NINDS (National Institute of Neurological Disorders and Stroke), 160, 161–162
Nirmal, Arvind, 244
Nongovernmental organizations (NGOs), 80, 107–108
North America, 5–8, 37–38
North American popular music, 200
Norway: Bosnian refugees in, 34–35
Nostalgia, 120–127, 140
Nsasi (shaker), 84
Ntankeh, Roch, 205, 206

Office of Folklife Studies, 23
Olonkho epic poem performances, 204, 205–206
Olsen, Paul Rovsing, 56
Orientalism, 226–229, 263

Orientation, epistemological, 8
Ortner, Sherry, 231, 232, 233, 240
Outcastes Welfare Association (Bahiskrit Hitakarini Sabha), 243
Outcasts. *See* Dalits
Ownership of songs, 305–309, 312–314

Parai (Tamil frame drum), 224–225, 231–233, 243
  oral system of drumming, 245
  This Is a Music: Reclaiming an Untouchable Drum, 238–242, 245
Participant activism, 241
Participant observation, 69
Participatory ethnographic film, 222
Partnerships
  CASES methodology, 80–81
  community, 78–79
  in fieldwork, 113, 140
Pathology, 164
Payap University, 212
PDD-NOS (pervasive developmental disorder not otherwise specified), 160
Peace, 7, 58
Peace Kawomera (Delicious Peace) Fair Trade Coffee cooperative, 79, 82–90, 83f, 93–95
Pedagogy. *See* Music education
Pekmezović, Ševko, 122–127, 123f
Performance. *See also specific performances*
  cultural, 278–279
  public, 115–120, 116f, 118f
  research through practice for, 226–227
Performative authenticity, 281, 297–298
Perlman, Marc, 226
Personal motivation, 71–73
Personal-political-possible story-ing, 253–254
Person-is-political story, 253
Peru, 318
  Ministry of Culture, 282–283, 292–293, 305–310, 314, 315–316, 320
  National Institute of Natural Resources (INRENA), 301
  Q'eros Nation *(Nación Q'eros)*, 275–277, 276f, 283
  Quechua Q'eros, 278–279
Pervasive developmental disorder not otherwise specified (PDD-NOS), 160
Petrović, Ankica, 55, 121–122

Pettan, Svanibor
  on advocacy and activism, 80–81, 82–83
  on applied ethnomusicology, 27
  on intercultural mediation, 139, 142
  on minorities, 100–101
  War, Exile, Everyday Life: Cultural Perspectives, 120
Phenomenological approach, 224
Phule, Jyotirao, 223
Pidgins, 195
Pinkuyllu flute, 280f, 286–287, 319
Place: construction through music in diaspora, 128–129
Podhale, 114
Poland: refugees from, 104–105, 106t
Polish crisis, 104–105
Politics
  assertions of cultural value, 223–224
  cultural, 220–221, 223–224
  of distraction, 267–268
  personal-political-possible story-ing, 253–254
  person-is-political, 253
Polyvocal narrative approach, 148
Pommer, Josef, 115
Popley, H. A., 228
Popular music, 199–200
"Position Statement against the Use of Music as Torture," 28
Postcolonial circumstances, 59
Postcolonial ethnomusicology, 9, 25. *See also* Decolonization
Poverty, 187–188
Prabhakar, M. E., 244
Prague spring, 104–105
Preservation. *See specific cultures, types, and topics*
Price, David, 226
Priorities, 212
Project conceptualization, 75–78, 76f
Promotion: public performance for, 115–120
Property, intellectual, 312–314
Protection songs, 320
Prototype theory, 190–191
Public ethnomusicology, 8
Public folklore, 23–25
Public performance, 115–120, 116f, 118f
Public programs. *See specific programs*
Public-sector ethnomusicology, 7–8
Punjabi popular music, 199–200

Q'eros identity, 283–285
Q'eros Nation *(Nación Q'eros),* 275, 283. *See also* Quechua Q'eros
  location, 275–277, 276f
  songs, 277
Q'eros River, 272–320, 276f
Quechua Q'eros
  active resistance, 273
  active voice, 315
  ayni (reciprocity), 273–275, 287–288, 297–299, 315, 320
  background, 275–278
  indigenous tourism with, 280f, 285–299, 287f, 289f–290f, 315–318
  music, 278–279
  population, 320
  spiritual tourism with, 319, 320
  tourist exchanges, 285–299, 287f, 289f–290f, 319
  and Wachiperi, 318–319
Queensland Conservatorium Research Centre, 188, 207
Queros-Wachiperi (Comunidad Nativa Queros-Wachiperi), 301, 310
  Casa de la Memoria (Memory House), 307, 310
  CD production, 309–314, 312f, 316–317, 317f
  population, 320
Quertehuari Walter, 308, 309–311
Quick and dirty health sketch, 201–202
Quispe, Francisco, 284–285, 291
Qureshi, Regula, 243

Racism, 131, 254
Racy, Jihad, 198–199
Rajasekaran, Jesudasan, 225
Ramnarine, Tina, 129
Rap music, 137
Rasmussen, Ljerka Vidić, 55
Reciprocity, 272–275, 319
  ayni, 273–275, 287–288, 297–299, 315, 320
  Harakbut (Wachiperi), 275, 300–301
  Quechua Q'eros, 297–299
Recordings, CD, 118
  Bosnia: Echoes from an Endangered World, 121–122
  Cantos Wachiperi: Familia lingüística Harakbut, Grupo étnico Wachiperi, 313f, 314
  Deep Forest, 197

Recordings (cont.)
  Delicious Peace, 70, 82–90, 93, 94
  Sevdah in Vienna, 127
  Wachiperi production, 309–314, 312f, 316–317, 317f
Reflexivity
  self-reflexivity, 221, 238
  uncomfortable, 253–254
Refugees
  Bosnian, 34–35, 104–105, 106t, 109, 120–127, 140
  from Czechoslovakia, 104–105, 106t
  from former Yugoslavia, 106t, 109
  from Hungary, 104–105
  from Poland, 104–105, 106t
Regional genres, 203b
Relationships, negotiated, 72
Religion, in university, 71–72
Relocation, 120–127. See also Migration and migrant communities
Remo, 165
Repair the World (NGO), 78
Research. See also specific researchers and projects
  agendas for, 189–190
  consultant-researcher cooperation models, 140
  impact of advocacy on, 93–94
  for its own sake, 18
  minorities, 100–101
  pure vs. applied, 5
  through performance practice, 226–227
  urban area as field of, 130–134
Reshetnikov, Pyotr, 205–206
Resistance, active, 273
The Resonant Community, 34, 41
Response-ability, 255, 266
Reyes, Adelaida, 100, 102–103, 120–121, 128, 130
Rhodes, Willard, 15–16, 54
Rice, Timothy, 55, 140
Rich, Adrienne, 96
Richardson, L., 254
Richter, Zachary (Zach), 171, 172–173, 177
Ricoeur, Paul, 198
River Q'eros, 272–320
R-Kan, 134–137, 134f
Robinson, Michael, 279, 280, 297, 319
Rock of Our Salvation Evangelical Free Church (Chicago, IL), 194

Roma
  in Austria, 108–109, 109–120, 112t, 140
  Bogdal on, 109–110
  Burgenland, 116, 117
  diversity of, 111, 112t
  ethnicity of, 114–115
  "Exceptional Gypsies," 115–117, 116f
  as Gypsy, 109–110
  Hemetek on, 110
  identity markers, 112–113
  Kalderaš-Serbian, 116, 118
  Lovari, 111, 116, 118–119
  national identity, 113
  public performance as promotion for, 115–120, 116f, 118f
  Serbian, 117, 118, 118f
  Silverman on, 110
  Sinti, 116
Roman (language), 119
Romani culture, 111–113
Romani language, 111–113
Romani music, 111–113, 117
Romani Routes. Cultural Politics and Balkan Music in Diaspora (Silverman), 110
Romano Centro, 117, 119–120
Romanticism, 110
Roma Verein zur Förderung von Zigeunern, 115–116
Rosch, Eleanor, 190
Russell, Ian, 99, 113
Russenorsk, 195
Ryan, Chris, 296

Safeguarding
  List of Intangible Cultural Heritage in Need of Urgent Safeguarding (UNESCO), 188, 204, 305, 307–308
  of songs, 305–309, 314, 320
Sağlam, Hande, 130, 131
Sambamoorthy, P., 228
Santa Rosa de Huacaria, 301, 303–304, 310
  Casa de la Memoria (Memory House), 307
  population, 320
Santería, 198
Savage Man Savage Beast, 30
Saz, 132
SAZ-Verein Wien, 132–133, 132f
Scheduled caste. See Dalits
Schippers, Huib, 56, 188, 300

Scholarship, value-free, 226–227
Schultz, Anna, 243
SDS. *See* Society for Disability Studies
Seeger, Anthony (Tony), 307, 308
   on copyright laws, 313–314
   early ethnomusicology work, 12, 311
   on loss of small traditions, 188
   on music cultures being "disappeared," 300
   Suyá collaboration, 73–74, 311
Seeger, Charles, 12
Seeger, Ruth Crawford, 12
Self-actualization, 199
Self-advocates, 162–163, 169–172
Self-reflexivity, 221, 238
Serbia, 40–41
Serbian Roma, 117, 118, 118f
Service, 87–88
Service learning: lessons from, 73–74
Sevdah in Vienna (Bajrektarević and Hemetek), 127
   "Dunjaluče," 123–124
   "Kraj tanana šadrvana," 125–126
Sevdalinka, 109, 120–127, 140
Shadows in the Field (Barz and Cooley), 140, 259
Sheehy, Daniel, 315
   on applied ethnomusicology, 25, 32, 115, 223, 261
   on approaches to problems, 72
   on community empowerment, 85
   on conscious practice, 34, 224, 261
   on ethnomusicology, 243
   on history of applied ethnomusicology, 11
   two aspects of applied ethnomusicology, 115
Shelemay, Kay Kaufmann, 72, 74
Shifting genres, 203b
Shirky, Clay, 211
Shudras, 223
Siberian Sakha people, 195–196
Siebers, Tobin, 166
SIL International
   Ethnologue, 190
   Ethnomusicology and Arts Group, 211–212
   International Academic Coordination team, 212
Silva, Carlos, 170
Silverman, Carol, 110, 140
Sinclair, Jim, 166–167, 177
Sinti Roma, 116

Skyllstad, Kjell, 41
Slobin, Mark, 139–140, 238
Slovenia, 39–40, 42–43
Smith, L. T., 263, 265
Smithsonian Folklife Festival, 5, 316
Smithsonian Folkways Recordings, 70, 82, 86, 89–90
   Delicious Peace, 70, 82–90, 93, 94
Smithsonian Institution, 23–24
Société française d'ethnomusicologie, 207
Society for Applied Microbiology, 55
Society for Applied Philosophy, 55
Society for Applied Spectroscopy, 55
Society for Disability Studies (SDS), 156
   Artism Ensemble concert (Orlando, 2013), 169–172, 172–173
Society for Ethnomusicology (SEM), 5, 155
   current applied ethnomusicology activity, 27
   founding and early history, 14, 15–16
   Indigenous Music Special Interest Group, 207
   interests of members, 206–207
   and International Council for Traditional Music, 53–54
   Section on Applied Ethnomusicology, 26, 207
Solomon, Olga, 161
Solomon, Tom, 129, 136–137
Soneji, Devesh, 243
Songs and singing
   aysariykuy, 288, 291, 298
   Bagisu circumcision songs, 82
   esütateika protection songs, 320
   esüwa healing songs, 303–309, 314, 320
   ewasütuteika protection songs songs, 320
   ownership of, 305–309, 312–314
   Q'eros-tourist exchanges, 288–291, 289f, 290f, 298
   safeguarding, 305–309, 314, 320
   subaltern singing (and drumming), 230–233
Songs for Peace Project, 200
Soundararajan, Thenmozhi, 244
Sound archives, 7
South America, 37
South Asia. *See also* India
   classical ten percent, 224–225
   cultural politics, 220–221
   ethnomusicology of, 220–221

South Asia (*cont.*)
  Hindustani music, 220–221, 224–225
  Karnatak music, 220–221, 224–225
  marginalized music, 220–245
  music, 220–221
  Tamil folk music, 234–238
  This Is a Music: Reclaiming an Untouchable Drum, 238–242, 245
Southeast Asia, 37
Sound, 7, 8
Spinny chairs, 156–159, 175–177
Spiritual beliefs, 71
Spiritual tourism, 319, 320
Spivak, Gayatri, 231
Starbucks, 94
Stimming, 158
Stoecker, Randy, 73
Stojka, Ceija, 111, 112f, 117
Stojka, Harri, 118
Stojka, Karl, 116
Stokes, Martin, 103–104, 122, 128
Story-ing, 253–254
Stout, Allegra, 171, 181
Strategic essentialism, 140
Straus, Joseph, 166, 180
Study Group on Applied Ethnomusicology, ICTM, 104, 140, 207
Study Group on Music and Minorities, ICTM, 101–104, 139, 140, 142
The Study of Ethnomusicology, 19
Stumpf, Carl, 12
Subaltern action theory, 230–231
Subaltern cultures, 86–87
Subaltern singing (and drumming), 230–233
Subramanian, Lakshmi, 243
Sundar, Pavitra, 244, 245
Survey, community arts, 213–215
Sustainability, 5, 59
  CASES methodology, 90–91
  of music, 303
  Titon on, 74, 178, 303
Sustainable Futures for Music Cultures project, 188
Suyá people, 73–74, 311, 314
Sympathetic listening, 221
Širola, Božidar, 40
Štrekelj, Karel, 40

Talam, Jasmina, 55n11
Talmud, 70
Tamil Dalit, 58
Tamil folk music
  as Dalit theology, 234–238
  Rajasekaran's studies of, 225
Tamil frame drum (*parai*), 224–225, 231–233, 238–242, 243
  oral system of drumming, 245
  This Is a Music: Reclaiming an Untouchable Drum, 238–242, 245
Tamil Nadu Theological Seminary (TTS), 234–238, 244
Tapia, Marisela, 192
Taquile island, 284–285
Taquileños, 284–285
Tarab, 198, 199
Tarantismo, 198
Tarfon, Rabbi, 70
Terada, Yoshitaka, 243
Terminology
  applied, 261
  for Dalits, 223, 242, 243, 244
  decolonization, 258–259
  return to coherence in, 189–191
  specialized, 198
Testimonials, 205–206
Thanksgiving Coffee Company, 83, 86, 93
Theater productions, 118
Theology
  Black Theology, 244
  Dalit, 233–234, 234–238
  Dalit liberation theology, 234–238, 243
  Dalit theology movement, 244
Therapeutic approach, 208–210
Third revolution, 78
This Is a Music: Reclaiming an Untouchable Drum, 238–242, 245
Threatened genres, 203b
Tikkun olam, 70, 96
Titon, Jeff Todd
  on applied ethnomusicology, 3–9
  on authenticity, 282
  on field research, 72
  on self-reflexivity and transformation, 238
  on sustainability and activism, 74, 178, 303
Tok Pisin, 195
Torture: use of music as, 28
Tourism, 115

community-based, 284–285
  eco-tourism, 320
  esoteric, 284
  indigenous, 272–320, 280f, 287f, 289f–290f
  mystical, 284
  New Age, 284
  Q'eros-tourist exchanges, 285–299, 287f, 289f–290f, 319
  spiritual, 319, 320
Tourism and Indigenous Peoples (Butler and Hinch), 279
Tradition(s)
  artistic
    foundational concepts, 189–192
    health assessment, 187, 200–202, 202–206
  living, 198, 282
  loss of small traditions, 188
  national, 113
  Ricoeur on, 198
Training, 213. *See also* Education; Music education
Trance states, 233. *See also* Ecstatic states
Transformative musical meaning/action, 223–224
Trauma, cultural, 5
Trautmann, Thomas, 227
Trejo, Kelsey, 295
Tryon, Elizabeth, 73
Tschernokoscheva, Elka, 138
TTS (Tamil Nadu Theological Seminary), 234–238, 244
Tuck, E., 264, 265, 268
Tufts University, 74, 94
Turkish immigrants, 105, 106t, 109, 127–139, 141, 142
  Bausinger on, 138
  challenging discourses on, 137–139
  construction of place, ethnicity, and identity through music, 128–129
  ethnic and religious backgrounds, 130, 131f
  hip-hop youth culture, 134–137
  Mansur Bildik work for, 132–134, 133f
  Tschernokoscheva on, 138
Turkish rap, 137
Turner, Victor, 193, 293

UCLA, 243
Uganda, 70f

Abayudaya (Jewish) community, 70, 70f, 75–82, 76f, 87–93
  advocacy in, 69–96
  CASES methodology in, 78–91
  Peace Kawomera (Delicious Peace) Fair Trade Coffee cooperative, 79, 82–90, 83f, 93–95
Ugarte, David, 305, 307
UGEL *(Unidades de Gestión Educativa Local)*, 307
Ultime grida dalla savana, 30
The Unheard Voices: Community Organizations and Service Learning (Stoecker and Tryon), 73
Unidades de Gestión Educativa Local (UGEL), 307
United Nations Educational, Scientific, and Cultural Organization (UNESCO), 6
  Commission on Intangible Cultural Heritage, 207
  Intergovernmental Committee on Intangible Cultural Heritage, 212
  List of Intangible Cultural Heritage in Need of Urgent Safeguarding, 188, 204, 305, 307–308
  National Inventory of Intangible Cultural Heritage (Austria), 119, 142
  Wachiperi song revival and, 299–314
  World Heritage Sites, 315–316
United States
  applied ethnomusicology in, 9–29
  cultural conservation in, 23–24
  Department of Homeland Security, 94
  ethnomusicology in, 9–29
  folklore, 23–24
  higher education, 78
Universidad Nacional de San Antonio Abad del Cusco (Cusco University), 283, 320
University
  engaged, 71–72
  religion in, 71–72
University of Ljubljana, 33, 53, 56
University of Michigan, 243
University of Music and Performing Arts Vienna: Institute of Folk Music Research and Ethnomusicology, 139, 141
University of Washington, 243

Untouchables. *See also* Dalits
  This Is a Music: Reclaiming an Untouchable Drum, 238–242, 245
Urban ethnomusicology, 100, 130–134
Usner, Eric Martin, 71–72, 78

Valuation
  musical value, 225, 238–239
  political assertion of cultural value, 223–224
Value-free scholarship, 226–227
Van Gennep, Arnold, 193
Van Willigen, John, 17–18
Vass, G., 259
Veršnik, Vojko, 89–90
Vienna Gypsy Music School, 120
Vigorous genres, 203b
Viswanathan, T., 229
Vocabulary, 189–191. *See also* Terminology
Voice
  active, 315
  polyvocal narrative approach, 148
Volksgruppe, 105, 112–113, 119
Volksgruppengesetz (Ethnic Groups Act) (Austria), 105, 113
Vranitzky, Franz, 113

Waade, A. M., 281, 285–286, 297, 298
Wachiperi language, 275, 299, 300
Wachiperi people, 299–314, 315–316, 318
  active resistance, 273
  background, 275–278, 300–302
  Cantos Wachiperi: Familia lingüística Harakbut, Grupo étnico Wachiperi, 313f, 314
  CD production, 309–314, 312f, 316–317, 317f
  dress, 307–308
  esütateika protection songs, 320
  esüwa healing songs, 303–309, 314, 320
  ewasütuteika protection songs, 320
  indigenous tourism with, 282–283
  "Kapiro," 303
  location, 275–277, 276f
  population, 319, 320
  and Q'eros, 318–319
  Queros-Wachiperi (Comunidad Nativa Queros-Wachiperi), 301, 310, 320
  reciprocity, 275, 300–301
  Santa Rosa de Huacaria, 301, 303–304, 310, 320
  song ownership and safeguarding, 305–309
  song revival, 299–314
  songs, 277, 303
Walker, Nick, 164, 177
Wang, N., 281–282
War, Exile, Everyday Life: Cultural Perspectives (Pettan), 120
Weidman, Amanda, 243
Wesleyan University, 243
Western music, 220–221
Wetzler, Laura, 83–84
White Settler Colonial, Ms., 255, 256–258, 267. *See also* Decolonization, Professor; Ethnomusicology, Dr. A
Whittenburg, Zachary, 192
Wide-awakeness, 258, 267–268
"Wien 10!" (R-Kan), 134, 135–136
Wilderness Travel, 319
Willard, Augustus, 228
Winter, Penni, 161, 162, 163, 177
Wolf, Richard, 243
Wong, Deborah, 32, 226–227
World Arts M.A., 212
World Heritage Sites, 315–316
World Intellectual Property Organization (WIPO), 7
World music, 22. *See also specific artists, promoters, types*

Xenophobia, 105–106, 130, 131

Yang, K. W., 264, 265, 268
Yonaje, Manuel, 278f, 302, 302f, 303, 310–311, 312f, 317–318
Youth culture, 134–137, 134f
Yugoslavia, 40
Yupanqui, Demetrio Tupac, 283

Zar, 198
Zavala, M., 267–268
Zebec, Tvrtko, 43
Žganec, Vinko, 40

www.ingramcontent.com/pod-product-compliance
Ingram Content Group UK Ltd.
Pitfield, Milton Keynes, MK11 3LW, UK
UKHW050410240426
12048UKWH00020B/1448